THE HANOVERIAN SUCCESSION

The Hanoverian Succession

Dynastic Politics and Monarchical Culture

Edited by

ANDREAS GESTRICH and MICHAEL SCHAICH
German Historical Institute London

ASHGATE

© Andreas Gestrich, Michael Schaich and the contributors 2015

All rights reserved. No part of this publication may be reproduced, stored in a retrieval system or transmitted in any form or by any means, electronic, mechanical, photocopying, recording or otherwise without the prior permission of the publisher.

Andreas Gestrich and Michael Schaich have asserted their right under the Copyright, Designs and Patents Act, 1988, to be identified as the editors of this work.

Published by
Ashgate Publishing Limited
Wey Court East
Union Road
Farnham
Surrey, GU9 7PT
England

Ashgate Publishing Company
110 Cherry Street
Suite 3-1
Burlington, VT 05401-3818
USA

www.ashgate.com

British Library Cataloguing in Publication Data
A catalogue record for this book is available from the British Library

The Library of Congress has cataloged the printed edition as follows:
The Hanoverian Succession : dynastic politics and monarchical culture / edited by Andreas Gestrich and Michael Schaich.
    pages cm
Includes bibliographical references and index.
    ISBN 978-1-4724-3765-5 (hardcover) -- ISBN 978-1-4724-3766-2 (ebook) -- ISBN978-1-4724-3767-9 (epub) 1. Hanover, House of. 2. Great Britain--History--1714-1837. I. Gestrich, Andreas. II. Schaich, Michael.
    DA480.H256 2015
    941.07--dc23
                                                                            2014045096

ISBN: 9781472437655 (hbk)
ISBN: 9781472437662 (ebk – PDF)
ISBN: 9781472437679 (ebk – ePUB)

Printed in the United Kingdom by Henry Ling Limited, at the Dorset Press, Dorchester, DT1 1HD

Contents

List of Illustrations   *vii*
Notes on Contributors   *ix*
Acknowledgements   *xv*

1   Introduction   1
    Michael Schaich

PART I   DYNASTIC LEGACIES

2   The Hanoverian Monarchy and the Legacy of Late Stuart
    Kingship   25
    Ronald G. Asch

3   The House of Brunswick-Lüneburg and the Holy Roman
    Empire: The Making of a Patriotic Dynasty, 1648–1714?   43
    Martin Wrede

PART II   REPRESENTING PROTESTANTISM

4   George I, the Hanoverian Succession, and Religious Dissent   73
    David Wykes

5   Hanover-Britain and the Protestant Cause, 1714–1760   89
    Andrew C. Thompson

6   The Hanoverians and the Colonial Churches   107
    Jeremy Gregory

PART III   IMAGE POLICIES

7   The Hanoverian Monarchy and the Culture of Representation   129
    Tim Blanning

8   'Every Inch *Not* a King': The Bodies of the (First Two)
    Hanoverians   147
    Robert Bucholz

9   Monarchy, Affection and Empire: The Hanoverian Dynasty
    in Eighteenth-Century America   171
    Brendan McConville

10 Visions of Kingship in Britain under George III and George IV   187
    G.M. Ditchfield

PART IV   CONTESTED LOYALTIES

11 The Hanoverian Succession and the Politicisation of the
    British Army   207
    Hannah Smith

12 Jacobitism and the Hanoverian Monarchy   227
    Gabriel Glickman

13 The Alternative to the House of Hanover: The Stuarts in
    Exile, 1714–1745   251
    Edward Corp

14 Radical Popular Attitudes to the Monarchy in Britain during
    the French Revolution   261
    Amanda Goodrich

Index   *279*

List of Illustrations

3.1 *Monumentum Gloriae Ernesti Augusti Principis Electoris Brunsvicensis Primi ...* (Hanover, 1704), frontispiece showing the apotheosis of the first elector of the House of Hanover, Ernest Augustus.   55

8.1 King George I, by Georg Wilhelm Lafontaine (1680–1745)   152
8.2 King George II, after Robert Edge Pine (c. 1730–1788)   153
8.3 Portrait of George I, after Godfrey Kneller, print made by Jacob Houbraken (1746)   157
8.4 Peter Bull as George I in *Saraband for Dead Lovers* (Ealing, 1948)   164
8.5 *A Cheap and Easy Method of Improving English Swine's Flesh by a German Method of Feeding* (London, 1743)   165

Notes on Contributors

Ronald G. Asch teaches as Professor of Early Modern History at the University of Freiburg. His research areas include British and German history from the sixteenth to the eighteenth century; the comparative history of nobility and court culture in early modern Europe; and early modern monarchy as an institution. Among his numerous publications on these and other topics are *The Thirty Years War: The Holy Roman Empire and Europe 1618–1648* (Macmillan, 1997); *Nobilities in Transition: Courtiers and Rebels in Britain and Europe c. 1550–1700* (Arnold, 2003); *Die Stuarts* (Beck, 2011); and *Sacral Kingship between Disenchantment and Re-enchantment: The French and English Monarchies 1587–1688* (Berghahn, 2014).

Tim Blanning was Professor of Modern European History at the University of Cambridge until his retirement in 2009. He remains a Fellow of Sidney Sussex College and has been a Fellow of the British Academy since 1990. He has published extensively on the political and cultural history of Europe in the eighteenth and nineteenth centuries, and is also general editor of *The Oxford History of Europe* and *The Short Oxford History of Europe*. His book *The Culture of Power and the Power of Culture* (Oxford University Press, 2002) was shortlisted for the British Academy book prize for 2003 and won a German prize as the best book in any language published in 2002 on early modern Europe. *The Triumph of Music: Composers, Musicians and Their Audiences, 1700 to the Present* (Penguin, 2008) has been translated into German, Portuguese and Spanish. Most recently he has published *The Romantic Revolution* (Weidenfeld & Nicolson, 2010).

Robert Bucholz is a Professor of History at Loyola University, Chicago. His research focuses on early modern Britain and London and the British court and royal household from 1660 to 1901. Among other works he has published and edited (with Joseph Ward) *London: A Social and Cultural History 1550–1750* (Cambridge University Press, 2012); (with Newton Key) *Early Modern England 1485–1714: A Narrative History* (Wiley-Blackwell, 2nd edn. 2009); and (with Caroline Levin) *Queens and Power in Medieval and Early Modern England* (University of Nebraska Press, 2009). He is also the Project Director for the Database of Court Officers 1660–1837: http://courtofficers.ctsdh. luc.edu/. Currently, he is working on his new book *Power, Pomp and Pleasure: A Political, Social and Cultural History of the British Court 1660–1901*, written both for an academic and popular audience.

Edward Corp is Emeritus Professor of British History at the University of Toulouse. He is the foremost expert on the Jacobite exile after 1689, and has curated and written the catalogues of two major exhibitions: *La Cour des Stuarts à Saint-Germain-en-Laye au temps de Louis XIV* (Château de Saint-Germain, 1992) and *The King over the Water, 1688–1766* (Scottish National Portrait Gallery, 2001). His other publications include *A Court in Exile: The Stuarts in France, 1689–1718* (Cambridge University Press, 2004); *The Jacobites at Urbino: An Exiled Court in Transition* (Palgrave Macmillan, 2009); *The Stuarts in Italy, 1719–1766: A Royal Court in Permanent Exile* (Cambridge University Press, 2011); and *I giacobiti a Urbino: la corte in esilio di Giacomo III re d'Inghilterra* (Il Mulino, 2013), a revised and expanded edition of *The Jacobites at Urbino*. He has also edited *The Stuart Court in Rome: The Legacy of Exile* (Ashgate, 2003).

G.M. Ditchfield is Professor of Eighteenth-Century History at the University of Kent. He is a specialist in the political and religious history of eighteenth-century Britain. His current research involves the history of parliament, changes and continuities in religious thought in the later eighteenth century, and dissenting education and reform movements. The work he has already published focused on the significance of religious issues in parliament. It has also taken account of movements for political and ecclesiastical reform and the nature of monarchical and parliamentary authority between c.1750 and c.1800, with particular reference to the reign of George III, which he dealt with in his book *George III: An Essay in Monarchy* (Palgrave Macmillan, 2002). He has edited *The Letters of Theophilus Lindsey (1723–1808)* (2 vols, Boydell, 2007–2012). Among his current projects is an edition of the correspondence of Archdeacon Francis Blackburne (1705–1787).

Andreas Gestrich is Director of the German Historical Institute London. Before he joined the institute he was Professor of Modern History at Trier University. His present research interests comprise the history of family, childhood and youth, the history of poverty and poor relief, media history, and the social history of religious groups. His publications include, among others, *Absolutismus und Öffentlichkeit: Politische Kommunikation in Deutschland zu Beginn des 18. Jahrhunderts* (Vandenhoeck & Ruprecht, 1994); *Familie im 19.*

und 20. Jahrhundert (Oldenbourg, 1999); (ed. with Lutz Raphael) *Inklusion/ Exklusion: Studien zu Fremdheit und Armut von der Antike bis zur Gegenwart* (Lang, 2004); and (ed. with Christiane Eisenberg) *Cultural Industries in Britain and Germany: Sport, Music and Entertainment from the Eighteenth to the Twentieth Century* (Wißner, 2012).

Gabriel Glickman is Assistant Professor of Early Modern British History at Warwick University. His research interests concentrate on politics and religion in Britain and its Empire c. 1660–1750. His first book, *The English Catholic Community 1688–1745: Politics, Culture and Ideology*, was published in 2009. He has since contributed articles to the *Journal of Modern History*, *Historical Journal*, *English Historical Review* and *Parliamentary History*.

Amanda Goodrich is a lecturer in Eighteenth-Century History at the Open University. Her research focuses on eighteenth-century and early nineteenth-century political ideas in a cultural context. Presently Amanda is working on a forthcoming book for the Pickering & Chatto, Enlightenment World Series, *Henry Redhead Yorke, Colonial Radical: Politics and Identity in the Atlantic World, 1790-1813*. Her most recent publications include *Debating England's Aristocracy in the 1790s: Pamphlets, Polemics and Political Ideas* (Boydell and Brewer, 2005); 'Understanding a Language of Aristocracy, 1700–1850', *Historical Journal* (2013); 'Radical "Citizens of the World" 1790–1795: The Early Career of Henry Redhead', *Journal of British Studies,* 53 (2014); and an introductory chapter to *Georgians Revealed: Life, Style and the Making of Modern Britain* (British Library, 2013).

Jeremy Gregory is Professor of the History of Christianity at the University of Manchester. His current research explores the position of the Church of England in North America, and particularly in New England from the late seventeenth to the late eighteenth centuries. His publications so far have contributed to the debates concerning the role of the Church of England in particular, and religion in general, in English social, cultural, political and intellectual history from the mid-seventeenth to the mid-nineteenth century. In that context he has edited, among others, *The Speculum of Archbishop Thomas Secker, 1759–1768* (Boydell, 1995); and, furthermore, a large number of books and essay collections on the Church and eighteenth-century religious life, including *Restoration, Reformation and Reform, 1660–1828: Archbishops of Canterbury and Their Diocese* (Oxford University Press, 2000) and (ed. with Jeffrey Chamberlain) *The National Church in Local Perspective: The Church of England and the Regions, 1660–1800* (Boydell, 2003).

Brendan McConville is a full Professor at Boston University, and Director of Graduate Study. His research focuses on the intersection of politics and social developments in early America. He is the author of *These Daring Disturbers of the Public Peace* (Cornell University Press, 1999; University of Pennsylvania, 2003) and *The King's Three Faces: The Rise and Fall of Royal America, 1688–1776* (Omohundro Institute of Early American History and Culture/University of North Carolina Press, 2006). At the moment he is writing a major study on the history of the American Revolution.

Michael Schaich is Deputy Director of the German Historical Institute London. He specialises in seventeenth- and eighteenth-century British and German history. His current research focuses on the symbolic representation of the British monarchy and state during the seventeenth and eighteenth centuries. He has published *Staat und Öffentlichkeit im Kurfürstentum Bayern der Spätaufklärung* (Beck, 2001) and edited several volumes of collected essays, among others, *Monarchy and Religion: The Transformation of Royal Culture in Eighteenth-Century Europe* (Oxford University Press, 2007) and (with R.J.W. Evans and Peter H. Wilson) *The Holy Roman Empire, 1495–1806* (Oxford University Press, 2011).

Hannah Smith is a tutor and Fellow of St Hilda's College, Oxford, and lecturer in history, University of Oxford. Her first book was entitled *Georgian Monarchy: Politics and Culture, 1714–1760* (Cambridge University Press, 2006). She has co-edited two collections of essays: *Civilians and War in Europe, 1618–1815* (Liverpool University Press, 2012) and *Religion and Women in Britain, 1660–1760* (Ashgate, 2014). She is currently writing a book on the British army, politics and society from 1660 to 1750.

Andrew C. Thompson is a lecturer on eighteenth-century British and European history at Queens' College, Cambridge. His PhD on the interaction of religion and foreign policy in Britain and Hanover in the first half of the eighteenth century was published as *Britain, Hanover and the Protestant Interest, 1688–1756* (Boydell and Brewer, 2006). He is particularly interested in the impact of religious ideas on foreign policy and the nature of eighteenth-century diplomatic thought. More broadly, he studies the interaction of culture, politics, the court and identity in Protestant Europe. Most recently he has written *George II: King and Elector* (Yale University Press, 2011) as well as a number of articles on eighteenth-century politics and diplomacy.

Martin Wrede is Professor of Modern History at the Université Pierre-Mendès-France, Grenoble. His main research interests cover the history of the early modern nobility, the study of Franco-German relations and the political culture of early modern Europe. Among his publications are *Das Reich und seine Feinde: Politische Feindbilder in der reichspatriotischen Publizistik zwischen Westfälischem Frieden und Siebenjährigem Krieg* (von Zabern, 2004) and *Ohne Furcht und Tadel – für König und Vaterland: Frühneuzeitlicher Hochadel zwischen Familienehre, Ritterideal und Fürstendienst. Studien zu Beharrungswillen und Anpassungsvermögen einer traditionalen Elite* (Thorbecke, 2012). He is also the editor of *Die Inszenierung der heroischen Monarchie: Frühneuzeitliches Königtum zwischen ritterlichem Erbe und militärischer Herausforderung* (de Gruyter, 2014).

David Wykes is the Director of Dr Williams's Trust and Library. He is a historian of late seventeenth- and early eighteenth-century dissent, and late eighteenth- and early nineteenth-century rational dissent and Unitarianism. He has a particular interest in dissenting academies and the contribution made by dissent to business, society and politics. He is currently working on a study of religious dissent during the 25-year period after the Glorious Revolution. He is the author of many articles, including 'Religious Dissent, the Church, and the Repeal of the Occasional Conformity and Schism Acts, 1714–1719', in Robert D. Cornwall and William Gibson, eds, *Politics, Religion and Dissent, 1660–1832* (Ashgate, 2010). With Isabel Rivers he has co-edited *Joseph Priestley: Scientist, Philosopher, and Theologian* (Oxford University Press, 2008) and *Dissenting Praise: Religious Dissent and the Hymn in England and Wales* (Oxford University Press, 2011).

Acknowledgements

The year 2014 marked the tercentenary of the succession of the Hanoverian dynasty to the British throne and the start of the personal union between England and Hanover, which created a link between the two countries that lasted for more than 100 years until its dissolution in 1837. In order to commemorate this event the Historische Kommission für Niedersachsen and Bremen and the German Historical Institute London teamed up to organize two international conferences which took place in Osnabrück (28–31 March 2012) and London (11–13 October 2012) respectively. The local organizers were Ronald G. Asch (University of Freiburg) and Thomas Vogtherr (University of Osnabrück and chair of the Historische Kommission) for the Osnabrück symposium and the two present editors for the London gathering.

The chapters in this volume started life as papers at these conferences and have been reworked for publication. Other contributions to the two meetings have been published separately in a German-language volume of collected essays edited by Ronald Asch. In the run-up to both events we greatly benefitted from the advice and help of numerous colleagues. In particular we want to thank Professor Stephen Taylor from the University of Durham, whose suggestions for themes and speakers helped to draw up the programme of the London conference, and the participants in a series of meetings organized by the Historische Kommission für Niedersachsen and Bremen in Hanover where first ideas were discussed. Thanks are due to Angela Davies for translations and editorial help. We would also like to thank our editor at Ashgate, Tom Gray, who has shown unfailing understanding and has been supportive of the volume from the beginning. Finally, our thanks go to the contributors to the volume, who bore all our requests with patience and grace.

Andreas Gestrich and Michael Schaich
London

Chapter 1

Introduction

Michael Schaich

I

History has not treated the Hanoverians kindly. For a long time they have been passed over quickly in general accounts of British history, as meek successors to the more colourful Stuarts and the invariably feted Tudors.¹ As luck would have it, their accession to the British throne in 1714 came at a point when, in the aftermath of the Glorious Revolution, the ascent of parliament was well advanced and seemed – at least with the benefit of hindsight – almost unstoppable. The royal court, so it was assumed, had to give way to the lobbies and corridors of Westminster as the stage on which political history was played out. Simultaneously, the British Isles experienced a 'revolution in everyday life that took place between 1714 and 1830' and was to transform society fundamentally: urbanisation, the rise of the public sphere and the triumph of a consumer culture with all the tell-tale signs of polite behaviour, the reign of fashion and the cult of celebrities came to be the hallmarks of the Georgian period.² Small wonder, then, that the history of monarchy in the eighteenth and early nineteenth centuries was subsumed within the master narrative of

---

¹ The old *Pelican History of England* which appeared between 1950 and 1978 had volumes on *Tudor England* (by S.T. Bindoff) and *Stuart England* (by J.P. Kenyon), but labelled the successor volume (by J.H. Plumb) rather indifferently – *England in the Eighteenth Century*. The as yet unfinished *New Oxford History of England* has one volume on *The Later Tudors: England 1547–1603* (by Penry Williams, 1995), while the titles of the three volumes which cover the Hanoverian period all allude to the nation or the people of England: *A Land of Liberty? England 1688–1727* (by Julian Hoppit, 2004); *A Polite and Commercial People: England 1727–1783* (by Paul Langford, 1989); *A Mad, Bad, and Dangerous People? England 1783–1846* (by Boyd Hilton, 2006).

² The most recent and very powerful statement of this view can be found in the British Library exhibition 'Georgians Revealed: Life, Style and the Making of Modern Britain', open to the public during the winter of 2014, and its accompanying catalogue (London, 2013); the quotation is from the website to the exhibition: http://www.bl.uk/whatson/exhibitions/georgiansrevealed/index.html (accessed 14 July 2014).

the onset of modernity, which left precious little space for the role of kings who, on top of everything else, were open to the charge of being of foreign extraction. Interestingly, the verdict of German historians on the dynasty was equally unfavourable. The Guelphs, as they were known in their home lands, were accused of sacrificing the interests of the electorate of Brunswick-Lüneburg on the altar of dynastic status elevation, thereby prompting a long-term descent into political and cultural decline.[3]

Nor did the Hanoverians fare better as individuals. George I (1714–1727) and George II (1727–1760) were deemed dull, dim-witted and boorish by British contemporaries and later scholars alike.[4] Even their bodies were distorted in pictorial and verbal representations to match their assumed mental and intellectual backwardness, as Robert Bucholz demonstrates in this volume. Many of their subjects and most historians also suspected them of loathing their new kingdom and still pining for their old territories. At best, the first two Georges were credited by posterity with keeping a low profile and not making any serious political blunders. George III (1760–1820) enjoyed a better reputation during his lifetime. He was applauded by many for his moral rectitude and his domestic portrayal of the royal family; but then he was the first Hanoverian to be born and educated a Briton, as he was keen to stress in his inaugural address to parliament in 1760.[5] Even his popularity, however, was far from universal or enduring. There were long and repeated periods of outright criticism during his reign and the judgement of later scholars and writers has sometimes been scathing, making George III, in the words of John Cannon, 'one of the most controversial and criticised monarchs in British history', whose

---

[3] The multi-volume history of the run-up to the personal union between Britain and Hanover by Georg Schnath, the leading historian of Hanoverian regional history during much of the twentieth century – *Geschichte Hannovers im Zeitalter der neunten Kur und der englischen Sukzession 1674–1714*, 5 vols (Hildesheim, 1938–1982) – is a swansong on the end of Hanoverian political significance. The notion of Hanover's decline after 1714 can still be found very recently; see, e.g., Heide Barmeyer, 'Die Personalunion England-Hannover: Ihre Entstehung, Etablierung und Fortsetzung aus Hannoverscher Sicht', in Rex Rexheuser, ed., *Die Personalunionen von Sachsen-Polen 1697–1763 und Hannover-England 1714–1837: Ein Vergleich* (Wiesbaden, 2005), pp. 275–98.

[4] For the traditional image of the first two Georges see their modern and more sympathetic biographers: Ragnhild Hatton, *George I* (1978; New Haven, 2001), p. 300 and passim (who explodes many myths about the first Hanoverian in the course of her narrative); and Andrew C. Thompson, *George II: King and Elector* (New Haven, 2011), pp. 3–4, 7–8 and 97–100 (on the source of much hostile writing about George II, John Hervey's court memoirs).

[5] See John Brooke, *George III* (St Albans, 1974), pp. 156 and 612.

standing improved only slowly since the 1930s.⁶ His wayward son, George IV (1820–1830), on the other hand, squandered much of the emotional attachment that the dynasty had commanded under his father through his private affairs and pompous behaviour, while William IV (1830–1837), the last Hanoverian king, is usually seen as an unremarkable post-script to a rather tiresome era in the history of the British monarchy.⁷

And yet, the Hanoverians can also be cast in a distinctly positive light. They were arguably one of the more successful royal dynasties. Not the least of their achievements was to steer the ship of state clear of the rocks on which the Stuarts had foundered twice during the seventeenth century. They navigated the difficulties of Britain's scattered religious landscape in a way unimaginable only a few decades earlier and always produced enough offspring to keep the family business going. There were no major religious or succession crises, which had been such a common feature of the previous two centuries; nor for that matter did the Georges face revolutions (apart, perhaps, from the War of American Independence to which we will return) or were forced into exile. On the contrary, against the backdrop of what had happened during the tumultuous century before 1714 it is rather striking that, as rulers imported from the continent and faced with a difficult dynastic legacy, as Ronald Asch explains, they managed to integrate themselves into British political culture and re-establish the monarchy as a national institution which was beyond principled criticism for most of their reign. In addition, they presided over one of the most significant periods in British political and economic history. They oversaw the rise of Britain to world power status and the birth of a new territorial empire after 1756 which was to reinforce the old empire of trade and commerce and would eventually compensate for the loss of the American colonies in the 1780s. At the same time they upheld Britain's political and military engagement in Europe, securing it the position of arbiter in continental affairs.⁸

Why, then, is the image of the Hanoverian dynasty so overshadowed by jaundiced statements and clichés? Part of the answer certainly lies in the

---

⁶ John Cannon, 'George III', in H.C.G. Matthew and Brian Harrison, eds, *Oxford Dictionary of National Biography*, 60 vols (Oxford, 2004), XXI, pp. 833–53, here pp. 849–52, the quote at p. 849. See also G.M. Ditchfield, *George III: An Essay in Monarchy* (Basingstoke, 2002), pp. 4–21.

⁷ See, e.g., Frank O'Gorman, *The Long Eighteenth Century: British Political and Social History 1688–1832* (London, 1997), pp. 277 (on George IV) and 360 (on William IV, 'an elderly man without much political passion').

⁸ See Brendan Simms, *Three Victories and a Defeat: The Rise and Fall of the First British Empire, 1714–1783* (London, 2007).

eighteenth century, when critics of the Georgian monarchy put many of these stereotypes into circulation. Fear of undue influence by foreign politicians and courtiers close to the royal family, suspicions about a waste of English resources for the electorate of Hanover – which, in any case, was seen as an albatross around the neck of ministers and diplomats – and dread of the possible import of autocratic forms of government by monarchs supposedly used to absolutist rule were widespread after 1714.[9] Still, in 1800, as G.M Ditchfield reminds us in his chapter, the electorate could be used as the *bête noir* of British politics, although the volume of the criticism might have been turned down. Throughout the eighteenth century there was a visceral dislike of the German dominions as an alien adjunct to the British monarchy. It did not help that at least up to the middle of the eighteenth century the Hanoverians had to put up with the propaganda of the exiled Stuarts and their supporters. Many of the more scurrilous blots on the image of individual members of the Hanoverian family can be traced back to Jacobite writings and were later on readily accepted by historians.[10]

Equally important in explaining the long-standing bias against the Georgians is the composite nature of their kingship. The conjunction of two or more legally independent states under one common ruler, as was the case with Britain and Hanover between 1714 and 1837, is a regular occurrence in early modern Europe and of necessity shaped the self-image and political approach of rulers charged with the task of holding these unions together. Historians living and working under the impression of the end of the nation-state have been increasingly aware of the phenomenon since the 1970s.[11] The insights gained from the multiple kingdoms of the sixteenth and seventeenth centuries, however, took a long time to filter through to the analysis of the Georgian monarchy and are still not yet fully developed. Until very recently most studies took no notice of the fact that the Hanoverians – not unlike their Stuart predecessors – ruled over composite states and had to adjust their policies to this situation. British historians failed to recognise the extent to which the Georges were (and were seen to be) kings

---

[9] Bob Harris, 'Hanover and the Public Sphere', in Brendan Simms and Torsten Riotte, eds, *The Hanoverian Dimension in British History, 1714–1837* (Cambridge, 2007), pp. 183–212.

[10] In addition to Robert Bucholz's chapter in this volume see, e.g., Hatton, *George I*, p. 300.

[11] See the groundbreaking essays by H.G. Koenigsberger, 'Dominium Regale or Dominium Politicum et Regale: Monarchies and Parliaments in Early Modern Europe', in id., *Politicians and Virtuosi: Essays in Early Modern History* (London, 1986), pp. 1–25 and J.H. Elliott, 'A Europe of Composite Monarchies', *Past and Present*, 127 (1992), pp. 48–71.

of Great Britain *and* electors of Hanover and disparaged many of their decisions as self-serving and opportunistic, while their German counterparts regarded the Anglo-Hanoverian union as a mere dynastic link which was of little political consequence (apart from pushing the electorate indirectly on a downward trend) and thus did not require proper examination.[12] Both camps failed to realise the complexities which the Hanoverians had to navigate were they to do justice to their role as sovereigns of two, albeit unequal, partners.

It should not come as a surprise, therefore, that the most important re-evaluations of the Georgian monarchy in recent years have come from historians who recognised the significance of the dual nature of Hanoverian kingship. Hannah Smith's inquiry into the cultural underpinnings of monarchy and the continuing relevance of the royal court under the first two Georges, Brendan Simms and Torsten Riotte's volume of collected essays which for the first time considered the implications of the 'Hanoverian Dimension' for British politics more generally, Clarissa Campbell Orr's studies of Queen Charlotte and her entourage and Andrew Thompson's rehabilitation of George II as a capable and, above all, still powerful figure central to the political process are all cases in point.[13] The Hanoverians emerge from these studies in a decidedly more positive light than previously thought. Clearly they were quite successful at commanding the loyalty of large parts of their subjects; they discharged their duties in a conscientious and, by and large, skilful manner; and their reign presented politicians in London and Hanover with opportunities as well as problems in pursuing the interests of a composite state. The reassessment of the Hanoverians has thus been under way for a few years now and is bound to continue (and become more public) with the spate of exhibitions in London and Hanover in 2014 to mark the tercentenary of the Protestant succession.

While the publications accompanying these celebratory events are mainly devoted to royal patronage of the arts and processes of communication and cultural transfer within the personal union,[14] the chapters in this volume aim

---

[12] See Torsten Riotte, 'Britain and Hanover', in Peter H. Wilson, ed., *A Companion to Eighteenth-Century Europe* (Oxford, 2008), pp. 354–67, here pp. 354–5, and Andrew Thompson's introductory remarks to his chapter in this volume.

[13] Hannah Smith, *Georgian Monarchy: Politics and Culture, 1714–1760* (Cambridge, 2006); Simms and Riotte, eds, *The Hanoverian Dimension*; Clarissa Campbell Orr, 'Queen Charlotte, "Scientific Queen"', in ead., ed., *Queenship in Britain, 1660–1837: Royal Patronage, Court Culture, and Dynastic Politics* (Manchester, 2002), pp. 236–66; ead., 'Queen Charlotte and Her Circle', in Jonathan Marsden, ed., *The Wisdom of George III* (London, 2005), pp. 162–78; Thompson, *George II*.

[14] See Desmond Shawe-Taylor, ed., *The First Georgians: Monarchy and Art 1714–1760* (London, 2014), and Katja Lembke, ed., *Als die Royals aus Hannover kamen: Hannovers*

to shed light on the mechanisms at the heart of the Georgian monarchy from a slightly different angle. They concentrate on the various ways in which the Hanoverian monarchs dealt with the problems arising from the diversity and heterogeneity of the territories over which they ruled and the competing claims made on these lands. Concentrating on the realms of religious affiliations, monarchical representation and political discourses, the individual contributions to this volume discuss the different dynastic legacies which the German dynasty embodied as well as encountered in 1714. They explore the widely diverging confessional obligations of their subjects that the monarchs had to integrate; the conflicting worlds of princely self-fashioning and commercial image-making; and the competing ideological programmes threatening to dislodge the Hanoverians' claim to rule. Along the way the chapters take in all parts of the Georgian composite monarchy, from the German dominions to the American colonies – although, due to the current state of research, the British perspective still dominates. Whatever chapter is considered, however, the hybrid identity of a ruling dynasty in eighteenth-century Europe will be thrown into sharper relief. Historians of early modern monarchies usually tend to homogenise the messages which rulers conveyed to the outside world in an effort to instil a sense of logic and inevitability into the policies of princely self-legitimation.[15] The Hanoverian dynasty, by contrast, furnishes us with an example of a ruling house whose self-representation and conception of itself was the site of contested identities and competing strategies – a model which might be more common in the *société des princes* than is sometimes acknowledged.

II

This problem of contested identities becomes obvious when we turn to the one feature of Hanoverian rule which is usually acknowledged as the new dynasty's undisputed strength – its profession of the Protestant faith. As is well known, only their seemingly impeccable Protestant credentials secured Electress Sophia and her descendants the succession to the British crown. The fact that merely a generation earlier some senior members of the Guelph dynasty had converted to

---

Herrscher auf Englands Thron 1714–1837 (Dresden, 2014). They accompany the exhibitions at the Queen's Gallery, London, and the Niedersächsisches Landesmuseum and Museum Schloss Herrenhausen, Hanover, respectively.

[15] The most cited example is Louis XIV; see Peter Burke, *The Fabrication of Louis XIV* (New Haven, 1992) and, more recently, Nicolas Milovanovic and Alexandre Maral, eds, *Louis XIV: L'homme et le roi* (Paris, 2009).

Catholicism had been conveniently forgotten by the time the Act of Settlement was passed in 1701. After 1714, in any case, the Hanoverians were keenly aware of their dependence on the Protestant religion, and acted accordingly. As Hannah Smith and others have shown, and several chapters in this volume confirm, the (self-)portrayal of the royal family bore unmistakable religious overtones: the first two Georges were depicted as Protestant soldier-kings, while George III was a paragon of personal piety and devotion.[16] It did not go amiss that compared to the Stuart queens the Hanoverian consorts turned out to be assets rather than liabilities in confessional terms. They might have been recruited from obscure German princely families and not from the royal houses of France and Portugal, the dynastic homes of Henrietta Maria and Catherine of Braganza, the wives of Charles I and Charles II respectively. Their religious record, however, was beyond any reproach. Far from being Catholic or showing any sympathies for the 'popish religion' like their more prominent Stuart predecessors, George II's consort Queen Caroline, for example, had spurned the crown of the Holy Roman Empire when asked to marry a Habsburg prince, the future Charles VI, to stay true to the religious convictions of her ancestors. This at least was the story that was spun by her admirers to great effect.[17] The other Hanoverian queens did not achieve the same martyr-like status, but they still lived their Protestant faith and presented a united confessional front to the outside world. Even in politics the Hanoverian kings pursued Protestant aims, at least to a degree. They had gone to England with the reputation of having fought Louis XIV and defended the Protestant religion within the Holy Roman Empire, despite the odd flirtation with the French – as Martin Wrede's chapter illustrates. Once installed on the British throne they embarked on several missions to rescue continental Protestants from Catholic persecution, even threatening to intervene if necessary.[18] In this respect the electorate's political ambitions to lead the Protestant party within the Holy Roman Empire and British statesmen's interests in addressing public concerns about the fate of

---

[16] Hannah Smith, 'The Idea of a Protestant Monarch in Britain, 1714–1760', *Past and Present*, 185 (2004), pp. 91–118; ead., *Georgian Monarchy*, pp. 19–58.

[17] For Queen Caroline see Andrew Hanham, 'Caroline of Brandenburg-Ansbach and the "Anglicisation" of the House of Hanover', in Clarissa Campbell Orr, ed., *Queenship in Europe, 1660–1800* (Manchester, 1991), pp. 13–48 and Joanna Marschner, *The Queen: Collections and Connoisseurship at the Early Georgian Court* (London, 2007).

[18] See Andrew Thompson's chapter in this volume and his *Britain, Hanover and the Protestant Interest, 1688–1756* (Woodbridge, 2006). For the wider context Tony Claydon, *Europe and the Making of England, 1660–1760* (Cambridge, 2007) and Stephen Conway, *Britain, Ireland and Continental Europe in the Eighteenth Century: Similarities, Connections, Identities* (Oxford, 2011).

fellow Protestants converged and gave the combined British–Hanoverian state a unifying purpose.

To a large extent, then, loyalty to the Hanoverian dynasty rested on the feeling of a shared Protestantism. Often, however, the common religious outlook amounted to no more than a virulent anti-Catholicism which, given British obsessions with popery and arbitrary power, provided the most basic and efficient bond between rulers and ruled, as Tim Blanning forcefully brings to mind in his contribution to this volume. Beneath the veneer of a broadly defined Protestantism beckoned pitfalls and difficulties which it is easy to miss if we do not probe more deeply into the religious identity of the Georgian monarchy. There can indeed be few other European princes who ruled over a comparable diversity of faiths and confessional allegiances as the Hanoverians. The presence of a sizeable Catholic population, mainly in Ireland, but as a small minority also in England, and from 1763, with immense political consequences, in Canada was only part of a wider problem. The appeal to a common Protestantism concealed (and was meant to conceal) the array of Protestant denominations that populated the lands of the Hanoverians: apart from the Anglican Church there were the politically and socially influential dissenters in England; the Presbyterian established Church in Scotland; the Lutherans in Hanover; and a mixture of all these creeds in the American colonies, to name just the most influential groups. Clearly, the Hanoverian composite state was a multi-confessional enterprise which the monarchs had to hold together somehow.

How difficult this was is often obscured by the much-vaunted success of the Georgian monarchy in appealing to a wide Protestant consensus. Examined more closely, however, numerous complications and obstacles come into view which the Hanoverians had to master, not to mention the cases in which they failed to uphold religious unity and cohesion. A few examples might suffice to illustrate this. One of the more immediate problems for the Hanoverians, for instance, was their role as head of several, at least in theory, mutually exclusive established churches. Besides the Anglican Church they also headed the Scottish Presbyterian and the Hanoverian Lutheran churches, which made them, in the memorable words of Brendan Simms, 'confessionally schizophrenic'.[19] In practice the problem only arose with regard to the religious establishments of England and Hanover since no Georgian monarch ever set foot on Scottish soil before 1822, by which time the problem had lost its urgency. The first three

---

[19] Simms, *Three Victories*, p. 85.

Georges, however, seem to have been acutely aware of their dilemma.[20] After 1714 George I and George II regularly returned to the electorate to take care of the government there. During these stays in Germany they behaved to all intents and purposes as Lutherans, habitually attending Sunday service at court. Once back in England, they visited the Anglican Chapel Royal, where they also received communion twice a year. Without any apparent personal qualms they changed their confessional allegiances as they saw fit, conforming to the rules of the country they happened to find themselves in. George III, by contrast, discontinued this practice. Staunch Anglican that he was, he must have felt unable to perform the same balancing act, which is one reason why he never visited Hanover, sending his sons in the 1780s and 1790s instead. For his predecessors, however, confessional cross-dressing was certainly a price worth paying to maintain the religious equilibrium in different parts of their multiple kingdoms.

It is also easily forgotten that the self-proclaimed Protestantism of the Hanoverians was not accepted unconditionally by their new subjects. The dissenters were without any doubt among the most fervent supporters of the Hanoverian succession in 1714, as David Wykes' chapter elucidates. But, as Wykes also makes clear, they had high hopes of the new dynasty and expected tangible political concessions – not least the repeal of the penal laws. When, in deference to the Anglican Church, George I could not follow up on his initial signals of goodwill he and his son had to work hard to cultivate the dissenter community lest they withdrew their support. How tenuous the relationship was became fully apparent after 1770: under George III and his unassailable Anglicanism the alliance between dynasty and dissent was allowed to slip, with the inevitable result that nonconformist criticism of the monarchy grew significantly and rapidly. The same mechanism can be observed on an even greater scale in the American colonies, the topic of Brendan McConville's and Jeremy Gregory's chapters. Here again the first two Georges enjoyed considerable popularity not just among Anglicans but also the substantial nonconformist groups. They were hailed as defenders of the 'Protestant interest' and – closely linked with this – English liberties. Some clergymen, such as the Congregationalist Cotton Mather, even referred to the policy of religious toleration which the dynasty had observed in its German heartlands, thus underlining the extent to which the composite Georgian monarchy was seen as one joint religious space.[21] Despite

---

[20] For the following see Michael Schaich, *Die vielen Gesichter des Königs: Die Inszenierung von Herrschaft in der britischen Monarchie während des 17. und 18. Jahrhunderts* (forthcoming), ch. II.3.c.

[21] For Cotton Mather see Jeremy Gregory's chapter in this volume.

this track record and their former enthusiasm, however, colonists turned abruptly against the monarch in 1774 when royal assent for the Quebec Act, which extended toleration to Catholics, was seen as a betrayal of the Protestant cause. The higher the expectations of the dynasty, it seems, the harsher the punishment once disillusionment set in. The loss of the American colonies was, as McConville and Gregory suggest, to a considerable extent the result of a failure in managing conflicting confessional demands made on the Hanoverians.

Add to this the omission to integrate the Scottish churches into the monarchical orbit before 1745 and its devastating consequences in the Jacobite rebellion of that year, a point made by Gabriel Glickman in this volume, and the limitations of Hanoverian pan-Protestantism become manifest. Despite their general success in projecting the image of a Protestant dynasty the Hanoverians clearly struggled to fulfil all the demands made on them. Confessional heterogeneity had been a structural problem of most composite monarchies, and it certainly was one in the multiple states of the Anglo-Hanoverian world.[22] Interestingly, George I and George II seem to have been better placed to deal with these challenges than George III, on whose watch some of the more significant blunders in religious policy between 1714 and 1837 happened. Is it too far-fetched to suggest that the experience of the Holy Roman Empire may have had something to do with the greater degree of flexibility in the earlier period? Did the multi-confessional environment of the Old Reich better prepare the first two Georges for the task of reconciling different confessional demands? In any case, the chapters in this volume point to a more nuanced reading of the by now well-worn narrative of the Protestant underpinnings of Hanoverian kingship, one that takes the contradictions and ambivalences within the overall Protestant identity of the dynasty more seriously.

III

A similar argument can be made for the secular self-representation of the Hanoverians which has often been denigrated. Here the comparison with the Tudors and Stuarts plays a major role.[23] Set against the magnificent palaces built by Henry VIII and enlarged and altered by his successors, the great collections

---

[22] Elliott, 'Europe of Composite Monarchies', pp. 58–9.
[23] See now Kevin Sharpe, *Selling the Tudor Monarchy: Authority and Image in Sixteenth-Century England* (New Haven, 2009); id., *Image Wars: Promoting Kings and Commonwealths in England, 1603–1660* (New Haven, 2010); id., *Rebranding Rule: The Restoration and Revolution Monarchy, 1660–1714* (New Haven, 2013).

of paintings and works of art amassed by Charles I and the rich cultural life of the courts of Elizabeth I, Charles I and Charles II, the Hanoverians indeed look rather ungainly. Their list of cultural achievements – which includes the rebuilding of Kensington Palace and Buckingham House as well as the employment of George Frideric Handel – is rather modest.[24] This dichotomy should not, however, tempt us to write off the Hanoverian self-representation too early. First of all, it has to be said that even under the Stuarts periods of cultural efflorescence at court were intermittent, narrowly circumscribed by financial constraints.[25] Secondly, the Hanoverian court has been rescued recently from the verdict of earlier generations of historians and restored to its rightful place as an important centre of social, political and cultural life in Hanoverian England.[26] Political careers still depended on a regular presence in the vicinity of the monarch, while social cachet could be acquired at the regular levees and assemblies. It should not surprise us that the entourages maintained by George I and George II were more numerous and costly than those of their immediate predecessors, giving the lie to all claims of a decline in the fortunes of the eighteenth-century court.[27]

Quite apart from such comparisons, the more understated language of Hanoverian regality – the style of 'frugal monarchy', as Tim Blanning calls it – can be seen as a conscious decision to reflect changing political and social circumstances as well as dynastic priorities. The triumphalist tone of Stuart image policy had already run into trouble in the seventeenth century[28] and would not have found much favour with the polite and commercial classes of eighteenth-century Britain. It is no coincidence that Charles II's grandiose plans to erect a 'new Versailles' in

---

[24] For the role of music during the Hanoverian period see the contributions to the 2013 conference '"The Power of Musick" – Music and Politics in Georgian Britain', in *Göttinger Händel-Beiträge*, 15 (2014), pp. 5–226.

[25] See Ronald G. Asch, 'Monarchische Repräsentation und politische Kultur in England im 17. Jahrhundert: Mangel an höfischem Luxus oder Defizit sakraler Legitimation?', in Werner Paravicini, ed., *Luxus und Integration: Materielle Hofkultur Westeuropas vom 12. bis zum 18. Jahrhundert* (Munich, 2010), pp. 251–68.

[26] Hanham, 'Caroline of Brandenburg-Ansbach'; Hannah Smith, 'The Court in England, 1714–1760: A Declining Political Institution?', *History*, 90 (2005), pp. 23–41; Nigel Aston, 'The Court of George II: Lord Berkeley of Stratton's Perspective', *Court Historian*, 13 (2008), pp. 171–93; Clarissa Campbell Orr, 'Popular History, Court Studies and Courtier Diaries', *Court Historian*, 17 (2012), pp. 1–15.

[27] See J.C. Sainty and R.O. Bucholz, *Officials of the Royal Household 1660–1837*, part 1: *Department of the Lord Chamberlain and Associated Offices* (London, 1997), pp. lxvi–lxx.

[28] See the chapter by Ronald G. Asch in this volume.

Winchester faltered,[29] while George I's refurbishment of Kensington Palace by William Kent was admired by contemporaries.[30] Enlightened ideas and discourses also dictated changes in how monarchs publicised themselves. The 'royal touch', the miraculous method of healing the scrofula – much practised by Stuart monarchs such as Charles II, James II and Queen Anne – might still have been immensely popular by 1714, but George I's decision to let the custom fall into oblivion must be read as a deliberate act of distancing himself from a charismatic, almost Catholic understanding of kingship. This was grist to the mill of Jacobite detractors who saw in the renunciation of such a central monarchical ritual further proof of the new dynasty's illegitimacy. In the long run, however, the more sober interpretation of kingship, which also found expression in other ceremonial changes,[31] was probably more to the liking of eighteenth-century British society and fitted the bill of a parliamentary and parsimonious monarchy better than the absolutist style of the past.

However, it would be wrong to assume that the Georgians just cut back on representation or did not care much about how they were perceived. On the contrary, as a foreign dynasty which had inherited a complex set of kingdoms and colonies they and their supporters went to great lengths, albeit not always successfully, to legitimate their rule and inscribe themselves into broader royal traditions. These efforts are not yet fully understood, but some suggestions, mainly based on the chapters in this volume, can be made.[32] To start with, the Hanoverians were certainly not averse to splendour and ostentation. They might not have built grand palaces, but the interiors of their princely abodes could bear comparison with any other royal residence in Europe. Contemporary visitors regularly commented on the brilliance and grandeur of the rooms, their furniture, works of art and precious tapestries.[33] Most importantly of all,

---

[29] See Simon Thurley, 'A Country Seat Fit for a King: Charles II, Winchester and Greenwich', in Eveline Cruickshanks, ed., *The Stuart Courts* (Stroud, 2000), pp. 214–39.

[30] See Edward Impey, *Kensington Palace: The Official Illustrated History* (London, 2003), pp. 55–73. It is telling that there is no modern history of the official residence of the Hanoverians, St James's Palace, whereas the Tudor and Stuart palaces have all received proper treatment, mainly by Simon Thurley.

[31] See Schaich, *Die vielen Gesichter*, ch. II.3.

[32] It is indicative that most studies of British royal ceremonial and image policy stop in 1714 at the latest. Kevin Sharpe's three-volume *opus magnum* which was always intended to go only up to 1714 is a good example of this.

[33] See, e.g., César de Saussure, *Letters from London 1725–1730*, trans. by Paul Scott ([Newnham], 2006), p. 71. In this respect the Hanoverians continued a practice which had been characteristic of the British court since the sixteenth century. See Malcolm Smuts, 'Art and the Material Culture of Majesty in Early Stuart England', in id., ed., *The Stuart Court in*

London court society was among the most dazzling in Europe. Dress mattered hugely at the British court, with the foreseeable result that court costume was expensive and exquisite.[34] Portraits of Queen Caroline in robes studded with precious stones and jewels display the example set by the royal family and duly followed by its courtiers.[35] Numbers mattered too, of course. Contemporary observers regularly commented on the throng of visitors (or their absence) to the state apartments in St James's Palace.[36] Whereas other princely dynasties in the eighteenth century sought aggrandisement through palace building, the Hanoverians (like the Habsburgs in Vienna) celebrated themselves via a numerous, magnificently dressed and high-aristocratic entourage.

Increasingly, the task of selling the dynasty to a broader public was also assumed by forces and institutions outside the monarch's control. The rise of the public sphere and the commercialisation of British society led to a cult of the monarch that Linda Colley has described for George III.[37] Earlier instances can also be found. Tim Blanning in his chapter refers to the example of 'Rule, Britannia', which was commissioned by Frederick Lewis, George II's unloved son, and became hugely popular in a short period of time. What is more, the involvement of agencies acting on their own behalf became particularly important in the colonies. Clergymen of all persuasions as well as printers and authors were crucial in promoting the image of the Georges in colonial America, as McConville and Gregory explain.[38] The influx of monarchical portraits, bibles and liturgical objects donated by the dynasty and shipped to the dominions by the Anglican Church as well as the general trade in goods which bore the

---

Europe: Essays in Politics and Political Culture (Cambridge, 1996), pp. 86–112, in particular pp. 90–93, 107–10.

[34] Hannah Greig, 'Fashion and Faction: The Politics of Court Dress in Eighteenth-Century England', in Isabelle Paresys, ed., *Se vêtir à la cour en Europe 1400–1850* (Villeneuve-d'Ascq, 2011), pp. 67–90.

[35] See, e.g., the illustration in Roy Strong, *Coronation: A History of Kingship and the British Monarchy* (London, 2005), p. 393.

[36] A vivid description of the bustle at court is to be found in Lucy Worsley, *Courtiers: The Secret History of Kensington Palace* (London, 2010), pp. 19–21.

[37] Linda Colley, 'The Apotheosis of George III: Loyalty, Royalty and the British Nation 1760–1820', *Past and Present*, 102 (1984), pp. 94–129; ead., *Britons: Forging the Nation 1707–1837* (New Haven, 1992), pp. 195–236. For the concept of the public sphere see Andreas Gestrich, 'The Public Sphere and the Habermas Debate', *German History*, 24 (2006), pp. 413–30; id., 'The Early Modern State and the Rise of the Public Sphere: A Systems-Theory Approach', in Massimo Rospocher, ed., *Beyond the Public Sphere: Opinions, Publics, Spaces in Early Modern Europe* (Bologna, 2012), pp. 31–52.

[38] See their chapters below and, in addition, Brendan McConville, *The King's Three Faces: The Rise and Fall of Royal America, 1688–1776* (Chapel Hill, 2006).

royal arms further strengthened the link between monarch and subjects. Taken together with the cycle of civic rituals organised on an annual basis by the imperial authorities these developments led to an unqualifiedly positive image of the Georges among colonists well into the 1770s. Their enormous popularity beyond the Atlantic stands, of course, in striking contrast to the criticism levelled against the first two Georges in England and simultaneously puts these strictures into perspective. The same can be said of the monarchy's German dominions, where the dynasty remained well liked throughout the personal union. The years after 1815, in particular, saw the emergence of a new identity in the recently elevated kingdom of Hanover which drew on the shared experience of the Napoleonic Wars in Britain and Hanover, the exchange of ceremonies across the North Sea and the political role of a common dynasty.[39] Perhaps an Anglo-centred scholarship has lost sight of the possibility that the constituent parts of the monarchy held different attitudes to the Hanoverians. Further research would certainly do well to cast the net wider and try to piece together a more comprehensive picture of the reputation of the dynasty in its different settings.

The question remains, however, whether there were any distinct features which set the self-representation of the Hanoverian dynasty apart from its predecessors. For the later eighteenth century there are certainly new trends which changed the image of the Georges, as G.M. Ditchfield's chapter amply demonstrates. A greater emphasis on philanthropic causes, on charitable giving and caring for the poor and less well off was combined with a more moralistic stance embodied in particular by George III and his wife Charlotte, although this new outlook was repeatedly undermined by the younger generation of royals and their lifestyle.[40] Interestingly enough, however, the most important vision of kingship which Ditchfield discerns for the later period of the Hanoverian dynasty still remained – apart from the overarching Protestant identity – a close association with the military. After 1815 the royal family may have had fewer occasions to brandish its martial credentials. Nonetheless the soldierly element is the one characteristic that runs through the self-representation of the Hanoverians from beginning to end. The early iconography of the Hanoverians was already dominated by the figure of the 'soldier king' – a revival of the chivalrous warrior of the Renaissance period, imbued with religious meaning, as becomes apparent in the analogy of the first Hanoverians with their namesake,

---

[39] Christine van den Heuvel, 'Georg IV. und Wilhelm IV.: Das Königreich Hannover und das Ende der Personalunion', in Lembke, ed., *Als die Royals*, pp. 180–201, here pp. 188–9, 191 and 196–7.

[40] See also Frank Prochaska, *Royal Bounty: The Making of a Welfare Monarchy?* (New Haven, 1995).

St George, who conveniently happened to be the national saint of England.[41] This image may have been created for them by their spin doctors and loyal supporters, but the first two Georges also held military life in high personal esteem. George I had seen action in his youth against the French and the Turks and commanded an army during the War of the Spanish Succession, while George II longed all his life for a major role on the battlefield – a dream finally fulfilled in 1743 when he led his troops in person into battle at Dettingen during the War of the Austrian Succession.[42] Both kings also made military reviews an important part of their public appearances, in Britain as well as Hanover, a fact easily forgotten in complaints about the supposed withdrawal of George I from public view during his reign.[43] Their successors, George III and George IV, may not have looked the part but they too hatched dreams of military glory in their youth (and in the case of George IV even later on, as Ditchfield writes with regard to the Napoleonic Wars) and kept close contact with all things military. George III in particular visited troops regularly and adopted the uniform as regular court dress,[44] while most of his brothers and sons spent at least some time in the army.

That the Hanoverians should have hit upon a military style of self-representation may seem a dubious and rather unfortunate choice for English monarchs. The Stuarts had for the most part not cultivated a martial image for themselves – and when they finally did so, under James II, things had gone terribly wrong. The spectre of a standing army, as is well known, was invariably linked with fears of absolutist or even tyrannical rule in British political discourse during the seventeenth and eighteenth centuries and automatically bred suspicion about the new rulers' true motives. There were, however, sound reasons – quite apart from individual preference – why the Hanoverians opted for this strategy. First of all, sheer pragmatism must have persuaded the new dynasty to rely on the armed forces. With the constant threat of a Jacobite invasion or uprising during the first 30 years of Hanoverian rule the army was the bedrock of the Georgian monarchy. The Protestant succession in 1714 already to a large degree depended, as Hannah Smith makes clear in this volume, on the officer

---

[41] Smith, 'Idea of a Protestant Monarch'; Smith, *Georgian Monarchy*, pp. 104–16, 182–5.

[42] Hatton, *George I*, pp. 34–5, 88–9 and 100–104; Thompson, *George II*, pp. 148–9.

[43] See Smith, *Georgian Monarchy*, pp. 113–15 and Joachim Niemeyer, *Die Revue der kurhannoverschen Armee bei Bemerorde 1735: Eine kulturgeschichtliche und heereskundliche Betrachtung zu einem Gemälde von J.F. Lüders* ([Berlin], 1985). I am grateful to Peter Wilson, Hull, for drawing Niemeyer's book and the extraordinary depiction of a military review which it analyses to my attention.

[44] Philip Mansel, 'Monarchy, Uniform and the Rise of the Frac 1760–1830', *Past and Present*, 96 (1982), pp. 103–32, here pp. 112, 115–19.

corps' decision to support George I (if needed even by a *coup d'état*) and not the Jacobite pretender. In the following years the army was systematically brought into line with the new dynasty and proved to be a loyal supporter of king and government during several Jacobite rebellions and numerous wars, priding itself on the pivotal role it had played in securing the Hanoverian succession and, by extension, Protestantism and English liberties.

In addition, the Hanoverians tried to conform to a model of heroic kingship which had been *de rigueur* for many continental dynasties at least since the Renaissance.[45] Glorifying the monarch as a military hero who protected his subjects had legitimised many a reign down the centuries and reached an apogee in the late seventeenth century with Louis XIV and William III as the two main protagonists. The latter, in particular, provided an important point of reference for the first two Georges, who in numerous respects followed the example which the Prince of Orange had set during the first personal union between Britain and a continental country in the 1690s.[46] Seen from this perspective, George II's appearance on the battlefield of Dettingen loses some of its oddity as the last occasion when a British king pursued his enemies in person. It turns instead into the re-enactment of a long and cherished tradition of *rois-connétables* who had demonstrated their personal courage and willingness to sacrifice their life for the common good in military combat. It was George II's misfortune, however, that this tradition was already fading when he tried to revive it. The increasing professionalisation of armies and military conflict had made the fighting king a thing of the past. Frederick II of Prussia could stem the tide for a while because he did not just grace the battlefield with his presence, but commanded his armies with daring brilliance and some success. As a rule, however, military figures such as the Duke of Marlborough or later on James Wolfe became the heroes of the day in Britain. Most Hanoverian kings recognised this and refrained from taking an active part, instead associating themselves with the army in more indirect ways to further benefit from the glory that fell on the monarchy from military success. But a certain ambivalence and even risk associated with the martial self-representation of the dynasty remained, particularly towards the end of the period. Ditchfield points to the growing desire for peace in the population

---

[45] See now Martin Wrede, ed., *Die Inszenierung der heroischen Monarchie: Frühneuzeitliches Königtum zwischen ritterlichem Erbe und militärischer Herausforderung* (Berlin, 2014) and, in particular, the introduction by the editor, pp. 8–39.

[46] The best-known instance is certainly William III's decision to renounce the 'royal touch' which foreshadowed the practice followed by the Georges after 1714. See for William III Esther Mijers and David Onnekink, eds, *Redefining William III: The Impact of the King-Stadholder in International Context* (Aldershot, 2007).

at large since the War of American Independence and the powerful critique of militarism in radical circles during and after the Napoleonic Wars – not to mention the revival of the debate about standing armies. At the other end of the spectrum, popular generals and especially admirals could potentially outshine the monarch and relegate him to second place in public esteem. Nowhere did this become more apparent than in the celebrations of the death of Horatio Nelson in 1805–1806. The state funeral awarded to the victor of the battles of Trafalgar and the Nile was more popular and celebrated with greater aplomb than any royal funeral during the whole of the Hanoverian period.[47]

Finally, the role of Nelson and other famous admirals of the eighteenth and early nineteenth centuries raises the more general issue of whether the Hanoverians predicated their self-representation solely on the army or whether, and to what extent, they inscribed themselves into the maritime traditions of their new lands. Curiously, this theme has not been addressed by historians in any coherent way. And yet, one of the first and most powerful pictorial depictions of the new dynasty linked the Hanoverians closely to seafaring and colonial enterprise. The monumental glorification of George I and his descendants by Sir James Thornhill, completed between 1718 and 1724, adorns the rear wall of the Upper Hall of Christopher Wren's Royal Hospital for Seamen at Greenwich, now the Old Royal Naval College.[48] What space could have been more appropriate for demonstrating the close relationship between the royal arrivals from the continent and their new kingdoms' naval power than this celebration of British maritime strength?

It probably says more about the underdeveloped role of empire for British collective identity before 1756[49] than about the Georgian kings that there are few other examples of sustained interest in naval and colonial affairs under George I and George II. Only from the Seven Years War did attitudes seem to have changed fundamentally. George III's visits to Portsmouth and the fleet from the 1770s are rightly famous. Even before that time the king's two younger brothers had founded the tradition of royal princes serving in the navy, while during the

---

[47] Laurence W.B. Brockliss, John Cardwell and Michael S. Moss, 'Nelson's Grand National Obsequies', *English Historical Review*, 121 (2006), pp. 162–82; Holger Hoock, 'The British Military Pantheon in St Paul's Cathedral: The State, Cultural Patriotism, and the Politics of National Monuments, c.1790–1820', in Matthew Craske and Richard Wrigley, eds, *Pantheons: Transformations of a Monumental Idea* (Aldershot, 2004), pp. 81–106; Holger Hoock, ed., *History, Commemoration and National Preoccupation: Trafalgar 1805–2005* (Oxford, 2007).

[48] It is depicted on the cover of this volume.

[49] See, e.g., Marie Peters, 'Early Hanoverian Consciousness: Empire or Europe', *English Historical Review*, 122 (2007), pp. 632–68.

1790s one of George III's sons, Prince Edward, became the first representative of the dynasty in the colonies, in Canada – although this was more by accident than design. Royal interest in maritime discovery and the accumulation of colonial knowledge also picked up under George III. Through his scientific adviser, Sir Joseph Banks, George III was closely involved in the planning and promotion of voyages of discovery in the Pacific and took a personal interest in channelling some of the botanical specimens and ethnographic objects collected during these expeditions to his German dominions. There they were stored at the museum of the University of Göttingen, highlighting once more the composite nature of the Hanoverian monarchy.[50] It is thus a fitting conclusion to this line of argument that the celebrations to mark the centenary of the Hanoverian succession in 1814 contained a decidedly naval component, as Ditchfield points out: they sported a reconstruction of the victory at Trafalgar and commemorated the Battle of the Nile.

Thus again, the representation of the Hanoverian dynasty, considered here primarily through the military theme, was not without its contradictions and ambivalences. In part this was certainly due to the haphazard nature of Georgian image policy, a feature which was not exclusive to the British monarchy, or indeed the eighteenth century. In part, however, it also had to do with the diverse nature of the monarchy as such, which had to be many things to many people and drew on a wide range of home-grown and foreign traditions, customs and legacies.

IV

The difficulties of the Hanoverians were aggravated by one further problem that was peculiar to their rule. Throughout the crucial first third of their reign they faced a powerful rival discourse on monarchy, Jacobitism. No other major European ruling house had to deal with the presence and activities of an exiled dynasty which in the eyes of some observers had a better claim to the English crown than the electoral family. This challenge could take different forms. In

---

[50] See John Gascoigne, 'Blumenbach, Banks and the Beginnings of Anthropology at Göttingen', in Nicolaas A. Rupke, ed., *Göttingen and the Development of the Natural Sciences* (Göttingen, 2002), pp. 86–98; Thomas Biskup, 'The University of Göttingen and the Personal Union, 1737–1837', in Simms and Riotte, eds, *The Hanoverian Dimension*, pp. 128–60; and, with a more sceptical view of the circulation of knowledge between Britain and Hanover, Dominik Collet, 'Creative Misunderstandings: Circulating Objects and the Transfer of Knowledge within the Personal Union of Hanover and Great Britain', in *German Historical Institute London Bulletin*, 36,2 (2014), pp. 3–23.

the first place, it presented itself, as has already been mentioned, as a military threat which became real in invasions, foreign interventions, popular risings and political plots – from the revolt of 1715 and the Atterbury plot of 1722 through to Charles Edward Stuart's part conquest of the British Isles in 1745–1746. This provoked the most serious crisis of Hanoverian rule, but at the same time marked the actual end of Jacobitism as a viable political alternative, although this became obvious only later.[51] How real the danger was perceived to be is evident from the almost paranoid concern with alleged Jacobite conspiracies and schemes in reports by British diplomats and correspondence between ministers. This culture of fear at the heart of the Hanoverian state turned out to be one of the most significant consequences of Jacobitism for Hanoverian politics, as Gabriel Glickman emphasises in his chapter.

Equally important was the existence of a rival Stuart court on the continent. By the time George I acceded to the British throne the exile court had already been moved – at the instigation of the government in London – from Saint-Germain-en-Laye to Bar-le-Duc in Lorraine, only to move still further away from Britain to Avignon, Urbino and finally Rome in 1719, where it was to remain with the exception of a brief sojourn in Bologna (1726–1729) for the remainder of its existence.[52] Geographical distance, however, did not weaken the court's allure for the supporters of the Stuart cause, at least until 1747, or indeed the power of its self-representation. As Edward Corp explains in this volume, the exiled Stuarts worked hard to defend their claim to the British throne in symbolic terms. They maintained a court worthy of a king; received recognition of their royal title from the French and Spanish ambassadors in Rome; and challenged their Hanoverian rivals directly, for example, by continuing to touch for the 'king's evil' and awarding the old chivalric orders of the British kings – the Order of the Garter and the Order of the Thistle.[53] For decades there were thus two competing claims to the ceremonial legacy of the British monarchy casting doubt on the legitimacy of the Hanoverian dynasty – in particular in Scotland,

---

[51] See Daniel Szechi, *1715: The Great Jacobite Rebellion* (New Haven, 2006); Eveline Cruickshanks and Howard Erskine-Hill, eds, *The Atterbury Plot* (Basingstoke, 2004); Christopher Duffy, 'The Jacobite Wars 1708–1746', in Edward M. Spiers, Jeremy A. Crang and Matthew Strickland, eds, *A Military History of Scotland* (Edinburgh, 2012), pp. 348–82.

[52] Edward Corp, *A Court in Exile: The Stuarts in France, 1689–1718* (Cambridge, 2004); id., *The Jacobites at Urbino: An Exiled Court in Transition* (Basingstoke, 2009); id., *The Stuarts in Italy, 1719–1766: A Royal Court in Permanent Exile* (Cambridge, 2011); id., ed., *The Stuart Court in Rome: The Legacy of Exile* (Aldershot, 2003).

[53] See also Edward Gregg, 'The Exiled Stuarts: Martyrs for the Faith?', in Michael Schaich, ed., *Monarchy and Religion: The Transformation of Royal Culture in Eighteenth-century Europe* (Oxford, 2007), pp. 187–213.

which the exiled Stuarts wooed more energetically than the Hanoverians. As Corp points out, James III pursued a deliberate policy of sending images to the Gaelic fringe of himself and his children wearing, in an innovative move, the Garter and the Thistle together, while the court in London made little effort to integrate this part of the composite monarchy into its policy of representation.[54] More than anything else, however, the Hanoverians were vulnerable to Jacobite propaganda, as Robert Bucholz demonstrates in his inquiry into the depictions of the first two Georges. Portrayals of George I and George II by Jacobite partisans as fat and ugly were meant to belittle their intellectual capacities and question their suitability for the office of king. Whatever effect this may have had at the time, it has certainly shaped the image of the Hanoverians to the present day.

The Stuart threat was not confined to the realm of images, symbols and ceremonies, however. It shaped Hanoverian political culture in other ways too, as Gabriel Glickman indicates in his discussion of the problem. To begin with, it laid bare the tensions within the Hanoverian composite monarchy by providing, during the first half of the eighteenth century, a rallying point for all those who opposed the centralising tendencies of the government in London and preferred to keep the looser ties of an old-style composite monarchy. As a consequence Jacobitism presented a counter-model to the modernising agenda of the fiscal-military state which appealed to groups not just in Scotland or Ireland but also in England, if we think of the patriot opposition to Walpolean government. At the same time, Jacobite writings about kingship and legitimate rule were not static and backward looking as had been thought in the past. On the contrary, they evolved constantly and adapted to changing fashions in political discourse, thus keeping up the challenge to Hanoverian self-legitimation. They even made some members of the Hanoverian dynasty, such as the Prince of Wales, Frederick Lewis, adopt Jacobite rhetoric and ideas for modernising the monarchy – an example of learning from the enemy that again highlights the diverse nature of the Hanoverian political code. Finally, the existence of a rival set of loyalties forced the Hanoverians to rely on only one part of the political and social elite of the British Isles and exclude others – such as the Tories, the Scottish Episcopalians and the Irish Catholics – from participation in government. As a result, the Georgian monarchy assumed the appearance of a partisan monarchy. Only after 1760 did it bring dissatisfied members of the political nation back out of the wilderness. Here the reverse of what we have observed in religious

---

[54] For the rather haphazard inclusion of Scottish symbols in Hanoverian court ceremonial see Schaich, *Die vielen Gesichter*, ch. II.3.b.

policy was the case. This time it was George III who proved to be much more accommodating than his predecessors. With the end of the Stuart claim to power he took on the role of monarch above parties.[55]

This emerging consensus among the political establishment also meant that the second rival discourse which (re-)surfaced during the reign of the Hanoverians, republicanism, developed into a lesser danger than Jacobitism. To be sure, there had been severe criticism of monarchs by radicals since the later eighteenth century. The 1790s, for example, saw underground plotting, physical assaults on the person of the king and the raising of hopes that a republican experiment was imminent. But, in the end, as Amanda Goodrich argues, radicalism was targeting not the monarchy but the aristocracy. The voices of anti-monarchism were drowned out by the critics of corrupt elite government which left the institution of monarchy untouched. In an ironic reversal of fortunes, radical circles even strengthened the king's position by appealing to him as an impartial figure alone capable of reforming the constitution. Since, at the other end of the political spectrum, loyalist supporters of king and country during the 1790s had also exalted the monarchy into the cornerstone of the fight against revolutionary and later Napoleonic France, the Hanoverian dynasty was arguably in a stronger position than ever before.[56]

This picture of a settled dynasty which had turned the corner in the struggle for the attachment of its subjects, however, should not blind us to the fact that loyalties remained fickle and the period of monarchical bliss did not last. Radical criticism of the monarchy was renewed in the early nineteenth century, especially during the reign of George IV. The damage done by the Queen Caroline affair probably hit the dynasty harder than many attacks by Jacobite writers on George I and his son, as G.M. Ditchfield opines. The Hanoverians certainly remained controversial in the years around 1800, still giving rise to talk about the 'German leeches' in their entourage or the frequent appearance of a white horse, the heraldic beast of the Guelphs, in cartoons to lampoon the king.[57] In its German dominions, on the other hand, the dynasty enjoyed a more favourable reception

---

[55] For the wider party political context see O'Gorman, *Long Eighteenth Century*, pp. 277–86 and P.D.G. Thomas, *George III: King and Politicians, 1760–1770* (Manchester, 2002).

[56] From the vast literature on loyalism in the 1790s see Jennifer Mori, 'Languages of Loyalism: Patriotism, Nationhood and the State in the 1790s', *English Historical Review*, 118 (2003), pp. 33–58; Mark Philp, ed., *Resisting Napoleon: The British Response to the Threat of Invasion, 1797–1815* (Aldershot, 2006).

[57] The quotation is from the chapter by Amanda Goodrich in this volume. For the Hanoverian horse see Ulrike Weiss, 'Das Pferd und seine besondere Rolle in Großbritannien und Hannover', in Lembke, ed., *Als die Royals*, pp. 94–105.

once it had been reinstated after the defeat of Napoleon in 1813.[58] George IV, William IV and their representative in Hanover, the Duke of Cambridge, cultivated the image of a benign 'Landesvater' and aligned themselves with the forces of political reform. Fortified by a widespread enthusiasm for the English constitution among German intellectuals, the dynasty was widely perceived as a force for good. This public mood remained largely unchanged until 1837, when the personal union was dissolved due to different laws of succession on Queen Victoria's coming to the throne.

To the last, then, the Hanoverians left a far from coherent impression on the various components of their territories. They were perceived in sometimes strikingly different ways, hailed by some and run down by others. The schemes developed to improve the dynasty's public image also drew on a variety of sources and deployed different stratagems. It should have become clear in the course of this introduction that this volume is not intended to tell the success story of a dynasty on the occasion of the tercentenary of its accession to the British throne. Rather, it will analyse the various and often conflicting ways in which it presented itself to the outside world and in turn was portrayed by other groups, friend or foe. If there is any unifying principle in this story then it is the realisation that the Hanoverian policy of representation was of necessity ill-defined, allowing the rulers to address as many constituencies of their composite monarchy as possible.

---

[58] See van den Heuvel, 'Georg IV. und Wilhelm IV'.

PART I
Dynastic Legacies

Chapter 2

The Hanoverian Monarchy and the Legacy of Late Stuart Kingship

Ronald G. Asch

I

When George I ascended the British throne in 1714, the succession to the crown had been a matter of dispute for at least 28 years. Ever since the Glorious Revolution the claims of the senior branch of the Stuarts had been in conflict with those of James II's daughters, Mary and Anne, and those of William III, Mary's husband. But in many ways the succession had become a matter of dispute even earlier, in the late 1670s, when the Whigs had tried to exclude the Duke of York from becoming king after his brother's death. If anything, the Hanoverian claims to the crown (although based on the Act of Settlement of 1701) were even more controversial than those of William and Mary and Queen Anne, as the Hanoverians were only distantly related to the royal dynasty.

This was not the first time that the succession to the crown had been the subject of political conflicts. One need not go as far back as the Wars of the Roses in the fifteenth century to find precedents for attempts to replace one branch of the dynasty by another one. Henry VIII had excluded the Stuarts from the English succession altogether in 1543 – a passage of his last will which was ignored in 1603 when James VI of Scotland became king of England as James I.[1] Perhaps more to the point, Mary Stuart's claims to the crown which she was to bequeath to her son after her death in 1587 were rejected in England after 1558, still in keeping with Henry VIII's last will. In addition, the Act of Association of 1584 had excluded from the succession any persons who were involved in a plot against the reigning monarch, Elizabeth I, a clause which was aimed at Mary Queen of Scots. Only when James I came to power in 1603 was this tradition of tampering with the succession for political and confessional

---

[1] Howard Nenner, *The Right to be King: The Succession to the Crown of England, 1603–1714* (Basingstoke, 1995), pp. 13–33.

reasons seemingly abandoned. James claimed to be king due to an indisputable hereditary right, which was not subject to parliamentary scrutiny or any other human limitations.[2] His vision of kingship *iure divino* was designed to strengthen royal authority both against the threat which religious fanatics posed and the claims of parliament to be able to define or limit royal power.

This model of kingship came to grief in the civil war, but was revived after a fashion after 1660. The late 1670s in many ways presented a throwback to the 1580s: under Elizabeth's rule, the threat of a Catholic succession was countered by the Act of Association; under Charles II the Exclusion Bill was to serve a similar purpose. But it was much easier to exclude a pretender to the crown who was a foreigner and, what is more, a prisoner in England from the succession than the ruling king's brother, even if intentions to connive in his older brother's death were imputed to the future James II during the Popish Plot. Thus, the debate on the succession to the crown became radicalised in new and unheard of ways, more so than in the past. Although historians like Patrick Collinson have discovered hints of an incipient republicanism in the Act and Bond of Association in the 1580s,[3] such republican tendencies became much more explicit from the 1670s onwards. This was partly because England had, indeed, been a republic for 11 years after 1649. The memory of the Good Old Cause was very much alive in the 1670s and 1680s, but such tendencies were also a result of the fact that it had become more difficult than in the past to implement a change of dynasty without appealing to political principles which called into question unfettered royal authority as such, not just the succession of a particular pretender. This was all the more true as both William III and George I were foreigners; thus attempts to check the royal prerogative, more successful ultimately in the latter than in the former case, were also meant to safeguard England's position within a wider dynastic conglomerate, a multiple monarchy whose real centre was not necessarily in London, but rather in The Hague, or even possibly in remote Hanover as many feared before 1714, remembering

---

[2] Ibid., pp. 55–64.
[3] Patrick Collinson, 'The Monarchical Republic of Queen Elizabeth I', in id., *Elizabethan Essays* (London, 1994), pp. 31–57; John F. McDiarmid, ed., *The Monarchical Republic of Early Modern England: Essays in Response to Patrick Collinson* (Aldershot, 2007); cf. Jean-Christophe Mayer, ed., *The Struggle for the Succession in Late Elizabethan England: Politics, Polemics and Cultural Representations* (Montpellier, 2004), and David Cressy, 'Binding the Nation: The Bonds of Association, 1584 and 1696', in DeLloyd J. Guth and John W. McKenna, eds, *Tudor Rule and Revolution: Essays for G.R. Elton from His American Friends* (Cambridge, 1982), pp. 217–34.

only too vividly how William III had relegated England almost to the status of a Dutch province at times before his death.

However, to limit royal power in England was a much more difficult business than, for example, in countries like Poland, which had been an elective monarchy since the late sixteenth century, or in eighteenth-century Sweden, which was an aristocracy with a monarch as its head between 1718 and 1772. In England, both for Whigs and Tories, the role of the monarchy was far more than a merely secular one. For the Tories, who remained reluctant to abandon the idea of a monarchy by divine right,[4] the monarch remained at least potentially God's image upon earth, a ruler who was both king and priest and held an authority which was sacred in nature. But could such a power and position be entrusted to a ruler who was not a reliable supporter of the Church of England? The answer to this question had still been affirmative in 1678 and in 1685, but was much more doubtful in 1688 and in 1701.

But the position of the Whigs was hardly less complicated. On the one hand they stood to some extent in the tradition of the parliamentary side in the civil war, which had claimed to defend ancient liberties and the traditional constitution against the royal prerogative. On the other hand a weak monarchy, and even more so a weak state, could all too easily prove to be an insufficient defence against the pretensions of prelacy and clericalism in its various forms. Already in the late 1670s the Whigs had largely rejected the option of imposing limitations on the ecclesiastical power of a popish successor to the crown to prevent him from destroying the church by law established, for such limitations would – or so it seemed – have given too much power to the bishops and to the clergy in general.[5] Because Erastianism and a rejection of the temporal power of a clerical hierarchy of any sort was such an important ingredient in the Whig outlook on politics, the king's authority could not easily be limited, at least as long as the danger posed by prelacy and priestcraft was seen as a serious menace. Thus Mark Goldie has stated: 'Erastianism became a permanent counterbalance within Whiggism to the country ideal of distrust

---

[4] Mark Goldie, 'The Political Thought of the Anglican Revolution', in Robert Beddard, ed., *The Revolutions of 1688* (Oxford, 1991), pp. 103–36. For developments after 1688 see also Gerald M. Straka, 'The Final Phase of Divine Right Theory in England, 1688–1702', *English Historical Review*, 77 (1965), pp. 638–58 and Robert D. Cornwall, 'Divine Right Monarchy: Henry Dodwell's Critique of the Reformation and Defense of the Deprived Nonjuror Bishops', *Anglican and Episcopal History*, 68 (1999), pp. 37–66. I have dealt with the problems of late Stuart Kingship more fully in my *Sacral Kingship between Disenchantment and Re-enchantment: The French and English Monarchies 1587–1688* (London, 2014).

[5] Jacqueline Rose, *Godly Kingship in Restoration England: The Politics of the Royal Supremacy, 1660–1688* (Cambridge, 2011), pp. 233–4.

of the state. It helps explain the readiness of post-revolution Whiggism to sanctify and defend state power, and so explains the longevity in England of the idea of a national church.'[6]

The question of the succession to the crown and the more general debate over the role the monarch was to play in politics can indeed not be separated from the conflict between *sacerdotium*, however defined, and *imperium* or *regnum* which still played such a prominent role in seventeenth-century English and Scottish politics, much more so perhaps than in many other European countries. This becomes visible not only in the political philosophy of Thomas Hobbes, as Jeffrey Collins has recently pointed out once more, but also in practical politics after the Restoration.[7] The conflict was only to abate gradually after the virtual dissolution of Convocation in 1717. Because both 1688 and 1714 were a triumph not only for Protestantism but also for a specifically Erastian variety of Protestantism, the role of monarchy as the decisive cornerstone for the ecclesiastical settlement remained of crucial importance far beyond 1714.

However the particular role the monarch played after 1714 and the religious context of royal authority in general can only be understood adequately if one bears in mind the problems kingship had encountered after the Restoration. Hanoverian kingship was deeply marked by the legacy of the Stuart age.

II

The Restoration of 1660, although widely accepted, even welcomed, by many sections of the population, especially the social elite, had failed to create a model of kingship that was consistent and sufficiently coherent. When Charles II returned to England in 1660, he was confronted by a variety of expectations which were largely incompatible with each other. There were the moderate Presbyterians who had had a decisive share in re-establishing monarchy. They clearly wanted a godly ruler who governed in accordance with the law of the land and presided over a broadly based and comprehensive national church, whose structure, liturgy and theology were acceptable to those who saw themselves as the heirs of early seventeenth-century

---

[6] Mark Goldie, 'Civil Religion and the English Enlightenment', in Gordon J. Schochet, Carol Brobeck and Patricia Elizabeth Tatspaugh, eds, *Politics, Politeness and Patriotism: Papers Presented at the Folger Institute Seminar 'Politics and Politeness: British Political Thought in the Age of Walpole'* (Washington, DC, 1993), pp. 31–46, at p. 44.

[7] Jeffrey R. Collins, *The Allegiance of Thomas Hobbes* (Oxford, 2005), p. 279.

Puritanism and adhered to a strictly Calvinist tradition.[8] On the opposite side of the religious spectrum there were the royalist Anglicans who saw the church by law established as a necessary cornerstone of a traditional social and political order and wanted to return, if not to the Laudianism of the 1630s, at least to the wider anti-Puritan conformist movement of the early seventeenth century.[9] A sacral monarchy and episcopacy *iure divino* formed a close alliance in this perspective, although this was a political and religious marriage which was not without its particular tensions.

Finally there were those who had had their fill of religious fervour and detested nothing so much as the enthusiasm and narrow-minded moralistic ideals of the religious militants who had dominated English politics in the 1650s. But in the end they were critical of all clerical authority, including that of the Anglican clergy, certainly in so far as it threatened to interfere with their lives and politics. In fact, whereas before 1640 it had seemed self-evident to most that church and nation were largely co-extensive and that the secular community of ruler and subjects was in many ways identical with the ecclesiastical community of the faithful at a national level, this unity had been shattered by the breakdown of the established Church in the late 1640s and the 1650s. The failure of a religious settlement, which could form the basis for a truly comprehensive church in the 1660s, was bound to provoke calls for toleration and consequently for some degree of separation between church and state, however limited. From such a perspective there would no longer be one church as a divinely ordained institution, but different competing churches which were essentially associations created by men and women who shared the same religious conviction.[10]

Without depicting the decades after 1660 as a period of inexorable secularisation, there can be little doubt that those who wanted to defend the full panoply of traditional Christian dogma and metaphysics against its critics increasingly faced an uphill struggle.[11] We would look in vain in England for the

---

[8] Ronald Hutton, *The Restoration: A Political and Religious History of England and Wales, 1658–1667* (Oxford, 1985), pp. 143–8; John Miller, *After the Civil Wars: English Politics and Government in the Reign of Charles II* (Harlow, 2000), pp. 141–4; Mark Goldie, ed., *The Entring Book of Roger Morrice, 1677–1691*, vol. 1: *Roger Morrice and the Puritan Whigs* (Woodbridge, 2007), pp. 154–61. Cf. Tim Harris, *Restoration: Charles II and His Kingdoms, 1660–1685* (London, 2005), pp. 43–84.

[9] Paul Seaward, *The Cavalier Parliament and the Reconstruction of the Old Regime, 1661–1667* (Cambridge, 1989).

[10] John Marshall, *John Locke, Toleration and Early Enlightenment Culture: Religious Intolerance and Arguments for Religious Toleration in Early Modern and 'Early Enlightenment' Europe* (Cambridge, 2006).

[11] Blair Worden, 'The Question of Secularisation', in Alan Houston and Steve Pincus, eds, *A Nation Transformed: England after the Restoration* (Cambridge, 2001), pp. 40–60.

Crépuscule des mystiques, the twilight of mysticism which we find in France at the end of the seventeenth century, because English Protestantism was little given to mysticism as such in comparison to Counter-Reformation Catholicism in France. But a more moralistic, and one might say more pragmatic, less metaphysical concept of religion certainly posed problems for the very idea of sacral kingship in England in the late seventeenth century which had been so important for sustaining royalist resistance against the new republican order after 1649.

Of course the reestablished Church of England provided a bulwark against such attempts to subject religion to individual judgement and private reason and to disenchant the world of politics in this way. But its hold on society as a whole always remained somewhat tenuous after 1660 and, at times, in its battle against religious enthusiasm it subscribed itself to the rationalism which it rejected in other fields.[12] In any case, it was by no means always an easy let alone submissive ally of the Restoration monarchy. Many convinced royalists had sought after 1660 to reestablish a close cooperation between divine right kingship and a church governed by bishops who derived their own authority immediately from God. Only such a partnership could in their opinion guarantee that England would not again succumb to the forces of disorder and rebellion.[13] The old royalists who had been forced to lie low after 1649 wanted a king who accepted the legacy his father had left him and ruled church and state accordingly. Ideally, England should be ruled by a king whose ecclesiastical policy was guided by his episcopal councillors inspired by the memory of Charles I, who had died as a martyr for the Church of England, at least in the account *Eikon Basilike* and similar writings gave of his death. *Eikon Basilike*, however, while founding the cult of the martyr king, was a difficult text for Charles II to base his policies on. It tried to cast Charles I far too much in the role of the steadfast defender of episcopacy and the Book of Common Prayer and all it stood for. By confronting Charles II with an ideal he could never live up to, given the need to seek compromises with Presbyterians and other dissenters, it potentially undermined the Stuart monarchy after 1660; or, as Sean Kelsey has put it: 'Eikon Basilike ... contributed powerfully to the growing crisis of representation that beset the political discourse of the age.'[14]

---

[12] John Spurr, 'Rational Religion in Restoration England', *Journal of the History of Ideas*, 49 (1988), pp. 563–85; id., *The Restoration Church of England, 1646–1689* (New Haven, 1991), pp. 249–69.

[13] For the Anglican Church after 1660 see next to Spurr, *Restoration Church*, also I.M. Green, *The Re-Establishment of the Church of England, 1660–1663* (Oxford, 1978).

[14] Sean Kelsey, 'The King's Book: Eikon Basilike and the English Revolution', in Nicholas Tyacke, ed., *The English Revolution, c.1540–1720: Politics, Religion and Communities* (Manchester, 2007), pp. 150–69, at p. 163.

In a wider perspective English kingship under the later Stuarts was confronted by the problem that the legacy of the Reformation was ever more difficult to combine with a consistent model of monarchy. There was the idea of the king as a new Constantine trampling under his feet not just the pope but all lordly prelates going back to Henry VIII. This essentially anticlerical model of kingship had in the past been invoked to justify the rejection of the papal supremacy as much as the fight against the theocratic variety of Calvinism which Scottish Presbyterianism represented. But such a model was not easily compatible with a Tory vision of church and monarchy for which episcopacy *iure divino* and the autonomy of the church were so important. On the other hand, there was the model of sacerdotal kingship, with the ruler playing to some extent the role of a priest-king guided by his episcopal councillors, whose role was ultimately indispensable in giving credibility to this vision of monarchy. This model, however, imposed enormous constraints on the monarch's freedom of action in all matters of ecclesiastical policy, not to mention the fact that even among high Anglicans many theologians were now increasingly inclined to downplay the quasi-sacerdotal powers of a king whose support for the church was not beyond doubt.[15]

Charles II himself clearly felt uneasy about the more fulsome aspects of sacral monarchy and sacerdotal kingship despite his pronounced and unrivalled enthusiasm for healing the scrofula.[16] The way he conducted his private life could even be seen as a permanent denial of the idea that the royal body was in some sense sacred. His personal life, however, was by no means the only reason which made the relationship between the king and the Church of England and its bishops a rather complicated one fraught with tensions.[17] The bishops were rarely easy partners for the king. They had their own notions of how the king should exercise his royal supremacy.[18] During and after the civil war, supporters of episcopacy and the Church of England had learnt that they might have to live without the support of an anointed monarch who had demonstrated all

---

[15] On the theological framework for relations between king and church see Rose, *Godly Kingship* and Jeffrey R. Collins, 'The Restoration Bishops and the Royal Supremacy', *Church History*, 68 (1999), pp. 549–80.

[16] Anna Keay, *The Magnificent Monarch: Charles II and the Ceremonies of Power* (London, 2008), pp. 115–18, 211–13; cf. Harold M. Weber, *Paper Bullets: Print and Kingship under Charles II* (Lexington, KY, 1996), pp. 50–87. For miraculous healings in this period see now also Peter Elmer, *The Miraculous Conformist: Valentine Greatrakes, the Body Politic and the Politics of Healing in Restoration Britain* (Oxford, 2013).

[17] See Rose, *Godly Kingship*, pp. 89–104, 154–62.

[18] J.R. Jones, *Charles II: Royal Politician* (London, 1987), pp. 46–51; Spurr, *Restoration Church*, pp. 147–8.

too clearly that he was prepared to seek a compromise with the enemies of the church, that is, Scots Presbyterians.[19]

A more secular vision of kingship, which downplayed the role of the king as supreme governor and head of the established Church, would perhaps have allowed the king to distance himself from the religious controversies of the age and to appear as a neutral arbiter standing above the confessional strife. However such a secular vision of kingship was unacceptable even to those who mistrusted Charles II and his brother as guardians of the Protestant faith. The danger that a monarchy, which by being secularised lost its authority in ecclesiastical matters, would be overshadowed by a powerful and intolerant clerical hierarchy seemed too great.[20]

In any case Charles II was only able to overcome the Whig opposition to the legitimate succession by a firm alliance with traditional Anglican royalism and the bishops of the established Church, who were as eager to promote divine right episcopacy as divine right monarchy.[21] Nevertheless, even during the last years before Charles II's death his commitment to this alliance was never entirely unqualified.[22] Although the vision of monarchy which court art now projected had stronger and clearer religious and sacral connotations than in the past, it remained somewhat unclear whether these connotations were exclusively Anglican in nature, and what role Catholicism would play at court. The messages conveyed by ceremony, sermons, art and poetry produced at or for the court were in every sense deeply contradictory. Certainly the meanings of symbolic images of royal authority had always been ambivalent. To some extent this was part of their strength – quite different audiences could identify with them because they were so ambiguous.[23] But at Charles II's court the contradictions often

---

[19] Rose, *Godly Kingship*, pp. 73–88, 130–40, cf. Anthony Milton, '"Vailing his Crown": Royalist Criticism of Charles I's Kingship in the 1650s', in Jason McElligott and David L. Smith, eds, *Royalists and Royalism during the Interregnum* (Manchester, 2010), pp. 88–105, and id., 'Sacrilege and Compromise: Court Divines and the King's Conscience', in Michael J. Braddick and David L. Smith, eds, *The Experience of Revolution in Stuart Britain and Ireland* (Cambridge, 2011), pp. 135–53.

[20] Mark Goldie, 'Danby, the Bishops and the Whigs', in Tim Harris, Paul Seaward and Mark Goldie, eds, *The Politics of Religion in Restoration England* (Oxford, 1990), pp. 75–105, and Paul Seaward, 'Shaftesbury and the Royal Supremacy', in John Spurr, ed., *Anthony Ashley Cooper, First Earl of Shaftesbury, 1621–1683* (Farnham, 2001), pp. 51–76.

[21] Harris, *Restoration*, pp. 211–328.

[22] Grant Tapsell, *The Personal Rule of Charles II, 1681–85* (Woodbridge, 2007), pp. 58–9.

[23] Laurence M. Bryant, 'Royal Ceremony and the Revolutionary Strategies of the Third Estate', in id., *Ritual, Ceremony and the Changing Monarchy in France, 1350–1789*

overshadowed the image of authority itself. Libertinage, satire and mockery of all conventions on the one hand and solemn divine right rhetoric on the other hardly ever created a coherent harmonious representation of kingship.[24]

III

With James II's accession these ambiguities seemed to come to an end. The image which kingship, court culture and royal policy projected became much clearer but also more controversial. Far from being indifferent in religious matters, James was a confirmed Roman Catholic.[25] In retrospect, James's real claim to a place in history seems to be his success in destroying in less than four years everything his brother had achieved since 1678: the alliance with the hierarchy of the Church of England; the loyalty of the Tories; and the widespread support which he enjoyed both in England and Scotland among all those who were prepared to pay a high price just to avoid another civil war.

In fact, James's keenest defenders could hardly argue that he was a clever and astute politician. The question, however, is what his vision of kingship was. Clearly this vision cannot easily be separated from his faith as a Catholic. For many historians James's obsession with his own salvation and the religious aspects of his role as a monarch shows that he was a man governed by bigotry and quixotic ideas of kingship as a religious mission. In England sacral monarchy had really come to an end with the execution of Charles I, and all attempts to revive it, especially if undertaken with such unmitigated fervour as James II showed, could only end in failure.[26] Other historians like Steve Pincus take James II's attempt to create a new model of Catholic kingship more seriously. If we follow

---

(Farnham, 2010), pp. 283–320, at p. 287: 'The king performed and each party could "read" a royal gesture in his own way: indeed a considerable part of his power came from allowing ambiguous and different interpretations of the same phenomenon among those who depended upon his decision, direction and support.' With regard to court and state ceremonies during the *ancien régime* in France.

[24] Matthew Jenkinson, *Culture and Politics at the Court of Charles II, 1660–1685* (Woodbridge, 2010), pp. 239–40. For the late Stuart court cf. however now Kevin Sharpe, *Rebranding Rule 1660–1714: The Restoration and Revolution Monarchy* (New Haven, 2013).

[25] For James II see John Callow, *King in Exile. James II: Warrior, King and Saint* (Stroud, 2004), and id., *The Making of King James II: The Formative Years of a Fallen King* (Stroud, 2000), as well as John Miller, *James II: A Study in Kingship* (London, 1978).

[26] See for example Monique and Bernard Cottret, 'La Sainteté de Jacques II et les miracles d'un roi défunt', in Edward Corp, ed., *L'autre exil: Les Jacobites en France* (Paris, 1993), pp. 79–106, and Bernard Cottret, 'Ecce Homo: La crise de l'incarnation royale en

Pincus, James II was not such a bad politician after all. His policies were 'neither foolish nor unrealistic'. Rather, they provided at core a realistic model of a sort of 'catholic modernity' which had found its apogee in Louis XIV's France.[27] 'Modern' for Pincus means primarily rational, efficient, with the capacity to create new structures of power and authority not hampered by mere tradition.

However, Pincus' attempt to depict James II as a king fighting for an ultimately secular absolutism which was inspired by France and its state church is based on a one-dimensional interpretation of royal government and baroque kingship in France. Not least, Pincus ignores the multi-layered character of French Gallicanism, which allegedly inspired James's policies. Gallicanism can by no means be identified with the ecclesiastical face of political absolutism, given that it was deeply rooted in conciliarism.[28] Moreover, by downplaying the religious element in the opposition against James II, Pincus tries to construct 1688 as a merely secular battle for liberty and constitutionalism.

James seems to have been convinced that sacral monarchy – and he certainly saw his role as a king as one which was divinely sanctioned and similar in some ways to that of a priest – could only work if it was based on the ruler's personal religious commitment and piety.[29] His brother had played with the trappings of sacral monarchy. He had submitted to all the rituals which were part of this vision of kingship, such as attendance at church and the healing of the scrofula, for example, but he remained convinced that ritual was enough and could stand on its own. But to some extent this was a model of kingship that no longer

---

Angleterre (1649–1688–1701)', in Maria-Christian Pitassi, ed., *Le Christ entre Orthodoxie et Lumières* (Geneva, 1994), pp. 77–99.

[27] Steve C.A. Pincus, *1688: The First Modern Revolution* (New Haven, 2009), p. 122.

[28] Jotham Parsons, *The Church in the Republic: Gallicanism and Political Ideology in Renaissance France* (Washington, DC, 2004); Alain Tallon, *Conscience nationale et sentiment religieux en France au XVIe siècle* (Paris, 2002); Francis Oakley, *The Conciliarist Tradition: Constitutionalism in the Catholic Church, 1300–1870* (Oxford, 2003), pp. 141–81; cf. Aimé-Georges Martimort, *Le Gallicanisme de Bossuet* (Paris, 1953); and for Pincus' own position Steve C.A. Pincus, 'The European Catholic Context of the Revolution of 1688–89: Gallicanism, Innocent XI and Catholic Opposition', in Alan I. Macinnes and Arthur H. Williamson, eds, *Shaping the Stuart World, 1603–1714* (Leiden, 2006), pp. 79–114.

[29] James's personal piety is not that easy to fathom for the years before he went into exile, but it was certainly inspired by contemporary French Catholicism; see Miller, *James II*, pp. 58–60. For James's piety and devotions in exile see Edward T. Corp, *A Court in Exile: The Stuarts in France, 1689–1718* (Cambridge, 2004), pp. 234–43. See also James II, *Royal Tracts in Two Parts the First Containing the Select Speeches, Orders, Messages, Letters, etc. of His Sacred Majesty Upon Extraordinary Occasions, ... The Second Containing Imago Regis or the Sacred Image of His Majesty in His Solitudes and Sufferings, Written During His Retirement in France* (Paris, 1692).

worked in the late seventeenth century, certainly not in England where religious sensibilities, even outside the communities of dissenters, had been so strongly shaped by the legacy of Puritanism. Ritual had to be founded in some sort of credible conviction, otherwise it lost its persuasiveness and could all too easily be rejected as mere show and play-acting.[30] The problem with James's religious fervour was that the personal religious commitment which was to give credibility and coherence to his role as a sacerdotal king was not an Anglican but a Catholic one and, thus, to all intents and purposes, incompatible with the creed of the church by law established.

In other respects, however, James II was quite capable of using the traditions of the Church of England and the teaching of its theology for his own purposes. At the core of James's vision of kingship and also, strangely enough, of his idea of toleration, was the conviction that as a ruler he was both *rex et sacerdos*, that he had virtually priestly powers and could, although a Catholic, use his position as head of the Church of England not just to appoint his clients and supporters as bishops and to transform university colleges into Catholic seminaries but also to impose a policy of toleration without reference to parliamentary statutes. He felt entitled to force Anglican clergy to comply with this policy due to his exalted semi-sacerdotal position.[31] Official and semi-official publications justifying his Declarations of Indulgence in 1687 and 1688 are highly revealing for this vision of kingship. Among the semi-official tracts which were disseminated in 1687–1688 to justify James's decision to suspend the laws against recusants and dissenters was one entitled *The King's Right of Indulgence in Spiritual Matters*, which was based on a memorandum originally written by Bulstrode Whitelocke in the 1660s and revised in 1672. This tract argued that the 'King of England is not only a *mixt* Person, but in some sense he may be termed a Spiritual Person'. The very fact that the king was not just crowned but anointed demonstrated 'a kind of Sacredness'.[32]

If, however, the character of the king as a spiritual person were denied, then 'he could not so properly be Head of the Church in England'. What is more, as head of the church the king must be presumed to have the same power to grant

---

[30] For this problem see Asch, *Sacral Kingship*, p. 144.
[31] Cf. Rose, *Godly Kingship*, pp. 235–9 and Callow, *King in Exile*, pp. 307–9.
[32] *The King's Right of Indulgence in Spiritual Matters, with the Equity Thereof, Asserted, by a Person of Honour and Eminent Minister of State Lately Deceased* (London, 1688), p. 37. The tract had originally been written by Bulstrode Whitelocke for Charles II in 1663, but not published; see Rose, *Godly Kingship*, pp. 169–70, 185, and Mark Goldie, 'Toleration and the Godly Prince in Restoration England', in John Morrow and Jonathan Scott, eds, *Liberty, Authority, Formality: Political Ideas and Culture, 1600–1900* (Exeter, 2008), pp. 45–65.

indulgences as the pope had had before the Reformation, and so it was up to him to decide to what extent individuals or entire communities and churches should enjoy liberty of conscience.[33] It is somewhat surprising to see supporters of a Catholic monarch acting as head of a Protestant church attributing the same powers to the king as Henry VIII's theologians, in particular, Archbishop Cranmer, had claimed for the Tudor monarch in rebellion against Rome: that is, the capacity to act both as prince and priest and as a sort of lay patriarch with the full panoply of powers which the pope had enjoyed in the past. However, it was precisely this sort of Caesaro-papism which was at the heart of James's concept of kingship, at least as far as his church policy was concerned, as Jacqueline Rose has recently demonstrated.[34] This approach may seem so self-contradictory that it was bound to fail, and fail it did indeed. However, there was a vociferous minority of Anglican divines who were prepared to supply the king with all the arguments he needed to underpin this sacerdotal kingship, and his policy of toleration could potentially appeal to certain sections of the dissenter community as well.[35]

What sealed James's fate was not so much his Catholic faith as such, but the fact that he was seen in the end as an unpatriotic ruler, even more so than his brother, which was quite an achievement in itself. He had tried to promote an idea of English patriotism which was based on loyalty to the monarchy and acceptance of religious plurality within England, and not on Protestantism as the core of national identity as Scott Sowerby has recently emphasised.[36] But in the end this was seen as a mere ploy to make England subservient to France.

---

[33] *The King's Right*, p. 38.

[34] Jacqueline Rose, *Concepts of Royal Ecclesiastical Supremacy in Restoration England* (PhD thesis, University of Cambridge, 2007), p. 230, ead., *Godly Kingship*, pp. 220–24.

[35] On supporters of James's policy, in particular Thomas Pierce and Samuel Parker, see Rose, *Godly Kingship*, pp. 139–40, 228, and Gordon J. Schochet, 'Between Lambeth and Leviathan: Samuel Parker on the Church of England and Political Order', in Nicholas Phillipson and Quentin Skinner, eds, *Political Discourse in Early Modern Britain* (Cambridge, 1993), pp. 189–208. For sympathy among dissenters see Mark Goldie, 'John Locke's Circle and James II', *Historical Journal*, 35 (1992), pp. 557–86.

[36] Scott Sowerby, 'Of Different Complexion: Religious Diversity and National Identity in James II's Toleration Campaign', *English Historical Review*, 124 (2009), pp. 29–52. According to Sowerby, English men and women by no means agreed on one particular concept of national unity (as Pincus assumes), but William III's programme of falling back on mainstream Protestantism as central to national identity proved victorious. James II had attempted to stretch a concept of national identity that had ultimately proved to be inelastic (p. 52); cf. Steve C.A. Pincus, '"To Protect English Liberties": The English Nationalist Revolution of 1688–1689', in Tony Claydon and Ian McBride, eds, *Protestantism and National Identity: Britain and Ireland, c.1650–1850* (Cambridge, 1998), pp. 75–104, in

IV

In 1688 James II was replaced by a king who claimed, with sufficient plausibility in the eyes of many observers, to be a godly prince, acting in the name of providence to save both Protestantism and English liberty from the French tyrant and his English henchmen, very much in the tradition of Elizabeth I. His vision of monarchy was not a predominantly secular one, but it lacked the elements of sacerdotal kingship which had been so important to James II. Moreover, William III's model of monarchy was more easily compatible with an Erastian and radically Protestant anticlericalism, which had gained ground in the 1670s and 1680s, than James's vision of sacral monarchy.[37]

Of course, William III had to be cautious in presenting himself exclusively as a godly fighter against popery; he owed his success in the battle against France to a considerable extent to his alliance with the emperor and other Catholic powers. It would not do to overemphasise the confessional elements of his kingship, at least at an official level, quite apart from the fact that William III was personally tolerant and that many of the soldiers fighting for him in his multi-national army were, indeed, Catholics. Sermons given in England or his other British kingdoms might stress that William, unlike his two predecessors, was a pious king and the sworn enemy of idolatry in all its forms. But the official image was that of the classical hero, modelled more on the mythological figure of Hercules than on biblical and historical examples, which were more strongly associated with the confessional divisions of early modern Europe. In some sense William III's image was that of the traditional soldier-king and royal hero – but perhaps with the difference that his life and actions were always depicted as being devoted to a higher cause.[38] Honour and prestige may have been important enough to William III, but his kingship was centred less exclusively on personal glory and dynastic reputation than was the case with his great counterpart and enemy, Louis XIV. William III's role as a military hero was never independent of his service to the common good and the greater cause of both liberty and religious freedom. In this sense, as in other respects, how he was depicted perhaps followed the example which Cromwell had set as a republican hero more than

---

particular p. 85; and, for the general background, Tim Harris, *Revolution: The Great Crisis of the British Monarchy, 1685–1720* (London, 2007), pp. 239–307.

[37] Tony Claydon, *William III and the Godly Revolution* (Cambridge, 1996).

[38] Ulrich Niggemann, 'Herrschermemoria als Norm und Symbol: Zum Umgang mit der Erinnerung an Wilhelm III. im England des frühen 18. Jahrhunderts', *Zeitschrift für Historische Forschung*, 39 (2012), pp. 1–37, at pp. 6–8.

the tradition of the dynastic ruler as a conqueror and chivalrous warrior-king in search of glory and military victory for their own sake.[39]

But William III was a hard act to follow. What is more, it is doubtful whether the king's attempt to win support for his rule in Britain was entirely successful. Many of his subjects seem to have seen him as too aloof, too obsessed with waging war against France with British money and British soldiers, and, worst of all, as too Dutch and not British or English enough, in particular after his wife's death.[40] Queen Anne's reign was a welcome interlude, especially for the Tories, as she was a Stuart and a staunch supporter of the Church of England. Partly because she was a woman, the warlike and heroic elements in the prevailing image of kingship receded into the background, although there had been queens in the past, in particular Elizabeth I (who had, however, been unmarried and childless), who had quite strongly emphasised these aspects of their role as a ruler.[41]

It was perhaps all the more difficult for the Hanoverians, and for George I in particular, to find a convincing new image for monarchy which would appeal to their new subjects. They could hardly go back to the image of the king as an almost priestly figure which the Stuarts in exile had cultivated. In fact, they ceased to heal the scrofula, a practice which Queen Anne had revived during her reign. But nor could George I pose in quite the same way as William III had done, as a God-sent heroic deliverer from the dangers of popery and tyranny.[42] In fact, for their supporters the Hanoverians now became more the mere protectors of the Protestant religion than charismatic saviours and deliverers. The king was more a 'fellow Christian who had particular duties in showing his subjects how they should lead virtuous and pious lives', as the Finnish historian Pasi Ihalainen has put it in his study of eighteenth-century

---

[39] Craig Rose, *England in the 1690s: Revolution, Religion and War* (Oxford, 1999), pp. 22–4.

[40] For criticism of William's reign see for example Mark Goldie and Clare Jackson, 'Williamite Tyranny and the Whig Jacobites', in Esther Mijers and David Onnekink, eds, *Redefining William III: The Impact of the King-Stadholder in International Context* (Aldershot, 2007), pp. 177–99, as well as Charles-Edouard Levillain, 'Cromwell Redivivus? William III as Military Dictator: Myth and Reality', ibid., pp. 159–76.

[41] Anne Somerset, *Queen Anne: The Politics of Passion* (London, 2012).

[42] For the monarchical culture during the early Hanoverian period see Hannah Smith, *Georgian Monarchy: Politics and Culture, 1714–1760* (Cambridge, 2006), in particular pp. 19–55, who does emphasise, however, the elements of continuity with the emphatically Protestant kingship of William III. See also below the chapters by Brendan McConville, G.M. Ditchfield, David Wykes, Andrew C. Thompson and Jeremy Gregory.

political sermons, and less a providential saviour of God's chosen people.[43] This change, however, was not yet entirely visible during the reign of George I and only became fully apparent later.

Does this leave us in the end with the old master narrative of an inevitable disenchantment of monarchy as an institution, combined with a long-term secularisation of politics? Did the 'prose of bureaucracy' or, in the English case, of parliamentary oratory finally replace the 'poetry of the prince', as Marcel Gauchet, the French historian and sociologist, has put it with regard to the change of political culture in late seventeenth- and early eighteenth-century Europe?[44] This interpretation would at best be based on half-truths, although it may indeed be true that 'George I was initially accepted more as an idea and as a symbol than as man or monarch', as Julian Hoppit has written, emphasising the lack of personal charisma from which the first two Hanoverian kings suffered.[45]

As we have seen, the crisis the Stuart monarchy faced between 1678 and 1688 initially led less to the secularisation of kingship and the culture of authority in which it was embedded than to the reconfessionalisation of monarchy: first, in the early 1680s in the direction of a high Anglican vision of politics, and after 1688 in the sense of a more militantly Protestant model of monarchy. There was much less room now for the role of the ruler as priest-king in the traditional sense, but politics by no means became secular and post-confessional in nature as such. This holds good at least for the first half of the eighteenth century. England was not alone in experiencing a process whereby attempts to conceive monarchical authority in broader, post-confessional or trans-confessional terms were rescinded and abandoned, and rulers committed themselves again fully to a vision of politics defined in more narrowly confessional ways. The Emperor Charles VI in Vienna after 1711 and the Prussian King Frederick William I after 1712 both offer examples of a more militantly confessional attitude in the early eighteenth century, as Louis XIV of France had done in the last three decades of his reign when he had become more ostentatiously pious and devoted to the church and had pursued his own domestic crusade against Protestants.[46] Thus

---

[43] Pasi Ihalainen, *Protestant Nations Redefined: Changing Perceptions of National Identity in the Rhetoric of the English, Dutch and Swedish Public Churches, 1685–1772* (Leiden, 2005), p. 348.

[44] Marcel Gauchet, *Le désenchantement du monde: Une histoire politique de la religion* (Paris, 1985), p. 285.

[45] Julian Hoppit, *A Land of Liberty? England 1689–1727* (Oxford, 2009), p. 384.

[46] Sylvène Édouard, 'Le messianisme de Louis XIV: Un modèle espagnol?', in Gérard Sabatier and Margarita Torrione, eds, *¿Louis XIV espagnol? Madrid et Versailles, images et modèles* (Versailles, 2009), pp. 255–70; Alexandre Maral, *Le Roi-Soleil et Dieu* (Paris, 2012), pp. 227–32. For Charles VI see Bernd Rill, *Karl VI.: Österreich als barocke Großmacht* (Graz,

the early eighteenth century was marked by ambiguities and contradictory tendencies. The trend of reasserting confessional allegiances stood side by side with the diminishing influence of traditional ecclesiastical authorities and the church as a self-governing body enjoying political power, in England as much as in some continental countries.[47]

The year 1688 certainly marked the defeat of a vision of politics for which an alliance between a national church ruled by an episcopal hierarchy *iure divino* and a king who was himself both *rex* and *sacerdos* had been essential. The long conflict between *sacerdotium* and *imperium* ended with the victory of the latter. An Erastian, parliamentary model of the royal supremacy triumphed over any claims the church could make to be a self-governing corporation. It was significant that Convocation ceased to meet in the eighteenth century, although the Non-jurors, who presented an important aspect of English Jacobitism, rejected this subordination of the church to a secular authority. But then they ended up on the losing side of history.[48]

Although the Glorious Revolution undermined the position of the church as an institution ordained by God, it had not, however, negated the religious mandate of the monarch as long as he exercised this mandate not in the name of an Anglican or Catholic prelacy, as the Stuarts had done in the eyes of their critics, but in the name of religious freedom and an enlightened Protestantism, which at least for many Whigs proved its credentials by being strongly anticlerical.[49] In the long run the monarchy remained an important symbol of the link between the political and social order on the one hand and religion on the other. Until 1828 it remained a crucial obstacle to the emancipation of Catholics and dissenters, and its religious role regained a new vitality in the late

---

1992); cf. also Joachim Whaley, *Germany and the Holy Roman Empire*, vol. 2: *From the Peace of Westphalia to the Dissolution of the Reich, 1648–1806* (Oxford, 2012), pp. 150–58.

[47] For England as a confessional state in the eighteenth century see the cautious and balanced assessment by Andrew C. Thompson, 'Early Eighteenth-Century Britain as a Confessional State', in Hamish Scott and Brendan Simms, eds, *Cultures of Power in Europe during the Long Eighteenth Century* (Cambridge, 2007), pp. 86–109; cf. Jeremy Black, 'Confessional State or Elect Nation: Religion and Identity in Eighteenth-Century England', in Claydon and McBride, eds, *Protestantism and National Identity*, pp. 53–74.

[48] For these changes see Justin Champion, '"My Kingdom is Not of This World": The Politics of Religion after the Revolution', in Tyacke, ed., *The English Revolution*, pp. 185–202, and Andrew Starkie, *The Church of England and the Bangorian Controversy, 1716–1721* (Woodbridge, 2007), in particular pp. 103–11. See also Paul Kléber Monod, *Jacobitism and the English People, 1688–1788* (Cambridge, 1989), pp. 17–23.

[49] Mark Goldie, 'Priestcraft and the Birth of Whiggism', in Phillipson and Skinner, eds, *Political Discourse*, pp. 209–31.

eighteenth century when political radicalism seemingly linked to heterodox religious positions seemed to threaten the very fabric of society.[50] George III was not a sacral monarch in the way Charles I and James II had aspired to be. But he was not only a strong defender of the religious settlement achieved in 1688/89 and confirmed in 1701 and 1707 (with the Act of Settlement and the Union with Scotland) but also of Christian morality, a role which William III and his queen had already played under different circumstances in the 1690s.[51]

After 1688 England found its way to a new religious settlement which combined Christian morality and Protestant providentialism with a certain amount of anticlericalism and toleration. The anticlericalism had been inherent in the English Reformation right from the start as much as the tendency to emphasise God's radical transcendence and therefore to call into question the capacity of human institutions like monarchy to represent his authority on earth. Neither of these tendencies can therefore be considered as merely the expression of a secular Enlightenment.[52] Moreover, while the monarch ceased to claim a quasi-sacerdotal role for himself in the traditional way in the eighteenth century, his person and office still embodied the close union between Protestantism and national culture, regarding both England and – after 1707 – Britain. That this Protestantism could mean different things to different men and women – for some it was perhaps not always easy to distinguish from a post-dogmatic providential deism – was no new phenomenon as such. It had been typical of the history of the Church of England and those religious communities existing in its shadow ever since the Elizabethan settlement.[53]

---

[50] Linda Colley, *Britons: Forging the Nation 1707–1837* (New Haven, 1992), pp. 204–27.

[51] Jonathan C.D. Clark, *English Society 1660–1832* (Cambridge, 2000), pp. 256–83, 300–17, and G.M. Ditchfield, *George III: An Essay in Monarchy* (Basingstoke, 2002), pp. 77–106.

[52] Justin A. Champion, *The Pillars of Priestcraft Shaken: The Church of England and Its Enemies 1660–1730* (Cambridge, 1992), pp. 170–75; cf. id., *Republican Learning: John Toland and the Crisis of Christian Culture, 1696–1722* (Manchester, 2003), pp. 91–115.

[53] For attempts to redefine the position of the Church of England and the other Protestant denominations in England in regard to continental Protestantism see Tony Claydon, *Europe and the Making of England 1660–1760* (Cambridge, 2007), pp. 313–53.

Chapter 3

The House of Brunswick-Lüneburg and the Holy Roman Empire: The Making of a Patriotic Dynasty, 1648–1714?

Martin Wrede*

On 30 August 1679, just six months after the Holy Roman Empire's war against France had been settled, Sophia of Hanover visited the French court at Fontainebleau. At this time she was merely the wife of Prince-Bishop Ernest Augustus of Osnabrück. Travelling under the protection of an intentionally transparent incognito, 'Madame d'Osnabruc' received all the honours that she was due, and a few more as well. After all, she not only represented an important German princely house, but was also the aunt of Princess Palatine Elizabeth Charlotte, wife of the Duke of Orléans.[1] At court, she first met the Dauphin and Prince Conti, on both of whom she passed brief but scathing judgement in her memoirs.[2] The next day Sophia was received by the king himself, and this meeting at least was satisfactory for both sides. The king, Sophia reported, 'went

---

* Trans. Angela Davies, German Historical Institute London.
[1] Carl Möller, 'Sophie von der Pfalz: "Madame d'Osnabruc" und Garantin der Erhöhung des Welfenhauses', in Franz-Joachim Verspohl, ed., *Das Osnabrücker Schloß: Stadtresidenz, Villa, Verwaltungssitz* (Bramsche, 1991), pp. 117–30; Dirk van der Cruysse, *Madame sein ist ein ellendes Handwerck: Liselotte von der Pfalz, eine deutsche Prinzessin am Hofe des Sonnenkönigs* (3rd edn; Munich, 1995), pp. 69–75. Biographical information on Sophia of Hanover can be found in Mathilde Knoop, *Kurfürstin Sophie von Hannover* (Hildesheim, 1964). On Osnabrück see Mark Alexander Steinert, *Die alternative Sukzession im Hochstift Osnabrück: Bischofswechsel und das Herrschaftsrecht des Hauses Braunschweig-Lüneburg in Osnabrück 1648–1802* (Osnabrück, 2003).
[2] The Dauphin was 'insipid', Conti 'very mediocre', Adolf Köcher, ed., *Memoiren der Herzogin Sophie nachmals Kurfürstin von Hannover* (Stuttgart, 1879; reprint Osnabrück, 1969), p. 120. See also Sophie de Hanovre, *Mémoires et lettres de voyage*, ed. by Dirk van der Cruysse (Paris, 1990).

out of his way, in his conduct as well as in his conversation, to let me see that he was one of the most courteous princes in the world'.³ Louis even found kind and respectful words for the members of the Guelph dynasty who had been at war with the French king only a few years earlier:

> His Majesty ... told me everything agreeable that one could say to please, even reminding me of the battle which the dukes had won against him. He also said that he had been well aware of who his enemies had been. I replied that since they had not been fortunate enough to have his goodwill, they had at least tried to gain his esteem.⁴

Ernest Augustus of Osnabrück and George William of Celle, the two dukes in question, had fought against France in the Dutch War, and with some success. In August 1675 they had won a significant victory in the Battle of Conzer Brücke near Trier, at which the *maison militaire*, the French royal guard, had been routed in open battle and the enemy commander, Marshal François de Blanchefort de Créqui, taken prisoner.⁵

Sophia and Louis both agreed, however, that an end should now be put to hostilities. As their conversation continued, the king extolled his own military power which, he thought, would deter the German princes from taking up arms against him again in future. He went on to praise the beauty and spirit of Sophia's and Ernest Augustus's daughter, and together they considered French marriage plans for her.⁶ In addition to Sophia, the French court was host to the crown prince of Saxe-Eisenach, a prince of Brunswick-Wolfenbüttel and a duchess of

---

³ 'n'oublia rien dans ses manières ny dans ses discours pour me faire voir que c'estoit un des princes du monde le plus poli', Köcher, ed., *Memoiren der Herzogin Sophie*, p. 121.

⁴ 'S. Mté ... me dit tout ce qu'on peut dire d'agréable pour plaire jusqu'à me faire souvenir de la bataille que Mess. les ducs avoient gagnée contre luy, et dit qu'il s'éstroit bien apperçu qu'il les avoit eus pour ennemis. Je répliquay, comme ils n'avoient pas esté assez heureux d'avoir ses bonnes grâces, qu'ils avoient tâché de s'acquérir au moins son estime', Köcher, ed., *Memoiren der Herzogin Sophie*, p. 121.

⁵ See Jean-Charles Fulaine, *Le duc Charles IV de Lorraine et son armée, 1624–1675* (Metz, 1997), pp. 245–7; A. Janke, *Die Belagerungen der Stadt Trier in den Jahren 1673–1675 und die Schlacht an der Conzer Brücke am 11. August 1675* (Trier, 1890); G. Weber, 'Der Bericht des lüneburgischen Feldpredigers Georg Berkkemeyer über die Feldzüge von 1674 bis 1679', *Zeitschrift des historischen Vereins für Niedersachsen* (1898), pp. 1–51, at 19–25.

⁶ Köcher, ed., *Memoiren der Herzogin Sophie*, p. 121. The marriage plans for Sophia Charlotte (ideally) focused on the 'insipid' Dauphin. See Hanovre, *Mémoires et lettres de voyage*, p. 148 and van der Cruysse, *Madame sein ist ein ellendes Handwerck*, pp. 261–2.

Mecklenburg, the latter from the French house of Montmorency-Bouteville, but all guarantors of the newly achieved concord.[7]

This episode can be read as testimony to the transnational aristocratic society of pre-modern Europe in which common values, such as fighting wars bravely or keeping a splendid court, transcended political opposition. Or it could be seen as evidence for the more or less patriotic integration of a princely house into the re-stabilized order of the Holy Roman Empire after 1648. These two variants, as will be shown here, are by no means contradictory; on the contrary, they are directly connected. The Guelphs were a dynasty that, even before 1714, could transcend political, even national, borders. But they also fitted into the imperial system renewed in the Peace of Westphalia and, where required, showed themselves to be (more or less) 'patriotic' within it.

To speak of 'the Guelphs', however, is imprecise. Although the dynasty had consolidated since the end of the Thirty Years War, it could not be compared with the Brandenburg Hohenzollern, the Bavarian Wittelsbach or even the Saxon Wettin dynasties in terms of power. It had gained little from the Peace of Westphalia, apart from the right to provide every second prince-bishop of Osnabrück, alternating with a Catholic. Since 1662 this had been Duke Ernest Augustus, the youngest son of Duke George of Calenberg. At first, he was put in the shade by his older brothers, who ruled in the duchies of Calenberg (Hanover) and Lüneburg respectively. Lüneburg, which had fallen to the Calenberg family in 1648 after the extinction of the local line, was ruled at first by Duke Christian Louis and, after his death in 1665, by George William, who initially ruled Hanover but had then preferred to take the vacated (and more profitable) Lüneburg. According to the rules of the house, he left Hanover to his next youngest brother, John Frederick. On the latter's death in 1674 he was succeeded by Ernest Augustus, who moved from Osnabrück to Hanover and established lasting and effective rule there. It was his son and heir, Elector George Louis (later to be King George I), who in 1705 brought the rule of Hanover and Lüneburg together into one hand, on the death of his uncle (and father-in-law), George William. A reversion to the partitions of the past was precluded by the introduction of the right of primogeniture established by Ernest Augustus between 1682 and 1691.

Apart from these members of the cadet branch of the house of Guelph (known as the Lüneburg line), there was also the older and therefore higher ranking, but politically insignificant, line that ruled the duchy of Brunswick-Wolfenbüttel. Here, too, there were many subdivisions and co-rulerships

---

[7] Köcher, ed., *Memoiren der Herzogin Sophie*, pp. 111, 119, 122.

between brothers with the same rights of inheritance. While the older and younger lines of the house had at first tried to work together after 1648, this unity of purpose had been broken by the political ambitions of Duke and then Elector Ernest Augustus. The cousins in Wolfenbüttel were not prepared to be pushed into the background by the younger Lüneburg and Hanoverian line of the house. In the end, however, they had no choice. We will come back to this.[8]

I *Teutschlinge* and Francophiles

Given the complex structure of the Guelph dynasty and the conflicts of interest and rivalries inevitably associated with it, it is not surprising that the Guelphs did not give a uniform response to the 'patriotic' and anti-French demands made by the Holy Roman Empire in the last third of the seventeenth century. In fact, the comparatively unanimous rejection of Louis XIV's politics by the Empire, the imperial princes and the public was a new development that could not necessarily have been foreseen at the beginning of the 1660s. In 1662 Louis had still been praised as 'consolidator of Christianity' and 'daily upholder of the German peace' in a pamphlet,[9] and in 1664 the Rhenish Alliance, the basis of French influence in the Empire, had been extended (for the second time). The part played by the French in defeating the Turks and in the victory of Saint Gotthard on the river Raab in 1664 can be seen both as demonstrating this position of power and as its high point. Louis XIV had some reason to present himself as the real conqueror of the Turks and true protector of the Empire – and, of course, he did so.[10]

Since the War of Devolution (1667–1668) and France's incursion into the Spanish Netherlands, however, this had changed. In 1672 the outbreak of the Dutch War deprived France of the basis of its influence in the Empire. In 1674 the Imperial Diet declared Louis XIV an enemy of the Empire. A patriotic press did not hesitate to disparage the foreign ruler, court and country, and most of

---

[8] A brief survey of the various lines, territories and rulers in Hans-Georg Aschoff, *Die Welfen: Von der Reformation bis 1918* (Stuttgart, 2010).

[9] 'Befästiger der Christenheit' and 'tägliche[r] Erhalter des Teutschen Friedens', *Deß Aller-Christlichsten Königs Friedhaltendes Gemüth mit den Ständen des Teutschen Reiches* (n.p., 1662), p. 6.

[10] Martin Wrede, 'Türkenkrieger – Türkensieger: Leopold I. und Ludwig XIV. als Retter und Ritter der Christenheit', in Christoph Kampmann et al., eds, *Bourbon–Habsburg–Oranien: Konkurrierende Modelle im dynastischen Europa um 1700* (Cologne, 2008), pp. 149–65, at 160–61.

the imperial princes – including the two Guelphs already mentioned – now supported the emperor and mobilized the forces of the Empire against the French threat.[11]

At first, however, Louis XIV still had a few partners or servants in the Empire and among the imperial princes. In the Dutch War he received military assistance until 1673 from the Bishop of Münster, Christoph Bernhard von Galen, who invaded Groningen and Friesland. And the two Wittelsbach electors, Ferdinand Maria of Bavaria and Max Heinrich of Cologne, persisted in an ultimately pro-French neutrality beyond 1674 – as did, for example, Duke John Frederick of Hanover. The imperial loyalty and patriotism of the Guelphs was anything but uniform.[12]

The Guelphs were wise, however, not to support the French side openly because *Teutschfranzosen* or *Teutschlinge*, as German Francophiles were known, not only had a bad press but also were put under political pressure. Pamphleteering and politics merged into each other here, as did the political and cultural mobilization against France, although the long-term achievements of the latter were extremely limited.[13] John Frederick of Hanover thus did not enter the first rank of Francophiles. This was filled, ahead of Christoph Bernhard von Galen, by the Fürstenberg brothers, Wilhelm Egon and Franz Egon, the two leading ministers of the Elector of Cologne, Max Heinrich. From the point of view of imperial patriots, they achieved notoriety in that position. Wilhelm von Fürstenberg, incidentally, was among the German onlookers at the reception of 'Madame d'Osnabruc' at the court of Fontainebleau.[14]

The anti-French pamphlet literature of the Dutch War and the Nine Years War (in German historiography better known as the War of the Palatine Succession) did not shy away from criticizing the aristocracy as a whole. This criticism took the form of warnings. The German princes and the aristocracy,

---

[11] See further Anton Schindling, *Die Anfänge des Immerwährenden Reichstags zu Regensburg: Ständevertretung und Staatskunst nach dem Westfälischen Frieden* (Mainz, 1991), pp. 182–226; Karl Otmar von Aretin, *Das Alte Reich 1648–1806*, 3 vols (Stuttgart, 1993–1997), vol. I, pp. 61–85, 116–42; Martin Wrede, *Das Reich und seine Feinde: Politische Feindbilder in der reichspatriotischen Publizistik zwischen Westfälischem Frieden und Siebenjährigem Krieg* (Mainz, 2004), pp. 324–33.

[12] Georg Schnath, *Geschichte Hannovers im Zeitalter der neunten Kur und der englischen Sukzession, 1674–1714*, 5 vols (Hildesheim, 1938–1982), vol. I, pp. 50–80; Aretin, *Das Alte Reich*, vol. I, pp. 253–65.

[13] Wrede, *Das Reich und seine Feinde*, pp. 407–15.

[14] Köcher, ed., *Memoiren der Herzogin Sophie*, pp. 122, 129. On the treatment of the 'Egons-Gesellen' in the contemporary pamphlet literature see Wrede, *Das Reich und seine Feinde*, pp. 435–8.

it was claimed, were particularly exposed to the temptations of French manners and fashions. They therefore had to be especially vigilant and protect themselves from the vain baubles and bustle emanating from France, its court and king. The Grand Tour to France was a bad thing, while the acceptance of fencing masters, dancing masters and language teachers into German aristocratic families even endangered the 'essence' of the Fatherland. These foreigners demanded high pay, confused all the senses, played nasty tricks and were spies.[15] This recognizably drew on the register of early seventeenth-century condemnations of French influence on German culture (*Alamodismus*), and linked it with traditional criticisms of the aristocracy and court on the one hand, and an increasingly aggressive Francophobia on the other. Although the rhetoric was pointed, it did not threaten political danger.[16]

The public outcry over the few princes who sympathized with France, or even concluded pacts with the French, however, was of a different quality. In Münster, Christoph Bernhard von Galen did a political about-face and withdrew from the French alliance under pressure from the emperor, the Empire – that is, his compeers – and also from his subjects. The public denunciation of 'unpatriotic' politics played a part in this decision.[17] Max Heinrich of Cologne found himself in a similar situation.[18] The fact that the Fürstenberg brothers now became the most hated men in the Empire – after Louis XIV and perhaps his minister, Louvois – also inevitably had an impact on the other members of this dynasty: they now had to distinguish themselves by their ostentatious loyalty to the emperor.[19]

---

[15] Anonymus Wahrmund, *Der Abgezogene Frantzösische Staats-Rock und Teutsche Schutzmantel* ... (n.p., 1675); *Teutsche Wächter-Stimme Uber das gefährliche Hahnen-Geschrey* ('In Teutschland', c.1674). Dating from the Nine Years War see e.g. *Das an der Teutschen Colica Danieder liegende Franckreich* ... (Freystatt [sic], 1690).

[16] Wrede, *Das Reich und seine Feinde*, pp. 407–15.

[17] Wilhelm Kohl, *Christoph Bernhard von Galen: Politische Geschichte des Fürstbistums Münster 1650–1678* (Münster, 1964), pp. 370–72, 378, 417–18. On similar situations in Bavaria see Michael Doeberl, *Bayern und Frankreich vornehmlich unter Kurfürst Ferdinand Maria* (Munich, 1900), pp. 498, 502. Cf. Martin Wrede, 'Der Kaiser, das Reich, die deutsche Nation und ihre Feinde: Natiogenese, Reichsidee und der Durchbruch des Politischen im Jahrhundert nach dem Westfälischen Frieden', *Historische Zeitschrift*, 280 (2005), pp. 83–116.

[18] Wrede, *Das Reich und seine Feinde*, pp. 436–40. Instead of concentrating on the Wittelsbach prince-bishop, the anger in imperial patriotic writings was directed at the Fürstenberg brothers, who, as his ministers, practically controlled politics in the electorate of Cologne.

[19] Esteban Mauerer, 'Die "Egoniden" zwischen Frankreich und dem Kaiser: Zum Umgang mit abweichendem politischen Verhalten im Haus Fürstenberg im 17. und 18. Jahrhundert', in

This was not the case for the Guelphs, however, where the lines of conflict within the dynasty emerged ever more clearly.[20] Apart from what Georg Schnath called his 'grotesque portliness',[21] Duke John Frederick was in many respects the ideal figure of a power-hungry imperial prince of middling importance, ambitious and timid in equal measure. Thinking of his own advantage, he constantly vacillated between the various sides in the conflicts with Louis XIV but shied away from taking any risk. He had no direct heir, however, and the contrast with his younger brothers, who were fixated on succeeding him, was underlined by his conversion to Catholicism.[22] His brothers had already rendered him incapable of taking any serious political action by the beginning of the Dutch War, and not only because of his doubtful loyalty to the Empire. All that was left for John Frederick, therefore, was to pocket the French subsidies to maintain his own army and, in order not to endanger these payments, to extricate himself from his imperial responsibilities as far as possible.[23] On his death in the year of the Peace of Nijmegen (1679), he left his brother Ernest Augustus a reasonably well-ordered house and principality. Not all was well with his posthumous reputation, however, as his name was not associated with any genuine political achievement. His exceptionally splendid funeral served the self-affirmation of his successor and marked a new beginning for the dynasty.[24] The younger brothers, Ernest Augustus and George William – known as the Herzberg brothers after the place of their birth – became the figureheads of new Guelph greatness, largely because of their imperial patriotism, or the appearance of it.

Martin Wrede and Horst Carl, eds, *Zwischen Schande und Ehre: Erinnerungsbrüche und die Kontinuität des Hauses. Legitimationsmuster und Traditionsverständnis des frühneuzeitlichen Adels in Umbruch und Krise* (Mainz, 2007), pp. 81–96.

[20] Schnath, *Geschichte*, vol. I, pp. 50–103.
[21] Ibid., p. 23; see likewise ibid., p. 21 ('immense obesity').
[22] Ibid., pp. 20–25.
[23] Ibid., pp. 58–84. See also Aretin, *Das Alte Reich*, vol. I, pp. 247–51, 262–3.
[24] Schnath, *Geschichte*, vol. I, pp. 126–8. According to Schnath, John Frederick's most enduring achievement was to recruit Leibniz for the Hanoverian service. His heirs, of course, were the ones to profit from this. On the succession and the internal state of the Guelph territories see Gerd van den Heuvel, 'Niedersachsen im 17. Jahrhundert', in Christine van den Heuvel and Manfred von Boetticher, eds, *Geschichte Niedersachsens*, vol. III, 1: *Politik, Wirtschaft und Gesellschaft von der Reformation bis zum Beginn des 19. Jahrhunderts* (Hanover, 1998), pp. 119–220, at pp. 149–59. On John Frederick's funeral Jill Bepler, 'Ansichten eines Staatsbegräbnisses: Funeralwerke und Diarien als Quelle zeremonieller Praxis', in Jörg Jochen Berns and Thomas Rahn, eds, *Zeremoniell als höfische Ästhetik in Spätmittelalter und Früher Neuzeit* (Tübingen, 1995), pp. 183–97.

II Victorious Heroes for Emperor and Empire

The exact site of the defeat of the Roman general Varus by Germanic tribes in the Battle of the Teutoburg Forest in AD 9 has been contentious for decades, if not centuries.[25] In 1675, however, it was in some respects quite clear: it was at the Conzer Brücke near Trier. At least this is how the imperial patriotic press and Guelph panegyric saw it. According to a pamphlet of this sort, after the defeat of his military commander, the duc de Crequi, Louis XIV had 'torn his hair / banged his head against the wall / and cried out wistfully: Vare! Vare! redde Legiones meas!'[26] This identified the locality of a second, modern Varus battle, seemingly no less important than the first: namely, the one that, among other things, had seen the loyal Guelph dukes, George William and Ernest Augustus, as victors over a French army. Historically this identification could not necessarily be justified; in terms of propaganda, however, it was obvious.

The pamphlet in which this appeared cannot be assigned Guelph provenance. Its aim was to provoke anti-Roman and anti-French sentiment, to invent a national tradition founded on, among other things, the Battle of the Teutoburg Forest and, based on it, the celebration of all 'manly Germans'.[27] It provides no information about the dukes' self-stylization, but it reveals some of the points on which Guelph self-presentation drew: loyalty to the Empire, serving the emperor and, not to be forgotten, a hefty dose of Francophobia. These were, in the end, the essential norms of political discourse in the Holy Roman Empire during the wars of Louis XIV.[28] And both Ernest Augustus and George William adapted them with great success. A political and rhetorical programme of praise for the Guelph princes can be found in several of the writings attributed to the courts in Osnabrück and Celle, which celebrate the return of the victorious rulers after the battle, thus placing the dukes themselves, their politics and behaviour in the field in the right light – that is, an unswerving commitment to the emperor, the Empire and the German nation.

Among the many German baroque poets who have rightly been forgotten must be counted Otto Friedrich Bärninger, Friedrich Funck and Johannes Faes from Osnabrück or Lüneburg respectively. They all delivered verses to order,

---

[25] Rainer Wiegels and Winfried Woesler, eds, *Arminius und die Varusschlacht: Geschichte, Mythos, Literatur* (2nd edn, Paderborn, 1999).

[26] 'sich die Haare geraufft/ den Kopff wider die Wand gestossen/ und wehmütig geschrien: Vare! Vare! redde Legiones meas!', *Die Federn stieben/ Der Hahn mauset sich ...* (n.p., [1675]), Aii v.

[27] 'mannhafften Teutschen', ibid., Aii r.

[28] Wrede, *Das Reich und seine Feinde*, pp. 537–60.

praising their ruler, and we can only hope that they did not do so in vain. The quality and influence of their writings were quite modest; but the occasional verse, while of little literary or aesthetic value, is revealing and interesting when interpreting the political culture of a period.[29] Bärninger, for example, was the author of a panegyric entitled *Unterthänigster Willkommen An die Hochwürdigsten/ Durchleuchtigsten Fürsten und Herren/ Hn. Ernest-Augustus/ Hn. Georg Wilhelm/ Und Hn. Georg Ludwig*, which was printed in Osnabrück in 1675 and referred to the victory on the Conzer Brücke. It celebrated the 'joyeuse rentrée' of the ruler, Ernest Augustus, his eldest son and older brother and in this way linked acclamation to a political programme.

The bravery and personal courage of the 'German Achilles' (Ernest Augustus), the 'new Odysseus' (George William) and especially the 'young Guelph lion' George Louis (Ernest Augustus's eldest son and future British king, George I) are vigorously celebrated in Bärninger's verses. Bravery and pugnacity, here and elsewhere, are princely virtues that can be taken for granted and are, in principle, sufficient unto themselves[30] – but only up to a certain point. In Bärninger's work, as in the political culture of the Empire in general at that time, there was a further, higher purpose behind these virtues, namely, service to the emperor, the Empire and the nation. Only against this background do the princes' feats of arms attain their real splendour; only from here is their political position legitimized again. Bärninger's final tribute is, at the same time, a challenge:

> If you continue to protect us
> Us and the dear fatherland
> We will soon be at peace;
> If only Your blessed hand
> May henceforth protect us in a fatherly way
> No tyrant will be able to assail us.[31]

---

[29] Erich Trunz, *Weltbild und Dichtung im deutschen Barock* (Munich, 1992).

[30] All quotations from Otto Friedrich Bärninger, *Unterthänigster Willkommen An die Hochwürdigsten/ Durchleuchtigsten Fürsten und Herren/ Hn. Ernest-Augustus/ Hn. Georg Wilhelm/ Und Hn. Georg Ludwig/ ... Hertzoge zu Braunschw. und Lüneb. ... Als Dieselbe ... Mit glorwürdigster Victorie bey Dero Fürstl. Residencen glücklich wieder angelanget* (Osnabrück, 1675). On the military expertise and heroic *habitus* of the early modern prince see Martin Wrede, ed., *Heroische Monarchie? Ritterliches Erbe, militärische Herausforderung, politische Krise des europäischen Königtums, 15.–19. Jahrhundert* (Munich, 2014).

[31] 'So fahret fort uns zu beschützen/ Uns und das liebe Vatterland/ So werden wir bald ruhig sitzen; Ach macht daß Eure Gnaden-Hand/ Uns fernerhin mag vätterlich beschirmen/ So wird und kan uns kein Tyrann bestürmen', Bärninger, *Unterthänigster Willkommen*, iiii v.

A condition of success, of course, was concord among the German princes. The suggestion that there could be exceptions is not merely hinted at but made abundantly clear. Anyone who 'betrays' the Fatherland is rhetorically cast out of the national community:

> The righteous boldly claim a German heart
> For better or for worse
> In order to defend golden freedom
> This heart remains faithful to the Fatherland:
> Anyone who does not want to defend the Fatherland
> Should not, therefore, be nurtured by it.[32]

The Guelphs, by contrast, are presented as heroic fighters for the Fatherland and its 'freedom', which means the Empire's free, libertarian order based on the Peace of Westphalia.[33] And their real glory derives not from fighting and victory as such, but from the recognition of their achievements by the imperial majesty:

> Our great emperor
> The most powerful prince LEOPOLD
> Praises these Lüneburg houses
> For their constant loyalty to the imperial eagle.[34]

For Bärninger from Osnabrück, his territorial ruler, Prince-Bishop Ernest Augustus, and his heir, Prince George Louis, occupy a prominent place at the pinnacle of the Lüneburg dynasty, while other authors – obviously subjects of Celle – give this place to Duke George William. But George William in particular is exposed as not so much a hero in his own right, but as the emperor's champion. Friedrich Funck's *Triumphirender Lorbeer-Kranz* calls him the 'emperor's hero' and his military intervention is described as a personal knightly service towards the head of the Empire:

---

[32] 'Ein Teutsches Hertz fällt dem Gerechten/ In Glück und Unglück kühnlich bey/ Die güldne Freyheit zu verfechten/ Bleibt es dem Vatterlande treu:/ Wer vor das Vatterland sich nicht wil wehren/ Den sol das Vatterland auch nicht ernehren', ibid.

[33] Georg Schmidt, 'Die "deutsche Freiheit" und der Westfälische Friede', in Ronald G. Asch and Martin Wrede, eds, *Frieden und Krieg in der Frühen Neuzeit: Die europäische Staatenordnung und die außereuropäische Welt* (Munich, 2001), pp. 323–48.

[34] 'Es rühmet unser Grosser Kayser/ Der mächtigste Fürst LEOPOLD,/ Daß diese Lüneburgschen Häuser/ Dem Adler stets so treu und hold', Bärninger, *Unterthänigster Willkommen*, iiii v.

The proper advice from good councillors to our White Horse [the armorial symbol of the Guelph dynasty] would be
To put on all its tack in its castle and palace
And use its power with Roman loyalty to bring peace to the great Leopold
The Empire and itself. On this advice,
The brave Guelph hero took up arms to resist the enemy
And bear witness to his deeds. He took to the field
And pitched his trusty tent near Leopold.[35]

In his *Sieg-prangenden Palmen*, Johannes Faes recognizes George William as a new Hector, and declares him to be 'Germany's delight'.[36] But the ultimate purpose of his struggle again seems to be to protect the emperor, Leopold I, and his fame:

The heroes proclaim Leopold's effort
Living they hand the laurels to the arms
Which burnish Leopold's efforts
In wars and in victories with eternal wreaths.[37]

---

[35] 'Der Rechtem Rähte Raht rieht unserm Weissen Rosse/ Daß es sich zäumete in seiner Burg und Schlosse/ Und führte seine Macht mit Römscher Treue zu/ Dem grossen Leopold/ dem Reich und sich zur Ruh./ Der tapffre Guelphen Held ergrieff auff solches Rahten/ Dem Feind zum Wiederstand/ zum Zeugniß seiner Thaten/ Der Waffen Gegenwehr/ Er rückte fort ins Feld/ Und schlug auff bey Leopold sein treues Hülff-Gezelt', Friedrich Funck, *Triumphirender Lorbeer-Kranz/ Mit welchem Der Gerecht-Kriegende und Gnädigst-Siegende Herr und Gott Zebaoth/ Den Durchleuchtigsten/ Hochgebohrnen Fürsten und Herrn/ H. Georg Wilhelm Hertzogen zu Braunschweig und Lüneburg/ ... als einen Tapffern und Keyser-Treuen Creiß-Obristen/ Glücklich beehret und rühmlich beschencket hat ...* (Lüneburg, 1675).

[36] 'Teutschlandes Wonne'. Johannes Faes, *Sieg-prangende Palmen/ Welche Dem Durchleuchtigsten Fürsten und Herrn/ Hn. Georg Wilhelm/ Hertzogen zu Braunschweig und Lünaburg/ Als Deroselben ... wider den Frantzösischen Marschall/ Mons. de Crequi .../ eine völlige Victorie erhalten ...* (Helmstedt, 1675), the quote at vi r.

[37] 'Es melden di Helden des Leopold Schaffen/ Si geben im Leben den Lorbeer den Waffen/ Di Waffen das Schaffen des Leopold glänzzen/ Im Krigen in Sigen mit ewigen Kränzzen', ibid., iii v–iv r. In the same sense *Das Gedämpffte Hahn=Geschrey Als Des Großmächtigsten Königs in Franckreich seine in Deutschland eingedrungene Waffen durch den Kayserl./ Österreichischen und der Hohen Alliirten Teutschen Fürsten rühmlichen Gegenstand/ Insonderheit Des Durchläuchtigsten Fürsten und Herrn/ H. Georg Wilhelms/ Zu Braunschweig und Lüneburg preißwürdige Kriegs=Actiones .../ Von Dero unterthänigstem Knecht* (Lüneburg, 1675).

The rhetorical effort that bound not only the duke but also his whole 'house of heroes'[38] to the emperor was not inconsiderable. Even if the aesthetic outcome was only moderately convincing, it was a way of accumulating political capital that could be used profitably in trade-offs with the imperial court, both when George William acquired the duchy of Lauenberg in 1689 and in Ernest Augustus's negotiations concerning the ninth electorate, which came to fruition in 1692.

Since the 1670s both princes had adapted to a political culture which once again related German patriotism to the office and person of the Roman-German emperor. The same applied, for example, to the elector of Brandenburg.[39] Bearing in mind the political and religious disruptions of the Thirty Years War, this might at first sight seem surprising; given the new pressure from France, it was almost inevitable. Only a new dependence on Vienna could promise protection against Louis XIV's aggressive politics. And the Empire, too, was still inconceivable without the emperor. The Habsburg rulers' 'return to the Empire' – not only political but also mental – was thus nothing but a return to normality.[40]

III Imperial Allegiance and Elevation in Rank

One precondition for success in this political climate of marked patriotism was a certain continuity in imperial allegiance, or in its dissimulation. The recently reignited Turkish war of 1683 gave the Guelphs and their compeers a chance to demonstrate this, as can be seen, for example, in the printed funeral books for the ruling dukes, especially in the case of Ernest Augustus in 1704.[41] This was a chance to point out, creditably and correctly, that troops from Brunswick-Lüneburg had already fought against the Turkish arch enemy in the siege of Candia (Heraklion) in the mid seventeenth century, although at that time probably more with an eye to Venetian subsidies than out of an interest in saving

---

[38] 'Haus der Helden', *Das Gedämpffte Hahn=Geschrey*, i v.
[39] Martin Wrede, 'Der Kaiser, das Reich und der deutsche Norden: Die publizistische Auseinandersetzung mit Schweden im Ersten Nordischen und im Holländischen Krieg', in Asch and Wrede, eds, *Frieden und Krieg in der Frühen Neuzeit*, pp. 349–73, and Wrede, *Das Reich und seine Feinde*, pp. 222–53.
[40] Schindling, *Die Anfänge des Immerwährenden Reichstags*, p. 224.
[41] *Monumentum Gloriae Ernesti Augusti Principis Electoris Brunsvicensis Primi ...* (Hanover, 1704). See for George William Nicolaus Baehr, *Die Letzte Lieb und Ehren-Pflicht Im Leichen-Klag- und Trost-Gedicht/ Als Ihre Hoch-Fürstliche Durchleuchtigkeit/ ... Herr Georg Wihelm/ Hertzog zu Braunschweig und Lüneburg/ ... Am 28. Aug. 1705 ... in die Ewigkeit ward versetzet ...* (Bremen, 1705).

Illustration 3.1 *Monumentum Gloriae Ernesti Augusti Principis Electoris Brunsvicensis Primi ...* (Hanover, 1704), frontispiece showing the apotheosis of the first elector of the House of Hanover, Ernest Augustus.

Source: Staats- und Universitätsbibliothek Göttingen, Sign. 2 H HANN I, 3998.

Christendom. Participation in the protection and relief of Hungary could also be cited. This had already found its way into an ambitious family portrait that can be dated to the first years of the Great Turkish War. Among other things, it depicts a number of captive and bound Turks, gathered at the feet of the Guelph dukes and princes victoriously returning home.[42] That two of Ernest Augustus's and Sophia's younger sons died in Hungary, however, was not made widely public. Two coins were struck for Prince Carl Philipp, but his brother, Frederick Augustus, was not commemorated in this way. He had fallen out with his father during the fierce dispute about the introduction of male primogeniture in Hanover (1682–1691), and as a dead hero he could no longer become an asset to the house.[43] Their father's funeral depiction, however, commemorates the two sons together in a few measured words, saying that they had both 'left their lives for Christianity in the emperors' service'.[44]

A third, patriotic imperial front on which the Guelphs were active lay much closer than Hungary: north Germany itself. In Ernest Augustus's funeral book, for instance, his achievements include *labores belgici* (struggle in Belgium, 1676–1678); *suppetiae rheno* (help on the Rhine, 1688–1689); and, especially prominently, *victoria treverensis* (the victory on the Conzer Brücke). In addition, the episodes from the Turkish War just named are mentioned: *Candia sustentata* (support for Crete, 1668–1669) and *Ungarica auxilia* (relief of Hungary). But the immediate environment provided a further point of reference for Guelph fame. The (repeated) protection of Hamburg and the Elbe against Denmark and the reinstatement of the Duke of Gottorf's rights in Holstein (*Albis servatus* and *restitutio holsatiae*) are mentioned. The acquisition of the duchy of Lauenburg by George William should also be cited in this context.[45]

---

[42] Illustration in Knoop, *Sophie*, table 12; Schnath, *Geschichte*, vol. I, table V. On Ernest Augustus's fixation on subsidies in the context of the Turkish War, like that of John Frederick before him, see Schnath, *Geschichte*, vol. I, p. 349. On Lüneburg's part in the Cretan War see Louis von Sichart, *Geschichte der königlich hannoverschen Armee*, 5 vols (Hanover, 1866–1898), vol. I, pp. 145–6.

[43] Schnath, *Geschichte*, vol. I, pp. 563–71; Thomas Schwark, 'Fortschritt oder Unrecht? Der Streit der Söhne um das Erbe im Fürstentum Hannover', in *Ehrgeiz, Luxus und Fortune: Hannovers Weg zu Englands Krone* (Hanover, 2001), pp. 50–67. For the commemorative coins on Carl Philipp see *Monumentum Gloriae Ernesti Augusti*, table II.

[44] 'vor die Christenheit in Kayserlichen Diensten das Leben gelassen'. *Monumentum Gloriae Ernesti Augusti*, p. 25. Similarly in Heinrich Bünting (continued by Philipp Julius Rehtmeier), *Braunschweig-Lüneburgische Chronica*, 3 vols (Braunschweig, 1722), vol. III, p. 1735.

[45] *Monumentum Gloriae Ernesti Augusti*, title page.

In the north, danger for the Empire and the Guelphs initially emanated not from Denmark but from Sweden, which entered the Dutch War as an ally of France. From 1675 this was to present a pressing challenge to Brandenburg in particular, but by no means exclusively. The Swedish duchies of Bremen and Verden were also Lüneburg's immediate neighbours, and, for George William at least, security against Sweden was a high priority. From the point of view of Hanover, where John Frederick was still ruling, things looked somewhat different. While Hanover was keen to get a share of Bremen-Verden, it found it difficult to extricate itself from its alliance obligations to Stockholm and Paris.[46]

Unlike Brandenburg, the court at Celle did not unleash an imperial patriotic pamphlet campaign against Sweden. For the Brandenburg elector, Frederick William, the expulsion of the Swedes from Pomerania and thus from Germany was the *grand dessein* of his rule.[47] Nothing similar applied to Duke George William. There was no prospect of gaining Bremen and Verden, bypassing Denmark. It was only British support after 1714 that would make this possible.[48] However, that Brunswick-Lüneburg was an important partner in the confrontation with the Swedish and, ultimately, the French enemy, and that it was important to tie the duchy to the 'good cause' of the emperor and Empire, was obvious by 1675 and left traces in publications, and not only because of the success in Trier. Thus the pamphlet *Ehr- und Freyheit liebende Gedancken Uber die Frage Mit welchem Theile ... ein vernünfftiger/ genereuser Teutscher Fürst ... es halten könne und solle?* sought loyalty to the Empire from both the electors of Brandenburg *and* the Brunswick-Lüneburg dynasties. Both were practically destined to drive the Swedes 'completely off German soil again and to confine them to their cliffs, as before'.[49]

This did not, of course, fully succeed, and the political fronts would soon change, as would the military threat. While the publication cited above counted Denmark among the estates most loyal to the Empire, this view could no longer be upheld just a few years later. The Guelph princes, united on this issue, thwarted a first Danish surprise raid on Hamburg in 1679 and a second in 1685,

---

[46] Schnath, *Geschichte*, vol. I, pp. 73–6.
[47] Wrede, *Das Reich und seine Feinde*, pp. 257–82; Ernst Opgenoorth, *Friedrich Wilhelm: Der Große Kurfürst von Brandenburg*, 2 vols (Göttingen, 1978), vol. I, pp. 150–53; vol. II, pp. 160–97.
[48] Lutz Erich Krüger, *Der Erwerb Bremen-Verdens durch Hannover: Ein Beitrag zur Geschichte des Großen Nordischen Krieges in den Jahren 1709–1719* (Hamburg, 1974).
[49] *Ehr- und Freyheit liebende Gedancken Uber die Frage Mit welchem Theile ... ein vernünfftiger/ genereuser Teutscher Fürst ... es halten könne und solle?* (n.p., 1675), the quote at Aiv r: 'von dem Teutschen Boden ... gäntzlich wieder abzutreiben/ und in ihre Klippen/ wie vorhin zu confiniren'.

by which time Ernest Augustus was ruling in Hanover. This was based on self-interest; its neighbours did not want Denmark to possess the most important trading and commercial city in north Germany.[50]

This self-interest, however, could also be interpreted, or presented, as a defence of the security and integrity of the Empire. Hamburg, the imperial city on the Elbe, could be protected from its expansionist neighbour, unlike Strasbourg, for instance, whose loss to France in 1681 was noted with interest in Hanover, and regarded as a call to action.[51] Ernest Augustus saw the annexation of the city as the first step towards further French expansion, and suggested immediate counter-measures, by which he initially probably only meant mobilizing troops. Against this background, the Guelphs were able to present their own expansionism in north Germany as serving the interests of the whole Empire. In like manner, the occupation of the duchy of Lauenburg by George William's troops in 1689 was declared a patriotic deed by the pamphlet literature. The cooperation between Denmark and France was public knowledge, it was argued: the latter was a 'public' enemy of the Empire; the former a 'covert' imperial enemy and in the pay of France. By securing the duchy after the extinction of the Ascanian line of Lauenburg, the pamphlets went on, the house of Brunswick had protected the whole of north Germany from a threatened Danish invasion, saved the Elbe from suffering the fate of the Rhine and upheld the imperial order.[52] To be sure, there was no sound legal title for the occupation and ultimate annexation of the small duchy. It would be difficult to argue politically or legally on the basis of the legacy of Henry the Lion, who had owned Lauenburg in the Middle Ages; this argument was too

---

[50] Schnath, *Geschichte*, vol. I, pp. 123–4, 381–90; Hans-Dieter Loose, ed., *Hamburg: Geschichte der Stadt und ihrer Bewohner. Von den Anfängen bis zur Reichsgründung* (Hamburg, 1982), pp. 279–80, 291, 301–7.

[51] *Der ... Straßburgische Staats-Simplicius/ Bestehend in XII außerlesenen ... Reise-Relationen/ Was nemblich der Autor ... Vor remarquable Staats-Constellationes Wegen Restituirung der importantesten Reichs-Stadt Straßburg/ observiret ...* (n.p., 1684), pp. 8–10; *Anderer Theil der Hamburger Groß-Mütigkeit Nebst deren Eröffneten Augen Uber der Bevorstehenden nun vermutheten Königl. Dennemärckischen harten Belagerung ...* (Hamburg, 1686), p. 3. See, with references to further sources, Wrede, *Das Reich und seine Feinde*, pp. 288–9. For the Hanoverian position see Schnath, *Geschichte*, vol. I, pp. 694–5.

[52] *Antwort Eines Sachsen-Lauenburgischen Edelmanns/ an seinen Vetter/ in Holstein/ Die Von der Cron Dennemarck begehrende Demolition des Orts Ratzeburg betreffend. Nach dem Holländ'schen in Lateinischen Litteren gedruckten Exemplar* (Bremen, 1693). See, with references to further editions, Schnath, *Geschichte*, vol. I, pp. 452–3; vol. II, pp. 64–5.

reminiscent of the pattern of the French reunions. The background of imperial patriotism was thus all the more important, especially after an armed success.[53]

The acquisition of the duchy on the Elbe was a substantial victory for Guelph politics, representing a considerable, but not over-large, expansion of power. Its modesty was what made it tolerable for the neighbours; indeed, allowed it to happen at all. More significant than the acquisition of Lauenburg was the elevation into the ranks of the electors, thus increasing from eight to nine the number of the most respected imperial princes who elected the emperor, and conferring on Brunswick the status of an electorate. As in the *causa* Lauenburg, arguments concerning imperial loyalty were used here, and the dynasty's past and future achievements for the emperor and the Empire were capitalized on, with some success, as the outcome shows.[54]

The document of 1692 by which Brunswick became an electorate refers, with appropriate pathos, to Guelph services to the emperor and the Empire and names these as the reason for the elevation in rank, associated with the expectation of rendering further such services. Both elements, services and expectations, formed part of the agreements between Vienna and Hanover that made the creation of a ninth electoral cap possible. All of this and the circumstances surrounding it have been superbly and exhaustively explored by Georg Schnath. The text of the document speaks naturally of the 'splendour of this ancient house', which the elevation in rank reflects, but it says more about the

> special, numerous and highly advantageous services, which the said two brother dukes have rendered the Holy Roman Empire of the German Nation, the whole of esteemed Christendom and the commonwealth in peacetime and at war, in unbroken loyalty, with careful zeal and, on several occasions at personal risk, and are willing to render again in future.[55]

---

[53] Armin Reese, *Die Rolle der Historie beim Aufstieg des Welfenhauses, 1680–1714* (Hildesheim, 1967), pp. 88–123; Schnath, *Geschichte*, vol. I, pp. 450–56; Wrede, *Das Reich und seine Feinde*, pp. 288–9.

[54] Schnath, *Geschichte*, vol. I, pp. 592–651.

[55] 'sonderbahre[n], viele[n] und sehr ersprießliche[n] Diensten, welche ermeldter beeder Herzogen Gebrüder Liebden dem Heil. Röm. Reich Teutscher Nation, der gesamten wehrten Christenheit und dem gemeinen Wesen in Kriegs- und Friedens-Zeiten in unverbrüchlicher Treue, mit sorgfältigem Eifer auch mehrmaliger Darsezung ihrer eigenen Person erwiesen und noch zu erweisen willens seynd', treaty between Hanover and Emperor Leopold I, 22 March 1692, quoted from Bünting, *Chronica*, vol. III, pp. 1736–7. On the form of the document see Schnath, *Geschichte*, vol. I, pp. 607–8.

The most important instance of 'personal risk' was the Battle of Conzer Brücke. The 'most expensive cap in world history' had therefore not only been 'bought' but also 'fought for', although not by Ernest Augustus alone. In other words, the electoral cap had also been paid for with the blood of the subjects who served under the Hanoverian standard. The early modern period was aware that the fame of a ruler involved the suffering of his people, but fame, rank and reputation were the unavoidable imperatives of politics.[56]

The electoral document, similarly, does not apply to Ernest Augustus alone. It refers to 'both dukes', and thus also includes George William. And in addition to the military aid provided by Hanover, that supplied by Celle was also a firm part of the contract. Ernest Augustus's funeral book also gives his older brother an important place. The aim of this publication was to increase the fame not only of the first elector in the Guelph family history as an individual, but also of the dynasty as a whole. The virtues of the deceased, therefore, were summed up under the heading of 'heroic generosity'.[57] In the original meaning of the word, this was a quality arising out of the noble's blood, which enabled him and spurred him on. The high-mindedness and great deeds of this prince, therefore, were the result of his belonging to the noble house of the Guelphs. Service to the German Fatherland, the credit for its protection and deliverance, were of no little value. The same claims were made for George I and George II, and we will return to this in the conclusion.[58]

IV Patriotic Rhetoric and Political Reality

To what extent, however, did rhetoric and reality match? Georg Schnath had already repeatedly hinted at how much Ernest Augustus, in particular, had been driven by tactical considerations in the twists and turns of his partisanships – and Schnath cannot be suspected of harbouring any aversion to his subject. In the work of Karl Otmar von Aretin, the history of Guelph politics reads in part

---

[56] François de Salignac de La Mothe-Fénelon, 'Les aventures de Télémaque', in id., *Oeuvres*, ed. by Jacques Le Brun, 2 vols (Paris, 1983–1997), vol. II, pp. 67–8. On the cost of the electoral cap and its historiographical evaluation see Schnath, *Geschichte*, vol. I, p. 650–51; Annette von Stieglitz, 'Der teuerste Hut des Reiches: Hannovers Ringen um die Kurwürde', in *Ehrgeiz, Luxus und Fortune*, pp. 68–83; Johannes Arndt, *Herrschaftskontrolle durch Öffentlichkeit: Die publizistische Darstellung politischer Konflikte im Heiligen Römischen Reich 1648–1750* (Göttingen, 2013), p. 303.

[57] *Monumentum Gloriae Ernesti Augusti*, pp. 16–18, 23 and passim, the quote at p. 36.

[58] Ibid., pp. 16, 20, 24 and passim.

like a chronicle of opportunism, extortion and betrayal of the Empire.[59] The list of unpatriotic blunders committed by Ernest Augustus and George William is, indeed, of considerable length, and we do not even need to mention John Frederick in this context.

Before the Peace of Nijmegen, for example, George William in particular pursued his own advantage rather egoistically, without caring much about the well-being of the Empire and the nation. In Bremen he tried, ultimately in vain, to keep as much as possible of what he had captured from Sweden. This egoism, however, was nothing that would have distinguished him in the least from his various allies, including the emperor. The political situation as the Dutch War was drawing to a close left little alternative.[60] The 1680s, therefore, marked by the Turkish War on the one hand and a brittle and undermined peace with France and the expectation of the next armed conflict in the west on the other, are more indicative in this respect.

In 1685, for example, Ernest Augustus, along with Electoral Brandenburg, was negotiating a subsidiary alliance with France, and continued these negotiations even after the Great Elector withdrew from them under the pressure of the looming crisis of the Palatine succession. The prospect of becoming France's well-paid bridgehead in the Empire instead of their Brandenburg rival did not particularly alarm the Guelphs (George William was involved in his brother's manoeuvres). The project failed, in the end, because of the excessive demands made by both sides: Hanover and Celle wanted more money than France could pay, and Louis XIV demanded greater services than the dukes wanted to render. They had suggested a clause, however, by which Louis XIV would have renounced any further conquest in the Empire, even of his Palatine inheritance.[61] Two years later an agreement was reached, at least with Hanover. The War of the Palatine Succession had not yet started, and the provisions of the treaty were rather restrained. Both sides assured each other of their good offices in preserving the peace and obtaining the electoral dignity (this topic was now on the agenda), and promised assistance in the case of attack by a third party. Hanover promised neutrality in a possible conflict over the Spanish succession, but in the case of a war declared officially by the Empire would provide its quota for the imperial army. That France would also pay subsidies was taken for granted. This agreement soon broke down over the question of relations with Denmark, which was allied with France but an enemy of the Guelphs, and over

---

[59] See Schnath, *Geschichte*, vol. I, pp. 135–6, 402–3, 519, 522; Aretin, *Das Alte Reich*, vol. II, p. 56.
[60] Schnath, *Geschichte*, vol. I, pp. 86–116; Aretin, *Das Alte Reich*, vol. I, pp. 260–71.
[61] Schnath, *Geschichte*, vol. I, p. 370.

the Glorious Revolution and Duke George William's active support for it.[62] The next alliance with France was not long in coming, but similarly remained a mere episode; it is remarkable, nevertheless, that it came about at all. The War of the Palatine Succession had in the meantime broken out, passionately involving the emperor and the Empire, and the expression of public hostility towards France reached its peak after 1688.[63] Like the breakdown of the earlier French alliance, the conclusion of the new one was determined by relations with Denmark, or rather concern about Lauenburg, an acquisition which was threatened from that direction. Hanover sought France's support on this issue, itself offering only neutrality. It was not a matter requiring active Hanoverian military intervention, and this was not expected by Louis XIV. But from the point of view of imperial law as well as imperial patriotism it was untenable, implying a refusal to meet imperial obligations, and thus nothing less than grave disloyalty towards the emperor and the other Estates.[64]

These 'blunders' on the part of the two Guelphs, of course, were balanced, and perhaps more, by a number of deeds that demonstrated loyalty to the Empire. The short duration of each pro-French episode also shows that it could not be maintained for long, and that this was probably not even intended. Establishing ties with France was a proven means of putting political pressure on the emperor. The crucial phase of the negotiations about the electoral cap fell into the early years of the War of the Palatine Succession; it is well known that Hanover threw its weight around here. Its elevation in rank was not a reward for good behaviour, but the result of a balancing out of interests and a trial of strength. The court in Celle, incidentally, may have been dominated by pro-French sentiment. Duchess Éléonore was known to be French, but as she was a Huguenot, the Francophile element in Celle would almost certainly not be particularly inclined to support Louis XIV's politics.[65] Ernest Augustus, however unscrupulous, was in principle clearly less pro-French than his older brother and predecessor had been. This becomes visible in his repeatedly pronounced partisanship for the emperor and the Empire, but also in the fact that he left his counsellor and librarian, Gottfried Wilhelm Leibniz, in peace. Since the end of the Dutch War and John

---

[62] Ibid., pp. 410, 421–30.
[63] Wrede, *Das Reich und seine Feinde*, pp. 402–4, 477–80.
[64] Schnath, *Geschichte*, vol. I, pp. 519–20. See the wording of the treaty ibid., pp. 761–5.
[65] René Marquis d'Arcy-Martel, 'Relation des cours de Brunswick Lunebourg en 1684' (end of mission report of the envoy, 1685), in Schnath, *Geschichte*, vol. I, pp. 721–30, at p. 729. See also Andreas Flick, '"Der Celler Hof ist ganz verfranzt": Hugenotten und französische Katholiken am Hof und beim Militär Herzog Georg Wilhelms von Braunschweig-Lüneburg', *Hugenotten* 72 (2008), pp. 87–120.

Frederick's death, Leibniz had found himself at the cutting edge of imperial patriotic Francophobia expressed in the press. The best-known product of this period, but certainly not the only one, was his *Mars Christianissimus* of 1683,[66] a mixture of fierce pride in the victory over the Turks outside Vienna and no less fierce contempt of an (imputed) Franco-Turkish alliance. Leibniz had little political influence and his *Mars Christianissimus* had a limited impact, but it reflects the state of information and the process of opinion-formation at the court in Hanover where it was written. Ernest Augustus may not have thought much of Leibniz as a political adviser, but his works demonstrate the extent to which Francophobia was accepted in the first elector's surroundings.[67]

Beyond this, it must be remembered that decision-making at the level of imperial and Guelph politics did not take place in a vacuum. What could be done politically was largely what could be said in public: that is, what could be written by journalists with an expectation of being listened to and applauded and what could be seen as legitimate by the author and readers. What could be said determined what could be done, but also what could even be thought.[68] In the wars with Louis XIV, the German side required, indeed, demanded imperial patriotism in both word and deed. Only declarations presenting one's own actions as patriotic granted legitimacy and created reputations, whether in Vienna, Berlin or Munich. The same applied in Hanover, Celle and Wolfenbüttel.[69] Since the Dutch Wars, imperial patriotism had been unequivocally defined: it encompassed the emperor and the imperial system, the order of German freedom and those who supported it. It rejected France and any potential *Teutschfranzosen*. In principle, the language of imperial patriotism

---

[66] Gottfried Wilhelm Leibniz, 'Mars Christianissimus', in id., *Sämtliche Schriften und Briefe*, series IV, vol. II (Berlin, 1963), no. 22, pp. 447–502. The edition used here is *Der Allerchristlichste Mars ...* ([Hanover], 1685). On its creation and dissemination see the introduction to the modern edition cited above and Martin Wrede, 'Leibniz und Frankreich: Feindbild und Vorbild', in Friedrich Beiderbeck, Irene Dingel and Wenchao Li, eds, *Umwelt und Weltgestaltung: Leibniz' politisches Denken in seiner Zeit* (Göttingen, 2015), pp. 277–92.

[67] Gerd van den Heuvel, 'Theorie ohne Praxis: Leibniz' Rolle in der Politik des Hauses Hannover', in *Ehrgeiz, Luxus und Fortune*, pp. 84–97; Carl Haase, 'Leibniz als Politiker und Diplomat', in Wilhelm Totok and Carl Haase, eds, *Leibniz: Sein Leben, sein Wirken, seine Welt* (Hanover, 1966), pp. 195–224. For a more positive view of Leibniz's political impact cf. Günter Scheel, 'Leibniz als politischer Ratgeber des Welfenhauses', in Herbert Breger and Friedrich Niewöhner, eds, *Leibniz und Niedersachsen* (Stuttgart, 1999), pp. 35–52. On his position at the Hanoverian court Gerda Utermöhlen, 'Leibniz im kulturellen Rahmen des hannoverschen Hofes', ibid., pp. 213–26.

[68] Willibald Steinmetz, *Das Sagbare und das Machbare: Zum Wandel politischer Handlungsspielräume. England 1789–1867* (Stuttgart, 1993).

[69] Wrede, *Das Reich und seine Feinde*, pp. 439–49.

determined what political options were available. Even if it did not exclude particular options, it could make them significantly more difficult.

Political rhetoric, however, could and did say the opposite of what it intended, or was prepared, to accept. Thus the well-being and peace of the German Fatherland is a motif that even adorns the treaties, reports and memoirs documenting the various attempts at rapprochement between the Guelphs and the French.[70] But there was no public defence of these tactics, which would have had little chance of success. In fact, they would have been counter-productive. Any prince who got involved with France in the 1680s knew that it was better not to draw too much attention to himself. A loss of respect was politically damaging. He had to consider the reaction of neighbouring rivals and the emperor on the one hand, and that of his subjects on the other. Johannes Arndt speaks of 'rulers being controlled by public opinion'.[71] This public did not consist only of the princes' compeers and their envoys to the Imperial Diet. We should remember the prince-bishop of Münster, pro-French at the beginning of the Dutch War, who came under pressure from his own provincial Estates after the first setbacks.[72] While it was possible to withdraw from these pressures in various ways, as Hanover and Celle demonstrate, this was risky and could eat away at one's reputation. The French subsidies had to offset this price. The example of Wolfenbüttel – the next alliance between the Guelphs and France was concluded by the older branch of the family – shows that this was not always the case. Wolfenbüttel's 1701 alliance with France arose out of opposition to the creation of a ninth electorate, that is, out of inner-dynastic rivalry. Duke Anton Ulrich could not accept that by being elevated to the rank of an elector, his 'junior' cousins in Hanover were ousting him from the formal leadership of the house. Added to this was probably a vague sympathy for Louis XIV on the part of Anton Ulrich, who had been intellectually and culturally influenced by France. As we know, this episode ended with the total collapse of Wolfenbüttel's position under pressure from Celle and Hanover, aided by the court in Vienna. Without further ado, the territory was militarily occupied at the beginning of the War of the Spanish Succession.[73]

---

[70] For example, a treaty of neutrality between France and Hanover, 27 Nov. 1690, in Schnath, *Geschichte*, vol. I, pp. 761–5.
[71] Arndt, *Herrschaftskontrolle*, in particular pp. 505–25.
[72] See above n. 17.
[73] See Schnath, *Geschichte*, vol. III, pp. 171–201, 364–80.

V Service to the Emperor, Loyalty to the Nation and the Freedom of the Aristocracy

This has not answered the question about the relative importance of the emperor, the Empire and the nation – the last two are often treated as synonymous – in the value system of an ambitious prince or elector. It is clear that they were not 'ultimate values', as the nation, for example, became in the nineteenth century, including among the aristocracy. For the aristocracy, as for princes in the early modern period, the ultimate value was the honour of their dynasty. All other factors had to be reconciled with this. If this is interpreted anachronistically, it is easy to misunderstand it as opportunism, lack of character or betrayal.[74]

A balance between these different values was relatively easy to achieve with regard to the emperor. Naturally there was tension and friction between the Guelphs and the court in Vienna. In the context of the struggle for the ninth electorate, Ernest Augustus repeatedly put the emperor under pressure. We could go so far as to speak of extortion.[75] Yet political proximity to the head of the Empire was attractive in itself. The panegyrics cited above identify the Guelphs as the servants of 'their' emperor, some in rather exaggerated language. Ostentatious service to the emperor, of course, would not have diminished the status of the servant, however high his birth. In a different context, Gerrit Walther has pointed out that for the French high aristocracy it was attractive and sensible to subordinate themselves to their *grand roi* in profound submission. By doing so they exalted the king, their lord, and thus, in turn, themselves.[76] The orientation towards the emperor could work in a similar way, and in some respects even better. The court in Vienna was less brilliant than that of Versailles, and Leopold I had much less charisma than his cousin, Louis XIV; but, at least

---

[74] On the nation as the ultimate value see Dieter Langewiesche, *Nation, Nationalismus, Nationalstaat in Deutschland und Europa* (Munich, 2000), p. 16. On the primacy of the honour of the house see Martin Wrede, *Ohne Furcht und Tadel – Für König und Vaterland: Frühneuzeitlicher Hochadel zwischen Familienehre, Ritterideal und Fürstendienst* (Ostfildern, 2012), pp. 223, 397–400. See Martin Wrede and Laurent Bourquin, eds, *Noblesses et nations à l'époque moderne: Loyautés, hiérarchies et égalité du XVIe au XIXe siècle* (Ostfildern, 2014). On the subordination of religion to the honour of the house see Ronald G. Asch, 'Religiöse Selbstinszenierung im Zeitalter der Glaubenskriege: Adel und Konfession in Westeuropa', *Historisches Jahrbuch*, 125 (2005), pp. 67–100. See Aretin, *Das Alte Reich*, vol. II, p. 56 with further references.

[75] Schnath, *Geschichte*, vol. I, pp. 592–609; vol. IV, pp. 472–5.

[76] Gerrit Walther, 'Protest als schöne Pose, Gehorsam als "event": Zur Formation des ludovizianischen Absolutismus aus dem Geist der Fronde', in Lothar Schilling, ed., *Absolutismus: Ein unersetzliches Forschungskonzept* (Munich, 2008), pp. 173–91.

within the Empire, the office and title of emperor still possessed great prestige. Attempts by French historians and jurists to diminish the imperial office in their writings show that this was also recognized on the other side of the Rhine.[77] To have served Leopold I was seen as an honour both in the Empire and beyond. Serving the emperor thus also elevated the house of Guelph and increased its honour. This pattern can be seen behind the writings of Bärninger, Funck and other panegyrists. The attractiveness of this situation lay not least in the fact that the emperor's princely subjects did not perceive his power and authority as oppressive – at least not after 1648.[78]

To subordinate oneself to the emperor as the peak of the earthly hierarchy thus made good sense; to place oneself within the German nation as a society tending towards egalitarianism less so. The *raison d'être* of princes and aristocracy was hierarchy and distinction. And yet we must take seriously the frequently recurring invocations of the 'noble German nation' and the 'German Fatherland' which characterized the political language of the times, even that used by princes.[79] They were not mere rhetorical set pieces, not among the Guelphs or their compeers, notwithstanding occasional expressions of dissatisfaction and attempts at extortion. But those expressions of dissatisfication could not and did not stand for a will to bring the whole system down – neither in the Holy Roman Empire nor in France where dissatisfaction among grandees was not entirely unknown.

In a letter to his daughter, the Duchess of Orléans, Charles Louis (Elector Palatine and brother-in-law of Ernest Augustus) complained about French aggression and declared that he was a 'German elector', 'did not want to become subject to a foreign nation' and wanted to enjoy 'the grace only of God, the Holy Roman Emperor and the Empire'. He addressed the imperial public in the same way.[80] Of course, he did this in the awareness of the positive impact that such

---

[77] Martin Wrede, 'Das Reich und seine Geschichte in den Werken französischer Staatsrechtler und Historiker des 18. Jahrhunderts', *Francia*, 27 (2000), pp. 177–211. On perceptions of the office of emperor see id., *Das Reich und seine Feinde*, pp. 160–66, 276–82, 350–55; id., 'L'état de l'Empire empire? Das Reich im Blick der französischen Historiographie im Zeitalter Ludwigs XIV.', in Matthias Schnettger, ed., *Imperium Romanum – irregulare corpus – Teutscher Reichs-Staat: Das Alte Reich im Verständnis der Zeitgenossen und der Historiographie* (Mainz, 2002), pp. 89–110.

[78] Aretin, *Das Alte Reich*, vol. I, pp. 64–85.

[79] Thomas Lau, *Teutschland: Eine Spurensuche im 16. Jahrhundert* (Stuttgart, 2010), pp. 35–49; Schmidt, 'Die "deutsche Freiheit"', pp. 334–40; Wrede, *Das Reich und seine Feinde*, pp. 435–49.

[80] 'nicht gern Anderer genadt alß Gottes, des Röm. Kaysers undt des Reichs', 'Copia Chur-Pfalz Antwortschreibens an der Hertzogin von Orléans Königl. Hoheit, vom 14.

a statement would have in the Empire. Yet Charles Louis *was* an elector, the Elector Palatine. He had fought for his position in the Empire, and saw in it his honour and that of his dynasty, which it was his task to preserve.

The notions of 'nation' and 'Fatherland' were especially popular between 1670 and 1714, during the ultimately successful battles to repulse the Turks and the French. But these ideas were also attractive in themselves, even to imperial princes, and offered a realistic option on which to base identity. In the early modern period, the Germans could not claim to be 'the elect nation', or even 'an' elect nation because, among other things, they were denominationally split.[81] Nonetheless, they saw themselves, as of right, as the leading Christian nation. It was the oldest, and thus the most venerable of all; it provided the emperor; and it was a bastion of Christianity against the Ottomans. If not 'chosen', the Germans had been marked out in a special way in the struggle against the arch enemy.[82] And, of course, the nation was hierarchically ordered internally; the high aristocracy of the Empire had every right and every chance to see themselves at its head.[83] It did not even need the construct of a separate aristocratic nation, as it was cultivated in France, in order to reassure itself of its own distinction.[84]

Beyond this, however, and perhaps more importantly, the early modern German nation offered 'its' aristocracy an especially well-tested point of reference

---

Julii 1674', in Eduard Bodemann, ed., *Briefwechsel der Herzogin Sophie von Hannover mit ihrem Bruder, dem Kurfürsten Karl Ludwig von der Pfalz* (1885; reprint Osnabrück, 1966), pp. 199–200. Charles Louis had forwarded his letter to his sister who, in her reply, reported the 'admiration' which it had aroused in her and in those around her (ibid., p. 200, 10 Aug. 1674). See also *Summarische Relation dessen/ Worin deß Pfaltzgrafens Churfürstl. Durchl. ... so wol von den Frantzösischen Commandanten und Guarnison der Vestung Philippsburg/ als auch sonsten der Königl. Arméen durchmarsch ... in viel wege beschwäret/ und unverschuldeter Dinge vergewaltiget ...* (n.p., 1674), pp. 19, 22, 26, 30.

[81] Georg Schmidt, 'Die frühneuzeitliche Idee der "deutschen Nation": Mehrkonfessionalität und säkulare Werte', in Heinz-Gerhard Haupt and Dieter Langewiesche, eds, *Nation und Religion in der deutschen Geschichte* (Frankfurt a.M., 2001), pp. 33–67.

[82] Martin Wrede, 'Die ausgezeichnete Nation: Nationale Identitätsstiftung im Reich Leopolds I. zwischen Feinden und Konkurrenten', in Eckhard Leuschner and Thomas Wünsch, eds, *Das Bild des Feindes: Die Konstruktion von Antagonismen und der Kulturtransfer zwischen Mittel- und Osteuropa und dem Osmanischen Reich im Zeitalter der Türkenkriege* (Munich, 2013), pp. 19–31.

[83] Horst Carl, 'Europäische Adelsgesellschaft und deutsche Nation in der Vormoderne', in Georg Schmidt, ed., *Die deutsche Nation im frühneuzeitlichen Europa* (Munich, 2010), pp. 181–200.

[84] Olivier Tholozan, *Henri de Boulainvilliers: L'anti-absolutisme aristocratique légitimé par l'histoire* (Aix-en-Provence, 1999).

that invited identification: namely, 'German freedom' as the basis of the Empire's political culture, which was aristocratic freedom first, not last. Freedom and autonomy, self-confidence and stubbornness on the part of the aristocracy and princes were able to develop in a special way within the Empire – differently from any of its neighbours, but better, it was thought.[85] German freedom also had much to offer non-nobles: among other things, legal protection, security of property and a form of orderly confessional co-existence. And in the view of contemporary commentators writing on the Empire, this was enough to distinguish the whole nation in a special way, aristocracy and princes at its head. Absolutism and slavery prevailed in France; in Germany, freedom.[86] 'Land of the free and home of the brave', as the 'Star-Spangled Banner' puts it; for patriots of the Empire, there was no question where this was to be found around 1700. Of course, national self-attributions are sometimes interchangeable.

In the case of the German nation, the German princes, whose power and reputation was almost equal to that of a king, could also become characteristic features of an identity. At the beginning of his work cited above, Otto Friedrich Bärninger self-confidently declaimed:

> Germany has its own potentates
> Equal to kings in power and dignity
> If we speak together with one voice
> The whole world may well fly into a rage with us then.[87]

This figure, standing 'alone in a world of enemies', was to be widely imitated in Germany, as is well known. As a way of boosting public self-confidence, however, it was neither original nor restricted to Germany. Louis XIV translated it as 'nec pluribus impar'.[88]

---

[85] Carl, 'Europäische Adelsgesellschaft', pp. 187–90.
[86] Wrede, *Das Reich und seine Feinde*, pp. 357–74.
[87] 'Teutschland hat selber Potentaten/ An Macht und Würden Köngen gleich: Wann wir einmüthiglich zusammen stimmen/ So mag die ganze Welt auff uns ergrimmen', Bärninger, *Unterthänigster Willkommen*, i v.
[88] This motif can be seen as echoing the notion of being a chosen people. The nation and the dynasty could also find each other reflected in it together. On France see Alexandre Yali Haran, *Le lys et le globe: Messianisme politique et rêve impérial en France aux XVIe et XVIIe siècles* (Seyssel, 2000). On the British variant see Tony Claydon and Ian McBride, eds, *Protestantism and National Identity: Britain and Ireland c. 1650–c. 1850* (Cambridge, 1998); Martina Mittag, *Nationale Identitätsbestrebungen und antispanische Polemik im englischen Pamphlet, 1558–1630* (Frankfurt a.M., 1993). On the catchphrase in the run-

VI A Patriot for the Empire on the British Throne? Conclusion and Outlook

The imperial princes were never far from referring to the emperor and Empire, Fatherland and nation, and this was also true of the Guelphs. These were the values and authorities that granted legitimacy and, ultimately, provided the foundation for political existence within the system of 'German freedom'. That princes tried to combine recourse to them with their own advantage or to derive advantage from them – whether it was a ninth electoral dignity or the acquisition of a duchy on the Elbe – went without saying. To seek this advantage outside the imperial system, outside German freedom and beyond the nation was not in all cases impossible, but always risky. This option was chosen when the honour of the dynasty required it or when, to express it in less pathetic terms, the odds were favourable. It was always the exception to the rule defined by the political culture of the Empire, a deviation from the example provided by the majority of ancestors and compeers. On the other hand it was not to be expected that the Guelphs, Wittelsbachs or Habsburgs should have internalized the belligerent Francophobia displayed by the authors of the pamphlets, even culturally. Even their subjects only backed it to a limited extent.[89] As far as the princes were concerned, the primacy of the honour of the dynasty was uppermost on their mind. If the opportunity arose to marry a dauphin, there was an obligation to try. Naturally, therefore, they took the road to Versailles as soon as it was possible again after a military conflict with Louis XIV – like Sophia of Hanover in 1679.

The succession to the British throne in 1714 naturally changed the patriotic self-representation of the dynasty and ruler, although not immediately and not fundamentally. The heroic honorary titles of both George I and George II deriving from the Turkish and French wars continued in use: Trier, the Conzer Brücke, the Lüneburger on Morea and Crete.[90] Services to the Empire also continued to be remembered: in the case of George II, even in the War of the

---

up to the First World War see Hans-Ulrich Wehler, *Deutsche Gesellschaftsgeschichte*, 5 vols (Munich, 1987–2008), vol. III, pp. 1145–68.

[89] Wrede, *Das Reich und seine Feinde*, pp. 474–83.

[90] For George I and George II see August Wilhelm von Schwicheldt, *Aller-Unterthänigste Lob und Ehren-Rede, Welche, als der Aller-Durchlauchtigste, Großmächtigste König, Fürst und Herr, Herr George, König von Groß-Britannien Dero Allerhöchstes Geburths-Fest ... erlebt, ... auf der Welt-berühmten Julius-Universität ... öffentlich gehalten worden* (Wolfenbüttel, 1726), A 2r, B 2v–B 3r; Johann Conrad Stephan Hölling, *Die ... in dem Glorwürdigsten und Hochseligen Könige und Herrn/ Herrn Georg dem Ersten/ ... erstorbene und in dem Allerdurchleuchtigsten und Großmächtigsten Könige und Herrn/ Herrn Georg dem Andern ... belebete Hoffnung ...* (Bremen, 1727). See Ragnhild Hatton, *Georg I.: Ein deutscher*

Austrian Succession, when the victory of Dettingen was proclaimed a service to the Empire and (the real, that is, Habsburg) imperial house; and in the Seven Years War, when Hanoverian writers exaggeratedly presented Vienna's alliance with Versailles as the ingratitude of the House of Habsburg.[91]

At the same time, a different, more confident, even paternalistic position had to be assumed towards the emperor and the Empire. Ernest Augustus and George William had been champions of the emperor – and junior partners. The British monarch could no longer appear solely as the emperor's knight and vassal. He now also became his benefactor and fatherly protector. Not only had he protected him from the Turks and the French, but also he had literally given him kingdoms. And in doing so, he had also protected the Empire from harm. In his German territories, the king-elector continued to be seen as a leading figure in the German nation, an expression of its virtues and a natural part of it.[92]

It is well known that the foreign dynasty's German background was not necessarily an asset for it in its new kingdoms. But it also had advantages in Britain. That the Guelphs were – more or less – pronounced patriots for the Empire who had rendered services to the emperor, the Empire and the German nation was of little significance across the Channel. But as German imperial princes they not only brought the right denomination with them, but also the added benefit that since 1674 they had always fought on the right side, that is, against the Turks and the French. Their various dalliances with the latter could easily be ignored. And if we add the dragon fought by St George – the fact that the Guelph king shared a name with the English patron saint was also noticed in the Empire[93] – then the country and the ruler shared three common enemies. And it is well known that nothing brings people – and even a people and their prince – together better than common enemies.[94]

Kurfürst auf Englands Thron (Frankfurt a.M., 1982), pp. 32–3; Mijndert Bertram, *Georg II.: König und Kurfürst* (Göttingen, 2004), pp. 47–8.

[91] Wrede, *Das Reich und seine Feinde,* pp. 500–501, 516–17.

[92] Christian Friedrich Weichmann, *Die glorieusen Thaten Des Aller-Durchleuchtigsten und Großmächtigsten Fürsten und Herrn/ Herrn Georg Des Ersten/ Königs in Groß-Britannien* (Lauenburg, 1719).

[93] Schwicheldt, *Aller-Unterthänigste Lob und Ehren-Rede,* E 1 v.

[94] Hannah Smith, *Georgian Monarchy: Politics and Culture, 1714–1760* (Cambridge, 2006), pp. 26–7, 106–8, 182–5. On 'negative integration' see Martin Wrede, 'Feindbild', in Friedrich Jäger, ed., *Enzyklopädie der Neuzeit,* 16 vols (Stuttgart, 2005–2012), vol. III, cols 878–90.

PART II
Representing Protestantism

Chapter 4

George I, the Hanoverian Succession, and Religious Dissent

David Wykes

Religious dissenters (those Protestants who refused to conform to the Church of England) greeted the accession of George I with joy and relief, but also with expressions of loyalty.[1] In one of the best-known accounts, the prominent London dissenting minister Thomas Bradbury claimed to have been the first person to proclaim George I as king. Preaching on 1 August 1714 at his meeting house in Fetter Lane he had news of Queen Anne's death signalled to him by the dropping of a handkerchief from the gallery. In the final prayers after the sermon, to the consternation of his congregation unaware of the news, he gave thanks for the deliverance of the three kingdoms from the evil councils and designs of their enemies, and implored divine blessings upon his majesty King George and the house of Hanover. He then gave out the 89th psalm: 'I will sing of the mercies of the Lord for ever'! He is said subsequently to have preached on the text 2 Kings ix, v. 24: 'Go, see now this cursed woman'. The latter anecdote is possibly apocryphal, though it was certainly characteristic of Bradbury's bombastic behaviour which on frequent occasions upset his contemporaries. The account of Bradbury's proclamation of George I may also not be reliable, for the first reference dates from the early nineteenth century.[2] There are, however, plenty of

---

[1] I am grateful to Professor G.M. Ditchfield for his comments on a draft of this chapter. I also wish to express my thanks to the Keeper of Western Manuscripts, Bodleian Library, University of Oxford; the Archivist of the American Antiquarian Society, Worcester, Massachusetts; the County Archivist, Hertfordshire Archives and Local Studies; and to the Trustees of Dr Williams's Library for permission to cite from the records in their keeping.

[2] Walter Wilson, *The History and Antiquities of Dissenting Churches and Meeting Houses, in London, Westminster, and Southwark*, 4 vols (London, 1810), III, pp. 513–14. The source is said to have been Bradbury's grandson, the Rev. Dr Robert Winter, minister of New Court, Carey Street, 1806–1833. For Bradbury's controversial reputation, see the threat from Convocation to prosecute him for his sermon on the anniversary of the Restoration (29 May) in 1715: *Weekly Packet*, 25 June–2 July 1715, no. 156; *British Weekly Mercury*, 25 June–2 July 1715, no. 522.

documented accounts of dissenters expressing their support for the new dynasty. The Non-juror Thomas Carte, writing from Dorset on 18 August, reported in disgust that '[t]he Presbyterians of Sherburn called K. G. Their King, & say, now is their Time'. Accounts of the proclamation of King George in the west of England record similar expressions of loyalty by dissenters.[3]

Hannah Smith in her book *Georgian Monarchy* has demonstrated that there was considerable and widespread support for George I and the new dynasty, and she has shown the variety of ways in which individuals and communities enthusiastically demonstrated their loyalty: by promoting local celebrations of royal anniversaries, through bell-ringing, bonfires, illuminations and the drinking of the king's health; by circulating verses and preaching sermons; and by the display of the new king's arms and portrait in churches and public buildings, with the king's image circulating even more widely through cheap prints and on earthenware pots, mugs and dishes.[4] But did this support represent real enthusiasm for George I and the Hanoverians, or more pragmatic considerations such as political expediency? Certainly there is evidence that supporters in the provinces demonstrated their loyalty without much encouragement from the new regime, often with considerable initiative and energy. But the evidence is ambiguous, suggesting in some cases more obvious self-interest.

This chapter sets out to extend the recent work on the culture of loyalty by focusing in detail on the response by dissenters to George I and the Hanoverian accession. Dissent certainly featured in Hannah Smith's book; many of the sermons cited in *Georgian Monarchy* were in fact by dissenters. Sermons will play a central role in this account too, but also loyal addresses to the crown, and the High Church reaction to dissenters and their demonstrations of loyalty. It will cover not just the response of dissenters to the new monarch, but also George I's attitudes towards dissenters, particularly their political aspirations. Dissenters undoubtedly claimed to be amongst the most loyal supporters of the Hanoverian succession, and they provided some ringing endorsements of the new king; but was their support driven by anything other than a fear of the return of the Stuarts and of Catholicism?

Dissenters had every reason to welcome George I. They had been under attack from the Tories for more than a decade, culminating in new legislation to curtail their involvement in public life: namely the passing of the Occasional Conformity Act in 1711, intended to prevent dissenters from taking the

---

[3] Bodleian Library, Oxford (hereafter Bodl.), MS Ballard 18, fo 67v, Thomas Carte, Brympton, to Arthur Charlett, 18 Aug. 1714; *Flying Post*, 14–17 Aug. 1714, no. 3529.

[4] Hannah Smith, *Georgian Monarchy: Politics and Culture 1714–1760* (Cambridge, 2006).

Anglican sacrament in order to qualify for office; and, more seriously, the Schism Act in 1714, which sought to prevent dissenters from educating their own children or students for the ministry. They came to believe, with justice, that even the Toleration Act was under threat, and with it their continuing existence.[5] In 1711 the dissenters had found themselves betrayed by their Whig political allies, who agreed to support the Occasional Conformity Bill in the House of Lords, which they had until then opposed, as a result of a bargain struck with the Earl of Nottingham over the peace negotiations. Despite pleas for support the dissenters were told bluntly that the agreement 'was the only way to prevent the Peace; and we should be relieved in some other way'.[6] Yet those dissenters who held political office were pressed by the leading Whigs to abstain temporarily from attending public worship at their meeting houses rather than resign their posts, an appeal backed by the Hanoverian representative in England, Christoph Friedrich Kreienberg, who told them 'how far the interest of his master, and of the Hanover family' depended upon them continuing in their posts.[7] In addition, dissenters had been amongst the most consistent supporters of the Hanoverian succession as a result of their commitment to Protestantism. Dissenters had a peculiar concern as a result of their hatred of popery, and acute anxiety (also shared by many churchmen, Tories as well as Whigs) that the failure of the Hanoverian succession would herald a return of the Stuarts and lead to the imposition of Catholicism and the extirpation of Protestantism. Although by the 1701 Act of Succession parliament had established the Hanoverian claim, there was no guarantee it would be unchallenged or indeed succeed. The question of the Protestant Succession dominated politics in the last year of Anne's reign,

---

[5] Geoffrey S. Holmes, *British Politics in the Age of Anne* (London, 1967), pp. 103–4, 475 n. 94; Dr Williams's Library, London (hereafter DWL), MS 38.17, Benjamin Stinton, 'A Journall of the Affairs of the Antipaedobaptists Beginning with the Reign of King George, whose Accession to ye Throne was on ye First of August, 1714', fo 15r; James E. Bradley, 'Nonconformist Schools, the Schism Act, and the Limits of Toleration in England's Confessional State', in Jordan J. Ballor, David Sytsma and Jason Zuidema, eds, *Church and School in Early Modern Protestantism: Studies in Honour of Richard A. Muller on the Maturation of a Theological Tradition* (Leiden, 2013), pp. 597–611.

[6] Edmund Calamy, *An Historical Account of My Own Life*, ed. by J.T. Rutt, 2 vols (London, 1829), II, p. 244.

[7] Ibid., pp. 243–4, 245–6; 'Four Letters: Relating to the removal of the incapacities of Protestant dissenters', no. VI in *A Collection of the Occasional Papers for the Year 1718* (London, 1719), III, pp. 4–5; The National Archives, Kew, SP 35/8, no. 110, Sir John Fryer to James Stanhope, 13 Apr. 1717.

provoking a final period of heightened tension, followed by joy and relief at George I's apparently peaceful accession.[8]

Sermons by Dissenters on the King's Accession

Sermons were central to the religious life of dissenters and, not surprisingly, published sermons form a major source for the response by dissenters to George I and the new dynasty.[9] According to the prominent London Baptist minister Benjamin Stinton, who wrote an historical account of the period:

> This signall Deliverance of the Nation [the accession of George I], was publickly acknowledged by many of ye Moderate Religious Clergy of ye Church of England; But ye Dissenting Congregations Universally rejoiced in this Salvation, and prais'd God for his preventing goodness.

Stinton continued:

> Many were the books & Sermons yt ... came forth on this account; wherein was set forth the Danger we were in[,] the Seasonableness of our Deliverance, & the Happiness we might expect under our Protestant Sovereign if our sins prevented not.[10]

Dissenters were to stress the providential nature of George I's peaceful accession despite the efforts of the enemies of the Protestant Succession. For Nathanael Harding, preaching to an assembly of Protestant dissenters in Plymouth on the day of King George's coronation, 'the peaceable Accession of a Good and Lawful Prince to the Throne, and his Settlement', was 'no casual Event, but the Lord's doing'.[11] For Benjamin Stinton, in the sermon he published, the happy accession showed 'how seasonably the Protestant Succession has by Divine Providence

---

[8] Holmes, *British Politics*, pp. 82–7.

[9] This study is based on a survey of all the published sermons by dissenters for the first five years of George I's reign, identified using the *English Short-Title Catalogue*; *The Monthly Catalogue, 1714–1717*, English Bibliographical Sources. Series I, no. I (London, 1964); *Early Nonconformity, 1566–1800: A Catalogue of Books in Dr. Williams's Library, London* (Boston, MA, 1968), known as 'Bibliography of Early Nonconformity' and compiled by Miss G. Woodward and Roger Thomas, 12 vols in three parts: subject catalogue, vol. II.

[10] DWL, MS 38.17, Stinton, 'Journall', fo 15r.

[11] Nathanael Harding, *A Sermon Preach'd at Plymouth to an Assembly of Protestant Dissenters, on their Lecture-Day, the 20th of October, 1714* (London, 1714), pp. 9, 10.

took place'.¹² Others echoed the nation's remarkable deliverance through 'the Goodness of our God'.¹³ Sermons also catch the fear and uncertainty of the final months of the old queen. Many ministers remarked on the extraordinary transformation of the nation's affairs and reminded their congregations of their earlier desperate situation:

> I am sure you have not yet forgot your Fears of a Popish Successor, or the fervent Cries and Vows which were offered up to Heaven under Apprehension of Danger. Our Friends abroad were in Agonies for us; Good Men in all Parts of our own Land were besieging Heaven with their Prayers for the Protestant Succession.¹⁴

Samuel Clark reminded his congregation at St Albans that in the last year of Queen Anne's reign 'it pleased God for our Sins to suffer our Hopes in a great measure to be blasted', and they had thus found themselves on 'the brink of Ruin'.¹⁵

A major theme was the use of biblical exegesis, and many drew on the Old Testament story of Adonijah to justify recent political events. Solomon was anointed king of Israel by his father David, though Adonijah was the eldest surviving son: a succession that dissenting ministers were careful to stress had been determined by the will of God:¹⁶

> Tho' God had deputed Solomon by Name, and David had fixed the Succession upon him; yet Adonijah would break through the Settlement, and advance himself. He claimed the Crown by Right of Primogeniture, looked upon the Kingdom as his Birth-right; because he was the eldest Son.¹⁷

For Harding, Adonijah was 'a bold and daring Pretender' who would have 'step'd into the Throne' before Solomon. John Archer, preaching at Tunbridge Wells a week after George's accession, improved upon his text, telling his audience that:

---

¹² Benjamin Stinton, *A Discourse of Divine Providence: Occasion'd by the Demise of Her Late Majesty Queen Anne, and the Happy Accession of Our Present Sovereign King George to the Throne of Great Britain, &c.* (London, 1714), p. 24.

¹³ Jonathan Owen, *An Occasional Sermon upon the Proclamation of King George, on the First of August, 1714* (London, [1714]), p. 16.

¹⁴ Harding, *Sermon*, pp. 21–2.

¹⁵ Samuel Clark, *A Sermon upon Occasion of the Death of Her Majesty Queen Anne: Preach'd to a Congregation of Dissenters, at St. Albans: Aug. 22. 1714* (London, 1714), pp. 20, 21.

¹⁶ Owen, *Occasional Sermon*, p. 4; John Archer, *The Kingdom Turned About: A Sermon Preached at Tunbridge-Wells August 8. 1714. on Occasion of his Present Majesty King George's Happy Accession to the Throne* (London, 1714), pp. 9–10.

¹⁷ Harding, *Sermon*, pp. 10–11.

Adonijah's Assertion of his Right to the Kingdom of Israel, gives us an Occasion to take Notice of the Frivolousness of the Pretence of those, who have been for divers Years paving the Way for that insolent Pretender, who has so long taken to himself the Stile of King of these Realms.[18]

He drew attention to the efforts by such men to undermine the Hanoverian settlement.

Only dissenters seem to have advanced the story of Adonijah so vigorously. They noted further examples in ancient Israel where the eldest son did not inherit: in the house of Isaac Jacob was raised above Esau, the first-born; and in the house of Jacob Reuben, the eldest, was disgraced in favour of Judah. Saul, the first king of Israel, was descended from Benjamin, the youngest of Jacob's sons. When God removed Saul for his wickedness, David, the youngest son of Jesse, was named instead. Although the kingship continued in the line of David to the Captivity, ministers were not certain that the eldest son always succeeded. Archer pointed out in short 'how little the Title of the eldest Son was favoured in the Kingdom of *Israel* or *Judah*, especially where God took upon himself the Nomination of the Successor'.[19] For Jonathan Owen, minister of the congregation meeting at Pewterers' Hall, Lime Street, the accession of Solomon to the throne of Israel was according to the will of God: it 'matter'd not the line of Primogeniture, nor did they regard the absurd Noise of indefeasible Right'.[20]

Dissenters did not rest their arguments on Old Testament exegesis alone. Harding saw that hereditary right could not stand as providence would not suffer it: '*Solomon* (tho' a younger Brother) is God's King, and the Peoples. The Elder Branches of the Royal Family are laid aside, and he is settled on the Throne, by the Joyful Concurrence of the whole Nation, in their Representatives.' Then, in an extraordinary piece of special pleading, he continued: 'So that he had not only an immediately Divine Right, but a Parliamentary one, or what was Equivalent thereto'.[21] Harding also observed that princes with better claims to the throne by inheritance were passed over to make way for George I and the house of Hanover, 'whose superior Merit and purer Religion drew the Eyes of our Legislators, and procured a sure Title to the Kingdom'. Moreover, '[t]his Just and Rightful Title God hath confirmed, by bringing our Sovereign peaceably to the Throne'.[22] As Archer noted, the friends of the Pretender asserted that

[18] Archer, *Kingdom*, p. 11.
[19] Ibid., p. 16.
[20] Owen, *Occasional Sermon*, p. 4.
[21] Harding, *Sermon*, p. 11.
[22] Ibid., p. 13; cf. Clark, *Sermon*, p. 22.

hereditary right could not be limited by act of parliament; that no one had the right to rule as king, but who is next in blood: 'Thus did Adonijah claim.'[23]

Dissenters sought to remind the king that their enemies had been the enemies of the Protestant Succession; that under the late queen the doctrine of an indefeasible hereditary right had been cried up, leaving the Protestant Succession in the greatest danger of being broken.

> To carry on these Designs, the Spirit of Envy and Persecution was reviv'd amongst the People; and those Incroachments that were made upon the Act of Toleration, caus'd some to fear, and others to hope, that in a little time it would be wholly taken away: And the more Zealous were hereby incourag'd to threaten the Dissenters with the demolishing of their Places of Worship, driving their Teachers into Corners, and banishing out of the Land all that dar'd to dissent from their Church.[24]

Ministers were to point out that dissenters had been the most loyal supporters of the Hanoverian interest and had suffered for it, and to express the hope that their liberties would now be secured to them.[25]

It is clear dissenters took advantage of the opportunities that occurred during the first few months to demonstrate their particular enthusiasm and loyalty to the Hanoverian line with sermons to mark the king's accession, his safe arrival in England and his coronation. In addition to these personal initiatives dissenters were also enthusiastic in taking part in the day of public thanksgiving held on 20 January 1714–1715 for the peaceable accession of the new king, and many of these sermons were published.[26] Besides thanksgiving days to mark special public events there were also four official fast days held each year: the anniversary of the execution of Charles I (30 January 1649); the Restoration of Charles II (29 May 1660); the double commemoration on 5 November of the failure of the Gunpowder Plot (1605) and the successful landing of William of Orange at Torbay (1688); and the anniversary of the accession of the

---

[23] Archer, *Kingdom*, p. 13. For an account of the laws governing succession under the Stuarts, and the challenges to an indefeasible hereditary right by parliamentary sanction leading to the Hanoverian succession, see Howard Nenner, *The Right to Be King: The Succession to the Crown of England, 1603–1714* (London, 1995).

[24] Stinton, *Discourse*, pp. 21–2.

[25] Owen, *Occasional Sermon*, p. 20; Clark, *Sermon*, p. 22.

[26] *London Gazette*, 7–11 Dec. 1714, no. 5284. Among the dissenters who published sermons were Bradbury, John Sprint, John Thomas, Simon Browne, Samuel Wright, Nathanael Harding, Henry Sanders, John Bowden, Thomas Masters, Stickland Gough, John Billingsley, Thomas Harrison, Thomas Simmons and John Tomlyns.

reigning monarch. Historians recognise that historical anniversaries and royal events were appropriated by the different political and religious parties. High Churchmen and their supporters observed the execution of Charles the Martyr on 30 January. In turn dissenters celebrated the providential deliverance of the nation from popery on 5 November, and it became the main anniversary in their religious calendar. Thomas Bradbury preached a November the fifth sermon to his congregation every year, which he published. In 1714 his subject was appropriately *The True Happiness of a Good Government*. Marking November the fifth could be contentious. Josiah Eveleigh of Crediton in Devon was forced to publish the sermon he had delivered that day against a divine hereditary right to clear himself from misrepresentation, after rumours that he had cast aspersions on the Church of England had led to a riot in the evening.[27] Dissenters also marked George I's birthday (28 May), but less commonly the birthdays of other members of the royal family – though in 1717 Jeremiah Owen ingeniously used the Princess of Wales's birthday on 1 March to celebrate the festival of St David.[28] A great many of the thanksgiving sermons delivered on royal occasions or public fast days to the society that supported the Lord's Day Morning Lecture at Little St Helen's Presbyterian meeting in Bishopsgate, London, were subsequently published at the society's expense. A majority marked the king's accession (1 August) rather than his birthday. Even after George I's death, August the first continued to be commemorated by the society as 'Being the Happy Day of the Accession of the Illustrious House of Brunswick to the Throne of Great Britain'.[29]

---

[27] Josiah Eveleigh, *The Dissenters Joy in the Preservation of the Church of England: A Sermon, Preach'd in Crediton in Devon, ... On Nov. 5. 1714. When a Riot Happen'd There in the Evening; and Now Publish'd upon Occasion of a Late Trial of the Said Riot, &c. With a Preface, Containing an Argument against the Divine Right of an Uninterrupted Lineal Succession* (Exeter, [1714]), 'Preface' [unpaginated]. See also the disturbance at Axminster, Devon, on 5 November, Paul Kléber Monod, *Jacobitism and the English People, 1688–1788* (Cambridge, 1989), p. 179.

[28] Jer[emiah] Owen, *The Goodness and Severity of God, in His Dispensations, with Respect unto the Ancient Britains, Display'd: In a Sermon Preach'd to an Auditory of Protestant Dissenters, at Haberdasher's Hall in London, on March the 1st, 1716. Being the Anniversary of the Birth of Her Royal Highness the Princess of Wales, and the Festival of St. David. Wherein is Contain'd, A Brief Historical Account of the State of that Ancient People, and the Several Revolutions they Underwent from their Origin down to these Present Times* (London, [1717]).

[29] Edward Godwin, *The Wonderful Works of God, an Obligation to Continual Gratitude: A Sermon Preach'd at Little St. Helen's, to the Society which Support the Lord's Day Morning Lecture There: Upon the First of August, 1727. Being the Happy Day of the Accession of the Illustrious House of Brunswick to the Throne of Great Britain. Publish'd as the Request of the Society* (London, 1727).

The anniversary of the Restoration, having declined in popularity following the 1688 Revolution, was revived after 1714 to become a major focus for disturbances by Jacobite supporters of the exiled Stuarts.[30] It was an unfortunate coincidence for the Hanoverians that George I's birthday (28 May) fell on the day before, providing the Jacobite mob with the opportunity for two days of disturbances. In London in May 1715, on the first occasion that the new king's birthday was celebrated, the Jacobite mob committed outrages on both days, despite the precautions taken for preserving the peace. The dissenters were the focus for most of the abuse. In Highgate, on the night of the king's birthday, after the inhabitants 'had with great Loyalty and Joy celebrated the Anniversary of his Majesty's Birth, with Illuminations and Bonfires &c.', the High Church rabble went to the Presbyterian meeting house and 'carry'd off the Casements of the Windows, and did further Mischief'. The following night 'the Rabble not only betook themselves to their old Trade of breaking Windows ... Others made Bonfires in which they burnt the Effigies of Persons in the habit [clothes] of Dissenting Ministers'.[31] Similar disturbances occurred at Oxford and Abingdon. At Oxford on the king's birthday the mob broke open the Presbyterian meeting house and 'fell to pulling down the Pews, &c. They put the Constable who came to keep the Peace into the Pulpit, and roll'd him up and down.' The following night 'the Tumult was greater than the Night before; they now fell foul on the Quakers and Anabaptist Meeting, which they gutted and brought the Goods into the open Street and burnt them'. The Presbyterian meeting house at Abingdon was also attacked.[32] The earlier disturbances on King George's Coronation Day (20 October 1714) were far more serious and an even more obvious affront to the new king. As on other occasions, dissenters experienced much of the trouble.[33]

The disturbances and the riots that took place during the summer of 1715 in London, the West Midlands and the North-West were some of the most serious in eighteenth-century England. Dissenters were clearly the object of the mob's hostility. Over 40 meeting houses were badly damaged or destroyed. In Manchester the mob demolished the meeting house brick by brick over a period of five days.[34] It would be easy to argue that dissenters were the focus of

---

[30] Ronald Hutton, *The Stations of the Sun: A History of the Ritual Year in Britain* (Oxford, 1996), p. 290; Monod, *Jacobitism*, pp. 181–2.
[31] *Flying Post*, 28–31 May 1715, no. 3651.
[32] *St. James's Post*, 30 May–1 June 1715, no. 55; *British Weekly Mercury*, 28 May–4 June 1715, no. 518. There were similar disturbances a year later; see *Flying Post*, 7–9, 14–16 June 1716, nos 3812, 3815.
[33] Monod, *Jacobitism*, pp. 173–8.
[34] *Flying Post*, 18–21 June 1715, no. 3660.

these attacks because of their loyalty to the Hanoverians, and certainly dissenters themselves in their petition to the crown for redress were to claim they were attacked because of 'their Zeal and firm Adherence to your Majesty and your Government'.[35] This is not, however, the whole explanation. Dissenters were the subject of hate in their own right. They were portrayed by High Churchmen as a threat to the security of the Church of England, and many meeting houses were also attacked in 1710 following the trial of the High Church incendiary Henry Sacheverell. The Jacobite rising of 1715 represented a much more serious threat to the Hanoverian regime than the riots, particularly as the government had great difficulty in many regions in raising sufficient forces to oppose the rebels. From a detailed study of Preston in Lancashire, Mark Parry has argued that the Hanoverian monarchy depended upon dissenters for its survival both in 1715 and 1745, because of the reluctance of the local gentry to assist with the county's defence. Parry sees dissenters as one of the few reliable constituencies supporting the Hanoverian regime, and that in 1715, without their support, he argues, the position of the government would have been very precarious.[36]

Loyal Addresses to the Crown

Dissenters had other ways of expressing their support for the new king in addition to sermons. The Committee of the Three Denominations (of Presbyterians, Congregationalists and Baptists), which represented the interests of dissenters, was one of the very few private bodies with the privilege of addressing the crown and of being received before the throne: a privilege shared only by the City of London, Oxford and Cambridge universities and the London clergy. They had the right to read their own address and to receive a response from the monarch.[37] The privilege was of considerable importance in providing access to the throne, but it also provided occasions for public demonstrations of support, allowing dissenters to express their loyalty, and to remind the king and his ministers that their past support and continuing loyalty were worthy of reward. How the address was presented, and how it was received by the crown, also provided an important public demonstration of dissenting loyalty and where they stood in

---

[35] *London Gazette*, 16–20 Aug. 1715, no. 5356.
[36] Mark Parry, 'Whigs, Dissenters and Hanoverian Loyalism in Preston during the Jacobite Rebellions of 1715 and 1745', *Transactions of the Historic Society of Lancashire and Cheshire*, 158 (2009), pp. 1–28, at pp. 4, 8, 13–14.
[37] 'Address of the Body of Dissenting Ministers to the King on his Accession: with the King's Answer', *Monthly Repository*, 15 (1820), p. 314 n*.

the royal favour. Shortly after the king's arrival in London the Committee met to prepare a loyal address, which it was agreed should be attended by all the London dissenting ministers. Consequently, on 28 September they met in the City, at Samuel Rosewell's meeting house in Silver Street, '& from thence (in Gentlemen's Coach's [sic])' lent by their wealthy supporters, they proceeded as a body to St James's Palace, where they were 'handsomely rec'd by the Court and Introduced into the Royall presence' by the Duke of Devonshire. According to Edmund Calamy, 'there were near an hundred ministers' present.[38]

The address was read by the Rev. Dr Daniel Williams, the senior minister present. It congratulated the king on his peaceable accession and safe arrival, 'the Merciful Return of many Ardent Prayers'. It continued by tactfully recalling George's descent from the king and queen of Bohemia, 'those Renowned Patrons of the Protestant Religion', and George's own zeal 'for the same Religion, your known Affection to the Liberties of Europe, and the Rights of Mankind'. It referred to the Act of Succession and to King William of 'Immortal Memory' who procured it, and to the steadfast adherence of the dissenters to the settlement despite the dangers: 'Our Zeal herein has been own'd to be very conspicuous, by those Noble Patriots, who now surround your Throne.' Having promised the support of the dissenters against all pretenders whatsoever, and their prayers for the king, the prince and princess of Wales, and all the branches of his family, the address ended with the hope that it might be 'your Majesty's Glory to protect the Protestant Religion, to suppress the Profaneness of the Age, to heal the Divisions of your People, to assert the Rights of the Injur'd Abroad, and to Preserve the Balance of Europe'. The address therefore mentioned all the key concerns of the Protestant dissenters, which they had expressed in their sermons. The king briefly acknowledged the address.[39]

All the ministers present then had the honour of kissing his majesty's hand, before being presented to the Prince of Wales, 'who received them in a very handsom manner Promising them his favour and friendship and then admitted them to the Hon.:ʳ of kissing his hand also'.[40] A week later there were addresses from the Presbyterian ministers and laymen of Northern Ireland and from dissenters in Dublin and the south of Ireland.[41] In the months that followed there were many similar addresses from dissenting ministers and congregations in England: from Berkshire, Bristol, Oxfordshire, Hampshire, Somerset, Wiltshire, Norfolk,

---

[38] DWL, MS 38.17, Stinton, 'Journall', fos 22r–23v; Calamy, *Historical Account*, II, p. 300.
[39] *London Gazette*, 28 Sept.–2 Oct. 1714, no. 5264.
[40] DWL, MS 38.17, Stinton, 'Journall', fo 23v.
[41] *Evening Post*, 2–5 Oct. 1714, no. 805.

Suffolk, Gloucestershire, Devon, Cornwall, Essex, Nottingham and the county, Bridport and Dorset, and Yorkshire – all acknowledged in the *London Gazette* or reported in the Whig press.[42] The decision that the London ministers should accompany the address, all clothed in black cloaks and arriving together in gentlemen's coaches, created a considerable display that was noted by many at court.[43] In turn the dissenters undoubtedly took much heart that the address was publicly so well received by both the king and the Prince of Wales. They also noted that the address itself was published in the *Gazette*.[44]

There were other more obvious demonstrations of the king's apparent sympathy for dissenters and his willingness to redress their grievances. Dissenters noted the new king's answer to the address of both Houses of Parliament, and in particular his declaration at his first Privy Council, on 22 September, that he would support and maintain the Churches of England and Scotland as by law established: 'which I am of Opinion may be Effectually done without the least Impairing the Toleration allowed by Law to Protestant Dissenters, so Agreeable to Christian Charity, and so Necessary to the Trade and Riches of this Kingdom'.[45] Nonetheless the declaration was concerned with reassuring the Church of England and the Church of Scotland rather than the dissenters. The king gave only a brief formal acknowledgement to the address presented a few days later by Daniel Williams on behalf of the dissenters, noting their expressions of loyalty and promising his protection, though it is clear dissenters were pleased by their reception at court and the publication of their address.[46] By contrast the king's declaration in Council 'not a little grated on ye High flown party to have ye C of E set upon a Level with ye C of Scotland, wch they upon all occasions so much contemn'd'.[47] The king also rewarded those dissenters who had supported the Hanoverian interest during Queen Anne's reign. In November 1714 John Fryer, who was one of those who at

---

[42] *London Gazette*, 19 Oct., 13, 16, 30 Nov. 1714, 4, 11, 25 Jan., 8 Feb. 1714/15, 3 May 1715; *Flying Post*, 16 Dec. 1715, 3 Feb., 12 Mar. 1714/15.

[43] Bodl., MS Ballard 36, fo 161r, [James Greenshields], London, to [Arthur Charlett], 2 Oct. 1714; Ragnhild Hatton, *George I: Elector and King* (London, 1978), p. 173.

[44] Bodl., MS Ballard 36, fo 162v, Greenshields, London, to Charlett, 6 Nov. 1714.

[45] *Journal of the House of Lords, 1714–1717* (London, 1834), XX, pp. 14–15; *London Gazette*, 21–25 Sep. 1714, no. 5262; Thomas Harrison, *A Sermon Preach'd the 20th of January 1714/15: Being the Solemn Thanksgiving-day for the Happy Accession of Our Gracious Sovereign King George* (London, [1715]), pp. 18–19; Calamy, *Historical Account*, II, pp. 298–9.

[46] *London Gazette*, 28 Sept. 1714, no. 5264. There is no evidence to support Ragnhild Hatton's claim that George I promised at his first Privy Council and in his reply to the dissenters' address that he would repeal the Occasional Conformity and Schism Acts: Hatton, *George I*, p. 199.

[47] Bodl., MS Eng. hist. d. 90, fo 36r.

the request of the Hanoverian representative had stopped attending his meeting house in order to continue in office, was given a baronetcy.[48]

In the months that followed dissenters were to be disappointed by the slow progress taken to repeal the various penal statutes against them, particularly in view of the high hopes they had entertained as a result of the king's apparent support. By the summer of 1716 dissenters had a number of grievances besides the government's failure on repeal. They had suffered badly from the Jacobite mobs, many of their meeting houses had been destroyed, and they became increasingly angry over the delay in paying the compensation they had been promised. As a consequence, while others made loyal addresses on the conclusion of the rebellion, 'they did not think their addressing now so seasonable'. 'The Ministry appearing cold to y[m], they ... were willing to let y[m] see, they were not insensible y^t they were not well us'd'.[49] A further grievance involved dissenting ministers who found themselves assessed under the Land Tax on their salaries for preaching. Jenkin Lewis, Congregational minister at Southwold in Suffolk, was expected to pay £8 out of his small salary of £40, and saw it as 'a persecuting of some of those y^t are the Kings best friends'. Despite pleas for help from their supporters in parliament, Lewis and his fellow ministers were disappointed.[50]

Early in 1717 the Committee of the General Body of the Three Denominations decided to present a loyal address to George I following his safe return from Hanover, but they had some difficulty in agreeing upon the form of words it should take:

> some were for having us Speak plainly of the hardships the Dissenters lay under & of the little regard that was had to them Notwithstanding their Stedfast Loyalty to his Ma[jes]tie ... Others thought an address of this nature would come better from the Laity than the Ministers.[51]

---

[48] *London Gazette*, 16–20 Nov. 1714, no. 5278.

[49] Calamy, *Historical Account*, II, pp. 354–5; Bodl., MS Eng. Hist. d. 90, fo 43r. An address had been prepared, but it was not presented; for a copy see DWL, Baxter Treatises, V, fo 186, 'The Humble Address of ye Protestant Ministers' [June 1716].

[50] DWL, MS 38.96, Jennings papers, J[enkin] L[ewis], Southwold, to [Matthew] Clark, Crouchet Friars, London, 23 Apr. 1716; see also John Sammon, Presbyterian minister at Mayfield, Sussex (*The Shift Shifted*, 4 Aug. 1716); and Edmund Taylor, Presbyterian minister at Alton, assessed at £15, to be tried at the Assizes for Hampshire (*Weekly Packet*, 1 June 1717). Ministers finally obtained relief at law rather than through parliament, when the Court of Common Pleas determined that they were not liable to be taxed on their salaries under the Land Tax: *Weekly Packet*, 15 Feb.; *St James's Evening Post*, 15 Feb. 1717/18.

[51] DWL, MS 38.17, Stinton, 'Journall', fos 70v–71r.

After some revision an address 'without any Complaints or Reflections' was drawn up and presented to the king by Edmund Calamy, one of the leading Presbyterian ministers. After kissing the king's hand, Calamy used the opportunity to lobby the Earl of Stanhope about the compensation for their meeting houses. Begging a word with 'Mr Secretary at the other end of the room', he was 'followed and surrounded', as previously arranged, by the other ministers accompanying the address. 'He', Stanhope, 'assured us, that as he was going into the Treasury, in a little time, so, upon his honour, he would take care that our's should be among the first money paid. He gave us leave to signify this much to our friends, and was as good as his word.'[52] Stanhope was the king's minister who was most sympathetic to dissenters. Payment did much to improve relations with the government.

It seems clear that the king's own sympathies were in favour of toleration and relief, and that despite the political difficulties he persisted in his efforts to relieve dissenters.[53] Contemporaries were certainly convinced the king favoured dissenters and their political goals. Churchmen who were Hanoverian supporters were alarmed at the king's open partiality towards dissenters and expressed their fears that it would alienate churchmen, already disaffected by the nomination of Benjamin Hoadley to the bishopric of Bangor in March 1716. The prominent Whig politician John Smith, MP for East Looe (1715–1723), in his speech opposing the vote for measures against Sweden in April 1717, asked:

> Is it not a Mistake, to take this Opportunity to create Divisions, and render some of the King's best Friends suspected and obnoxious? Is it not a Mistake, in short, to form Parties and Cabals, in order to bring in a Bill to repeal the Act against Occasional Conformity?

Stanhope, in reply, told the House that 'he had, some time ago, the King's Orders to draw up an Act of Indemnity'.[54] Dissenters certainly believed the king was

---

[52] Calamy, *Historical Account*, II, pp. 368–9; British Library, London, Add MS 50959, Autobiography of Edmund Calamy (1671–1732), fos 164v–165r.

[53] Hatton, *George I*, pp. 289, 173. See p. 349, note 7, where Friedrich Wilhelm von der Schulenburg's letters of 2 April and 12 May 1717 are quoted as evidence of George's determination to keep his promises to the dissenters.

[54] *The Historical Register, Containing an Impartial Relation of all Transactions for the Year 1717* (London, 1718), p. 165. See also Christ Church, Oxford, MS Arch. W. Epistl. 20, fo 477v, William Nicolson, Bishop of Carlisle, to William Wake, Archbishop of Canterbury, 21 Nov. 1717.

their friend, but that attempts to grant them relief were thwarted by 'some of his Great Ministers [who] ... are Great Whiggs in ye State but Tories in ye Ch[urch]'.[55]

There is in addition direct evidence of the king's own views. On 18 March 1717, William Nicolson, Bishop of Carlisle, who spoke German, told the king of the bishops' opposition to the repeal of the Occasional Conformity and Schism Acts. The king asked the reason why, and was told by Nicolson, '[p]robably because it had so lately become law'. The king then asked: 'Have not the Dissenters deserved well since?'[56] William Wake, Archbishop of Canterbury, was also told that it was 'the King's earnest desire to have the Dissenters eased'. A few days later, on 23 March, Nicolson dined with William Cowper, the Lord Chancellor, and six other bishops. Cowper asked them how they stood about repeal. He was also informed that the majority of bishops were against it. Cowper, though, believed that the king 'had set his heart on passing it'; he therefore asked the bishops present to consider whether some expedient could be found 'to atteyn the same good end the K[ing] proposed ... the uniting and strengthening the Prot[estant] interest, &c. and the making some publ[ic] acknowl^t to the Dissent^s who had been faithfull to the K[ing] to a man'.[57]

Conclusion

The support dissenters gave to the Hanoverian succession can be readily demonstrated through their sermons, their loyal addresses, and even their willingness to take up arms in defence of the crown. In turn there is evidence of George I's support for dissenters and their political aspirations. Nevertheless, their history did not make dissenters very convincing monarchists even if they were committed to the Hanoverians and to the Protestant Succession. Although the Presbyterians, the largest and most respectable body of dissenters, had been appalled by the execution of Charles I and the rule by the saints, and had worked for the restoration of Charles II, they were damned by High Churchmen and

---

[55] American Antiquarian Society, Worcester, MA, MS62–4507, Curwen Family Manuscript Collection, 1637–1808, Box 2, folder 2, Benjamin Colman, Boston, to [John Higginson], 18 June 1717.

[56] Geoffrey S. Holmes and Clyve Jones, eds, *The London Diaries of William Nicolson, Bishop of Carlisle, 1702–1718* (Oxford, 1985), p. 651 (18 Mar. 1716/7).

[57] Hertfordshire Record Office, DE/P/F131, fo 11, notes of a conference between Lord Cowper and the bishops, [23 Mar. 1717], in attempt to ascertain the bishops' views on the repeal of the Occasional Conformity Act; Holmes and Jones, eds, *London Diaries of William Nicolson*, pp. 652, 704–5 (23 Mar. 1716/17).

Tories with the separatists as king-killers, republicans and fanatics. Opening the door to dissenters, it was alleged, would ensure the destruction of the Church of England and the monarchy. In 1714 dissenters had rested considerable, and in the end unrealistic, hopes on George I for the repeal of the Test and Corporation Acts and other penalties against them. The crown was quick to realise that whatever sympathy it may have felt for dissenters and their desires for relief, it could not afford to antagonise churchmen. Despite continuing disappointments over repeal, dissenters remained loyal to George I and George II, as the laudatory sermons preached on their deaths by dissenters help demonstrate. Dissenters were as committed to the government in 1745 as they had been in 1715; on both occasions they raised volunteers from their congregations to fight the rebels.

During the 1770s there was a growing belief amongst dissenters that the king's ministers were increasingly wicked and corrupt. Jim Bradley has argued that the mishandling of the Wilkite controversy, the failure of the campaigns by dissenters for relief from subscription (until they received some limited concessions in 1779), and the breakdown of relations with the American colonists turned many dissenters towards opposition to government. Historians studying the electorate have reached similar conclusions.[58] George III was a convinced Anglican, whose faith was characterised by his commitment to the Doctrine of the Trinity. While he accepted the Toleration Act, he was against any attempt to weaken the position of the Church. He opposed most efforts to relieve dissenters from their political disabilities.[59] Dissenters were to become increasingly vociferous critics of the king and his ministers. Historians have noted the irony that whereas dissenters had their meeting places ransacked and destroyed in 1714 because of their loyalty to the Hanoverians, the same meeting houses were destroyed when Joseph Priestley and his friends were attacked in Birmingham in July 1791 for their supposed lack of loyalty.

---

[58] James E. Bradley, *Religion, Revolution and English Radicalism: Nonconformity in Eighteenth-Century Politics and Society* (Cambridge, 1990); John A. Phillips, *Electoral Behaviour in Unreformed England* (Princeton, 1982), pp. 289–305; Frank O'Gorman, *Voters, Patrons and Parties: The Unreformed Electoral System of Hanoverian England, 1734–1832* (Oxford, 1989).

[59] See the chapter by G.M. Ditchfield in this volume.

Chapter 5

Hanover-Britain and the Protestant Cause, 1714–1760

Andrew C. Thompson

Confessional conflict was a central theme of early modern life in both Britain and Hanover. Like succession and security, it was an important concern for the new Hanoverian dynasty after 1714. Moreover, debate over religious persecution provides an interesting example of the functioning of the Anglo-Hanoverian composite state in practice and the nature of the Personal Union. Analysing the interest that the early Hanoverian monarchs displayed in persecuted Protestants also provides a means to think about questions of self-perception and presentation.

Much of the older historiography which surrounds the Personal Union tended to emphasise the points of difference and departure between the two entities, arguing in essence that the union was merely personal and did not extend beyond the accidental and contingent sharing of a ruling family.[1] Looking at the ways in which those on both sides of the North Sea seemed willing to engage in the defence of co-religionists within central Europe provides a means to question this perception.[2] Even if British intervention on behalf of

---

[1] This view is classically articulated in Ernst von Meier, *Hannoversche Verfassungs- und Verwaltungsgeschichte, 1680–1866*, 2 vols (Leipzig, 1898–1899), I, pp. 122–3 and Adolphus William Ward, *Great Britain and Hanover: Some Aspects of the Personal Union* (Oxford, 1899), pp. 1–2. A more recent example, among many, is Heide Barmeyer, 'Die Personalunion England-Hannover: Ihre Entstehung, Etablierung und Fortsetzung aus Hannoverscher Sicht', in Rex Rexheuser (ed.), *Die Personalunionen von Sachsen-Polen 1697–1763 und Hannover-England 1714–1837: Ein Vergleich* (Wiesbaden, 2005), pp. 275–98, at p. 275. For a suggestion that this perspective was limited, see Ragnhild M. Hatton, *The Anglo-Hanoverian Connection, 1714–1760: The Creighton Trust Lecture 1982* (London, 1982), pp. 2–3. There is a useful overview and compelling case made for a broader perspective in Nick Harding, *Hanover and the British Empire, 1700–1837* (Woodbridge, 2007), pp. 1–14.

[2] Andrew C. Thompson, 'The Confessional Dimension', in Brendan Simms and Torsten Riotte (eds), *The Hanoverian Dimension in British History, 1714–1837* (Cambridge, 2007), pp. 161–82, at p. 162.

persecuted European Protestants had not been one of the original intentions of the link between Britain and Hanover, it rapidly became one of the tangible consequences of it. Yet, the union itself was, even at the start, conceptualised as a mechanism which could profitably be used to defend Protestant interests at home and further afield. In this sense looking at Britain's role in intervening on behalf of co-religionists affords an opportunity to consider how the connection with Hanover was justified and legitimated at a dynastic level, as well as the chance to consider the contribution that ideas might have made to a broader discussion about British strategic culture and its position within the European states system in this period.[3]

The chapter begins by setting out the context for confessional politics in the Holy Roman Empire during the early eighteenth century. This entails not only charting Hanover's rise to a position of prominence but also looking at the structures within the early modern *Reich* that were available to deal with confrontation between Protestants and Catholics. The responsibilities that followed from the gaining of electoral status by the Guelph dynasty in the late seventeenth century, as well as the changing balance of power in north Germany, are important here; but it is also worth looking at the role that religion played in the lives of the Guelphs themselves to see how far this was a matter of statecraft and how far one of personal conviction. Having established the parameters of interest in defending persecuted Protestants, it will then be possible to look at the mechanics of intervention and consider several examples of policy in action. The purpose here is to look at the ways in which a concern for defending Protestants could resonate with, but also come into conflict with, other political aims and highlight some of the choices and compromises that had to be made. There might have been good reasons to intervene on any number of occasions, but for intervention to take place there was a need not just for good evidence of persecution but also a realistic chance of success and an ability to do so without creating broader political problems.[4] A providential sense of Protestant duty was not enough – the politics needed to be right too.

---

[3] Andrew C. Thompson, *Britain, Hanover and the Protestant Interest, 1688–1756* (Woodbridge, 2006), pp. 1–24.

[4] For a broader reflection on the conditions necessary for successful intervention, see D.J.B. Trim and Brendan Simms, 'Towards a History of Humanitarian Intervention', in Brendan Simms and D.J.B. Trim (eds), *Humanitarian Intervention: A History* (Cambridge, 2011), pp. 1–24.

I

The role that confession played in the early modern *Reich* is a useful starting point for a discussion of Anglo-Hanoverian Protestant politics. The Peace of Westphalia (1648) brought an element of structure and order to relations between the confessions within the *Reich*. It has often been taken by international relations theorists and some historians as an inaugurating period in which the sovereignty of the state became the paramount concern within international relations and, consequently, interference in the internal affairs of another state became virtually impossible.[5] Some more recent work has suggested that this impression is misleading and that the possibility of intervention over matters such as religion remained, even if it was considered undesirable.[6] However, there were more concrete reasons why the peace treaties signed at Osnabrück and Münster in 1648 are relevant here. These are related to the arrangements that had been put in place to regulate relations between the confessions in their aftermath.

If the Thirty Years War brought an end to an era in which religious differences were settled through open conflict, then it might be said that the Peace of Westphalia saw not the disappearance of religious conflict but rather its transfer to another sphere. The move was from the battlefield to the courtroom. The treaties set up seemingly clear guidelines for determining how the religious composition of the *Reich* was to be regulated.[7] Building on earlier principles that promoted a convergence between the religion of rulers and ruled, the treaties established a *Normaljahr* which would serve as the basis on which the future religious direction of the *Reich* was to be determined. This year – and 1624 was selected – was designed to set the religious map of the *Reich* in stone. It was chosen not for any particular significance of its own but mainly because it was roughly half way between the periods of early Protestant gains at the war's commencement and the height of Catholic success prior to Gustav Adolph's

---

[5] See Brendan Simms, '"A False Principle in the Law of Nations": Burke, State Sovereignty, [German] Liberty, and Intervention in the Age of Westphalia', ibid., pp. 89–110, at p. 89–91. For a similar set of reflections on the need to rethink assumptions about the character of the 1648 settlement as a turning point in international history, see David Onnekink and Gijs Rommelse, 'Introduction', in David Onnekink and Gijs Rommelse (eds), *Ideology and Foreign Policy in Early Modern Europe (1650–1750)* (Farnham, 2011), pp. 1–9.

[6] D.J.B. Trim, '"If a Prince Use Tyrannie towards His People": Interventions on Behalf of Foreign Populations in Early Modern Europe', in Simms and Trim (eds), *Humanitarian Intervention*, pp. 29–66.

[7] There is an excellent summary of the background in Karl Härter, *Reichstag und Revolution, 1789–1806* (Göttingen, 1992), pp. 52–65.

intervention on the anti-Imperial side. The confession of territories in 1624 was assumed to be normative for the future, as was the possession of churches.

Disputes over religious affairs could be dealt with by using a variety of mechanisms. The early modern *Reich* was a relatively loose structure where power was based more around precedent than formal institutions. Nevertheless, there were some options that could be utilised to complain about religious disputes. There were two Imperial courts – the *Reichshofrat* (Imperial Aulic Council) in Vienna and the *Reichskammergericht* (Imperial Chamber Court) in Wetzlar.[8] Judicial process could be slow and there was the additional complication that an increasing number of territories were choosing to assert their territorial sovereignty by seeking to ban appeals to Imperial institutions. There was also the problem, mentioned before, of the acceptability of intervening in the internal affairs of a sovereign, or semi-sovereign, territory. Another option would be to make use of pressure applied at the regional level of the *Reichskreise* (Imperial circles). This could be surprisingly effective, with collective action by neighbours leading to resolutions of disputes on some occasions.[9]

Yet the best way of dealing with issues of concern was probably to make use of the formal representative institution of the *Reich* – the *Reichstag* (Imperial Diet) in Regensburg.[10] In common with many such institutions in early modern Europe, the *Reichstag* had originally only been summoned at the pleasure of the ruler, but from 1663 it had been in permanent session in Regensburg (parliaments in England, Scotland and Ireland in this period were, it should be noted, still more occasional than permanent).[11] In terms of business, there were the typical sorts of task to be performed – discussions of declaring war and making peace and providing the resources for funding military campaigns

---

[8] There is a good short account of both institutions in Karl Otmar von Aretin, *Das Alte Reich, 1648–1806*, 3 vols (Stuttgart, 1993–1997), I, pp. 85–91 (*Reichshofrat*) and pp. 142–8 (*Reichskammergericht*).

[9] This is one of the important themes to emerge from Patrick Milton, 'Protective Intervention in the Holy Roman Empire in the Early Eighteenth Century' (PhD dissertation, University of Cambridge, 2013).

[10] Good introductions to the workings of the *Reichstag* can be found in Anton Schindling, 'The Development of the Eternal Diet in Regensburg', Supplement to *Journal of Modern History*, 58 (1986), pp. 64–75 and Johannes Burkhardt, 'Verfassungsprofil und Leistungsbilanz des Immerwährenden Reichstags: Zur Evaluierung einer frühmoderen Institution', in Heinz Duchhardt and Matthias Schnettger (eds), *Reichsständische Libertät und Habsburgisches Kaisertum* (Mainz, 1999), pp. 151–83.

[11] Karl Härter, 'The Permanent Imperial Diet in European Context, 1663–1806', in R.J.W. Evans, Michael Schaich and Peter H. Wilson (eds), *The Holy Roman Empire, 1495–1806* (Oxford, 2011), pp. 115–35 for an important comparative discussion.

through the imposition of taxation amongst others. There were three representative colleges – the electors themselves, the princes and the Imperial towns. It was the task of the various colleges to respond to formal proposals from the emperor. Simple majorities within each body could decide the outcome in all matters other than those to do with religion.[12]

This was an important and well-known exception in procedure. The Westphalian treaties had provided for direct negotiation between the two confessional groups (for these purposes the split was straight Protestant/Catholic, without a further division between Lutherans and Calvinists), regardless of the relative numerical size of the two parties.[13] The *Reichstag* itself recognised the existence of two separate bodies to represent Protestant and Catholic interests – the *Corpus Evangelicorum* and the *Corpus Catholicorum*.[14] In circumstances where it was thought appropriate for the religious division of negotiations to take place the *ius eundi in partes* was invoked and matters proceeded accordingly.[15] What had begun as a simple expedient to expedite efficient settlement of contentious issues took on a different character over time, though.

The balance of power in the electoral college and the *Reichstag* more generally at the end of the Thirty Years War favoured the Catholics, but the gap became more pronounced as the seventeenth century progressed. One of the reasons for this was the success of the Counter-Reformation in winning back souls to the mother church, but there were more mundane explanations as well. Over time, the patronage resources that the Catholic side had to offer were considerable, not least in the form of potential employment and promotion for younger sons within the *Reichskirche*.[16] Additionally, conversion to Catholicism also enhanced considerably the chances of being able to marry into some of the *Reich*'s major

---

[12] For further details, see Aretin, *Alte Reich*, I, pp. 130–42. There is a helpful summary in English of the *Reich*'s structures in Joachim Whaley, *Germany and the Holy Roman Empire*, 2 vols (Oxford, 2012), II, pp. 53–65.

[13] Aretin, *Alte Reich*, I, pp. 44–56 and Whaley, *Holy Roman Empire*, I, pp. 621–6.

[14] In addition to the works cited in fn. 13, further general insight on the activities of the *Corpus Evangelicorum* can be gained from Ulrich Belstler, 'Die Stellung des Corpus Evangelicorum in der Reichsverfassung' (doctoral dissertation, University of Tübingen, 1968). For a more recent work that looks at the tactics of the two confessional groupings, see Peter Brachwitz, *Die Autorität des Sichtbaren: Religionsgravamina im Reich des 18. Jahrhunderts* (Berlin, 2011).

[15] Härter, 'Permanent Imperial Diet', p. 127 points out that the procedure was used infrequently but the threat was an important bargaining tool.

[16] W.R. Ward, *Christianity under the Ancien Régime, 1648–1789* (Cambridge, 1999), pp. 54–6; Whaley, *Holy Roman Empire*, II, pp. 66–9.

families and, particularly, the Imperial family itself.[17] This meant that the late seventeenth century saw a wave of princely conversions to Catholicism, the most significant of which was the conversion of the Wettin family in 1697, following Augustus II's decision that Poland was worth a mass. The effect of all this, along with the extinction of the Protestant line of Pfalz-Simmern and their replacement by their Catholic Pfalz-Neuberg cousins, was that it was becoming rather difficult by the end of the seventeenth century for the Protestants within the *Reich* to achieve their aims collectively at the *Reichstag*.[18] Consequently, it is not entirely surprising that they utilised the weapons available to them as best as they could, claiming that issues that were only tangentially related to religious concerns really needed to be settled by direct negotiation between the two sides, rather than following the *Reichstag*'s normal (and therefore Catholic-favouring on a purely arithmetical basis) procedures.

This decline in Protestant power is one of the contexts in which the rise of Hanover to electoral status needs to be viewed. There is not space to develop fully the importance of George I's father, Ernst August, for effecting the transformation of a rather disparate group of north-west German duchies into one of the foremost powers within the *Reich* at this point.[19] One of the things that are worth noting, though, is that there was no inevitability about Hanover's rise to a position of principled defender of German Protestantism. Like many other middle-ranking German princes of the time, Ernst August was perfectly prepared to see his troops working for the highest bidder or the person whom he thought would be most useful to him in achieving his aim of consolidation and enhancement of status for his territories. Consequently, at various points, Ernst August flirted with the idea of conversion to Catholicism himself, mindful of the advantage that it might win him with either Louis XIV, who was continuing to seek an extension of French influence within the *Reich*, or the Imperial

---

[17] George I's cousin, Wilhelmine Amalia, became the wife of Joseph I and Holy Roman Empress. Her father, Duke Johann Friedrich, had converted to Catholicism after the Westphalian settlement. Charles VI's bride, Elizabeth Christine, came from the Wolfenbüttel branch of George's family. Her conversion to Catholicism in 1707 was a matter of considerable public debate. See Georg Schnath, *Geschichte Hannovers im Zeitalter der neunten Kur und der englischen Sukzession, 1674–1714*, 4 vols (Hildesheim, 1938–1982), IV, pp. 192–6.

[18] The difficulties that Augustus II's conversion posed for Protestants within the *Reich* is the central theme of Adolph Frantz, *Das Katholische Directorium des Corpus Evangelicorum* (Marburg, 1880).

[19] See Ragnhild Hatton, *George I: Elector and King* (London, 1978), ch. 2 for a summary of this process.

Court.[20] Part of the price that Ernst August had to pay for attaining electoral status was the concession of freedom of worship to the Catholic community in Hanover, which led eventually to the construction of a new church in the Calenberger Neustadt – the delay may be attributable to George I's reluctance to follow through on the concessions made by his father in the electoral treaty, so the new church was not dedicated until 1718.[21]

Ernst August's wife, the Electress Sophia, was also a supporter of church-building outside the old centre of Hanover but her preference was for supporting the Reformed congregation instead, founded in 1697 for both locals and Huguenot exiles.[22] The importance of Sophia's Protestantism for the future fate of her family was to become crucial, of course. James II had been forced from the British thrones in 1688, in significant measure due to his personal and political Catholicism.[23] The seventeenth-century English had developed a passionate fear of what they termed 'popery and arbitrary government', arguing that the former led inevitably to the latter and undermined other freedoms as well.[24] The birth of a son to James in June 1688, somewhat against expectations, heightened Protestant fears that the switch in monarchical confession was not going to be temporary, and consequently something needed to be done to secure a Protestant future. The Glorious Revolution of 1688 placed a Protestant, William of Orange, and James's eldest daughter, Mary, on the thrones. The Bill of Rights (1689) stated quite categorically that, henceforward, the monarch could neither be a Catholic nor married to a Catholic, claiming it was 'inconsistent with the Safety and Welfare of this Protestant Kingdome to be governed by a Popish Prince'.[25] Mary died childless in 1694, leaving her younger sister, Anne, as her brother-in-law's successor. Yet even before Anne came to the throne it was already apparent that there would be no succession from within the Stuarts into the next generation and alternative arrangements would have to be made. This left Sophia and her family as William's nearest Protestant relatives, and the Act

---

[20]   Schnath, *Geschichte Hannovers*, I, pp. 488–91 for one example.
[21]   Ibid., I, pp. 631–5, and III, pp. 67–9.
[22]   Ibid., III, pp. 66–7.
[23]   A theme eloquently explored in Tim Harris, *Revolution: The Great Crisis of the British Monarchy, 1685–1720* (London, 2006), ch. 5.
[24]   For a discussion of how this rhetoric could also be deployed against Louis XIV, see Tony Claydon, *Europe and the Making of England, 1660–1760* (Cambridge, 2007), pp. 152–92. For how far similar trends were discernible in the *Reich*, see Martin Wrede, *Das Reich und seine Feinde: Politische Feindbilder in der reichspatriotischen Publizistik zwischen Westfälischem Frieden und Siebenjährigem Krieg* (Mainz, 2004), pp. 481–3.
[25]   http://www.legislation.gov.uk/aep/WillandMarSess2/1/2/introduction [accessed 19 March 2013].

of Settlement (1701) duly confirmed Sophia and the 'heirs of her body being Protestant' as the future of the English throne.[26] Confession was, therefore, becoming a tool to achieve political advancement and dynastic enhancement.

The leading members of the Guelph family held a spectrum of personal religious views. Sophia herself was reluctant to give in to pressure from English diplomats in the aftermath of the signing of the Act of Settlement to have the Book of Common Prayer used within her household. She had received 12 copies but argued that there were not enough English speakers at court to justify so many.[27] When asked a few years later about why she did not use the German version (something that was becoming popular at the Prussian court), she responded that she found it boring and she had no need, as she still knew the liturgy by heart from her childhood.[28] Her eldest son, George I, was a reasonably orthodox Lutheran, although traces of his personal belief are difficult to uncover within his surviving correspondence – though there is a case from 1686 when he commented that the death of a group of Catholic nobles in Venice might be seen as the working of divine providence.[29] It is clear, though, that he wanted both his eldest son, George, and his grandson, Frederick, brought up in a strictly religious environment, where biblical study, prayer and attendance at divine worship formed a key part of the curriculum.[30] There is little evidence of the confessional indifference of, say, Frederick II of Prussia.[31] Like most rulers in this period, the Guelphs were aware of the value of the religious prop to the secular prince. While they may have displayed a degree of enlightened scepticism about the power of priests, neatly encapsulated in the term 'priestcraft', there was a double reason for them to take Protestantism seriously. Their claim to the British thrones was reliant on their faith. Yet the position of the Hanoverian electorate within *Reich* politics was also becoming increasingly intertwined with confessional concerns as well.

---

[26] http://www.legislation.gov.uk/aep/Will3/12–13/2/contents [accessed 19 March 2013].

[27] Schnath, *Geschichte Hannovers*, IV, p. 57.

[28] Ibid., IV, p. 205.

[29] See the letter from George to his mother, Sophia, Venice, 12 July 1686, reproduced in Georg Schnath, 'Briefe des Prinzen und Kurfürsten Georg Ludwig (Georgs I.) an seine Mutter Sophie 1681–1704', *Niedersächsisches Jahrbuch für Landesgeschichte*, 48 (1976), pp. 249–305, at p. 264.

[30] Andrew C. Thompson, *George II: King and Elector* (New Haven, 2011), p. 16.

[31] Frederick's princely education was as religiously orientated as his cousin's and uncle's but his indifference was clear, even at a young age. Increasing his exposure to religious ideas proved counterproductive; see Theodor Schieder, *Frederick the Great*, ed. and translated by Sabina Berkeley and H.M. Scott (Harlow, 2000), p. 18.

The confessional balance within the *Reich* had shifted in the late seventeenth century. Hanover's advancement to electoral status in 1692 meant that it joined Brandenburg and Saxony as Protestant powers within the electoral college, shifting the balance from six to two, in favour of the Catholics, to six to three in their favour. Yet Augustus's conversion in 1697 put further pressure on the Protestant position.[32] The Wettin dynasty wanted to rise above electoral status and become a royal house in its own right. The Hohenzollern were to accomplish something similar by becoming kings in Prussia in 1701 and the Guelphs eventually joined the royal club too in 1714. The status race in north Germany was a contributory factor to an increased interest in Protestant politics as a means to raise political profile. Saxony, as the senior Protestant electorate, had traditionally acted as the leader of Protestant interests at the *Reichstag* and had assumed direction of the *Corpus Evangelicorum*. The agreement that Augustus had reached over Poland left the confessional status of Saxony intact, but both Prussia and Hanover quickly became wise to the opportunities that the *Corpus* might provide.[33] Status enhancement and confessional concern could go hand in hand – providing leadership for Protestants within the *Reich* would draw smaller territories into their orbit and show the Habsburgs that they were powers that needed to be respected and taken seriously.[34]

None of this would matter, of course, if there were not issues and concerns about which Protestants were exercised.[35] One of the most important in the early eighteenth century related to the so-called Ryswick clause.[36] The peace settlement that brought the Nine Years War to an end in 1697 included, as its fourth clause, the provision that although there was to be a thorough restoration to the status quo ante bellum, this was not to apply to those churches where Catholicism had been introduced during the period of French occupation of the Palatinate. Additionally, where decisions had been made that compelled Protestant and Catholic communities to share buildings or where a physical division of the church had taken place, then these provisions were to be maintained as well.[37]

---

[32] For the background, see Aretin, *Alte Reich*, II, pp. 54–73.

[33] Frantz, *Katholische Directorium*, pp. 3–19.

[34] On the broader context for these developments, see also Gabriele Haug-Moritz, 'Kaisertum und Parität: Reichspolitik und Konfessionen nach dem Westfälischen Frieden', *Zeitschrift für historische Forschung*, 19 (1992), pp. 445–82.

[35] Whaley, *Holy Roman Empire*, II, pp. 150–57 for the general context.

[36] Aretin, *Alte Reich*, II, 41–51 and Thompson, *Britain, Hanover*, pp. 54–5.

[37] This arrangement was known as a 'Simultaneum'. See Christoph Schäfer, *Das Simultaneum: Ein staatskirchenrechtliches, politisches und theologisches Problem des Alten Reiches* (Frankfurt a.M., 1995).

The difficulties that these arrangements posed were several. First, it was resented intensely by Protestant communities within the Palatinate itself who felt that they had had to deal with a double dose of disappointment with the succession of the Catholic line of the electoral house in 1685 and then the non-restitution of what had been taken from them during the war.[38] For Protestant powers outside the Palatinate the imposition of the fourth clause raised questions about their ability to influence the emperor during the process of negotiating peace treaties.[39] Some felt that Saxon leadership of the *Corpus* had been insufficiently robust and there was a general sense that the balance of power within the *Reich* seemed to be swinging against Protestants. There was also concern about the signal that such an arrangement sent. It seemed to contradict the ideas embodied in the Westphalian treaties that the confessional issue had been settled finally and definitively, and instead seemed to suggest that territorial princes were possessed of considerable prerogative rights themselves and therefore had the ability to alter the confessional arrangements within their territories as they saw fit.[40] The defence of the Westphalian treaties and the need to ensure that international agreements were upheld was to prove an important and consistent theme in Anglo-Hanoverian defences of Protestant interests in the first half of the eighteenth century.[41]

II

What strategies, then, did Britain-Hanover adopt when it came to matters of confessional concern in the post-1714 period? One point that needs to be made is that a division of labour, of sorts, emerged as to how matters were to be dealt with diplomatically. Prior to 1714, there had been regular, if not quite continuous, British diplomatic representation at the *Reichstag* in Regensburg. The advent of the Personal Union brought this to an end, but it did not mean that the British lost interest in or information about the workings of the *Reichstag*. Instead, Hanoverian representatives at Regensburg were tasked with

---

[38] Thompson, *Britain, Hanover*, pp. 63–4.
[39] Aretin, *Alte Reich*, II, pp. 163–72 for the importance of the Ryswick clause for *Reich* politics during the War of the Spanish Succession.
[40] Dieter Stievermann, 'Politik und Konfession im 18. Jahrhundert', *Zeitschrift für historische Forschung*, 18 (1991), pp. 177–99, at p. 181.
[41] For one example, see British Library, London, Add Ms 37376, fo 164, James Stanhope to Charles Whitworth, the Göhrde, 27 Oct. 1719, for the suggestion that Britain should become a guarantor power of the Westphalian treaties.

sharing their dispatches with other British diplomats within the *Reich*, and the king in London was just as acquainted as the ministry in Hanover about what was taking place at the Diet. A number of the British diplomats within the *Reich*, such as Charles Whitworth who served in Berlin in the late 1710s and early 1720s, had built up considerable experience of the workings of Imperial politics.[42] Knowledge of confessional points of contention and historic grievances was relatively widespread; but, more importantly, when particular issues and crises emerged British diplomats could rely upon detailed (some might say encyclopaedic) accounts of past wrongs to help them place their negotiations in context.

The ways in which British and Hanoverian approaches could interact and reinforce each other is perhaps best illustrated by looking at some examples of policy in action. There has long been a sense that particular issues of confessional concern were still evident in the early eighteenth century. These were, however, frequently dismissed as hangovers from a bygone age, inappropriate to a new era of enlightenment.[43] More recently, though, there has been a move to see the period from the late 1710s onwards as one in which *Reich* politics was 'reconfessionalised'.[44] This view, and it is one that has considerable merit, argues that there was a consistency of response to a set of seemingly diverse issues such as shared church use, religious freedom and princely conversion. At the heart of that response was the *Corpus Evangelicorum* in Regensburg and the attempts it made to monitor the situation within affected territories. Alongside that was an effort to ensure that the Westphalian settlements were upheld, even if this meant

---

[42] For an overview of Whitworth's career, see Janet M. Hartley, *Charles Whitworth: Diplomat in the Age of Peter the Great* (Aldershot, 2002). His involvement in the *Reich* is considered in more detail in Andrew C. Thompson, 'Britain, Hanover and the Politics of the Peace of Rastatt-Baden', in Heinz Duchhardt and Martin Espenhorst (eds), *Utrecht – Rastatt – Baden 1713/14: Ein europäisches Friedenswerk am Ende des Zeitalters Ludwigs XIV.* (Göttingen, 2013), pp. 71–89.

[43] Michael Maurer, *Kirche, Staat und Gesellschaft im 17. und 18. Jahrhundert* (Munich, 1999), p. 1.

[44] For important statements on the 'reconfessionalisation' thesis, see Gabriele Haug-Moritz, 'Corpus Evangelicorum und deutscher Dualismus', in Volker Press (ed.), *Alternativen zur Reichsverfassung in der frühen Neuzeit?* (Munich, 1995), pp. 189–207. For a longer term perspective on confessional tensions within the *Reich*, see also Gabriele Haug-Moritz, 'Protestantisches Einungswesen und kaiserliche Macht: Die konfessionelle Pluralität des frühneuzeitlichen Reiches (16. bis 18. Jahrhundert)', *Zeitschrift für historische Forschung*, 39 (2012), pp. 189–214.

involving the external guarantor powers – France and Sweden. In both aspects of this campaign, Britain-Hanover was intimately engaged.[45]

One of the spurs for this Protestant reaction was the continued pressure exerted on Protestants in the Palatinate. The fact that it was the Palatinate that provided the spark is interesting. Unlike the other major Protestant electorates, the Palatinate was historically Calvinist rather than Lutheran. Working on behalf of the Palatine Protestants represented working for general Protestant interests, rather than specifically confessional ones. This was something that some were uneasy about – some of the representatives of the Saxon duchies were instructed to express displeasure at Regensburg about the *Corpus* working for a seemingly non-orthodox cause.[46] Others saw the aid being offered as a chance to extract a quid pro quo. Working to help the Reformed must go hand in hand with concessions on their part to help the small Lutheran communities in the region.[47] Yet, in a sense, both of these approaches are a reminder of a central truth. This was a form of political Protestantism and political imperatives about rights, legality, freedom of worship and the like were as important as debates about more abstract theological issues for determining outcomes.[48]

The issue of specific concern in the Palatinate in 1719 was twofold.[49] One was the ban that the elector had placed on the publication and use of the Heidelberg catechism, one of the historic statements of Calvinist faith. Karl Philipp was annoyed both by the content of the catechism and the fact that a recent edition had appeared bearing the electoral arms, implying official sanction for it. The latter was probably an oversight, but there was not much that could be done about the former – the content was offensive to Catholics, describing the mass as a blasphemy against Christ's true sacrifice and calling it both the work of the devil and a cursed idolatry.[50] Karl Philipp's other complaint was about the shared

---

[45] Thompson, *Britain, Hanover*, pp. 73–4, at p. 92.
[46] Ibid., pp. 67–8.
[47] Ibid., pp. 74–5.
[48] Wolf-Friedrich Schäufele, *Christoph Matthäus Pfaff und die Kirchenunionsbestrebungen des Corpus Evangelicorum, 1717–1726* (Mainz, 1998) illustrates some of the difficulties in seeking a more irenic approach, as a means to facilitate political action, in the face of embedded confessional tensions in Saxony and Hamburg.
[49] Thompson, *Britain, Hanover*, pp. 61–2. The broader history of the emergence of religious complaints in the Palatinate can be traced in Hans von Hymmen, 'Der erste preussiche König und die Gegenreformation in der Pfalz' (doctoral dissertation, University of Göttingen, 1904) and Alfred Hans, *Die Kurpfälzische Religionsdeklaration von 1705* (Mainz, 1974).
[50] *The Heidelberg Catechism: Containing the Principles of the Christian Religion, for which the Protestants in the Palatinate have Long been Persecuted by the Jesuits* (London,

use of the Heiliggeistkirche in Heidelberg. He regarded it as a court church and was irritated that the Catholic community had to make do with the choir as opposed to the nave. He also thought that it was an assault on his dignity that he did not have free access to his ancestral tombs which were situated in the nave.[51] Consequently, representatives of the local consistory were given a week to vacate the church at the end of August 1719 and, on 4 September, the dividing wall between the two halves of the church was removed and the Catholic community took possession of the whole.

The reaction to events in Heidelberg was swift. Within the contemporary press, accounts quickly appeared of what had happened, along with accusations of guilt and appeals for something to be done.[52] The Hanoverian representative in Regensburg, Rudolf Johann Freiherr von Wrisberg, saw this as an opportunity to promote Protestant interests more generally, something which was close to his heart, and undermine the position of the emperor.[53] He was anxious to see George I take the lead and effectively act as head of the *Corpus Evangelicorum*, even if the official direction still rested with Saxony. To that end, he was anxious to reassure the other Protestant representatives that George I would listen carefully to their concerns but also that he would be more effective in achieving a resolution, making clear that George I's royal status would count particularly. Given the ways in which information very rarely stayed secret for very long within Regensburg,[54] there may also have been a sense in which Wrisberg was hoping that the oxygen of publicity might be used to achieve a swift and favourable settlement.

The way that George I chose to react is interesting. He opted to dispatch a British diplomat, James Haldane, to negotiate directly with Karl Philipp in Heidelberg.[55] Haldane kept in regular contact with both Wrisberg and other British diplomats within the *Reich*, such as Charles Whitworth in Berlin and

---

1720), p. 21. The title and date of publication are a further indication of how seriously the crisis was taken within Britain.

[51] Hauptstaatsarchiv, Hanover (henceforth HStAH), Calenbergisches Briefarchiv (henceforth CB) 11, no. 1626, fos 1–2, Karl Philipp of the Palatinate to Privy Council, Heidelberg, no date. That a copy of Karl Philipp's complaints found its way to the Hanoverian government is indicative in itself.

[52] See, for example, *Europäische Fama*, 226 (1719), pp. 519–21 or *The Political State of Great Britain*, 18 Sept. 1719, pp. 196–223.

[53] Thompson, *Britain, Hanover*, pp. 66, 72, 77–9.

[54] For Regensburg as an 'information hub', see Susanne Friedrich, *Drehscheibe Regensburg: Das Informations- und Kommunikationssystem des Immerwährenden Reichstags um 1700* (Berlin, 2007).

[55] Thompson, *Britain, Hanover*, pp. 69–70.

François Louis de Pesme de Saint-Saphorin in Vienna. Dispatching a British diplomat sent an important signal about the commitment of Britain-Hanover as a whole to the issue. Wrisberg was keen to leverage British power and did so with some success. Another interesting aspect of the way in which the affair unfolded was how Wrisberg was also prepared to use it as a way to stress Hanoverian supremacy over Prussia. He was adamant that it was Hanover that should take the lead, and Frederick William I in Berlin was asked to support his uncle's efforts, rather than the other way round.[56]

The importance of generational and broader great power politics is worth underscoring. It was easier for George I to try to tell Frederick William what to do than it was to prove for his son. A certain amount of respect for elders and betters was assumed and given. George II hoped that the accession of Frederick II in 1740 might produce a reversion to type, given the difficulties he had encountered with Frederick's father and the son's well-known dislike of the paterfamilias.[57] In this, he was to be disappointed; but the point remains that Hanover was not prepared to accept Prussian leadership in the defence of German Protestantism. Rather, it was assumed that Prussia might accept Hanoverian leadership instead.

On the great power front, British advantages were clear – it was a European, rather than a regional, power and, in the aftermath of the Treaty of Utrecht, could also lay claim to a status on a par with France and Austria.[58] Signs of this can be seen in the concern expressed by British diplomats and ministers about the need to ensure that short-term concessions over the Palatinate did not have detrimental longer-term consequences for the fate of German Protestantism. They were also apparent in British talk about the desirability of becoming a guarantor power of the Westphalian treaties, thus increasing British leverage over central European affairs. One of the reasons for this might be related to the ways in which British attitudes towards government and authority were evolving. There were several strands to British arguments that justified interference in the internal affairs of other territories. One was the importance placed upon constitutional niceties and the upholding of treaties – if a group had certain rights defined by treaties, then these ought to remain. Another was the increasing importance attached to the rights of individual conscience, characteristic of the early enlightenment. Connected to this was a view that persecution was straightforwardly wrong and inappropriate, as conscience could not be coerced. It followed, therefore, that

---

[56] HStAH, CB 11, no. 2978, fo 10, Wrisberg to George I, Regensburg, 1 Jan. 1720.
[57] Thompson, *Britain, Hanover*, pp. 193–5.
[58] Derek McKay and H.M. Scott, *The Rise of the Great Powers* (Harlow, 1983), pp. 94–5.

those in authority who tried to change the minds of their subjects on religious matters forcibly were putting themselves in a state of war with their subjects, and other powers then had a legitimate right to intervene. As one contemporary put it, if a neighbour's house is on fire, one does not stand idly by; rather, one moves quickly to help put that fire out.[59] Attempts to put fires out needed to be measured and considered, however. While Frederick William I seemed willing and able to escalate matters over the Palatinate, threatening reprisals against Catholics within his territories and calling on all Protestant estates to band together in a military alliance, George took a slightly different view. Bringing Karl Philipp into line would require Imperial intervention and tactful diplomacy. Consequently, he favoured an approach based around both carrots and sticks, and Frederick William seems, in the end, to have taken the hint.[60]

Assessing different diplomatic and political tactics is, of course, partly a matter of taste. George I was ultimately unable to secure significant concessions over the Palatinate, and it might be argued that much more was achieved in the next cause célèbre to be considered, albeit briefly: the expulsion of Protestants from Salzburg in 1731. Once more, the traditional picture within the historiography is one of Prussian domination – a bold example of taking a stand and stepping in to rescue beleaguered co-religionists. This was certainly the impression cultivated at the time in a variety of media, both written and visual.[61] There is, of course, something to this. Prussia did welcome considerable numbers of refugees with open arms, and the numbers taken make the smaller contingents who found their way to Hanover itself and later, through the good offices of the Society for the Promotion of Christian Knowledge, to the new colony of Georgia seem rather paltry by comparison.[62] Yet, it is also worth remembering that it was sometimes easier to talk the talk, rather than walk the walk when defending Protestant interests. Prussia and the United Provinces were never backward in coming forward when criticising British and Hanoverian efforts to support

---

[59] Charles Owen, *An Alarm to Protestant Princes and People, who are All Struck at in the Popish Cruelties at Thorn, and Other Barbarous Executions Abroad* (London, 1725), p. 27.

[60] Thompson, *Britain, Hanover*, pp. 78, 96.

[61] For the impact in visual and print culture, see Angelika Marsch, *Die Salzburger Emigration in Bildern* (Weissenhorn, 1977) and Artur Ehmer, *Das Schriftum zur Salzburger Emigration 1731/33* (Hamburg, 1975). Christopher Clark, *Iron Kingdom* (London, 2006), pp. 141–4 provides a good account from the Prussian perspective, while Mack Walker, *The Salzburg Transaction: Expulsion and Redemption in Eighteenth-Century Germany* (Ithaca, 1992) shows the broader impact on German culture. He also shows (pp. 124–35) how important political considerations were to Prussia's response.

[62] Thompson, *Britain, Hanover*, pp. 159–64 for an account of this.

persecuted Protestants.⁶³ However, as with the Palatinate crisis, a crucial factor in ensuring a satisfactory resolution was Austria's willingness to do something. In 1731, as opposed to 1719–1720, the Protestant powers had significantly more leverage over the Austrians because Austria was very concerned about securing the approval of the *Reichstag* for the Pragmatic Sanction – the arrangements Charles VI was putting in place to guarantee his daughter's succession to his patchwork inheritance.

One final area provides a different sort of example of Britain-Hanover's interest in Protestants. Previous examples dealt with groups of sufferers who were relatively numerous and amorphous. There were also instances where things got a little more personal. George II, like any dynast of this period, thought carefully about appropriate marriages for his offspring. One of the difficulties that he faced was that the number of Protestant ruling houses was shrinking; so finding partners of appropriate status and confession for his children was a far from straightforward task. His daughters married into the Dutch and Danish royal families and one, Mary, married Friedrich, the eldest son of Wilhelm, Landgrave of Hesse-Kassel.⁶⁴ The connection with Hessen-Kassel was important militarily, given the size and strength of the landgrave's regiments.⁶⁵ The reasons behind the match had not therefore been entirely about companionship for Mary. Friedrich and Mary were frequent visitors to George when he travelled back to Hanover from London. However, when it became clear that Friedrich had converted to Catholicism, perhaps to ensure that he would be reunited with a particular mistress in the afterlife, paternal rage kicked in quickly.⁶⁶ George's response was to dispatch a diplomat to Kassel to ensure both that his daughter and her sons would be adequately compensated and protected and that some guarantees would be put in place about the future position of Protestantism within Hesse-Kassel itself, given that Friedrich was in line to inherit the territories.⁶⁷ George was anxious that any agreement would be considered and ratified by the *Corpus Evangelicorum*. A settlement was eventually reached that allowed for a separation, support for Mary, guarantees

---

⁶³ Ibid., p. 155. See The National Archives, Kew, State Papers 80/84, Robinson to Chesterfield, Vienna, 26 Jan. 1732, for details of Hamel Bruyninx, the Dutch representative in Vienna, and his complaints about Robinson's conduct.

⁶⁴ Thompson, *George II*, pp. 143–4.

⁶⁵ The marriage was a further step in an alliance policy that the Hanoverians had been pursuing since the 1720s. See Peter H. Wilson, *German Armies: War and German Politics, 1648–1806* (London, 1998), p. 207 for earlier efforts.

⁶⁶ Thompson, *George II*, p. 227.

⁶⁷ HStAH, Hann. 92, no. 1991, fo 27, George II to William of Hesse-Kassel, Kensington, [October 1754], draft.

of Protestant upbringing for the children and a broader framework that aimed to ensure that the Westphalian settlement was maintained.[68]

III

A number of important themes have emerged for explaining the involvement of Britain-Hanover in the politics of the *Reich* in the first half of the eighteenth century. The defence of Protestantism provided a collective cause and a means by which British and Hanoverian interests could be seen to be acting in concert. This was evident to ministers on both sides of the North Sea – indeed, in June 1714 the privy councillors in Hanover had advised the future George I that he needed to do all he possibly could to ensure that the succession was safeguarded because of the critical role that he had to play in maintaining the balance of power in Europe and defending the interests of Protestants in Britain and further afield.[69] This sort of language was common in both British and Hanoverian ministerial correspondence of the period and it was also visible within a broader circle of printed material, from sermons and pamphlets to newspapers and prints.[70] Talk of the responsibility that the Hanoverian monarchs had to prevent the growth of universal monarchy and defend the balance of power may have been a political commonplace – but it was a political commonplace with a broader point and resonance. It was also a reminder that both George I and George II needed to be seen to act decisively on behalf of Protestants. Their origins, in a sense, condemned them to intervene.

On the German side, interest in the travails of Protestants within the *Reich* was a means to gain traction and status. As a new electorate with pretensions to influence outside north-west Germany, attempting to lead the Protestant interest within the *Reich* was an engaging and potentially fruitful strategy. It was also another factor that complicated relations with Hanover's Prussian neighbour. Like Hanover, Prussia was keen to profit from Augustus II's conversion and the vacancy that this might create for leadership of the *Reich's* Protestants, both officially at Regensburg and more generally. Prussia's relations with Austria, like Hanover's, went up and down in this period. Competition with Austria might,

---

[68] Lord Chancellor Hardwicke's opinion on the legality of the ultimate settlement was sought. See ibid. fo. 238r, copy of Hardwicke to Holdernesse, Powis House, 13 Dec. 1754.
[69] The memorandum from the Hanoverian Privy Council to (the future) George I, dated 5 June 1714, is reproduced in Schnath, *Geschichte Hannovers*, IV, pp. 743–7.
[70] For examples in relation to the Palatinate crisis, see Thompson, *Britain, Hanover*, pp. 85–9.

on occasion, be a spur to cooperation between the Protestant electorates, but it could also serve as a way for Austria to play one off against the other, particularly after 1727. It was very easy, for example, for Austrian diplomats and officials to talk up the inappropriateness of British 'interference' in the internal affairs of the *Reich* and to argue that the British had neither the right nor the knowledge to intervene.

Yet, for all these complications, there remained strong reasons why British interests also suggested involvement, rather than neutrality. The Hanoverians' claim to the throne rested on their Protestant credentials. This was something that their propagandists never tired of stressing – anti-popery had strong and deep roots. While the events of 1714 are now commonly referred to as the Hanoverian succession, contemporaries thought in different categories. They prioritised confession over dynasty, frequently referring to the 'Protestant succession' instead.[71]

The approach that George I and George II favoured in relation to defending Protestant interests prioritised negotiation over crusading, upholding existing agreements and rectifying perceived legal wrongs over reprisals and violence. Politics mattered. There was a pragmatic realisation about what was achievable and, almost as importantly, what was not. To use modern political jargon, ultimately, it was about 'smart intervention'.

---

[71] Schnath, *Geschichte Hannovers*, IV, p. 435.

Chapter 6

The Hanoverians and the Colonial Churches

Jeremy Gregory

> We see ascending to the British throne ... a KING in whose Dominions Lutherans and Calvinists live easily with one another; and all Good Protestants have employments indifferently conferred upon them. A KING, so beloved by them that have hitherto been the Subjects of his Dominions, that they never think they over-do in Celebrating of Him. A KING ... [who] will discern and Pursue the True Interest of the Nations; and give the Best Friends of His House and the Nations cause to Rejoice ... Among, whom it is incredible, that the DISSENTERS, who have been so universally true to that, and his interest, should not be regarded as a Body of People, too true Britons, and Christians, to be Excluded from a share in the Common Joy of their Fellow-Subjects.[1]

So preached Cotton Mather, the leading New England Congregationalist minister and bitter enemy to the emergence of Anglicanism in the Puritan heartlands, in September 1714, a few weeks after the Hanoverian succession. A month later, a 'dutiful address' was sent to George I just after his coronation, signed by members of the Anglican churches at Boston, Newberry and Marblehead:

> Wee your Mats most dutyfull and Loyall subjects in this place of the Church of England as by law Established ... It's Our Misfortune to be removed to so great a distance from your Mats Royall Person whose comfortable Influences fall with director Rays upon your more happy subjects in Great Britain. It behoves us, therefore, to be constant in our Solicitations, As we doubt not to approve

---

[1] Cotton Mather, *The Glorious Throne: A Short View of Our Great Lord-Redeemer, on His Throne; Ordering by His Providence, All the Changes in the World: and Most Particularly, what has Occurr'd in the Death of Our Late Memorable Sovereign, and the Legal Succession of the British Crown, to the Illustrious House of Hanover. In a Sermon on that Great Occasion, at Boston in New England, 23 September 1714* (Boston, 1714), pp. 34–5.

ourselves in our Obedience, Loyalty, and Zeal for your service. Tho distance may make Us late with our addresses, Yet none of your Mats subjects shall appear more early and diligent with their Lives and Fortunes in defence of your sacred person and Government.[2]

These two quotations – one from a Congregationalist, the other from a group of Anglicans trying to make headway in Puritan New England – reveal something of the varied and competing, but also overlapping, expectations different religious groups in North America had of the Hanoverian succession. For Mather, what was important was the perceived toleration and coexistence amongst various reformed Protestant groups in Hanover which could be seen as a blueprint for what might be achieved elsewhere in the new king's empire, and this included fully integrating dissenting Protestants into the Hanoverian polity. In this, the new monarch would act for the benefit of all his (Protestant) peoples and their allies in other countries (who together would be his 'best friends'). The Anglicans, not surprisingly, emphasised in contrast the new monarch's role as Supreme Governor of the Church of England and highlighted the sacral nature of his kingship, seeing themselves as 'dutiful and loyall subjects' promising to outdo the rest of the people he ruled over in coming to his defence. It might be possible to discern a difference between 'contractual' and quasi 'divine-right' monarchy in these two short extracts,[3] yet we should be wary of reading too much into this since both emphasised their position as 'subjects', although the first emphasised that subjects could also be 'friends';[4] but in any case 'critical friends' could be loyal, and subjects, as George III would find out, could be rebellious. What is clear, however, are the enormous hopes both the New England Congregationalist leader and the Anglican parishioners put on their new king. It was this sense of opportunity and anticipation (and with it an inbuilt possibility of disappointment and failure to live up to those expectations) which shaped much of the relations between the Hanoverians and the colonial churches in the next half century.

---

[2] H.W. Foote, *Annals of the King's Chapel: From the Puritan Age of New England to the Present Day*, 2 vols (Boston, 1882), vol. I, p. 237.

[3] For 'contractual' and 'divine right' monarchy, see Mark Goldie and Robert Wolker, eds, *The Cambridge History of Eighteenth-Century Political Thought* (Cambridge, 2006), passim.

[4] For the interchange between 'subjects' and 'friends', see the discussion in James J. Caudle, 'Measures of Allegiance: Sermon Culture and the Creation of a Public Discourse of Obedience and Resistance in Georgian Britain, 1714–1760' (PhD dissertation, Yale University, 1996), p. 494, where the Ciceronian imagery of 'the father of his people' could also become 'friend of his people'.

The links between the Hanoverian monarchs and the colonial churches have been obscured by the events of the mid 1770s and early 1780s. Because large numbers of those living in colonial America in the years after 1775 repudiated the authority of George III, including sizeable numbers belonging to the Church of England, and notably over half of the colonial American Church of England clergy,[5] who thereby broke their ordination oaths upholding the royal supremacy – where they had acknowledged the monarch to be 'the only Supreme Governor of this Realm and of all other His Highnesses Dominions and Countries'[6] – it has traditionally been commonplace to view the Hanoverians at best as very distant players in the American religious scene, being far removed from the religious concerns or ecclesiastical structures of their colonial subjects, or, at worst, as despots keen to use their relationship to the Church of England as a way of extending their power and influence in and over North America. Carl Bridenbaugh's massively influential *Mitre and Sceptre*, published in 1962,[7] articulated wilder Congregationalist fears about the combined strength and aspirations of Hanoverian throne and Anglican altar, depicting the Hanoverian monarchs and their Anglican clerical counterparts as hell-bent on subverting the rights of the colonies with the overarching aim of introducing popery to the British colonial New World. Bridenbaugh saw a narrowly unilateral relationship between the Hanoverians and the Church of England and read perceptions of that relationship by the Church's opponents, which were vociferously stated in some quarters from the mid 1760s, as emblematic of the entire period after 1714.

In actual fact, as a number of commentators from a variety of perspectives have shown, the multilateral involvement of the Hanoverians in the life of the colonial churches, and perhaps more importantly the ways in which those living in British North America saw their relationship with the Hanoverian monarchy, fits neither into the disinterested and far-removed nor into the power-seeking paradigm.[8] Although most of this chapter will focus on the interactions between the Hanoverian monarchs and the colonial Church of England, it is worth stressing

---

[5] Nancy L. Rhoden, *Revolutionary Anglicanism: The Colonial Church of England Clergy During the American Revolution* (New York, 1999), p. 24; John Woolverton, *Colonial Anglicanism in North America* (Detroit, 1984), p. 35.

[6] *The Form and Manner of Making, Ordaining, and Consecrating of Bishops, Priests and Deacons According to the Order of the Church of England* (London, 1717), p. 22.

[7] Carl Bridenbaugh, *Mitre and Sceptre: Transatlantic Faiths, Ideas, Personalities, and Politics, 1689–1775* (London, 1962).

[8] See Thomas S. Kidd, *The Protestant Interest: New England After Puritanism* (New Haven, 2004); Benjamin Lewis Price, *Nursing Fathers: American Colonists' Conception of English Protestant Kingship, 1688–1776* (Lanham, MD, 1999); Brendan McConville, *The Rise and Fall of Royal America, 1688–1776* (Chapel Hill, 2007).

at the outset the ways in which other Protestant denominations in British North America viewed the Hanoverian monarchs as their supporters and protectors. After all, the Hanoverian succession was billed as safeguarding 'the Protestant succession', and this brought buy-in from across the Protestant spectrum. What is striking, given the events after 1765, and Bridenbaugh's conspiracy-theory analysis, is the ways that non-Anglicans in North America in the years after 1714, in their loyal addresses, sermons, tracts and pamphlets, proclaimed their ardent loyalty to the first three Hanoverians, at least until the mid 1760s, and often until the early 1770s.[9] New England Congregationalists, for example, sometimes appealed to them over and against colonial governors, above all looking to the Hanoverian monarchs to defend 'the Protestant interest' in the colonies as well as in Europe.[10] The 'Protestant interest', while of course involving the Church of England (which some of its defenders liked to see as the best guarantor of Protestantism, although its opponents not always agreed and sometimes argued that the Church of England was antithetical to 'the Protestant interest'),[11] was a general coalition of all Protestant groups and the first two Hanoverians acquired a huge amount of support in North America if they could be seen to be defending it, as did George III in the early years of his reign. Benjamin Price, over 15 years ago, showed how non-Anglican groups in America gave the credit for the Hanoverian government's upholding of religious toleration to the monarchs themselves, and argued that the Hanoverians' reputation as guardians of their subjects' rights was in fact much more widely aired in New England, where they were often seen as model rulers, than in Old England, and where in the colonies the monarchs' defence of Protestantism was frequently synonymous with guarding the liberties of the individual.[12] Rather than being feared as purveyors of popery (as in Bridenbaugh's model), the Hanoverians were actually widely viewed throughout British colonial North America as the principal protectors on the globe of Protestantism and its related freedoms in a continent where, at least until the early 1760s, its fate was perceived as insecure and under attack from the Spanish and the French.

This perception of the Hanoverian monarchs as the protectors of all Protestant groups was both reinforced by and itself encouraged the situation whereby, during the reigns of the first three Georges, the colonies were seen

---

[9] Price, *Nursing Fathers*; McConville, *Royal America*.

[10] Andrew C. Thompson, *Britain, Hanover and the Protestant Interest, 1688–1756* (Woodbridge, 2006). See also, Carla Pestana, *Protestant Empire: Religion and the Making of the British Atlantic World* (Philadelphia, 2009).

[11] See the discussion in Tony Claydon, *Europe and the Making of England, 1660–1760* (Cambridge, 2007).

[12] Price, *Nursing Fathers*, pp. 12–13.

as welcoming to all shades of reformed belief. The period after 1714 saw Protestants from across Europe finding a haven in British North America, many indeed coming from the Hanoverians' native Germany – namely Lutherans, Moravians, Mennonites and 'the poor palatines' who suffered persecution from a reinvigorated German Catholicism. All these groups left a confessionalised Europe for the New World and settled especially in the middle colonies.[13] In any case, as James Caudle and others have pointed out, the Hanoverian regime should better be seen not as a 'confessional state', only upholding the Anglican Church, but rather as a 'bi-confessional state' since the Presbyterian establishment was preserved in Scotland.[14] This was something which Presbyterians in the middle colonies made much of in their attempt to strengthen their position, in some cases arguing from Scottish precedent that they too should have establishment status,[15] and this further extended support for the Hanoverians from outside the Anglican establishment.

In this understanding, it was the Hanoverians' Protestantism rather than their Anglicanism which made them valued rulers to much of British North America. In 1746 Charles Chauncy, a leading Old Light New England Congregational minister, during a time of unease about Jacobite and Catholic advances in both Old and New England urged his hearers (and readers) in words which in part were strikingly similar to those expressed by loyal Anglicans over 30 years earlier and quoted at the start of this chapter:

> Let us, my Brethren ... express our Love, and Gratitude, and Loyalty to our Sovereign, and Concern for the safety of his Kingdom. Let us be constant and importunate in our Supplications to God, that he would preserve the Person, and protect the Crown of our rightful and Lawful King; ... that he would mercifully save his people from Popery and Slavery; perpetuating to them the

---

[13] Stephen L. Longenecker, *Piety and Tolerance: Pennsylvania German Religion, 1700–1850* (Metuchen, NJ, 1994). See also Hartmut Lehmann, Hermann Wellenreuther and Renate Wilson, eds, *In Search of Peace and Prosperity: New German Settlements in Eighteenth-Century Europe and America* (University Park, PA, 2000), part IV.

[14] Caudle, 'Measures of Allegiance', p. 11. See also his 'James Boswell and the Bi-Confessional State', in William Gibson and Robert G. Ingram, eds, *Religious Identities in Britain 1660–1832* (Aldershot, 2005), pp. 119–46.

[15] Ned C. Landsman, *From Colonials to Provincials: American Thought and Culture, 1680–1760* (New York, 1997), p. 21 and his 'Nation, Migration and the Province in the First British Empire: Scotland and the Americas, 1600–1800', *American Historical Review*, 104 (1999), pp. 463–75, at pp. 471–2. See also his *Scotland and Its First American Colony, 1683–1765* (Princeton, 1985) on New Jersey.

Enjoyment of their Rights and Liberties, which distinguish them from other Nations of the Earth.[16]

Hanoverian monarchs were regarded, then, not only as champions of the Protestant religion; they were also seen as wardens of other rights and freedoms, at least as far as Protestants were concerned, which came as a concomitant of the fact that they were Protestant rulers. James Caudle has argued that dissenters in England saw George II if not as 'a nursing father' then certainly as a 'sheltering wing',[17] and much the same could be said of non-Anglicans in North America.

The Hanoverians' reputation for supporting religious liberty was such that Jonathan Belcher, the Governor of Massachusetts, when trying to support Quakers there against the Congregationalist establishment, told the colonial assembly that:

> it is one of the shining graces of His Majesty's reign that Dissenters of all denominations in Great Britain enjoy the toleration on its full ease and extent, and it should be your care to imitate the royal indulgence of our gracious sovereign, that none of our laws may carry in them a spirit of rigor or severity to those who may conscientiously differ from us in the mode of Divine worship.[18]

The process by which the Hanoverian monarchy during the 1760s and early 1770s came to be seen as an enemy to, rather than a bulwark of, 'the Protestant Interest' and 'Protestant Liberties' is of course a crucial explanatory factor for the ideological context for the War of Independence; but it needs to be stressed that this sentiment was in fact a surprisingly new one and did not represent how the Hanoverians were viewed for the first 50 years after the succession in 1714.

One indicator of the ways in which the Hanoverians were perceived in North America is to explore the imagery associated with them in loyal addresses, pamphlets and sermons from those across the Protestant spectrum, and this often came to the fore in thanksgivings for the accession of individual

---

[16] Charles Chauncy, *The Council of Two Confederate Kings to Set the Son of Tabeal on the Throne Represented as Evil … A Sermon Occasione'd by the Present Rebellion in Favour of the Pretender. Preached in Boston … 6 February 1745* (Boston, 1746), p. 43.

[17] Caudle, 'Measures of Allegiance', p. 497.

[18] 'Governor Belcher's Speech to the Massachusetts General Court, 9 September 1730', in *A Journal of the Honourable House of Representatives, at a Great and General Court of Assembly of His Majesty's Province of the Massachusetts Bay in New England* (Boston, 1730), p. 2.

monarchs or for victories in war.[19] Of course, it can be rightly queried how far the frequently extravagant language and sentiments expressed in these forms of discourse had any bearing on how the monarchs were actually viewed on the ground, or even in actuality by the writers or speakers themselves, although we should be wary of saying that they had no bearing on reality; and indeed it is likely that the seemingly high-flown rhetoric had the power to shape feelings, perceptions and, more crucially, expectations. At one level of course, the genres necessarily highlighted, emphasised and perhaps overrepresented the positive feelings and sentiments displayed towards the monarchs. Given that they were directed towards the king concerned, and often in the hope of receiving further support and protection, it would have been odd, if not foolish, to have expressed these in terms of critique. Nonetheless, it is striking to see how often North Americans presented the early Hanoverians as religious saviours and as warriors fighting on behalf of a religious people.[20] As Hannah Smith has shown, the Hanoverians in England were often viewed in the light of biblical types, and this was also true of the ways in which they were portrayed in British North America by all shades of Protestant opinion.[21] George II in particular was frequently associated with King David in English discourse (as William

---

[19]   For example, Benjamin Colman, *A Sermon Preach'd at Boston in New-England on Thursday the 23d. of August. 1716: Being the Day of Publick Thanksgiving, for the Suppression of the Late Vile and Traiterous Rebellion in Great Britain* (Boston, 1716); Thomas Foxcroft, *God the Judge, Putting Down One, and Setting Up Another: A Sermon upon Occasion of the Death of Our Late Sovereign Lord King George, and the Accession of His Present Majesty, King George II to the British Throne* (Boston, 1727); Jonathan Mayhew, *A Discourse Occasioned by the Death of King George II and the Happy Accession of His Majesty King George III. to the Imperial Throne of Great-Britain; Delivered Jan. 4th 1761* (Boston, 1761); Amos Adams, *Songs of Victory Directed by Human Compassion, and Qualified with Christian Benevolence: In a Sermon Delivered at Roxbury, October 25, 1759. On the General Thanksgiving, for the Success of His Majesty's Arms, 'More Particuarlly [sic], in the Reduction of Quebec, the Capital of Canada'* (Boston, 1759); Thomas Prince, *A Sermon Delivered at the South Church in Boston, N.E. August 14. 1746: Being the Day of General Thanksgiving for the Great Deliverance of the British Nations by the Glorious and Happy Victory near Culloden. Obtained by His Royal Highness Prince William Duke of Cumberland April 16. Last. Wherein the Greatness of the Publick Danger and Deliverance is in Part Set Forth, to Excite Their Most Grateful Praises to the God of Their Salvation* (Boston, 1746).
[20]   See the works cited above.
[21]   Hannah Smith, 'The Idea of a Protestant Monarch in Britain, 1714–1760', *Past and Present*, 185 (2004), pp. 91–118; ead., *Georgian Monarchy: Politics and Culture, 1714–1760* (Cambridge, 2010), p. 39.

III had been)[22] and North Americans were also keen to view him through a Davidic lens.[23]

But while their portrayal as protectors of Protestantism certainly accounts for a great deal of the popularity of the early Hanoverian monarchs in British North America, what is also crucial was their role as nursing fathers to the colonial Church of England. In many ways this is a curiously under-researched topic. Even James B. Bell's meticulous examination of Anglican developments in North America, especially activity sponsored by the Society for the Propagation of the Gospel in Foreign Parts (SPG), has almost nothing to say about individual monarchs and their part in supporting the colonial Church of England, despite its promising-sounding title, *The Imperial Origins of the King's Church*.[24] The Hanoverians are also virtually absent from John Woolverton's book-length study of colonial Anglicanism.[25] And yet, the Georges' involvement in, and importance to, the colonial churches is hard to overlook.

Between the Restoration and the Hanoverian succession, the Church of England had made some considerable advances in North America. Its legal position had been strengthened in a number of colonies, and in the South it was now taken for granted that it was the established Church (and this continued to be the case when the last colony, Georgia, was founded in the 1730s). By 1714 an impressive number of new churches had been built in parts of the continent, and, especially in Virginia, clergy were increasingly better trained and monitored; an Anglican college had been created (William and Mary College in 1693);[26] and, as far as some churchmen were concerned, the chance of securing a bishop in the colonies seemed more than wishful thinking. Queen Anne had given the idea her backing; a house had been bought in Burlington, New Jersey, for a bishop; and, in 1715, Archbishop Tenison left money in his will for a bishop

---

[22] For George II, see Caudle, 'Measures of Allegiance', p. 493; for William III, see Tony Claydon, *William III and the Godly Revolution* (Cambridge, 1996), pp. 37, 48, 56, 62, 128.

[23] Foxcroft, *God the Judge*, pp. 4, 5, 18, 29, 33, 34, 35; Mayhew, *A Discourse*, pp. 22, 36; Adams, *Songs of Victory*, pp. 9, 10, 15.

[24] James B. Bell, *The Imperial Origins of the King's Church in Early America, 1607–1783* (Basingstoke, 2004).

[25] Woolverton, *Colonial Anglicanism*.

[26] Jon Butler, *Awash in a Sea of Faith: Christianizing the American People* (London, 1990); John Nelson, *A Blessed Company: Parishes, Parsons and Parishioners in Anglican Virginia, 1690–1776* (Chapel Hill, NC, 2004). See also Joan Gundersen, *The Anglican Ministry in Virginia, 1723–1766: A Study of a Social Class* (New York, 1989); Thad W. Tate, 'The Colonial College', in Susan H. Godson et al., eds, *The College of William and Mary: A History*, 2 vols (Williamsburg, VA, 1993), vol. I, pp. 3–80.

in America,[27] and this became a budget line in the SPG's accounts. Furthermore, startling-seeming Anglican successes had occurred in those colonies which had traditionally rejected the Church of England, revealed by its arrival in 'Puritan New England'.[28] Both in North America and in the home country expectations were focussed on how the new monarch would continue, or live up to, the role set by his staunchly Anglican predecessor.

Hanoverian sustenance for the Church of England in North America could be expressed in a number of ways and could encompass a broad range of activities, from giving treasured gifts and financial aid to particular churches, to demonstrating and encouraging more general support. In addition, those churches could be identified, and identify themselves, with the Hanoverian monarchy in general, or with individual monarchs. If nomenclature is any indication of affiliation, it is worth noting that a number of Church of England churches built in the colonies from 1714 onwards were named 'St George', or were in other ways linked to the house of Hanover. These included: St George's, Schenectady, New York; St George's, Flushing, New York; St George's, South Carolina; St, George's, Dorchester Parish, South Carolina; Prince George's, Georgetown, South Carolina; St George's, Bermuda; St George's, Accomack, Virginia; St George's, Spotsylvania, Virginia; St George's, Pungoteague, Virginia; and St George's, Fredericksburg, Virginia (where George Washington's mother worshipped), or churches with other Hanoverian connections, such as Prince Frederick parish Church, South Carolina – the last two examples also emphasising the connection to Frederick, Prince of Wales and, until his death in 1751, the heir apparent.[29] And 'Georgia', the final colony to be created before independence, had established the Church of England by the 1750s. With the Hanoverians' dual role as Anglican nursing fathers and dissenting sheltering wings it is not surprising to find non-Anglican places of worship also named after 'St George' or 'Hanover', such as St George's, Orangeburg, South Carolina – the town itself named after Prince William of Orange, son-in-law of George II – which began as a German Lutheran church, only later becoming

---

[27] Edward Carpenter, *Thomas Tenison, His Life and Times* (London, 1948), p. 350.

[28] For a fuller account of the activities of the Church of England in North America up to 1714, see Jeremy Gregory, 'The Later Stuart Church and North America', in Grant Tapsell, ed., *The Later Stuart Church, 1660–1714* (Manchester, 2012), pp. 150–72 and Jeremy Gregory, 'Refashioning Puritan New England: The Church of England in British North America, c. 1680–c. 1770', *Transactions of the Royal Historical Society,* 6th ser. 20 (2010), pp. 85–112, esp. pp. 88–91, 93–4.

[29] For some of these, see Dell Upton, *Holy Things and Profane: Anglican Parish Churches in Colonial Virginia* (Cambridge, 1986), p. xvii; Louis Nelson, *The Beauty of Holiness: Anglicanism and Architecture in Colonial South Carolina* (Chapel Hill, NC, 2008), see index.

Anglican; and what was to be St George's Methodist church, Philadelphia, and was widely regarded as 'the cradle of American Methodism', founded in 1769. 'Hanover' County in Virginia was created in 1719, and this jurisdiction became central in debates about an Anglican establishment in America when Patrick Henry attacked the Parson's Cause to increase the clergy's tithe in tobacco in the early 1760s.[30]

The Hanoverian monarchs were also explicitly linked to other institutions which were seen as crucial to the development of Anglicanism in colonial America. King's College, New York, was established in 1754 by royal charter to uphold Anglican principles (not dissimilar to the founding of William and Mary College).[31] Likewise, King's Chapel, Boston, built in 1689, developing from a congregation established during the reign of James II, supported first by William and Mary and then Queen Anne, was so linked to the person of the monarch that it became known as 'Queen's Chapel' during her reign and later on received material and financial support from the first three Hanoverians.[32] The minister, vestry and churchwardens of King's Chapel played on the name of their church to solicit extra funding from the monarchy, for example asking Bishop Gibson in 1748 whether it would be worth their while writing to the king for contributions towards a new roof 'in favour of a Church the first in America and who at the publick charge erected a very handsome pew for his Majesty's governor'. In short, they said, 'a Church which has heretofore tasted of royal bounty and if we may judge by the name seems in some measure encouraged to expect it'.[33]

A major way by which the Hanoverian monarchs became associated with colonial churches was through the work of the SPG (1701).[34] The Society had

---

[30] Rhys Isaac, 'Religion and Authority: Problems of the Anglican Establishment in Virginia in the Era of the Great Awakening and the Parson's Cause', *William and Mary Quarterly*, 3rd ser., 30 (1973), pp. 3–36.

[31] David C. Humphrey, *From King's College to Columbia* (New York, 1976). See Robert G. Ingram, *Religion, Reform and Modernity in the Eighteenth Century: Thomas Secker and the Church of England* (Woodbridge, 2007), pp. 223–6.

[32] Foote, *King's Chapel*, p. 153.

[33] Ministers, Wardens and Vestry to Bishop Gibson, 25 July 1748, quoted in Kenneth Walter Cameron, *Letter-Book of the Rev. Henry Caner, SPG Missionary in Colonial Connecticut and Massachusetts until the Revolution: A Review of His Correspondence from 1728 through 1778* (Hartford, CT, 1972), p. 31.

[34] Standard histories of the SPG are C.F. Pascoe, *Two Hundred Years of the S.P.G., 1701–1900: Based on a Digest of the Society's Records* (London, 1901); H.P. Thompson, *Into All Lands: The History of the Society for the Propagation of the Gospel in Foreign Parts* (London, 1956); Daniel O'Connor et al., *Three Centuries of Mission: The United Society for the Propagation of the Gospel, 1701–2000* (London, 2000). See also J.K. Nelson, 'Anglican

received a royal charter from William III on its founding, and the Hanoverian monarchs kept up the close association. George I in 1718, following the precedent established by Queen Anne in 1711 and 1714, issued a royal letter endorsing a collection through the cities of London and Westminster – 'as also in the several large Towns trading to the Plantations in America, viz. Bristol, Plymouth, Whitehaven, Liverpool, Biddiford, Barnstable, Exeter and Newcastle upon Tyne'[35] – which raised over £3,698 for the Society's work in sending over and financially supporting Church of England clergy in the colonies, helping to pay towards church-building, giving funds for catechists and school masters and shipping bibles, Books of Common Prayer and other religious tracts and pamphlets to the new world. George II did the same in 1741, giving his 'Royal aid and favour' to support the work of the Society 'at a time when the Popish emissaries are very vigilant, and Active in perverting, and drawing over Our subjects to Popish superstition and idolatry'[36] – in effect seeing the work of the Society, and the Church of England more generally, as furthering 'the Protestant interest' in its battle against the forces of Roman Catholicism.

But perhaps the most common ways in which the Hanoverian monarchs were connected to the colonial churches were through the prayers said for the monarchs and royal family in the context of Church of England services in America, a weekly reminder of the relationship between the American congregations and their monarchs over 3,000 miles away. As Michael Schaich has noted, 'praying for the well-being of the royal family, and the King or Queen in particular, lent an air of domesticity to the religiosity surrounding the monarchy'.[37] Schaich has

---

Missions in America, 1701–1725: A Study of the Society for the Propagation of the Gospel in Foreign Parts' (PhD dissertation, Northwestern University, 1962).

[35] Edward Chandler, *A Sermon Preached Before the Incorporated Society for the Propagation of the Gospel in Foreign Parts; at Their Anniversary Meeting in the Parish–Church of St. Mary-le-Bow; on Friday the 20th of February, 1718* (London, 1719), p. 35. For the earlier royal letters, see White Kennett, *The Lets and Impediments in Planting and Propagating the Gospel of Christ: A Sermon Preach'd Before the Society for the Propagation of the Gospel in Foreign Parts, at Their Anniversary Meeting, in the Parish-Church of St. Mary-le-Bow, on Friday the 15th of February, 1711/12* (London, 1712), pp. 41–2; George Ashe, *A Sermon Preach'd Before the Incorporated Society for the Propagation of the Gospel in Foreign Parts; at Their Anniversary Meeting in the Parish-Church of St. Mary-le-Bow; on Friday the 18th of February, 1714* (London, 1715), pp. 30–31.

[36] Henry Stebbing, *A Sermon Preached Before the Incorporated Society for the Propagation of the Gospel in Foreign Parts; at Their Anniversary Meeting in the Parish-Church of St. Mary-le-Bow, on Friday, February 19, 1741–2* (London, 1742), pp. 63–4.

[37] Michael Schaich, 'Introduction', in id., ed., *Monarchy and Religion: The Transformation of Royal Culture in Eighteenth-Century Europe* (Oxford, 2007), pp. 1–40, at p. 29.

also observed that the central tenet of eighteenth-century thanksgiving services was of a ruler who needed the prayers of his subjects, which had the effect of making the sovereign seem more humane. It could be argued that something of this more humane, and more human, monarch, who needed the supplications of his people, lay at the heart of the prayers for the king in the Prayer Book services. At every Morning and Evening Prayer, Anglican congregations in the New World (as elsewhere) asked their 'heavenly Father, high and mighty, King of Kings, Lord of Lords, the only Ruler of princes, who dost from thy throne behold all dwellers upon earth', to

> behold our most gracious sovereign ... and so replenish him with the grace of thy Holy Spirit, that he may always incline to thy will, and walk in thy way; Endue him plenteously with heavenly gifts; grant him in health and wealth long to live; strengthen him that he may vanquish and overcome all his enemies; and finally after this life, he may attain everlasting joy and felicity.[38]

In the North American context, these words would have had an immediate resonance. In a continent which experienced almost constant warfare in the 50 years after the Hanoverian succession, against the French and the Spanish, as well as threats from native Americans, the plea that the monarch might 'vanquish and overcome all his enemies' would have had an especial meaning. Being repeatedly told on a weekly basis of the monarch and royal family may well have had an important function in creating an hierarchical imagined transatlantic community, helping to fashion an emotional bond between North American congregations and their king, and thereby connecting North American Anglicans to their ruler separated by the Atlantic Ocean. The services of the Book of Common Prayer were therefore a crucial instrument in establishing an imperial Hanoverian church by providing a regular forum for members throughout the empire to focus on the well-being of their Supreme Governor.

The association between the Hanoverians and the colonial churches was also expressed through material culture. Material connections with the lives of those monarchs were such that the pulpit of King's Chapel, Boston, was draped in black for mourning after a monarch's death.[39] Colonial Anglican churches normally had a royal coat of arms painted on boards near the altar,

---

[38] *The Book of Common Prayer and Administration of the Sacraments, and Other Rites and Ceremonies of the Church, According to the Use of the Church of England: Together with the Psalter or Psalms of David, Pointed as They are to be Sung or Said in Churches* (London, 1719), p. 22.

[39] Foote, *King's Chapel*, p. 237.

a visible signifier of the presence of the Hanoverian monarchs in the lives of their congregations.[40] In some of the flagship Anglican churches, such as King's Chapel, Christ Church and Trinity Church, Boston, highly prized gifts from the Hanoverians included folio versions of the King James Bible and the Book of Common Prayer to be used at the lectern and altar. Perhaps even more cherished were the gifts of communion silver, engraved with the names of the monarchs. In 1733, for example, George II sent over to Christ Church, Boston:

> 2 silver flagons, 1 royal bible, and 2 common prayer books bound in Turkey leather strung with blue garter ribbon trimmed with gold fringe, 12 common prayer books in calf gilt filleted and strung with blue ribbon, 1 chalice, 1 paten, 1 receiver, 2 cushions for the reading desk, 1 large cushion and cloth for the pulpit, 1 carpet and 1 altar piece, 20 yards of damask cloth for the communion table, 2 large surplices of fine Holland [linen].[41]

Gifts of communion silver, made in London, were particularly valued since they were engraved with the name of the church and the royal donor. Engraving and inscribing the chalices and other pieces of communion silver had the obvious function of marking the silverware as church property, but they also made the line of dependency clear between the communicants in North America and the king in England.[42] Likewise, the gifts of a folio edition of the King James Version of the Bible for use at the lectern (called a 'royal bible') and the Books of Common Prayers, bound in the perennially valued 'Turkey leather' with a gold-fringed blue garter ribbon (often associated with royalty), provided the church with the key liturgical texts without which services could not happen. The intimate relationship between the King James Bible and the Book of Common Prayer[43] was also enhanced by the fact that in these instances these were both royal presents, underlining the ways in which the Supreme Governor of the Church of England provided both the word of God and the liturgy to his subjects across the globe.

---

[40] Butler, *Sea of Faith*, pp. 100, 109.
[41] Massachusetts Historical Society, Boston, MS N–2249 (XT) Old North Church, Vestry Book, 1724–1802, vol. 2/0, p. 45, 7 Sept. 1733.
[42] Nelson, *Beauty of Holiness*, pp. 210–11.
[43] Jeremy Gregory, 'Transatlantic Anglican Networks, c. 1680–c. 1770: Transplanting, Translating, and Transforming the Church of England', in id. and Hugh McLeod, eds, *International Religious Networks* (Woodbridge, 2012), pp. 127–43, at pp. 133–7; see also my 'The Transatlantic Bible and Anglican Identity in Colonial North America', forthcoming.

It is worth observing that one probable result of the Hanoverians' special connection to the colonial Church of England was that in those colonies where the Anglican Church was not the established Church (particularly in 'Puritan New England'), the Church was successful in winning over people from other religious traditions; and to some extent this fuelled the impressive growth in numbers enjoyed by the Church of England in British North America in the years before 1770, making it the fastest growing denomination in the colonies.[44] There were, of course, a number of complex reasons why people might decide to conform to the church – and these included a reaction to the enthusiasm unbridled by the Great Awakening in the late 1730s and 1740s, the attractions of the Anglican liturgy and services as well as more opportunist and pragmatic self-identification with the British governmental elite, as well as with the monarchy.[45]

It is noticeable that the Anglican clergy in New England were especially ready to stress their royal connections, an emphasis which was followed through after 1775 when they were much more likely than their Virginian peers to remain loyal to George III.[46] Whilst the Virginian indifference to the monarchy can be exaggerated,[47] it is certainly true that some New England clergy demonstrated their loyalty to the monarchy as much as they could. Governor Thomas Hutchinson of Massachusetts observed in one of his meetings with George III when in England in 1774:

> The rector [at the chapel] is Dr Caner, a very worthy man also, frequently inculcates upon his hearers due subjection to Government, and condemns the violent, riotous opposition to it; and besides the prayers in the Liturgy, generally in a short prayer before sermon expressly prays for your Majesty, and for the chief Rulers in the province.

---

[44] Gregory, 'Refashioning Puritan New England', pp. 99–100. See also Jeremy Gregory, '"Establishment" and "Dissent" in British North America: Organising Religion in the New World', in Stephen Foster, ed., *British North America in the Seventeenth and Eighteenth Centuries* (Oxford, 2013), pp. 136–69, esp. pp. 160–66.
[45] See Gregory, 'Refashioning Puritan New England', pp. 99–109.
[46] Rhoden, *Revolutionary Anglicanism*, chs 4 and 5.
[47] Edward L. Bond, ed., *Spreading the Gospel in Colonial Virginia: Sermons and Devotional Writings* (Lanham, MD, 2004) and Lauren Winner, *A Cheerful and Comfortable Faith: Anglican Religious Practice in the Elite Households of Eighteenth-Century Virginia* (New Haven, CT, 2010).

The king enquired: 'Why do not the Episcopalian ministers in general do the same?' Hutchinson informed him: 'In general, sir, they use no other prayer before the sermon than a short collect out of the Liturgy.'[48]

Nevertheless, Hanoverian royal support for the colonial Church of England went only so far. Despite real indications that Queen Anne was personally committed to establishing a bishop for America, and despite the fact that members of the SPG continued to back this project – and even had a fund for it – the first three Hanoverians, perhaps mindful of their role as maintainers of the broader 'Protestant interest', and advised by their governments, took this idea no further.[49] Under Walpole and Newcastle the enterprise remained firmly on the back-burner, Walpole apparently stopping a petition for a bishop from 209 people in Boston in August 1727 from reaching the new George II.[50] In 1760 Henry Caner, the rector of King's Chapel, Boston, wrote to Thomas Secker, Archbishop of Canterbury, remarking that the 'success of the king's arms here seems to be our opportunity to reviving the scheme for a bishopric in America.'[51] When the idea became part of a more public debate, spurred on by the Congregationalist Jonathan Mayhew's investigation into the SPG's charter in the early 1760s, often rehearsing arguments made a couple of decades before,[52] the young George III and his government refrained from engaging in the discussion, although there was talk of the house built by Charles Apthorp in Cambridge, Boston, being the site of a proposed bishop's

---

[48] *The Diary of Letters of His Excellency Thomas Hutchinson* (London, 1883), p. 169, July 1774.

[49] S.J.C. Taylor, 'Whigs, Bishops and America: The Politics of Church Reform in Mid-Eighteenth-Century England', *Historical Journal*, 36 (1993), pp. 331–56. For an overview of attempts to have a bishop in the colonies, see F.L. Hawks, 'Efforts to Obtain the Episcopate Before the Revolution', in *Collections of the Protestant Episcopal Historical Society* (New York, 1851), vol. I, pp. 136–57. See also, Ingram, *Religion, Reform and Modernity*, pp. 234–59.

[50] Foote, *King's Chapel*, p. 353.

[51] Cameron, *Letter-Book*: Henry Caner to Archbishop Secker, 6 Oct. 1760.

[52] Jonathan Mayhew, *Observations on the Charter and Conduct of the Society for the Propagation of the Gospel in Foreign Parts; Designed to Shew Their Non-conformity to Each Other: With Remarks on the Mistakes of East Apthorp, M.A. Missionary at Cambridge, in Quoting and Representing the Sense of Said Charter, &c. As also Various Incidental Reflections Relative to the Church of England, and the State of Religion in North-America, Particularly in New-England ... To Which is Subjoined Apthorp's Considerations* (London, 1763); id., *A Defence of the Observations on the Charter and Conduct of the Society for the Propagation of the Gospel in Foreign Parts, Against an Anonymous Pamphlet Falsly Intitled, A Candid Examination of Dr. Mayhew's Observations, &c.: And Also Against the Letter to a Friend Annexed Thereto, Said to Contain a Short Vindication of Said Society* (Boston, 1763).

palace for his son, East Apthorp.⁵³ By 1770 it was reported that the clergy of New England had sent so many petitions to the king and senior clergy in England asking for a bishop in America that the Bishop of London had requested that they stop doing so.⁵⁴

In their role *vis-à-vis* the colonial churches, it could be reasonably argued that there was a tension between the Hanoverians' role as defenders of the Protestant interest and their role as nursing fathers of the Church of England. Given this, what is remarkable is that, for the period between 1714 and about 1765, and in some interpretations as late as perhaps 1774, these goals could in fact be seen to be operating simultaneously (if often independently) so that the seemingly different and competing Protestant visions of kingship articulated by Grayson Ditchfield elsewhere in this volume could in fact broadly coexist.⁵⁵ While the first two Georges did defend Anglican privileges, this could be seen within the wider role of maintaining and furthering 'the Protestant interest', and in this the Seven Years War was seen as a pan-Protestant alliance defending 'religion and liberty'. Nevertheless, the period after 1765, and especially after 1770, saw roles which had been compatible being regarded more and more as incompatible, as at first some, and then increasingly a large number of, North Americans viewed the Hanoverians' dual roles as Anglican 'nursing fathers' and Protestant 'sheltering wings' as antithetical rather than coexisting.⁵⁶ In the early 1770s there was concern that the British in North America had not used the years of peace to spread westwards to consolidate their power base and were in fact losing out to the French once again, and this put a strain on the way that George's role as defender of the Protestant interest was viewed in the colonies.⁵⁷

Undermining the Hanoverians' ability to fulfil the overlapping, but potentially strained dual roles of Protestant hero and Supreme Governor of the Church of England in North America, a crucial change in the way in which George III was perceived came with the passing of the Quebec Act in 1774,

---

⁵³ For the purposes of this chapter, what is also interesting is that although Mayhew railed against the SPG and the Anglican hierarchy, he was keen to ensure that he did not criticise the king: Mayhew, *Defence of the Observations on the Charter*, p. 25.

⁵⁴ Cameron, *Letter-Book*, Henry Caner to Rev. Dr Thomas Bradbury Chandler, 15 Feb. 1771.

⁵⁵ See the chapter by G.M. Ditchfield in this volume.

⁵⁶ James B. Bell, *A War of Religion: Dissenters, Anglicans, and the American Revolution* (Basingstoke, 2008); J.C.D. Clark, *The Language of Liberty, 1660–1832: Political Discourse and Social Dynamics in the Anglo-American World* (Cambridge, 1994), pp. 296–381; Gordon S. Wood, 'Religion and the American Revolution', in Harry S. Stout and D.G. Hart, eds, *New Directions on American Religious History* (Oxford, 1997), pp. 173–205.

⁵⁷ I am grateful to Professor Brendan Simms for alerting me to this.

to which he gave assent in June before it became law in October of that year. Clause 5 of the Act allowed the French Roman Catholics in the colony to 'have, hold and enjoy the free exercise of their religion' under 'the king's supremacy'. This was widely viewed in North America as a betrayal of George's coronation oath to support Protestantism, where the king had promised to 'maintain the laws of God, the true profession of the Gospell and the Protestant reformed religion established by law' as well as to 'preserve unto the bishops and clergy of this realme and to the churches committed to their charge all such rights and priviledges as by law doe or shall appertaine unto them or any of them'.[58] The coronation oath used by the Hanoverians was the one modified in 1689 for William and Mary, and this has been seen as ending a divine-right model of kingship and instead requiring the monarch to uphold the rights and privileges of their subjects.[59] It can be argued that the coronation oath's dual requirement of upholding reformed Protestantism as well as supporting the bishops and clergy of the established Church envisaged a convergence between Protestantism and the Church of England; but it also articulated the implicit tension between the two which was significant to dissenters in North America and elsewhere. Given George III's later refusal to agree to Catholic emancipation in the United Kingdom of Great Britain and Ireland in 1801 because it would violate the oath he had made at his coronation,[60] it is perhaps ironic that it was the perception in the colonies nearly 30 years previously that he had done just that which had already created a changed context for how he would be regarded in North America. Indeed, according to a recent analysis, the Quebec Act became a 'tipping point' for how George was viewed in the colonies.[61] Until then, however critical the colonists may have been of specific policies, or of the government at large, criticism of George himself had largely been limited to the age-old critique of the monarch being misled or duped by evil counsellors. As a reflection of this changing perception, on 12 September 1774 *The Boston Gazette* noted:

---

[58] http://avalon.law.yale.edu/18th_century/quebec_act_1774.asp.
[59] http://www.legislation.gov.uk/aep/WillandMar/1/6/contents; Schaich, 'Introduction', p. 32.
[60] G.M. Ditchfield, *George III: An Essay in Monarchy* (London, 2002), p. 104. Although he did allow relief acts for Roman Catholics, the king would not sanction complete religious emancipation because he wanted to maintain the constitution as it was when he was crowned.
[61] David Theobald, 'The Representation of George III in Republican Discourse between 1774 and 1776' (MPhil thesis, Cambridge University, 2012), p. 82. I am very grateful to David Theobald for letting me read his unpublished thesis, and I have drawn on it heavily in the rest of this paragraph.

> It is amazing that a Bill should be brought into Parliament for establishing popery and tyranny under the reign of a Prince of the House of Hanover to whom the people of England gave the crown for the ... purpose of preserving them from popery and arbitrary power![62]

David Theobald has argued that statements such as this emphasised the importance of government by contract, and the way this was aligned to Protestantism demonstrates how colonists could see 'republican' ideas as a concomitant of their religion.[63] *The Newport Mercury* had previously noted on 5 September that 'Popery has been lately established in some parts of the British dominions by a K*** and parliament pretending to be Protestants ... [It] ... does certainly tend to disestablish his Majesty's right to the crown.'[64] Meeting for the first time on the same date, the Continental Congress drafted a petition to the king, observing that his 'family was seated on the British throne to rescue and secure a pious and gallant nation from the popery and despotism of an ... inexorable tyrant'.[65] Although not yet going so far as to call George himself a 'tyrant', the possibility was implicit, and it was this rhetoric which would soon be found in Thomas Paine's *Common Sense* (1776).[66]

What is also striking – and another indication that we need to think of the relationship between the Hanoverian monarchs and the colonial churches as multilateral and polyvalent rather than as unilateral and monovalent – is the way that from 1775, as individual men and women and Church of England congregations struggled to come to terms with their allegiance, and anticipating the formation of what would become the Protestant Episcopal Church of America in the years after 1784, the Anglican liturgy could be adapted to the new circumstances. Examples of Books of Common Prayer with the prayers to the royal family crossed out in ink and the names of George Washington and the Convention inserted in their place, or written over them, indicate that what seemed to be an inexorable link between Anglican worship and the Hanoverian kings could change and mutate, and instead much of the Anglican liturgy

---

[62] 'London, 15th June', in Benjamin Edes and John Gill, eds, *The Boston Gazette and Country Journal* (Boston, 1774), Monday 12 Sept. 1774, p. 1.
[63] Theobald, 'Representation of George III', p. 43.
[64] Solomon Southwick, ed., *The Newport Mercury* (Newport, 1774), Monday 5 Sept. 1774, p. 3.
[65] William Bradford and Thomas Bradford, eds, *Journal of the Proceedings of the Congress Held at Philadelphia* (Philadelphia, 1774), 5 Sept. 1774, p. 139.
[66] Thomas Paine, *Rights of Man, Common Sense and Other Political Writings*, ed. by Mark Philp (Oxford, 1995), p. 35.

could be transposed, virtually intact, to the new regime.[67] During the War of Independence, Samuel Tingley, who served Church of England congregations in Maryland and Delaware, replaced the Prayer Book's 'O Lord, save the King' with the more pragmatic and politique but not necessarily any less heartfelt 'O Lord, save those whom thou hast made it our especial Duty to pray for'.[68] And another clergyman, apparently from habit saying a prayer for King George, is supposed to have said as an afterthought, 'O Lord, I mean George Washington'.[69]

The Hanoverians' relations with their colonial churches in some ways exemplified the tensions inherent in their peculiar religious position. George I succeeded to the British throne not because he was a member of the Church of England but because he was a Protestant. Yet being king meant that he was Supreme Governor of the Anglican Church. For 50 years (or more) after 1714, the Hanoverian monarchs managed to be seen both as supporters of 'the Protestant interest' in North America and backers of the colonial Church of England, although they and their governments, and indeed senior clergy within England, refrained from realising the desire of some colonial Anglicans for a bishop for America. To what extent it was George III's position as Supreme Governor of the Church of England that turned the colonies against him has been the subject of debate since the 1770s; in all likelihood the breakdown of the dual role of Protestant hero and Church of England leader was a consequence rather than a cause of the collapse of the Hanoverian empire in North America.

---

[67] For an example, see the Book of Common Prayer at Christ Church, Philadelphia, where prayers to the royal family were crossed out in 1776 by the Anglican patriot clergyman Jacob Duché; Christ Church Library, Philadelphia, Book V–600.

[68] Samuel Tingley to the Secretary of the SPG, 5 March 1782, in W.S. Perry, ed., *Historical Collections Relating to the American Colonial Church* (Hartford, CT, 1878), vol. V, p. 135. For the wider picture, see also David L. Holmes, 'The Episcopal Church and the American Revolution', *Historical Magazine of the Protestant Episcopal Church*, 47 (1978), pp. 261–91.

[69] Eben E. Beardsley, *The History of the Episcopal Church in Connecticut*, 2 vols (New York, 1866), vol. I, p. 313.

PART III
Image Policies

Chapter 7

The Hanoverian Monarchy and the Culture of Representation

Tim Blanning

The culture of representation of the Hanoverian dynasty was developed long before George I set foot in England. The tumultuous history of the previous century had led to a sharp change of style in 1688, as first William III and Mary II and then Anne I, and their advisers, showed that they had learned from the fate of Charles I and James II. However tumultuous the years between the Glorious Revolution and the Hanoverian Succession, the period demonstrated that a consensus had formed around four fundamental principles. The first was liberty. Apart from the hardcore Jacobites who learned nothing and forgot nothing, there was a general recognition that the ejection of the aspiring absolutist marked a watershed. As Bolingbroke put it in his *Dissertation upon Parties* in 1733: 'the Revolution is looked upon by all sides as a new era'. This belief became a central axiom of British politics in the eighteenth century, as a veritable litany of tributes testified, whether it was the Duke of Devonshire inscribing 'begun in the year of liberty 1688' above the fireplace of the Painted Hall at Chatsworth, or John Wilkes claiming 'from this most auspicious period, freedom has made a regular uninterrupted abode in our happy island'.[1]

The second was nationalism. This had long been a powerful force in English politics, whether cohesive under Henry VIII and Elizabeth I or disruptive under the first three Stuarts. Steve Pincus has been particularly emphatic on this point, writing that 'England's later seventeenth-century revolution was a nationalist revolution'.[2] Gilbert Burnet, Bishop of Salisbury, told his congregation in November 1689, and then the public when his sermon was printed, that 'we are all Englishmen, all of the same nation under the same laws, and the same

---

[1] Steve Pincus, *1688: The First Modern Revolution* (London, 2009), pp. 12, 490 n. 2.
[2] Ibid., p. 348. See also his article '"To Protect English Liberties": The English Nationalist Revolution of 1688–1689', in Tony Claydon and Ian McBride, eds, *Protestantism and National Identity: Britain and Ireland, c. 1650–1850* (Cambridge, 1998), pp. 75–88.

protection'.[3] Liberty and national identity were believed to be interdependent, of course. In an age when it seemed that one continental state after another was succumbing to the absolutist model of Louis XIV, England stood alone as a libertarian beacon. 'England', cried the Member of Parliament for Somerset, 'is the last monarchy that yet retains her liberties. Let them not perish now!'[4]

Also binding liberty to nation was the more material ideal of prosperity. In that same sermon, Burnet compared the teeming ports and booming manufactures with the poverty of the continentals, whose:

> ruined houses, their ragged clothes, their hungry looks, and their half-naked children, give evident proofs of the tyranny of their governments that can render the people extremely miserable, in spite of all that abundance which nature has set before them, while millions of people are pining away in want and beggary, that so a few may surfeit themselves with all the excess of fullness and vice.[5]

The most popular visual image of this imagined continental destitution was the wooden shoe believed to be the only kind of footwear worn east of Calais.[6] A good example was provided by William Hogarth in his etching 'The Invasion' of 1756 which shows a group of emaciated French soldiers roasting frogs outside an inn, with a sign reading 'Soup Meagre a la Sabot Royale', from which a wooden shoe hangs.[7] The obverse was a belief in English dietary superiority. In the late 1730s the French Abbé Le Blanc, visiting London, saw a play in which:

> the excellence and virtues of English beef were cried up, and the author maintain'd, that it was owing to the qualities of its juice that the English were so courageous, and had such a solidity of understanding, which rais'd them above all the nations in Europe; he preferred the noble old English pudding beyond all the finest ragouts that were ever invented by the greatest geniusses that France has produced; and all these ingenious strokes were loudly clapp'd by the audience.[8]

Again, it was Hogarth who provided the definitive (and very popular) visual statement of this prejudice in *O The Roast Beef of Old England, or The Gate*

---

[3] Pincus, *1688*, p. 348.
[4] G.M. Trevelyan, *England under the Stuarts* (Harmondsworth, 1960), p. 98.
[5] Pincus, *1688*, pp. 348–9.
[6] Michael Duffy, *The Englishman and the Foreigner* (Cambridge, 1986), p. 34.
[7] Joseph Burke and Colin Caldwell, eds, *Hogarth: The Complete Engravings* (London, 1968), p. 241.
[8] Duffy, *Englishman*, p. 34.

of Calais. Across the centre of the picture staggers a kitchen porter bearing a massive sirloin labelled 'For Madm. Grandsire at Calais', the owner of the port's English eating-house, where those embarking on the Grand Tour could enjoy one last square meal. It is watched with slavering gluttony by a fat friar and with amazement by two emaciated and ragged French soldiers, whose own pot of thin gruel (*soupe maigre*) is carried past in the opposite direction by servants wearing wooden clogs.[9]

In both of Hogarth's pictures the fourth driving principle of the Glorious Revolution is obtrusive – anti-Catholicism. In *The Invasion* it is a monk gleefully inspecting the instruments of torture and execution that will be accompanying the French army; in *The Gate of Calais* it is the priest bearing the Host through the streets as the locals kneel in veneration (which Hogarth and his fellow-Protestants viewed as idolatrous). Rejection of James II on confessional grounds was fundamental to the events of 1688–1689. As the constitutional convention that met in London in January 1689 proclaimed: 'it hath been found by experience, to be inconsistent with the safety and welfare of this Protestant Kingdom to be governed by a Popish Prince'.[10] English Protestants were hypersensitive to James II's proselytising because there was a general fear abroad that Catholicism was rampant throughout Europe. A late seventeenth-century pamphlet lamented that 'in the beginning of the last age, the Protestant interest in Europe was more than a match for the Roman Catholick ... But now, instead of this, is not the Protestant power destroyed almost over Europe?'[11] The revocation of the Edict of Nantes by Louis XIV in 1685 stoked fears across the Channel that England would be next. James II's simultaneous attempt to repeal the Test Acts, which excluded Catholics from public office, was believed to be a prelude to forced conversions. His professed adherence to religious toleration was not believed. In 1687 *The Dilucidator* warned that the example of Louis XIV 'made those of England fear that the King, after having rendered his religion powerful and ruling, would undertake to make them Catholics after the dragoon mode, as has been done to those of France'.[12] Once again, it was Hogarth who produced the

---

[9] Burke and Caldwell, eds, *Hogarth*, p. 217. The oil painting on which the engraving was based is now in the Tate Gallery, London. For the English obsession with beef, see Ben Rogers, *Beef and Liberty: Roast Beef, John Bull and the English Nation* (London, 2003), passim.

[10] Tony Claydon and Ian McBride, 'The Trials of the Chosen Peoples: Recent Interpretations of Protestantism and National Identity in Britain and Ireland', in eid., eds, *Protestantism and National Identity*, pp. 3–30, at p. 3.

[11] Quoted in Julian Hoppit, *A Land of Liberty? England 1689–1727* (Oxford, 2000), p. 214.

[12] Pincus, 'To Protect English Liberties', p. 84.

most memorable – and also the most shocking – image to illustrate this attitude, in the shape of *Transubstantiation Satirized*, which shows the Virgin feeding the infant Christ into a mincing machine, out of which pour wafers which a priest then administers to the faithful.[13]

The fears expressed of a recatholicisation of England did not die after 1688, however absurd they may have been. The presence of a significant Catholic minority in Scotland (c. 10 per cent of the population, but concentrated in the notoriously unruly Highlands), and an even more significant majority in Ireland, sharpened fears of a French invasion by the back door. After the great 'Irish Terror' of the winter of 1688–1689 had revived memories of the horrors of 1641, it was an anxiety that may have faded over time but never wholly disappeared.[14] At the turn of the century, there were only about 60,000 Catholics in the country, representing about 1 per cent of the total population, served by c. 650 priests.[15] Nevertheless, the confessional pot was kept on the boil by tales of Catholic persecution on the continent that were given plenty of publicity in the English press, notably the judicial murder of Protestants in the 'blood-bath of Thorn' (Toruń) in Poland in 1724, the expulsion of the Salzburg Protestants in 1731 and the persecution of Protestants in the Palatinate throughout the period.[16] In the English collective consciousness, Catholicism meant despotism, poverty, idolatry and French domination. Speaking in the House of Lords on 25 March 1679, Shaftesbury declared that 'Popery and slavery, like two sisters, go hand in hand, and sometimes one goes first, sometimes the other; but wheresoever the one enters, the other is always following close at hand.'[17] It is difficult to overestimate the importance of anti-Catholicism in England during the 'long eighteenth century' (1688–1832) because it involved so much more than religion. As Linda Colley has observed with characteristic trenchancy: 'the

---

[13] This is not reproduced in the Burke and Caldwell volume but can be found in Edward Ireland, *Graphic Illustrations of Hogarth: From Pictures, Drawings, and Scarce Prints*, 2 vols (London, 1794–9), I, pp. 122–3.

[14] Tim Harris, *Revolution: The Great Crisis of the British Monarchy, 1685–1720* (London, 2006), p. 298.

[15] Hoppit, *A Land of Liberty?*, p. 221.

[16] Andrew C. Thompson, *Britain, Hanover and the Protestant Interest, 1688–1756* (Woodbridge, 2006), pp. 15, 23, 44, 53–4, 74–5, 97–8, 110–15, 152–4. This important work is indispensable for an understanding of British politics during the period.

[17] Harris, *Revolution*, p. 31. When asked by a woman which was the right form of religion, Shaftesbury replied: 'Madam, wise men are of but one religion', 'Which one is that?', 'Madam, wise men never tell', quoted from Trevelyan, *England under the Stuarts*, p. 332.

absolute centrality of Protestantism to British religious experience in the 1700s and long after is so obvious that it has proved easy to pass over'.[18]

Colley also demonstrates in her ground-breaking book the importance of Francophobia. Memories of the pernicious influence of Charles I's queen, Henrietta Maria, had not faded when her nephew, Louis XIV, began his march to European hegemony. His cultural triumphalism, exemplified by Versailles, and aggressive Catholicism provoked a reaction of corresponding vehemence (and not just in England, it might be added).[19] The Marquis of Halifax's 'Trimmer', 'easily one of the most influential political characters of the 1680s', affirmed that such was the attachment of the English to their nation that 'before the French blood can be let into our bodies, every drop of our own must be drawn out of them'.[20] In the view of Sir Richard Cox, Lord Chancellor of Ireland and prolific author:

> I take him for an Englishman that is for securing our properties and maintaining the liberties of Europe against the French king ... I take him for a Frenchman, a Papist, a foreigner or anything that being born here and enjoying the freedom of an Englishman can ever entertain thoughts of changing this present government or making any interest for the French King or our late tyrant [James II].[21]

This prejudice expressed itself, among other ways, in fierce bellicosity. In the view of Steve Pincus: 'from the moment that James departed England, the English with almost-united voice called for war against France'.[22]

What was to give the French Revolution its special power was its combination of the three great abstractions of the modern world: state, nation and people.[23] The Glorious Revolution arguably had anticipated this achievement, for it also brought a massive expansion in the power of the state. The 'Second Hundred Years War' against France, which it unleashed, demanded an unprecedented increase in expenditure and the machinery to collect and administer it. This was nothing less than a revolution in government, which created a fiscal-military

---

[18] Linda Colley, *Britons: Forging the Nation 1707–1837* (London, 1992), p. 18.
[19] See, for example, Martin Wrede, *Das Reich und seine Feinde: Politische Feindbilder in der reichspatriotischen Publizistik zwischen Westfälischem Frieden und Siebenjährigem Krieg* (Mainz, 2004), pt. 3.
[20] Pincus, *1688*, p. 349.
[21] Ibid.
[22] Ibid., p. 363.
[23] I have discussed this in *The Pursuit of Glory: Europe 1648–1815* (London, 2007), pp. 337–55.

state and was 'the most important transformation in English government between the domestic reforms of the Tudors and the major administrative changes in the first half of the nineteenth century'. As John Brewer has demonstrated:

> Between 1688 and 1714 the British state underwent a radical transformation, acquiring all of the main features of a powerful fiscal-military state: high taxes, a growing and well-organised civil administration, a standing army and the determination to act as a major European power.[24]

What might have happened if England had stayed out of the continental wars after 1688 is difficult to assess. It is certain however that it was the need to finance those wars which made the monarchy limited, bureaucratic and parliamentary. It ceased to be personal, but it was also more powerful because now the great and growing economic power of the country could be tapped.[25] Or, in other words, it was not the Glorious Revolution but the Glorious Revolution's wars that created modern England (and later Britain).[26]

'State' and 'nation' were very much part of 1688 and its consequences, but so too was 'people'. It can now be seen how inadequate was J.H. Plumb's account which concentrated on the resentment of the gentry at infringements on their power in the localities.[27] Both of the major recent accounts of 1688, by Tim Harris and Steve Pincus respectively, stress the intensity and degree of popular participation: 'it was not so much William's invading army that brought James down ... but rather the people of England' (Harris) and 'The Revolution of 1688–89 was neither a *coup d'état* nor a foreign invasion but a popular revolution' (Pincus).[28] As the latter shows, the extent of popular involvement has been consistently underestimated. In fact, thousands took up arms in support of William and overall crowd activity was very similar to that experienced in other revolutions.

So state, nation and people were all involved in England a century before the French Revolution. Yet the post-revolutionary experiences of the two countries

---

[24] John Brewer, *The Sinews of Power: War, Money and the English State 1688–1783* (New York, 1989), pp. xvii and 137.

[25] Harris, *Revolution*, p. 492.

[26] Cf. 'It was not the French Revolution which created the modern world, it was the French Revolutionary wars', T.C.W. Blanning, *The Origins of the French Revolutionary Wars* (London, 1986), p. 211.

[27] J.H. Plumb, *The Growth of Political Stability in England 1675–1725* (London, 1967), ch. 2.

[28] Harris, *Revolution*, p. 276; Pincus, *1688*, p. 224.

proved to be very different. Neither England nor the other two kingdoms in 'these islands' (as the politically correct like to call the British Isles) followed France down the path of chronic political instability, state terror and military dictatorship, despite much turbulence, including a bloody but brief civil war in Ireland. This was due to the contrasting roles played by religion. In France, it was deeply divisive. As John McManners wrote:

> If there was a point at which the Revolution 'went wrong', it was when the Constituent Assembly imposed the oath to the Civil Constitution of the Clergy, 27 November 1790. This marked the end of national unity and the beginning of civil war.[29]

In England, on the other hand, Protestantism provided the underlying cement that held together the base, no matter how crazy a paving of party and sectarian hostilities appeared on its surface. Nonconformists or Presbyterians might well hate Anglicans, and *vice versa*, but they feared and hated Catholics more. The presence of an aggressively Catholic Pretender, first in France and later in Rome, reminded everyone of what could be expected if the Stuarts returned. The death of James II in 1701 meant that from now on Jacobites were seeking the installation of a young Catholic prince raised abroad and with no direct experience of England.[30] It was particularly unfortunate that James had tried to regain England by entering through the Irish back door. In the sonorous judgement of Macaulay: 'the effects of the insane attempt to subjugate England by means of Ireland was that the Irish became the hewers of wood and drawers of water to the English'.[31] The existential hostility between Protestants and Catholics in Ireland gave the English government an opportunity to play the role of 'the smiling third' (*der lachende Dritte*), which they were not slow to exploit. The rollercoaster ride of Irish Protestants in the seventeenth century, from near disaster in 1641 to deliverance in 1688–1690 persuaded them that the hand of God had been at work, that they had been specially chosen to do His work. So they came to see themselves as not 'a' but as *the* people of Ireland, for the Catholics, whether of Gaelic or Old English origin, they concluded, were hopelessly lost, never to rise again.[32]

The decision of the Old Pretender 'James III' that London was not worth renouncing a Mass – 'I have chosen my own course, therefore it is for others to

---

[29] John McManners, *The French Revolution and the Church* (London, 1969), p. 38.
[30] Hoppit, *A Land of Liberty?*, p. 283.
[31] Thomas Babington Macaulay, *History of England to the Death of William III*, 4 vols (London, 1967), I, p. 627.
[32] Thomas Bartlett, 'Protestant Nationalism in Eighteenth-Century Ireland', *Studies on Voltaire and the Eighteenth Century*, 335 (1995), pp. 79–88, at p. 81.

change their sentiments' was his quintessentially Stuart statement[33] – handed a precious advantage to his Hanoverian rivals; nor did his decision and that of his son, 'Bonnie Prince Charlie', to launch their invasions in 1715 and 1745 respectively from France via the Scottish Highlands do anything to dilute the patently foreign nature of their expeditions. It is worth remembering that in Scotland divisions between the Highlands, where 28 of the 50 clans were Jacobite, and the Lowlands were every bit as acute as those between the Highlands and England.[34] When the Old Pretender's second son, Henry, became a Catholic priest, and a cardinal to boot, the cost of a Stuart restoration became too high for all but a small and ever-diminishing number of Jacobite diehards. Vigorous persecution of Catholics in England might have kept the flame burning, but successive Protestant monarchs were too sensible. Macaulay observed that the difference between the fates of James II and William III could be summed up by their approach to dissent. The former said of one of his most fanatical opponents, 'Mr Johnson has the spirit of a martyr; and it is fit that he should be one', whereas William's dismissal of one of the most obstreperous of Jacobites was, 'he has set his heart on being a martyr; and I have set mine on disappointing him'.[35]

As this examination of the period between 1688 and 1714 has sought to show, Hanoverian representation did not have to be positive to be effective. All the Georges had to do was accommodate themselves to a political culture which was constitutional, materialist, nationalist and Protestant. They had been dealt as strong a hand as any incoming foreign dynasty had ever received; and – if they did not exactly make the most of it – they certainly played it satisfactorily. The sense of relief when the transition from Stuart to Guelph was completed with the coronation of George I on 20 October 1714 was vigorously expressed by public celebrations across the land. In a sermon preached (and printed) in 1727 after the king's death, Thomas Prince recalled:

> I shall never forget the Joy that swell's my Heart, when in the Splendid Procession at his Coronation ... That Royal Face at length appear'd, which Heaven had in that Moment sent to Save these Great Nations from the Brink of Ruin.[36]

---

[33] Edward Gregg, 'James Francis Edward (1688–1766)', *Oxford Dictionary of National Biography* (Oxford, 2004), online edn, May 2012 (http://www.oxforddnb.com/view/article/14594, accessed 19 February 2013).

[34] Hoppit, *A Land of Liberty?*, p. 249.

[35] Macaulay, *History of England to the Death of William III*, I, p. 604.

[36] Hannah Smith, *Georgian Monarchy: Politics and Culture 1714–1760* (Cambridge, 2006), p. 19. Much of what follows is taken from this exceptionally distinguished, original

That was more than a little hyperbolic, as in 1714 the War of the Spanish Succession had just come to an end with a resounding English victory over the hereditary enemy; but the French-sponsored Jacobite invasion of the following year certainly warned against complacency. Loyalist writers were keen to present both the new king and the Prince of Wales as valiant warriors who risked their lives in wars against the Turks, in the case of the former, and the French, in the case of the latter. It was a happy coincidence for Hanoverian public relations that George I's eldest son (the future George II) had been present at the Battle of Oudenarde in 1708. So had the Old Pretender, but he had been in the French army fighting against the English whose government he sought to usurp.[37]

If the new Prince of Wales was a Protestant hero, his wife, Caroline of Ansbach, was, if anything, even more renowned as a Protestant heroine,[38] for in 1704 she had turned down a proposal of marriage from Archduke Charles, who in 1711 became ruler of the Habsburg monarchy and Holy Roman Emperor, because she could not bring herself to convert to Catholicism. In 1714 John Gay published a poem entitled 'To a lady, occasioned by the arrival of the Princess of Wales', which celebrated this sacrifice with the line: 'She scorn'd an empire for religion's sake'. So famous did this line become that the rest of the poem has been neglected. Also worth quoting are the lines applied to her infant son:

> The son shall add new honours to the line,
> And early with paternal virtues shine.
> When he the tale of Audenard [sic] repeats,
> His little heart with emulation beats.[39]

And so is the passage which associates the new dynasty with prosperity. Looking back from an imaginary future at 'the glorious series of the Brunswick race', Gay finds:

> 'Tis thus secure in peace
> We plough the fields, and reap the year's increase:
> Now Commerce, wealthy goddess, rears her head,

---

and important study. Its author shows how much there is to be gained when historians of England take the trouble to master the German sources and secondary literature.

[37] Ibid., p. 21.

[38] On the importance of Protestantism to the new dynasty, see especially Andrew C. Thompson, 'The Confessional Dimension', in Brendan Simms and Torsten Riotte, eds, *The Hanoverian Dimension in British History 1714–1837* (Cambridge, 2007), pp. 161–82.

[39] *The Poems of John Gay* (London, 1822), p. 82.

> And bids Britannia's fleets their canvass spread;
> Unnumber'd ships the peopled ocean hide,
> And wealth returns with each revolving tide.[40]

Gay's poem may well have been a transparent bid for preferment, but it struck a chord with the public, going through four editions by the end of the year.[41] The contrast between this Protestant paragon and the Catholic wives of the three Stuarts (Henrietta Maria of France, Catherine of Braganza and Mary of Modena) could hardly have been greater. As Hannah Smith has written: 'From the time of her arrival in England in 1714, Caroline enjoyed a popularity which even her detractors found difficult to assail and which was crucial to the successful establishment of the dynasty in Britain.'[42] It was also a happy accident that the favourite first name of the Guelphs was 'George', allowing the pamphleteers and cartoonists to cross-refer to St George slaying the Catholic dragon. The author of 'The Welcome' (to George I), for example, revelled in the terror struck into the hearts of papists by the realisation that:

> Their Popish Dragon now must lose his Sting,
> Because St George our Champion is, and King.[43]

The style of kingship the Hanoverians brought with them assimilated naturally with post-1688 representation. The last two Stuarts and their consorts were certainly capable of baroque display – Hampton Court and the Painted Hall at Greenwich are proof of that – but in general there was a move away from the kind of exuberant representation to be found at Versailles or Schönbrunn. Along with divine right and absolutism, the sacral nature of monarchy was dropped. Although Queen Anne touched afflicted subjects for the 'King's Evil' (scrofula), including most famously the infant Samuel Johnson, William III and the Hanoverians all refused.[44] This was less self-evident than it might seem. At his coronation at Rheims in 1775, Louis XVI was to insist on carrying out the ceremony. Newly

---

[40] Ibid., p. 84.
[41] David Nokes, 'Gay, John (1685–1732)', *Oxford Dictionary of National Biography* (http://www.oxforddnb.com/view/article/10473, accessed 19 February 2013).
[42] Smith, *Georgian Monarchy*, p. 33. See also Andrew Hanham, 'Caroline of Brandenburg-Ansbach and the "Anglicisation" of the House of Hanover', in Clarissa Campbell Orr, ed., *Queenship in Europe, 1660–1815: The Role of the Consort* (Cambridge, 2004), pp. 276–99.
[43] Smith, *Georgian Monarchy*, p. 27.
[44] Hoppit, *A Land of Liberty?*, p. 41.

equipped with thaumaturgical powers, he laid hands on 2,400 scrofula-sufferers. Unimpressed, Voltaire wrote to Frederick the Great that he had lost confidence in the king of France's miraculous power on learning that one of Louis XIV's mistresses had died of scrofula, despite being very well touched by the king.[45] This attachment of the early Hanoverians to enlightened ideas also found its way into a practical interest in scientific advance, expressed for example in the decision of Queen Caroline to have her children inoculated against smallpox.[46]

George I was anyway temperamentally averse to extravagant display. He was very much a private man, disliking the bustle of court life, fuss and ostentation and preferring a simple life alone or with a few intimates, tended by his two Turkish servants, Mehemet and Mustapha.[47] Handicapped by his rudimentary knowledge of the English language, his ignorance of English conditions (he did not even know the ranks of the peerage when he arrived) and his lack of physical stature, he was both unable and unwilling to impose his personality on high society. He rarely showed himself to the people, travelled infrequently and never without specific purpose. As a result, the long-standing trend towards the strict separation of public and private in the life of the monarch was strengthened.[48] The English court lacked an architectural framework comparable with even a middling continental state. The main London palace, Whitehall, had been destroyed by fire in 1697 and had not been rebuilt. Everyone recognised the need for a new royal palace and many plans were drawn up, but nothing was actually done. St James's Palace was not an adequate replacement, consisting of a maze of small rooms. As James Ralph observed in 1734: 'so far from having one single beauty to recommend it, … 'tis at once the contempt of foreign nations, and the disgrace of our own'.[49] Plans came and went without being realised beyond another wing at this existing palace or a new suite of rooms at another. In November 1741 the Prussian Baron Bielfeld was deeply unimpressed: 'The court here is the residence of dullness. The old palace of St James's, or the king's lodging-house; crazy, smoky and dirty, is sufficient of itself to inspire melancholy ideas.' He added that since the death of Queen Caroline in 1737 the king was rarely seen and so 'this life of perpetual retirement renders the court to the last

---

[45] Anton Haueter, *Die Krönungen der französischen Könige im Zeitalter des Absolutismus und in der Restauration* (Zurich, 1975), p. 257.
[46] Smith, *Georgian Monarchy*, p. 94.
[47] J.H. Plumb, *The First Four Georges* (London, 1956), p. 41.
[48] Ragnhild Hatton, *George I: Elector and King* (London, 1978), p. 139.
[49] John M. Beattie, *The English Court in the Reign of George I* (Cambridge, 1967; repr. 2008), p. 9.

degree spiritless, or rather, there is no court at all'.[50] In the visionary *London and Westminster Improved* of 1766, John Gwynn argued that 'public magnificence may be considered as a political and moral advantage to every nation' and that 'publick works of real magnificence ... [are] as necessary to the community as health and clothing to the human body'. But his plan to overhaul Paris-Versailles in the representational stakes by demolishing St James's Palace and Buckingham House and replacing them with two new palaces came to nothing.[51]

George I vetoed Vanbrugh's plans for a great baroque replacement for Kensington Palace along the lines of Blenheim, ordering instead a modest reconstruction with two of the storeys completed 'in the cheapest and plainest manner'.[52] George II was equally frugal, if not more so. Apart from the completion of a grand staircase at Hampton Court, his building works were all by way of restoration. The renovation of St James's Palace, which involved the removal of a number of commercial buildings that had accumulated around its walls, was initiated by the need to deal with the stench from the privies of a neighbouring tavern.[53] The most ambitious building project of his reign was the construction of new stables, which of course gave rise to the chiasm 'Kings lodg'd as Horses, and as Horses, Kings'.[54] The fact of the matter was that parliamentary control of finance meant that economy was a necessity. As Hannah Smith has pointed out, Charles II was only able to embark on the building of an English version of Versailles at Winchester because he was on Louis XIV's payroll.[55]

The first two Georges were very well placed both to benefit from and to consolidate the style of representation established after 1688 in the matter of religion and modesty. They also very wisely left the constitutional settlement alone. However much they may have chafed at the toils in which they found themselves, both men cooperated with the parliamentary monarchy they inherited. All the major gains of the Revolution were maintained. Although neither of the first two Georges had been raised as Anglicans, they sensibly left the messy but viable religious settlement alone: Anglican domination tempered by modest toleration. As John Locke claimed: 'Toleration has now at last been established by law in our country. Not perhaps so wide in scope as might be

---

[50] *Letters of Baron Bielfeld, Secretary of Legation to the King of Prussia, ... Translated from the German by Mr Hooper* (London, 1770), pp. 57–8.

[51] David Watkin, *The Architect King: George III and the Culture of the Enlightenment* (London, 2004), pp. 14–15.

[52] Smith, *Georgian Monarchy*, p. 68.

[53] Ibid., p. 70.

[54] Ibid., p. 71.

[55] Ibid., p. 72.

wished for ... Still, it is something to have progressed so far.'[56] At a time when France was being torn apart by the intra-Church feuding between conservatives and Jansenists, this was no mean achievement. Both kings were on the receiving end of much vicious party-political polemic from those who failed to secure the preferment they thought they deserved, and during Walpole's heyday George II was confronted by a 'patriot opposition'. Yet apart from the committed Jacobites, whose numbers and importance have often been exaggerated, the opposition was not systemic.

In London and, to a lesser extent elsewhere in their kingdoms, the Hanoverians found a cultural novelty – a large and rapidly growing public sphere. 'Bourgeois' it may have been, consistently oppositional it certainly was not. It was a neutral vessel in which every shade of opinion could find a berth, loyalist and Jacobite, royalist and republican. There were sharp pens writing for the opposition, and equally sharp pens writing for the crown and its government of the day. Again, the Hanoverians left well alone. Charles II had tried to close the coffee houses down, an attempt that ended in humiliating retreat. As Andrew Marvell observed in a poem entitled 'A Dialogue between Two Horses', with more wisdom than command of rhyme:

> When they take from the people the freedom of words,
> They teach them the sooner to fall to their swords.
> Let the City drink coffee and quietly groan;
> They that conquer'd the father won't be slaves to the son.[57]

George I arrived in the middle of a cultural revolution, expressed most obviously in the growth of literacy and corresponding explosion of printed matter of every kind. Around 45 per cent of the male and 25 per cent of the female population in England were literate in 1714, growing to 60 per cent and 40 per cent respectively by mid-century. Figures for London were much higher, of course, with 66 per cent of women literate by the 1720s. By 1739 there were 551 coffee houses in London in which all the latest news could be read and discussed.[58] In 1731 a French visitor, the Abbé Prévost, had reported:

> I have had pointed out to me in several coffee-houses, a couple of lords, a baronet, a shoemaker, a tailor, a wine-merchant and some others of the same sort, all sitting

---

[56] Hoppit, *A Land of Liberty?*, p. 33.
[57] Quoted in Blanning, *The Pursuit of Glory*, p. 331.
[58] John Brewer, *The Pleasures of the Imagination: English Culture in the Eighteenth Century* (London, 1997), pp. 35, 167.

round the same table and discussing familiarly the news of the court and the town. The government's affairs are as much the concern of the people as of the great. Every man has the right to discuss them freely. Men condemn, approve, revile, rail with bitter invectives both in speech and in writing without the authorities daring to intervene. The King himself is not secure from censure. The coffee-houses and other public places are the seats of English liberty. For two pence you have the right to read all the papers for and against the government and to take a cup of tea or coffee as well.[59]

In other words, monarchical representation was too important to be left to the monarchs. If an account of Hanoverian representation were confined to the latter, it would be short and thin. If George I has been rescued from Plumb's acid verdict – 'very stupid, and lacking interest in the arts, save music'[60] – lack of ambition and lack of means restricted his representational activity. His son had more money and more time; but, following a lavish coronation, he reverted to the parsimony of his predecessor, especially after the death of Queen Caroline.[61] In 1735 he was on the receiving end of a lesson on the independence of the public sphere, when the Tory MP Francis Seymour refused to remove his hat in the royal presence at the theatre, asserting: 'he should have thought it very wrong to have done anything of that sort in the King's palaces, but there were no kings at operas and playhouses where everybody might sit as they pleased'. Although suitably enraged, George did not insist.[62]

Protestant and – however grumpily – constitutional, the first two Georges faced a sterner task when it came to representing the English nation. Both men were patently – and audibly – German. By the time he succeeded, George I was an old man (54) by the standards of the day and his son already 31. The preference they showed for their electorate was demonstrated not least by their frequent and lengthy visits to the latter, which caused a great deal of offence in their new acquisition.[63] Also born and educated in Germany was the next generation, George II's eldest son, Frederick, who did not arrive in England

---

[59] Francesca M. Wilson, ed., *Strange Island: Britain through Foreign Eyes 1395–1940* (London, 1955), p. 86.

[60] Plumb, *The First Four Georges*, p. 39. Cf. Hatton, *George I* for his rehabilitation, which again demonstrates the importance of having a command of the German language when writing about Hanoverians.

[61] For a sympathetic but not uncritical biography of George II, see Andrew C. Thompson, *George II* (New Haven, 2011), by far and away the best biography available.

[62] Smith, *Georgian Monarchy*, p. 235.

[63] Brendan Simms, 'Hanover: The Missing Dimension', in id. and Riotte, eds, *The Hanoverian Dimension in British History 1714–1837* (Cambridge, 2007), pp. 1–9, at p. 5.

until 1728, when he was 21. However, he did grasp the opportunity to play the patriotic card, especially after he had fallen out with his parents in 1737. In particular he was both the beneficiary and the promoter of the cult of King Alfred (848–899), in reality only the ruler of the West Saxons and Anglo-Saxons but hailed by posterity as the first king of England. At his London residence, Carlton House, the prince had an octagonal temple built adorned with statues of Alfred and Edward the Black Prince.[64]

He also commissioned a masque, *Alfred*, first performed in 1740, with a libretto by James Thomson and David Mallet and music by Thomas Arne. The plot, such as it is, follows the king's recovery from hunted fugitive to triumphant vanquisher of the Danish invaders. Its purpose, however, was plainly political. Being performed the year after war against Spain began and with an undeclared war against France underway, it was a call to arms. In Act II, scene 3, for example, a hermit inspires the hard-pressed Alfred by conjuring up spirits from the future, including such hammers of the French as Edward III and the Black Prince. The greatest hero of the future, however, is William III, for it was he who banished that two-headed monster, superstition and absolutism (James II), and his crony 'vile Servility, that crouch'd and kiss'd the whip he trembled at'. The hermit sees the Glorious Revolution as the turning point in English history:

> From this great hour
> Shall Britain date her rights and laws restor'd:
> And one high purpose rule her sovereign's heart;
> To scourge the pride of France, that foe profess'd
> To England and to Freedom.[65]

What gave *Alfred* its immense and enduring power was neither the music nor the text, but the combination of the two for the closing chorus, which was to become perhaps both the most emotive and popular in all English music. There

---

[64] Simon Keynes, 'The Cult of King Alfred the Great', *Anglo–Saxon England*, 28 (1999), pp. 225–56, at p. 277. This substantial and revealing article appears to have been overlooked by most historians of eighteenth-century England. See also Oliver Cox, '"Rule Britannia!" King Alfred the Great and the Creation of a National Hero in England and America 1640–1800' (DPhil dissertation, University of Oxford, 2013) and id., 'Frederick, Prince of Wales, and the First Performance of "Rule Britannia"', *Historical Journal*, 56 (2013), pp. 93–154.

[65] *The Works of James Thomson, with His Last Corrections and Improvements*, 4 vols (London, 1766), III, p. 244.

is no need for a musical quotation, for the words of the refrain alone will be sufficient reminder of the melody:

> Rule, Britannia, rule the waves;
> Britons never will be slaves.[66]

With impressive economy, the six four-line verses manage to cover all the main characteristics of eighteenth-century British nationalism: divine assistance ('When Britain first at heav'n's command,/ Arose from out the azure main'); a unique capacity for liberty ('The nations, not so blest as thee,/ Must, in their turns, to tyrants fall:/ While thou shalt flourish great and free,/ The dread and envy of them all'); defiant resistance to continental despotisms ('Thee haughty tyrants never shall tame'); a flourishing agriculture and commerce ('To thee belong the rural reign;/ Thy cities shall with commerce shine'); global naval supremacy ('All thine shall be the subject main,/ And every shore it circles thine'); cultural excellence ('The muses still with freedom found;/ Shall to thy happy coast repair'); natural beauty ('Blest Isle! With matchless beauty crown'd'); and virile masculinity ('And manly hearts to guard the fair'). There was also an obvious domestic agenda. Against a king alleged to prefer Hanover to Britain, and who relied on the notoriously corrupt Sir Robert Walpole to manage parliament by illicit means, Frederick presented himself as a selfless British patriot.

Commissioned by a Hanoverian prince and popularised by the public, the success of *Rule Britannia* symbolised the symbiosis between the two and exemplified the mixed nature of Hanoverian representation. Under Frederick's son, who succeeded as George III in 1760, this powerful combination was to continue, albeit rocked hard by political instability in the 1760s and the American war in the 1770s. It was not until 1784 that calm waters were reached again.[67] George enjoyed a number of advantages denied or spurned by his two predecessors. He was not just Protestant, he was Anglican. His personal life was without blemish. His life-style was not just restrained, it was positively frugal. Above all he was English through and through. As he proclaimed in his first speech from the throne, delivered on 18 November 1760: 'born and educated

---

[66] Ibid., p. 253.
[67] Linda Colley, 'The Apotheosis of George III: Loyalty, Royalty and the British Nation 1760–1820', *Past and Present*, 102 (1984), pp. 94–129. I have also discussed the process in *The Culture of Power and the Power of Culture: Old Regime Europe 1660–1789* (Oxford, 2002), pp. 322–53.

in this country, I glory in the name of Britain'.[68] What he lacked early on was a reputation for respecting the traditional constitution, as the disappointed Whigs chose to mistake independence for subversion. Once he had dispelled that myth and learned the ropes as a politician, he was able to achieve a degree of popularity that far exceeded that of the first two Georges. Hanoverian representation however remained very much a private-public initiative.[69]

---

[68] John Brooke, *George III* (London, 1972), p. 88. There has been some confusion as to whether George said 'Britain' or 'Briton'. Brooke states firmly that the original draft quite clearly shows 'Britain' in the king's hand, but it was reported as 'Briton'; see ibid., p. 390 n. 7.

[69] I have discussed George III's style of representation in another conference paper: 'The Representation of Frederick II and George III: A Comparison', in Jürgen Luh and Andreas Pečar, eds, Öffentliche Tagung des Interdisziplinären Zentrums zur Erforschung der Europäischen Aufklärung an der Martin-Luther-Universität Halle-Wittenberg und der Stiftung Preußische Schlösser und Gärten Berlin-Brandenburg im Potsdam Museum – Forum für Kunst und Geschichte vom 28.–29. September 2012, http://www.perspectivia.net/content/publikationen/friedrich300-colloquien/friedrich_repraesentation/blanning_representation.

Chapter 8

'Every Inch *Not* a King': The Bodies of the (First Two) Hanoverians

Robert Bucholz[1]

The ruler's body – its care and comfort, adornment and presentation, safety and security – must always be at the centre of the state's concerns. Nowhere is this more true than in a personal monarchy, in which the sovereign's decisions and popularity are determinative. Historians have long been aware of the distinction between the sovereign's sacred, legal and constitutional body and his corporeal one, thanks in large part to the classic work of Ernst Kantorowicz, but most of the immediately ensuing research concentrated on the former. Actual, physical royal bodies were for many years left to popular historians, romance novelists and gossip columnists, part of a broad neglect of courts by academic scholars. Scholarly study of the court has taken off in the last few decades, as has the study of the body generally; but it is only in recent years that academics have begun to scrutinise the flesh and blood at the centre of the early modern state.[2]

This is surprising, given that the ruler's corporeal presence was long thought to represent, even em*body*, the state, receiving the honours and reverence that

---

[1] The author would like to express his gratitude to the participants in the 'Dynastic Politics, Monarchical Representation and the Union between Hanover and Britain Joint Conference' of the German Historical Institute London and the Historische Kommission für Niedersachsen und Bremen, held at the German Historical Institute London, 11–13 October 2012, and the members of the British-Atlantic Writing Group at Loyola University Chicago for their helpful questions, comments and suggestions. He would also like to thank Michael Schaich for his suggestion of the topic and subsequent editorial assistance; and Alan Burton, Elizabeth Coffman, Aaron Greer, J.B. Kaufman, Thomas Michalak, Massimo Moretti, Tim O'Sullivan and Agata Rutkowska for their assistance with the illustrations for his chapter.

[2] Ernst H. Kantorowicz, *The King's Two Bodies: A Study in Medieval Political Theology* (Princeton, 1957). For more recent work on royal bodies, see Paul Kléber Monod, *The Power of Kings: Monarchy and Religion in Europe, 1589–1715* (New Haven, 1999), ch. 2; Ellen M. McClure, *Sunspots and the Sun King: Sovereignty and Mediation in Seventeenth-Century France* (Urbana, 2006); Regina Schulte, ed., *The Body of the Queen: Gender and Rule in the Courtly World, 1500–2000* (New York, 2006); and n. 4 below.

we pay today to flags, founding documents, film stars and football players. This exalted treatment of the person of the monarch complicates Kantorowicz's seemingly neat distinction between public and private, legal and physical, immortal and mortal. It is a hallmark of modernity that the royal body has since been de-sacralised and de-mythologised; but people (including even scholars) do not seem to have abandoned entirely the ancient notion that physical appearance connotes more than bodily health and grooming, that it also reveals qualities of mind and character.[3] In a 2009 publication, I argued that Queen Anne's physical body, in particular her obesity, played an important role in her reception as a monarch, both by her subjects and, perhaps most decisively and derisively, by subsequent historians. Rare was the scholar who could comment on her girth without in the same breath disparaging her abilities; but historians who downplayed or ignored her physical attributes were far more generous to her rule and reign.[4]

This chapter applies the same lens to Anne's immediate successors. In the tercentenary of the Hanoverian accession, it is worth asking what British subjects made of the physical bodies of their new sovereigns after the somewhat sickly and disappointingly reclusive presence (or non-presence) of the last of the Stuarts. More specifically, how did supporters and detractors interpret and portray Hanoverian bodies; and what do those interpretations and portrayals say about contemporary and later expectations of the British monarchy (and its German occupants) at a crucial moment in their history? To address these questions, this chapter attempts to do three things: 1) establish, as much as possible at this distance in time, the ontological reality of the bodies of the first two Georges – what they were like and how they appeared to the unprejudiced eye; 2) determine how that reality was portrayed, used, obscured and distorted – that is, how the royal body was constructed and deconstructed, by supporters and opponents, in text and image, both contemporaneously and afterwards; and 3) assess what this might tell us about contemporary and later attitudes to the monarchy, Germans, bodies etc. In answer to the last two questions in particular, the reality of royal bodies – ultimately unknowable in any case – is less important than their portrayal in various media and their perception by diverse audiences. In fact, the real matter of this study lies in the distance between the former and

---

[3] For a brief history of this idea, see Roy Porter, *Flesh in the Age of Reason: The Modern Foundations of Body and Soul* (New York, 2003), ch. 14.

[4] Robert Bucholz, 'The "Stomach of a Queen" or Size Matters: Gender, Body Image, and the Historical Reputation of Queen Anne', in Carole Levin and Robert Bucholz, eds, *Queens and Power in Medieval and Early Modern England* (Lincoln, NE, 2009), pp. 242–72.

the latter. Put more simply, this chapter is far more about attitudes and fantasies than it is about the thing itself.

As is well known, the *later* Hanoverians provide a rich harvest for the historian of the body thanks to the proliferation of biting satirical cartoons and caricatures in the second half of the eighteenth century, its last two decades in particular. Add to this the extensive late Hanoverian patronage of court painters and the increasingly widespread dissemination of the royal image through mezzotint and print, and we have every reason to claim to know the bodies of the last four Hanoverian rulers of Great Britain pretty well. For example, George III – of aristocratic squint and fashionable *embonpoint* in youth; the genial and paternal, if somewhat doddering, 'Farmer George' at mid-life; and the pathetic invalid and shut-in of his later years – presents a familiar image at every stage. Nor was that image an uncongenial one, for many Britons at least. Most of the popular and satirical portrayals tend to be gently deflating, de-sacralising perhaps, but hardly de-legitimising. Rather, as Linda Colley, Marilyn Morris and others have shown, these almost affectionately critical presentations of the royal body seem to have increased sympathy for, and therefore the popularity of, the beleaguered king, both then and now.[5]

The gloves came off in portraying the king's sons, George IV in particular. As his body became the canvas on which he painted his own indulgences, caricaturists like Gillray and Cruickshank used it against him. Obviously, unusual physical features of any kind are a godsend to the satirist: Bill Clinton's belly and bulbous nose, Barack Obama's ears, Tony Blair's smile and, perhaps a little oddly, Angela Merkel's chin are recent examples. But when the physical trait seems to mirror or be the consequence of a character flaw (Clinton and his appetites provide the prime modern example), the satirical possibilities and political consequences expand exponentially. Thus, while Anne's appetite for food and its results were portrayed by her subjects and later historians as signs of a dull, sublunary mind, George IV's expanding girth became the symbol *par excellence* of a greedy, all-consuming ruler whose flights of ceremonial, sartorial and architectural fancy were bankrupting the nation. Here, fatness takes on a far more sinister aspect than it ever did for Queen Anne. The fact that Caroline of

---

[5] Linda Colley, *Britons: Forging the Nation 1707–1837* (London, 1992), pp. 210–12; ead., 'The Apotheosis of George III: Loyalty, Royalty and the British Nation 1760–1820', *Past and Present* 102 (1984), pp. 94–129; Marilyn Morris, *The British Monarchy and the French Revolution* (New Haven, 1998), esp. ch. 8. Many Americans saw and continue to see George III rather differently, of course; see, for example, Earl A. Reitan, *George III: Tyrant or Constitutional Monarch?* (Boston, MA, 1964); Brendan McConville, *The King's Three Faces: The Rise and Fall of Royal America, 1688–1776* (Chapel Hill, NC, 2006).

Brunswick also grew stout in later years made the royal pair 'partners in crime', despite George's implacable rejection of her as wife and queen.[6] The bodies of William IV and Queen Victoria, though also stout in later years, were treated more gently by their critics. In Victoria's case this undoubtedly had something to do with changing mores that she did much to foster, but it also reminds us that a distinctive physical appearance is not in itself enough to yield satire; it must be wedded to an obvious, or at least plausible, flaw in character. George IV's fatness became vicious because it was thought to be associated with the sins of greed and pride as well as gluttony.

In contrast, the first two Hanoverians seem to have got off lightly from the satirists. Admittedly, though royal bodies might appear in pictorial satire before the 1730s, they were rarely caricatured: for example, the satirical possibilities of Anne's size do not seem to have been exploited in this way even by her sharpest critics.[7] This reticence can be explained by the persistence of the old idea that the king (or queen) was a semi-sacred person and therefore could do no wrong; the related and not entirely inaccurate perception that the real issue was overpowerful ministers (Harley, Walpole), who thus became more appropriate targets of visual satire; and, perhaps most importantly, by the fact that caricature was a new art form in Britain in the first half of the eighteenth century.

But it is also true that Georg Ludwig and his son seem to have given their critics very little 'body' with which to work, whether in prose, poetry or paint. Recall Horace Walpole's famous written recollection of George I when Horace was a small boy: 'the person of the King is as perfect in my memory as if I saw him but yesterday'. But what follows describes the sovereign's dress and demeanour, not his physical features:

---

[6] For George IV's obesity, see J.H. Plumb, *The First Four Georges* (New York, 1967), pp. 137, 167, 177–8. For his perceived extravagance, see ibid., pp. 161–7, 177. For Caroline's weight, see p. 173. For their linkage in obesity and extravagance see George Cruickshank, *Two Green Bags* or *'Ah! Sure Such a Pair was Never Seen so Justly Form'd to Meet by Nature'* (1820), British Museum, London (henceforth BM), Satires 13735. Plumb makes the additional point that George IV's mistresses also grew fatter over the years, and that they, too, became objects of satire: *First Four Georges*, pp. 167–9.

[7] See Herbert M. Atherton, *Political Prints in the Age of Hogarth: A Study of the Ideographic Representation of Politics* (Oxford, 1974), pp. 34, 38, 110; Vincent Carretta, *The Snarling Muse: Verbal and Visual Political Satire from Pope to Churchill* (Philadelphia, 1983), pp. 42, 56, 177, 208; Ragnhild Hatton, *George I: Elector and King* (Cambridge, MA, 1978), p. 259; Jeremy Black, *George II: Puppet of the Politicians?* (Exeter, 2007), p. 16. Satirical poets did comment on Anne's appetite for food, if not her size, when she was a princess, but even this seems to have stopped when she became queen; see Bucholz, 'Stomach of a Queen', pp. 250–52.

It was that of an elderly man, rather pale, and exactly like his pictures and coins; not tall, of an aspect rather good than august, with a dark tie-wig, a plain coat, waistcoat, and breeches of snuff-colored cloth, with stockings of the same color, and a blue riband over all.[8]

When John Toland introduced their future king to English readers in 1705, he described 'a proper, middle-siz'd, well-proportion'd Man, of a gentile Address, and good Appearance'.[9] Indeed, to judge from the surviving statues and portraits taken from life, the physical appearance of George I and George II should have provided little grist for the satirical mill: for example, despite a well-remarked tendency towards jowliness in later life, both men seem to have remained fairly trim, undoubtedly a result of their enthusiasm for perambulation.[10]

Sympathetic observers will note the fine Guelph nose, and hands and faces set in expressions that are not, perhaps, entirely forbidding. Perhaps the only *real* physical attribute of the first two Georges that their opponents could use against them was their shortness of stature: hence the Jacobite song 'The Wee, Wee German Lairdie'.[11] In the end, their almost nondescript physical appearance may explain why professional historians, with the exception of J.H. Plumb, have tended to leave their bodies alone, foregoing the kind of verbal description that they have often applied to Anne or George IV. Perhaps as a result, I would argue, the *actual* physical appearance of George I and George II did not penetrate into the public consciousness in any distinctive way, either then or now.

This presented Jacobite and other opposition satirists with difficulties, but also possibilities. One option was to concentrate on the circle of seeming grotesques that made up the royal entourage: the famous Maypole and the Elephant and

---

[8] Quoted in John Heneage Jesse, *Memoirs of the Court of England from the Revolution in 1688 to the Death of George II*, 3 vols (Philadelphia, 1843), II, p. 212.

[9] John Toland, *An Account of the Courts of Prussia and Hanover* (London, 1705), p. 69. For physical descriptions by later historians, see Plumb, *First Four Georges*, pp. 38–9; Leonard W. Cowie, *Hanoverian England 1714–1837* (London, 1967), p. 43; Joyce Marlow, *The Life and Times of George I* (London, 1973), p. 21; Hatton, *George I*, pp. 25, 170–73.

[10] I wish to thank Dr Ulrike Weiss for the point about George I's jowliness: see Hatton, *George I*, p. 171. César de Saussure, *A Foreign View of England in the Reigns of George I and George II*, trans. and ed. by M. van Muyden (New York, 1902), p. 45 describes the king as 'very corpulent' in 1725, but this description is an outlier. For its refutation, see Hatton, *George I*, pp. 139, 170–71, 349 n. 3 and the late portrait by Georg Wilhelm Lafontaine. For the early Hanoverians walking, see ibid., pp. 133, 170, 264; Andrew C. Thompson, *George II: King and Elector* (New Haven, 2011), p. 100.

[11] For some good-humoured contemporary doggerel about George II's stature, see Jesse, *Court of England,* III, pp. 27–8.

Illustration 8.1　King George I, by Georg Wilhelm Lafontaine (1680–1745), RCIN 405247

Source: Royal Collection Trust/© Her Majesty Queen Elizabeth II 2013.

Illustration 8.2 King George II, after Robert Edge Pine (c. 1730–1788), RCIN 404629

Source: Royal Collection Trust/© Her Majesty Queen Elizabeth II 2013.

Castle, i.e., Madames Schulenburg (later Duchess of Munster and Duchess of Kendal) and Kielmannsegge (later Countess of Darlington and Countess of Leinster);[12] Peter the Wild Boy;[13] the exotic foreign appearance of Mehemet and Mustapha;[14] not to mention the size of the unwieldy Sir Robert Walpole,[15] Queen Caroline[16] and, later, the Duke of Cumberland.[17] As Horace Walpole noted:

[12] For most of the famous quotes and stories, see Plumb, *First Four Georges*, pp. 39–41. Schulenburg is described as 'a tall, thin, bony woman who had grown more interested in money and power than in the delights of the flesh'. For Kielmannsegge, Plumb turns to Horace Walpole's famous description: 'Lady Darlington, whom I saw at my mother's in my infancy, and whom I remember by being terrified at her enormous figure, was as corpulent and ample as the Duchess was long and emaciated. Two fierce black eyes, large and rolling beneath two lofty arched eyebrows, two acres of cheeks spread with crimson, an ocean of neck that overflowed and was not distinguished from the lower parts of her body, and no part restrained by stays – no wonder that a child dreaded such an ogress, and that the mob of London were highly diverted at the importation of so uncommon a seraglio!' See also Charles Mackay, ed., *The Jacobite Songs and Ballads of Scotland from 1688 to 1746* (London, 1861), p. 64: 'The Riding Mare', ll. 24, 27; Jesse, *Court of England*, II, p. 201; Justin McCarthy, *A History of the Four Georges*, 4 vols (New York, 1901), I, p. 7; Wolfgang Michael, *England Under George I*, vol. 1: *The Beginnings of the Hanoverian Dynasty* (London, 1936), pp. 81–5; Mairead McKerracher, *The Jacobite Dictionary* (Glasgow, 2007), *sub* George I. For more sympathetic descriptions, see Hatton, *George I*, pp. 50–51, 99, 135–8.

[13] See Lucy Worsley, *The Courtiers: Splendor and Intrigue in the Georgian Court at Kensington Palace* (New York, 2010), ch. 4, esp. pp. 89–91.

[14] See Hatton, *George I*, pp. 99–100, 132, 142; Worsley, *Courtiers*, pp. 78–81; John M. Beattie, *The English Court in the Reign of George I* (Cambridge, 1967), p. 55. For contemporary comment, see *Nostradamus's Prophecy* [London, 1715?], ll. 21–2; *Directions to a Painter* [London, 1716?], p. 2, l. 79; Mackay, ed., *Jacobite Songs and Ballads*, p. 136: 'Geordie Whelp's Testament', ll. 81–4.

[15] Plumb, *First Four Georges*, p. 70: 'Walpole was a short, dumpy man, weighing rather more than twenty stone'; see also ibid., pp. 71, 85. For contemporary depictions, see Atherton, *Political Prints*, pp. 203–5; Carretta, *The Snarling Muse*, pp. 124, 181–2, 188–92; M. Dorothy George, *English Political Caricature to 1792: A Study of Opinion and Propaganda* (Oxford, 1959), p. 87, plate 25.

[16] Even supposed supporters commented cruelly on Queen Caroline's increasing girth. Thus the Earl of Chesterfield, quoted by Lord Hervey: 'Great George escaped from narrow seas and storms/Now rides at large in Carolina's arms./Bold Jonah thus, as holy writ will tell ye,/A whale received at once into her belly.' Quoted in Black, *George II*, p. 158. Another squib by Chesterfield refers to George's 'haste to run/From blooming twenty to fat fifty-one'. See also Robert Walpole in [Clarke], *The Georgian Era: Memoirs of the Most Eminent Persons, Who Have Flourished in Great Britain from the Accession of George the First to the Demise of George the Fourth,* 4 vols (London, 1832–4), I, pp. 29–32; Plumb, *First Four Georges*, pp. 42, 58, 66; Charles Chenevix-Trench, *George II* (London, 1973), pp. 154, 158.

[17] See Thomas Wright, *Caricature History of the Georges, or, Annals of the House of Hanover* (London, 1876), pp. 168, 213; Paul Kléber Monod, *Jacobitism and the English*

They were food for all the venom of the Jacobites; and indeed nothing could be grosser than the ribaldry that was vomited out in lampoons, libels, and every channel of abuse, against the sovereign and the new court, and chanted even in their hearing about the public streets.[18]

On the one hand, these attacks were part of a traditional opposition critique of court extravagance. The alleged rapacity of the Hanoverian-Whig entourage (in some of the above cases, signalled by their gluttony or sexual depravity), consuming the country and the Stuart patrimony, was a favourite theme of Jacobite balladry in particular. Subsequent research has shown that the court of George I was, indeed, significantly more expensive than that of Queen Anne, and that of George II more expensive than that of his father in turn – all in a period of relatively low inflation.[19] But these critiques may also be seen as part of an eighteenth-century reaction against the sensuality of the Restoration court and society, itself part of a broader move to discipline the body and keep its passions in check.[20]

The other option available to the regime's critics was to elide the physical and psychological characteristics of George's courtiers into those of the king. An examination of the solander boxes in the National Portrait Gallery Archives indicates that in non-official portrayals (miniatures, delftware, title pages) George I is often given a very round face.[21]

People, 1688–1788 (Cambridge, 1993), p. 61. See also depictions of Handel, associated with the Hanoverian court, as a hog: Wright, *Caricature History*, pp. 244–5.

[18] *The Works of Horatio Walpole, Earl of Orford*, 5 vols (London, 1798), IV, pp. 284–5.

[19] For Jacobite ballads bewailing the metaphorical rape of British resources, see *The Plagues of Nod* [London, 1715?], esp. ll. 23–30; Mackay, ed., *Jacobite Songs and Ballads*, pp. 74 ('Jamie the Rover', ll. 17–18 of which compare George I to 'a huge black bull,/ That would devour us at his will'), pp. 133–4 ('Geordie Whelp's Testament', ll. 1–24). See also Atherton, *Political Prints*, p. 111; Hatton, *George I*, ch. 6. For the expense of the early Hanoverian courts, see J.C. Sainty and R.O. Bucholz, *Officials of the Royal Household 1660–1837*, part 1: *Department of the Lord Chamberlain and Associated Offices* (London, 1997), pp. lxvi–lxx and Figure 6: 'Average Annual Issues to the Household, 1660–1837', p. xcviii.

[20] See esp. Porter, *Flesh in the Age of Reason*, chs 4, 7–9, 13; id., 'Bodies of Thought: Thoughts About the Body in Eighteenth-Century England', in Joan H. Pittock and Andrew Wear, eds, *Interpretation and Cultural History* (New York, 1990), pp. 82–108, esp. pp. 88–94. I am grateful to Erin Feichtinger for this reference.

[21] I would like to thank Professor Karen Hearn for suggesting this approach and guiding me through the use of this source. This tendency towards facial puffiness is especially true of miniatures: see B. Arlaud, *George I* [sic] *Wearing the Order of the Garter* (1709); Charles Boit, *George I with the Order of the Garter* (1719); Bernard Lens, *George I* (1718), Victoria and Albert Museum, London, P.64-1987; Anon., *George I*, exhibited Christie's, South Kensington, 23–27 April 2006, no. 1305; Anon., snuffbox, *George I* (Geneva, c. 1770,

This popular tendency to portray 'pudding George' as somewhat heavier than in official portraits is significant. If it does not come from his physical body, from whence does it come? When Jacobite writers focused on the king, they generally drew an unflattering comparison with the Pretender, the titular James III. They did so by emphasising George's German identity and his failure to learn much English,[22] which somehow went hand in hand with portraying him as cruel, coarse and sensual, implying a far greater degree of indulgence in food, drink and sex than the official portrait images suggest.[23] This was where his body came in. George was depicted by his critics as a man bent on sublunary pleasures, unable to master his bodily appetites and, by implication, unfit to rule a country.[24] Take sex. From 1714 there was actual sex with kings taking place at the English court for the first time in a quarter century, and it was a godsend to the regime's critics. Apart from its presumed frequency, satirists harped on the allegedly appalling bodily appearance of the king's reputed mistresses, Schulenburg and Kielmannsegge in particular. In the *Epistle to Sir Scipio Hill* of 1720 both George's love of routine and his taste in women make the same point about his lack of refinement or imagination:

> To vast Balena [Kielmannsegge?] nightly he repairs.
> For her, his Wife and Children he removes,

---

in which the king is portrayed as very fat), exhibited Sotheby's, 9 Nov. 2000, no. L 00529. See also a Bristol delftware charger depicting George I (1714–1727), exhibited Sotheby's, 16 Oct. 1967, lot 75 and another exhibited Christie's New York, 23 Jan. 2009, lot 137; and George Vertue after Godfrey Kneller, the title page of John Chamberlayne, *Magnae Britanniae Notitia* (London, 1716). It might be objected that some of the identifications of these images as George I are doubtful, and in a few cases bear little resemblance to him; but the misidentification of these images of fat men as Georg Ludwig only strengthens the argument being made here that his body was often distorted in the public imagination.

[22] 'Thank, that thy King brought from a foreign land,/Cannot be understood, nor understand' from *On the Thanksgiving-Day* [London?, 1715], ll. 17–18.

[23] For cruelty, see *Rightful Monarchy: or Revolution Tyranny. A Satyr. Being a Dialogue Between High-Dutch Illustrious and Low-Dutch Glorious* ([London?], 1722), pp. 20–22, 30–31; *An Epistle to Sir Scipio Hill* [London, 1720?], ll. 23–9; *Directions to a Painter*, p. 2, ll. 70–74, 89–92; *The Character of Sultan Galga, the Present Cham of Tartary, Drawn by a Walachian, who Had Been His Favourite for Several Years* [London, 1718], p. 2. For coarseness, see *Epistle to Sir Scipio Hill*, l. 28. For drink, see *Rightful Monarchy*, pp. 3–4. For sensuality, food and sex, see below.

[24] For the eighteenth-century value for mastery of the body, see Porter, *Flesh in the Age of Reason*, esp. chs 4, 7, 13.

Illustration 8.3 Portrait of George I, after Godfrey Kneller, print made by Jacob Houbraken (1746)
Source: British Museum, London, 1977, U.1263/© Trustees of the British Museum.

And wallows in her Fat, and thinks he loves.[25]

From here, it was a short step to portray the king *himself* as fat. The result has confused even historians. Thus one scholar quotes a Jacobite satire depicting George and an obese mistress in bed, then adds to the confusion over his body by mistaking which mistress was being bedded:

> George's mistress, Melusine von der Schulenburg, whom he created Duchess of Munster in 1716 and Duchess of Kendal in 1719, was very fat [sic], *like her lover* [sic, my italics], and their size was a source of much Jacobite hilarity. In 'The Bed-Testor's Plot', George and Munster fall through a bed while fornicating when the structure collapses under their combined weight; the unhappy monarch cries out that it must be a Jacobite plot![26]

In fact, it was Kielmannsegge who was, apart from actually being George's sister, heavy. Schulenburg was notably tall and – like George – relatively trim. A number of writers seem to confuse the king's two famous female companions.[27] In any case, his apparent sexual attraction to women who did not fit conventional English standards of beauty added to the image of a coarse, tasteless voluptuary.[28]

---

[25] *Epistle to Sir Scipio Hill*, ll. 20–22. See also *Directions to a Painter*, p. 2, l. 97; *Character of Sultan Galga*, p. 2: 'If he gives any Preference to one Woman before another, she that hath most Flesh and Fat, is his Choice. His present Sultana-Concubine is of so vast a Bulk, that were she not the Fattest, she wou'd yet be the largest Woman in Tartary.' See also the testimony of Lord Chesterfield in Claudia Gold, *The King's Mistress: The True and Scandalous Story of the Woman Who Stole the Heart of George I* (London, 2012), p. 128. George II's tastes also seem to have run to full-figured women: see Thompson, *George II*, p. 136.

[26] Monod, *Jacobitism*, p. 58, quoting Bodleian Library, Oxford, Rawlinson MS. D 383, f. 77.

[27] Thus Basil Williams (*The Whig Supremacy 1714–1760* [Oxford, 1939], p. 146) writes of 'the Baroness von Schulenberg [sic], a lady of opulent charms, [and] the Baroness Kielmannsegge, whose scrawny figure was likened to a hop-pole by the ribald populace'. See also McCarthy, *Four Georges*, I, p. 266. Many older historians also seem to take as given that Kielmannsegge was a mistress, whether or not she was also a sibling: see Plumb, *First Four Georges*, pp. 39–41 and n. For the contemporary charge of incest, see *Rightful Monarchy*, p. 32.

[28] *The Weekly Journal or Saturday's Post*, no. 130, 27 May 1721, complained 'we are ruin'd by Footmen, Pimps, Pathicks, Parasites, Bawds, Whores, nay, what is more vexatious, old ugly Whores! Such as could not find Entertainment in the most hospitable Hundreds of old Drury.' For additional harping on the king's taste in mistresses, see *Directions to a Painter*, p. 2: 'But place his bulky whores behind his back' (l. 97); *The Character of Sultan Galga*, p. 2; Mackay, ed., *Jacobite Songs and Ballads*, p. 65 ('The Riding Mare', l. 24), pp. 67–9 ('The Sow's Tail to Geordie'), pp. 83–4 ('Petticoats Loose'), pp. 134–5 ('Geordie Whelp's Testament',

The widely told tale of George I's death – rumoured to have been precipitated by a bout of indigestion 'after gorging himself on a huge platter of melons' – confirms the verdict.[29]

The *Bed-Testor's Plot*, quoted above, also portrays the king as stupid. This assessment was common even among contemporary Whigs: Lady Mary Wortley Montagu labelled him 'an honest blockhead'; Lord Chesterfield called him 'an honest and dull German gentleman ... lazy and inactive even in his pleasures'; while the Tory Dr Johnson charged that George 'knew nothing and desired to know nothing, did nothing and desired to do nothing'.[30] Johnson is often accused of Jacobitism, and Jacobites particularly associated the king's alleged stupidity with his animal sensuality, attributing to him a 'base, poltroon, sordid mind' according to the popular ballad 'Geordie Whelp's Testament'.[31] These characteristics were linked, in turn, to his disastrous marital history: George was a 'Hum-drum Clown/Adorn'd with Capricornus Crown' according to *A Tale of a Man and His Mare* (1721), which, of course, cast doubt on the legitimacy of the rest of the line.[32] *Nostradamus's Prophecy* (1715) warned of the consequences:

> When a Throne is giv'n to an ignorant Fool,
> Whom wise Men laugh at, and whom Harlot's rule.[33]

---

ll. 52–3). For later opinion, see [Clarke], *Georgian Era*, I, p. 19: 'The taste exhibited by the prince, in the selection of his mistresses, was outrageously bad'; Jesse, *Court of England,* II, p. 201; McCarthy, *Four Georges,* I, p. 7; Williams, *Whig Supremacy*, p. 146; and Plumb, *First Four Georges*, pp. 39–40.

[29] Kay Mann, *The German Connection* (Bridgewater, 1993), p. 3. According to Hatton, *George I*, p. 282, the offending fruits were strawberries and oranges.

[30] All quoted in Cowie, *Hanoverian England*, p. 44. See also *A Sacred Ode to King George* [London?, 1714?], l. 35. 'Gathering Rant' refers to George I as 'Yon German cuif [simpleton] that fills the throne' (l. 5), in Gilbert S. MacQuoid, ed., *Jacobite Songs and Ballads* (London, 1887), p 141. In the *Dunciad*, Alexander Pope characterised father and son as follows: 'Still Dunce the second reigns like Dunce the first' (Book I, l. 6). For later expressions of this view, see McCarthy, *Four Georges,* I, p. 59; Plumb, *First Four Georges*, p. 39 and below.

[31] 'Geordie Whelp's Testament', l. 5, in Mackay, ed., *Jacobite Songs and Ballads*, p. 133.

[32] *A Tale of a Man and his Mare, Found in an Old Manuscript, Never before Printed* ([Edinburgh?], 1721), p. 5. 'O What's the Matter wi' the Whigs' opines 'Our king he has a cuckold's luck' (l. 29); 'Whurry Whigs Awa' refers to 'This beggar cuckold king' (l. 131), both in MacQuoid, ed., *Jacobite Songs and Ballads*, pp. 82, 129. See also *Directions to a Painter*: 'On his soure Brow ... /A Pair of well-spread Brow-Antlets set' (l. 83); and Murray Pittock, *Poetry and Jacobite Politics in Eighteenth-Century Britain and Ireland* (New York, 1994), p. 64. I am grateful to Amy Oberlin for the point about legitimacy.

[33] *Nostradamus's Prophecy*, ll. 36–7.

In *The Character of Sultan Galga, the Present Cham of Tartery* (1718) George's very physical demeanour marks him as a man out of his element, an imposter on the British throne:

> so little was he formed by Nature for a Throne, that he seems conscious of it himself, and never makes a worse Figure than when he appears with the Ensigns of Royalty; at which Seasons, he is observ'd to have that Sort of uneasy, awkward Look, that a Man hath, when he is ashamed of something about him, and afraid the Company shou'd discover it.[34]

These themes, largely derived from Jacobite propaganda, became commonplaces in the next century. Thus Clarke's *The Georgian Era* (1832) reasserts the king's 'licentious pleasures' and 'outrageously bad' taste in mistresses, and says of George himself that 'his decidedly foreign appearance and manners, when they became known, lowered him materially in public estimation'. This is followed by several anecdotes about the king's ignorance of doings at court and helplessness in the hands of his ministers.[35] Jesse's *Court of England* (1843) describes a 'seraglio of hideous German prostitutes' while stressing George's foreignness and supposed lack of dignity: 'A foreigner, as he was, in all his taste and habits; ignorant, debauched, and illiterate; inelegant in his person, and ungraceful in his manners.'[36] Justin McCarthy's *The Four Georges*, first published in 1884, describes '[a] dull, stolid, and profligate king, fond of drink and of low conversation, without dignity of appearance or manner' whose 'strongest taste was for ugly women ... heavy dining and heavy drinking'. For good measure, McCarthy also adds the canard that he was heavy: 'no-body pretended to feel any thrill of sentimental emotion towards *portly* [my italics], stolid, sensual George the First'.[37] Perhaps the most influential exponent of this image was Wolfgang Michael, whose *England Under George I: The Beginnings of the Hanoverian*

---

[34] *Character of Sultan Galga*, p. 1. Interestingly, the author gives 'Galga' credit for abstemious living: 'In his Diet he is temperate; not sumptuous in his Cloths: Uses little Exercise: Is regular in his Hours; and may, properly enough, be stiled a sober Man.' But his good health is equally attributed 'to the Inactivity of the Mind, as much as to the strength of his natural Constitution'. For the charge that George was awkward in public, see also Michael, *England Under George I*, p. 88; W.H. Wilkins, *The Love of an Uncrowned Queen: Sophia Dorothea, Consort of George I* (New York, 1906), pp. 47, 52.

[35] [Clarke], *Georgian Era*, I, pp. 18, 19, 20, 25–7.

[36] Jesse, *Court of England*, II, pp. 200–201. See also pp. 215–16: 'His general appearance was undignified; his address awkward.'

[37] McCarthy, *Four Georges*, I, pp. 7, 59, 61.

Dynasty was researched and written at the end of the nineteenth century, but only translated into English in 1936:

> King George was of medium height, and without real dignity in his appearance; his countenance, as seen in portraits, was heavy, broad, and lifeless, with a vacant look in his large eyes; he had a big and broad nose, an ugly mouth, and no trace of a moustache. His face, framed in a dark wig, might almost have been that of a woman, except for its selfish hardness.

In keeping with long-standing physiognomic theory, George's undistinguished appearance becomes a sign of intellectual mediocrity: 'he had inherited none of his mother's gifts, but had a solid understanding and a certain stock of ideas. He was slow in thought and action, and never rash in his decisions.'[38]

With war looming in 1939, Basil Williams's *Whig Supremacy* complained that the first two Georges came 'with characters well set in the German mould'. In the 1960s, even the judicious Dorothy Marshall opined 'it would have been difficult even for the modern propagandist press to have built him [George I] up as a figure of romance', not least because 'his two official mistresses were unattractive and greedy'.[39] As late as 1973, just five years before Ragnhild Hatton's influential reassessment, George II's biographer, Charles Chenevix Trench described his father as 'a lout and a bore'. Once again physiognomy mirrored personality: 'The countenance ... framed in a dark periwig, was commonplace. A big nose, an ugly mouth, a surly expression showed no liveliness or interest. George I's eyes, slightly bulging, were dull and vacant.' In the same year, Joyce Marlow finds him 'limited in intellect ... consuming vast quantities of food was a major obsession'.[40] This picture naturally made its way into the classroom: here is how Clayton and David Roberts characterised the first Hanoverian king of Great Britain in their *A History of England 1688 to the Present*, probably the most popular survey of English history for American undergraduates in the 1980s: 'George I was coarse, sensual, unsocial, and not very bright. He spoke English poorly and cared so little for Londoners that he wished to plant turnips in lovely St. James Park [sic].'[41]

---

[38] Michael, *England Under George I*, p. 80. See pp. 80–89 for critical description of his entourage and court style.

[39] Williams, *Whig Supremacy*, pp. 145–6, which also complained that the English people 'were shocked at the grossness of George I's amours'; Dorothy Marshall, *Eighteenth-Century England* (London, 1962), p. 75.

[40] Chenevix-Trench, *George II*, pp. 1, 39; Marlow, *George I*, p. 21.

[41] Clayton Roberts and David Roberts, *A History of England 1688 to the Present*, 2 vols (2nd edn, Englewood Cliffs, NJ, 1985), II, p. 428.

This image seeped into the popular record as well.[42] It was probably inevitable that romance writers, in particular, would embrace a Jacobite perspective – what could be more romantic than a king who never was or the failed escapade of the '45? It follows that the Hanoverians would be portrayed as the mirror images of the elegant, urbane Stuarts, slaves to the desires of their ungainly bodies. Perhaps the apogee (or nadir) of this view appears in R. Folkestone Williams's three-decker novel *Maids of Honour: A Tale of the Court of George I* (1845), which presents the first Hanoverian king of Great Britain 'as deficient in moral as he was in intellectual recommendations'; 'a character with whom delicacy and refinement were entirely unknown'; the maintainer of 'a harem of Hanoverian mistresses, whose persons were of so dominant an ugliness as to repel the most easily pleased'. All of this was signalled by his unprepossessing appearance:

> The individual seated in the chair was an elderly man plainly dressed, and still more plainly featured. He wore the usual heavy wig of innumerable curls; but it failed to confer dignity on a countenance, particular only for its want of refinement. Beetling brows, shaded eyes, in their general expression as dull as those of a dead fish; the lower part of the face was vulgar and sensual, and marked with wrinkles at the corners of the heavy mouth, indicative of distrust and apprehension.
>
> The ordinary look was grave even to sternness, changing frequently to suspicion; but the more careful observer might have noticed in the features a wild, uneasy expression, that spoke of a mind disturbed by some secret disquietude. The whole face was without a single gleam of intellect; it gave evidence neither of heart nor of mind; it seemed to belong to some member of the animal kingdom, as ignorant of human knowledge as incapable of human sympathies.
>
> The form was as ungraceful as the countenance was unprepossessing. Physical power had been given at the expense of symmetry, and broad shoulders, large extremities, short body, a protruding stomach, and thick legs, seemed rivalling each other which should contribute the greatest share of vulgarity to the general effect.

That effect is boiled down by the author into a single phrase: 'every inch *not* a king'.[43]

---

[42] See, for example, the popular (if not always accurate) guidebook by Mann, *The German Connection*, p. 2, which describes George I as 'low of stature, of features coarse, of aspect dull and placid'.

[43] R. Folkestone Williams, *Maids of Honour: A Tale of the Court of George I*, 3 vols (London, 1845), I, pp. 2–3, 16–17, 132–3. See also pp. 129–30: George I 'was as repulsive in aspect, as he was undignified in his carriage ... the Elector of Hanover was arbitrary, bigoted, avaricious, and profligate ... also stupid, obstinate, passionate, and vulgar ... he neither looked like a king, behaved like a king, nor thought like a king.' On pp. 53–4 a servant observes helpfully that 'an honest,

A corollary to this attitude towards Georg Ludwig is sympathy for his ex-wife, Sophia Dorothea of Celle, who is generally portrayed in romance as a sylph among swine. Thus, in Helen de Guerry Simpson's 1935 novel *Saraband for Dead Lovers*, the unfortunate princess prays to God to be delivered from marriage with the Hanoverian brute: 'Why, he's not even polite. He walks like a groom, and belches at meals. He scratches, I saw him, and his face is horribly fat already.'[44] Doris Leslie's *The Rebel Princess* (1970) is yet more explicit in conversation with her mother, the Duchess of Brunswick-Lüneburg: 'I'd sooner be married to a pig! He looks like a pig, he behaves like a pig and he is a pig! Oh Maman, how could you!'[45] On the wedding night in Simpson's novel, the fictional Georg Ludwig consummates the arranged marriage by first devouring a roast chicken and then committing rape upon his consort. In the somewhat sanitised 1948 film of *Saraband*, Ealing's first colour feature, George is played as a calculating brute by the hulking Peter Bull, who had a large, heavy face (see Illustration 8.4).[46] In contrast, Sophia Dorothea's love interest, Count Königsmarck, is played by the dashing Stewart Granger.

The physical George II should be less elusive than his father if only because his reign was longer, allowing for more depictions. Early portraits, such as those by Charles Jervas and Enoch Seeman, seem to tell a clear story: a man of short stature and slim-to-average build. Ridiculed by Jacobites as the 'Wee, wee German Lairdie', modern authors sometimes elide George II's short physical stature into a smallness of mind: thus, according to Basil Williams, he was '[a] choleric, obstinate little man with violent prejudices and a great sense of his own importance'.[47] Though it was often said that his parts were proportional,

---

cheerful face ain't so necessary to a king as it is to a coachman; so I don't pretend to blame King George on account of his want of handsomeness. His appearance might do very well for a throne, however ill it would become a coach-box.' The novel also contains the obligatory reflections on the ugliness of the king's mistresses and the 'two heathen Turks' (I, pp. 55–7, 135).

[44] Helen Simpson, *Saraband for Dead Lovers* (London, 1935), p. 58.

[45] Doris Leslie, *The Rebel Princess* (London, 1970), p. 23. See subsequent descriptions: on p. 30 the Countess of Platen opines 'He does look rather like a pig, especially nude'; on pp. 32–3 Sophia Dorothea describes Georg Ludwig as 'a sweaty-faced pig ... he's so ugly and horrible and fat!'; on p. 37 he is described as 'blond, heavily jowled and, despite his youth, paunchy'; on p. 103, dancing at a ball in 1689, 'for so fat a little man he was not ungraceful'; on p. 164 he is described as having a 'fat pudding face'; on p. 273 as 'this bloated, beery leery little man'.

[46] See Alan Burton and Tim O'Sullivan, eds, *The Cinema of Basil Dearden and Michael Relph* (Edinburgh, 2009), pp. 90–96. Interestingly and not entirely coincidentally, in his last film role, Bull would impersonate the famously fat Queen Anne in one of the most insulting royal portrayals ever offered on film, 1983's *Yellowbeard*.

[47] Williams, *Whig Supremacy*, pp. 343–4. See also Thompson, *George II*, p. 7; McKerracher, *The Jacobite Dictionary*, sub George II: 'Vain, small and dressy, he was always susceptible to

Illustration 8.4 Peter Bull as George I in *Saraband for Dead Lovers* (Ealing, 1948)

Source: Courtesy of STUDIOCANAL Films Ltd.

George's large head seemed to promise greater bulk, and later images imply this. For example, the portrait from circa 1753 by Thomas Worlidge shows a double chin and noticeable *embonpoint*; while prints on title pages often portray a very round-faced man. To these we might add the satirical prints *Solomon in His Glory* (c. 1738), which also gives the king a round, heavy face, and *Three Courtiers* (1731), which gives him bulk. A few of the equestrian portraits and those depicting the king at Dettingen portray him as somewhat fleshy but athletic. But other prints show a rather slim man.[48] In fact, the king's face and body did grow rounder over the years, but one would have to stretch the definition of stout to make it fit the 1758 full-length by John Shackleton or the 1759 image by Robert Edge Pine, which was said to have been particularly true to life (see Illustration 8.2).

---

flattery'. J.H. Plumb, *First Four Georges*, p. 65 writes: 'Like his father George was stupid but complicated'. For a more positive description, see Chenevix-Trench, *George II*, pp. 6–7.

[48] See John Wootton, *George II at the Battle of Dettingen* (1743) vs. *The Court Fright* (1744), BM, Satires 2606, and *A Very Extraordinary Motion* (1744), BM, Satires 2613.

Illustration 8.5 *A Cheap and Easy Method of Improving English Swine's Flesh by a German Method of Feeding* (London, 1743)

Source: British Museum, London, 1868,0808.3743/© Trustees of the British Museum.

It was during the reign of George II that popular satirical prints began to depict the royal body. Some of these likenesses appear to be rooted more or less in the king's actual appearance, but they are not true caricatures: while the king's body may be caught in a sexual act (*Solomon in His Glory* of 1738), a moment of anger (*The C[our]t Shittle-Cock* of 1740) or even defecation (*A Very Extraordinary Motion* of 1744), his physical appearance is not exaggerated to make a point about character. Though the royal body was frequently portrayed in such prints as thicker than it actually was, its proportions and features do not seem to signify anything beyond themselves, as they would do for his successors.[49]

---

[49] See, for example, *Three Courtiers* (1731), BM, Satires 1870; *The C[our]t Shittle Cock* (1740), BM, Satires 2451; *The Screen* (1742), BM, Satires 2539; *A Very Extraordinary Motion* (1744), BM, Satires 2613.

This does not mean that the king's body was not turned against him. As Paul Monod puts it, Jacobites saw George II as a re-run of George I: 'he was a fool, a tyrant, a "German Savage" and a servant of the devil, and at times he even inherited the turnip-hoe and cuckold's horns'.[50] Like his father, he was attacked for his sexual escapades: *The Festival of the Golden Rump* of 1737 portrays him as a satyr and *Solomon in his Glory* of the following year criticises him for seeking physical consolation from Amalie Sophie von Wallmoden, the future Countess of Yarmouth, so soon after Caroline's death.[51] But George II was also denigrated for his stiff self-importance, as in *A Cheap and Easy Method of Improving English Swine's Flesh by a German Method of Feeding* (1743); his choleric temperament in *The C[our]t Shittle-Cock* (1740); and his militaristic bearing and alleged disdain for learning and art in Alexander Pope's *The Impertinent, or, a Visit to the Court: A Satyr* (1733):

> The Captain's honest, Sirs, and that's enough,
> Tho' his soul's bullet, and his body buff.
> He spits fore'right; his haughty chest before,
> Like batt'ring rams, beats open ev'ry door;
> And with a face as red, and as awry,
> As Herod's hang-dogs in old tapestry,
> Scarecrow to boys, the breeding woman's curse,
> Has yet a strange ambition to look worse;
> Confounds the civil, keeps the rude in awe,
> Jests like a licens'd Fool, commands like law.[52]

In all three cases, it is the *carriage* of the royal body that reveals character. Thus 'Geordie Whelp's Testament' refers to 'my graceless son,/That awkward ass'.[53]

As with George I, this negative portrayal became the standard one in the nineteenth century: Jesse says of George II that 'he was distinguished by no

---

[50] Monod, *Jacobitism*, p. 59.
[51] See Black, *George II*, pp. 161–2.
[52] Alexander Pope, *The Impertinent, or a Visit to Court: A Satyr* [Satire IV after Donne] (London, 1733), ll. 262–71.
[53] 'Geordie Whelp's Testament', ll. 66–7, in Mackay, ed., *Jacobite Songs and Ballads*, p. 135. Atherton, *Political Prints*, p. 36 characterises George II's appearance in prints as follows: 'stiff, erect, goggle-eyed; with a high prominent nose; an inscrutable smile on the thin, tight lips'. See also Michael, *England Under George I*, p. 85. For George's character, behaviour and artistic patronage, see Black, *George II*, ch. 5, passim.

graces either of mind or person'; in Clarke's *Georgian Era*, he is the strutting fool who annually dons his Oudenarde uniform to parade before amused courtiers:

> Sure such a day was never known!
> Such a king! and such a throne![54]

And then there is the medium of modern popular cinema. In the 1948 film *Bonnie Prince Charlie*, the doomed Stuart prince is played by David Niven at the height of his urbane charm. In contrast, the Hanoverians are portrayed as coarse and ruthless: George II, played by the Czech actor Martin Miller, a paunchy, strutting boaster with a bad German film accent. But the hostile popular portrayal of the bodies of the first two Georges only reached its widest possible audience (and lowest depths) very recently with the appearance of Georg August in the 2011 Hollywood blockbuster, Disney's *Pirates of the Caribbean: On Stranger Tides*. The king's character is identified in the film only as 'King George', but it is pretty clear from the period dress and furnishings that it has to be George II. Indeed, he is so identified in the official Disney wiki, his character said to be inspired by 'the notorious king of the same name'. The wiki gives the king's distinguishing characteristics as 'Rude, greedy', his appearance as 'Obese, white wig'.[55] In the film, aptly described by one major critic as 'long, expensive

---

[54] Jesse, *Court of England*, III, p. 25; anonymous courtier, quoted in [Clarke], *Georgian Era*, I, p. 39. Jesse, *Court of England,* III, p. 27 is more complimentary about George's physical appearance: 'Though George the Second had never been handsome, his appearance in middle age is described as being neither unpleasing nor altogether undignified. His face, of which the distinguished characteristics were prominent eyes and an aquiline nose, wore a pleasing and good-humored expression; and his figure, though so short as almost to come under the denomination of diminutive, is said to have been extremely well proportioned.' See the similar description in Michael, *England Under George I*, p. 85. The nineteenth-century novelist R. Folkestone Williams (*Maids of Honour,* I, pp. 16–17, 163) sees this George as worse than his father, despite a somewhat more promising appearance: 'there sat a young man rather short of stature, and somewhat pinched in features. The expression of his countenance would have been repulsive, had not a sense of good humour, mixed with animal enjoyment visible in the lower part of his face, redeemed in a slight degree the narrow forehead and unintelligent eyes that made his ordinary look so very ordinary. There certainly was no one feature that could be styled handsome. But though plain, there was a deal of good nature in the countenance, that gave it a great advantage over the dull and harsh physiognomy of his father. For be it known that the portrait we have been attempting to sketch is that of the Prince of Wales.' '[H]is son the Prince of Wales, was allowed the merit of exceeding his august parent in the coarseness and vulgarity of his disposition.'

[55] http://disney.wikia.com/wiki/King_George_II. The wiki is not entirely inaccurate: the king is described as living in St James's Palace and his 'Likes' are listed as: 'Things going his way, giving orders'.

and bombastic', George II is played for laughs as a petulant child, hulking over his food and possessions, by the late, distinguished, and decidedly portly, British actor Richard Griffiths.[56]

What does this distorting mirror tell us? The obvious explanation for the skewed portrayal of the bodies of the first two Hanoverian monarchs of Great Britain would seem to be anti-German prejudice. We know that Britons called the Dutch 'butterboxes' in the seventeenth century, and portrayed them as heavy, dim and unsophisticated in eighteenth-century satirical prints.[57] How did they feel about Germans? Were Germans similarly associated with fatness, stupidity and oafishness in the early modern period? It is not entirely clear that they were. It is true that, according to Panikos Panayi, for most of the early modern period, Germans in England were associated either with Faustian mysticism or animal sensuality and coarseness. The latter stereotype survived into the eighteenth century, often manifesting itself in the portrayal of Germans as drunks. Thus Defoe: 'Drunkenness, the darling favourite of hell/Chose Germany to rule, and rules so well.'[58] This is consistent with much of the negative characterisation of George I, in particular, as described above, but it does not explain the attribution of fatness. A search of Eighteenth Century Collections Online (ECCO) under the terms 'fat German' reveals only six references in different works in the eighteenth century, the earliest being George Lillo's *Marina* of 1738. Is it significant that a search under 'fat Frenchman' for the same period – a period in which France obsessed English writers far more than the German states did – yields only two such references?

Perhaps the attribution of fatness was meant to convey the sense that the new, German line was depleting the country of resources. The last time that Germans had figured in English public discourse was during the controversy over the poor, displaced Palatines in 1709–1712. Ostensibly the victims of Louis XIV's military aggrandisement and religious persecution, these Rhineland Germans were portrayed by their critics as stupid, lazy and greedy, '[s]trangers that were come over to devour the Land' – just as George I and his entourage were later accused of doing.[59] It is possible that he and his son were stand-ins for English

---

[56] Roger Ebert, http://www.rogerebert.com/reviews/pirates-of-the-caribbean-on-stranger-tides-2011. The author's request to reproduce an image from the film of Mr Griffiths as George II was refused by the Disney Corporation; however, the image is readily available via Google Images by searching under 'Richard Griffiths, George II'.

[57] Atherton, *Political Prints*, p. 88.

[58] Quoted in Panikos Panayi, 'Germans in Eighteenth-Century Britain', in id., ed., *Germans in Britain since 1500* (London, 1996), pp. 29–48, esp. pp. 44–5; see also A. Shadwell, 'The German Colony in London', *National Review*, 26 (1896), p. 804.

[59] *A View of the Queen and Kingdom's Enemies, in the Case of the Poor Palatines* [London, 1711?], p. 6. See also William Cunningham, *Alien Immigrants to England*

feeling about needy continental war refugees, Britain's dependent German allies and perhaps war itself. After the middle of the eighteenth century, the only consistently negative portrayal of Germans in satirical prints is that of German mercenary soldiers.[60] For much of the period, Hanover was seen in Great Britain as a drain on British financial and military resources; is it so surprising that their German rulers would be seen that way too?

But why have the lies told above had such a long shelf-life? Conditioned by hostile portrayals that fit a Romantic Jacobite sensibility, and perhaps still bound by prejudice against Germans and against people of size, it would appear that, on some level, we *want* the early Hanoverians to be fat. While it is true that a moderate fleshiness was once seen as a sign of prosperity,[61] obesity has long been associated in the unthinking corners of the popular mind with gluttony, stupidity, laziness and an obsession with sensual pleasure. In the words of Roy Porter, 'grossness bespoke greed, lack of self-control and the vulgarity of temper associated with low life'.[62] These are all character traits frequently, if unfairly, attributed to the early Hanoverians – every inch not a king. When a monarch becomes fat it means either rapacious gluttony for everything life and a kingdom have to offer (Henry VIII, George IV) or stupidity (Anne and, in some portrayals, Victoria). Britain's intellectual monarchs are slim: Charles II, William III.[63] Is it any wonder that the foreign-born kings of the period 1714–1760 tend to be portrayed as both 1) dull disappointments, and 2) fat?

(2nd edn, New York, 1969), p. 251; Alison Olson, 'The English Reception of the Huguenots, Palatines and Salzburgers, 1680–1734: A Comparative Analysis', in Randolph Vigne and Charles Littleton, eds, *From Strangers to Citizens: The Integration of Immigrant Communities in Britain, Ireland and Colonial America, 1550–1750* (Brighton, 2001), pp. 481–91, esp. pp. 481, 485–7; H.T. Dickinson, 'The Poor Palatines and the Parties', *English Historical Review*, 82 (1967), pp. 464–85, esp. p. 473.

[60] See Atherton, *Political Prints*, p. 184.
[61] See Porter, *Flesh in the Age of Reason*, pp. 239–40; Wright, *Caricature History*, pp. 175–6, 209–10; William Hogarth, *Beer Street* (1751).
[62] Porter, *Flesh in the Age of Reason*, p. 239.
[63] Both Henry VIII and, possibly, George IV would appear to disprove the rule, but it is important to recall that our subject is popular stereotypes and reputations, not the considered views of scholarly biographers. For example, popular cinematic treatments – from Charles Laughton's star turn in *The Private Life of Henry VIII* (1933), through Peter Ustinov's portrayal of George IV in *Beau Brummell* (1954), to more recent treatments ranging from *Carry on Henry* (1971) to *The Tudors* (2007–2010) – stress the *appetites* of both men, not their intellectual interests. I am grateful to my colleague, Professor John Donoghue, for challenging me on this point.

Chapter 9

Monarchy, Affection and Empire: The Hanoverian Dynasty in Eighteenth-Century America

Brendan McConville

When Pennsylvanian Ebenezer Hazard travelled to Williamsburg, Virginia, in 1777, he toured the state capital's main church and public buildings. Hazard noted that the elegant coat of arms of the House of Hanover that had once hung at the entrance to the House of Burgesses had been burnt during the iconoclastic violence that finished the empire in 1776. Nonetheless, a full-length, life-size Van Dyck portrait of Queen Anne continued to hang in the capital's courtrooms. More astonishingly, similar-sized portraits of George II and his popular queen, Caroline, looked down on the Virginia house's would-be republicans in the main assembly room as they debated war and republican revolution.[1]

Well beyond July 1776, many in the American camp continued to venerate Protestant monarchs long past. Even as the war raged in 1778, a piece carried in the Norwich (Connecticut) *Packet* denounced the Scottish (tyrannical) influence in the British nation; especially appalling was the reappearance of tartan cloth and kilts in public! This sort of thing 'was forbid in the time of that real King, GEORGE the SECOND'. As late as 1787, Yale College had its portrait of George I prominently displayed.[2] For these Americans, even in the midst of a republican revolution, the post-1688 British monarchy commanded respect. George III might have been politically corrupted, but that did not mean monarchy per se was bad; nor did it lessen affection for the earlier monarchs in the Hanoverian dynasty, who had protected the colonists from France, Spain and Catholics in general.

---

[1] Historical Society of Pennsylvania, Philadelphia, Hazard Family Papers, *Ebenezer Hazard Journal*, 1 June 1777.

[2] Luigi Castiglioni, *Viaggio: Travels in the United States of North America, 1785–87*, ed. by Joseph and Nesta Ewan (Syracuse, NY, 1983), p. 248; *The Norwich Packet*, 22 June 1778, p. 4.

What Hazard saw in the Virginia House of Burgesses suggests that, even after independence, Americans still understood these earlier Hanoverian monarchs as just rulers. It is fair to say that, in many respects, provincial Americans had embraced the Hanoverians more enthusiastically than subjects in the home islands did, right up to the moment of independence. Provincials manifested none of the cynicism and passive hostility towards the Hanoverians so widespread in England, and in fact routinely expressed affection, even devotion, to George I and George II.

Why? Certainly there must be an explanation for such a historical anomaly, the enthusiasm for monarchy in a society that quickly gave way to an enthusiastically republican society.

I

This affection for monarchy in America rested on four factors that produced strong attachment to the Hanoverian dynasty. First, those in control of the primary forms of mass communication, the printers and writers of provincial print culture in all its forms, and the Protestant ministers who preached from the pulpits, devoted themselves to advocating for the Hanoverian dynasty from the moment George I ascended to the throne until the descent into chaos in 1774. Second, imperial authorities successfully established a cycle of public rites and political holidays that celebrated the Hanoverian rulers and Protestant monarchs generally. Such rites became common in towns and villages and relatively standardised in the course of the eighteenth century. Third, trade ties and consumption of British goods reinforced the connections to empire and allowed those ties to be personalised by the purchase of goods bearing the royal arms or royal likenesses. Finally, in George II Americans had a king who reigned for 33 years, personally led British troops in combat against the French and was understood as guiding the empire towards its great victory in the Seven Years War. Celebrated by the press and prayed for by preachers, he was the only monarch most Americans ever knew when he died in 1760, and his reign played mightily into understanding of what a king should be. And certainly, the hostility of his long-time nemesis, the deposed Catholic house of Stuart, only enhanced his stature. Collectively, these forces created a monarchical culture that even the Revolution itself could not immediately erase.

Contemporary Americans cherish press freedom, and volumes have gone into tracing its origins back into the colonial past. Generally, the tendency has been to root that freedom in the famous Zenger Crisis (1733–1735) in New

York City. More than one twentieth-century scholar has asserted that freedom of the press began then, though some revisions on that claim have occurred in recent decades. In regard to the empire and the Hanoverian dynasty, though, no freedom of the press existed. No vehicle in America could be used to publicly criticise the Hanoverian dynasty in print or in rite or ritual until 1775. For certain, a few papers outside the ring of government patronage or licensing control complained about royal governors or other appointees, became upset with suspending clauses in money bills and sometimes chafed under wartime requisitions or attempts to press colonials into the British navy. Even in these cases, though, all were quite careful to avoid criticising the empire or the royal family directly, or even implicitly.[3]

The realm of letters was relatively small in any event. Although general literacy was high, and among that generally literate population were a few Benjamin Franklins and Roger Shermans, the actual number of college-educated people who might have mounted a serious intellectual challenge to the Hanoverian dynasty was tiny. The number who actually wanted to do so was almost zero.

It is almost impossible to find, in the colonial print culture, any criticism of the Hanoverian dynasty. The eighteenth-century colonists saw Britain as defenders of international Protestantism or the Protestant interest, as it was known. The Hanoverians, their legitimacy resting on their Protestant genealogy, were seen as Protestant princes who bore the weight of this charge with uncommon grace. Threatened by the French and Spanish colonists and their native allies, and conceiving themselves as part of international Protestantism, American colonists embraced the more aggressive British foreign policy that came with the Glorious Revolution and the Hanoverian succession. The print culture was limited; the actively literate population was small and loyal; and the population as a whole approved of the key imperial policies that impacted foremost on their lives. Little wonder the print culture celebrated the Hanoverian dynasty.[4]

---

[3] See Alan Tully, *Forming American Politics: Ideals, Interests, and Institutions in Colonial New York and Pennsylvania* (Baltimore, MD, 1994), who gives a sound and solid discussion of Zenger. For older approaches, see Bernard Bailyn, *The Origins of American Politics* (New York, 1970). Leonard Levy, 'Did the Zenger Case Really Matter? Freedom of the Press in Colonial New York', *William and Mary Quarterly*, 3rd ser., 17 (1960), pp. 35–50, demonstrated that freedom of the press did not originate in the crisis.

[4] Brendan McConville, *The King's Three Faces: The Rise and Fall of Royal America, 1688–1776* (Chapel Hill, NC, 2006), pp. 159–65, discusses this issue at great length in relation to the Zenger Crisis, and the general tendency to read 'opposition' or proto-Americanism into the period's print culture. For the identification of the empire and the Hanoverian dynasty with the Protestant interest in Europe, see Thomas Kidd, *The Protestant*

This print culture was indeed designed, to the degree it had a self-conscious design, to inculcate loyalty to the Hanoverians. It also carried a powerful message about imperial history that intertwined that history with Protestant monarchy generally and the family and political history of the Hanoverian dynasty specifically in order to legitimate these German-speaking rulers. In these tellings, English and/or British history was driven by the realm's internal emergence from Catholic darkness and spiritual damnation, and from its repeated salvation from foreign Catholics and their Stuart minions' attempts to reintroduce popery and slavery. The Hanoverian dynasty was God's appointed guardian of this Protestant historical legacy and timeline, and the dynasty's family history demonstrated that they had been prepared by divine providence for this role. The message was transmitted in almanacs, newspapers, pamphlets and handbills, and it is difficult to find a serial publication that did not at one time or another carry some portion of this story; many carried portions of it in every issue.[5]

If the message needed amplification, it received it regularly from what was, in 1775, still the major mode of communication, the Sunday sermon delivered by Protestant preachers.[6] The network of Protestant pulpits in British America created and linked communities, shaped understanding of events and personalities and articulated and mediated social values. They were, as a number of scholars have noted, the primary source of information and worldview for the vast majority of British Americans. They hated and feared Catholics, and they supported the Hanoverian dynasty as champions against them.

The vast majority of the preachers in America were educated at Harvard, Yale and the College of New Jersey (Princeton), College of Rhode Island (Brown) and Rutgers, all dissenting colleges. But these dissenting preachers, like their counterparts in the Church of England, prayed for the king and the royal family every week, preached justification of the Hanoverian dynasty and the Protestant succession and denounced the threat of Catholic subversion within the empire, and foreign Catholic powers abroad. Royal arms often adorned their churches,

---

Interest: New England after Puritanism (New Haven, 2004), and Andrew Thompson, *Britain, Hanover and the Protestant Interest, 1688–1756* (London, 2006).

[5] For the broader process at work, see J.G.A. Pocock, 'The Limits and Divisions of British History: In Search of the Unknown', *American Historical Review*, 87 (1982), pp. 311–36, at p. 318 and passim; for an example of this in the period's print culture, see 'A Gratulatory Poem Received from a Friend ... ', *Boston Weekly News-Letter*, 28 July 1728. For a general discussion of the issue of empire and history, see McConville, *The King's Three Faces*, pp. 81–92, and Kidd, *The Protestant Interest*, passim.

[6] See also the chapter by Jeremy Gregory in this volume.

and in some cases their communion silver came as a royal gift, bearing the royal arms. Special sermons were delivered on the monarch's birthday, the anniversary of his coronation and other royal holidays.[7]

In short, the two primary means of communication available to the colonists – print and pulpit – sent a consistent message to the colonial population about the Hanoverian dynasty. And this arrangement of political beliefs about the Georges and their relationship to a Protestant historical timeline was closely linked to the emergence of a series of annual, formal, imperial holidays with increasingly elaborate rites. In fact, these depended on each other, the political rites visualising a Protestant-imperial timeline and celebrating the Hanoverian dynasty in the streets for all to see.

Colonials, especially those living in the port towns, often only needed to listen or look out of their windows to see this process at work – the imperialisation of public time, realised in celebration of the Hanoverian regime. A seemingly endless cycle of imperial holidays, the so-called red-letter days, defined public political life in British America's towns and villages, and these were centred on the lives and history of the Hanoverian dynasty and Protestant British monarchs generally. The king's birthday, the queen's birthday, Pope's Day (Guy Fawkes Day in Britain, 5 November), the Prince of Wales's birthday; the saint days symbolic of the nations that comprised the empire (St George, St Andrew, St Patrick, St David); the entrance and exit of imperial governors; the celebration of imperial victories and, in some areas, King William's birthday: these holidays were celebrated in public, and even lavish, manners.[8]

By the 1730s or 1740s there were 26 official imperial holidays. Some of these were marked in a simple fashion: raising the British flag, and perhaps firing a salute at noon. But even as early as 1730, significant elaboration had begun for those holidays that remembered the monarch or immediate members of the royal family. When the people of Charlestown, South Carolina, marked Queen Caroline's birthday in 1731, for instance, they made sure to make 'all demonstrations of joy suitable to the occasion'. There was a procession of the key government officials led by the royal governor, Robert Johnson, to the town's fort, where 'discharges of the Great Guns' marked the day as the

---

[7] For the best statement on the implication of this process, see Harry S. Stout, 'Religion, Communications, and the Ideological Origins of the American Revolution', *William and Mary Quarterly*, 3rd ser., 34 (1977), pp. 519–41.

[8] McConville, *The King's Three Faces*, pp. 49–80, passim, discusses the introduction and establishment of these rites in mainland British America.

officials drank the royal health. In the evening, the leading men threw a ball to close the remembrances.[9]

The rituals used to celebrate the important imperial holidays soon became largely standardised across British America. There would be a political procession like the one in Charlestown in 1731, involving the community leadership. Over time, militia parades came to accompany these processions, or precede them. Preachers gave sermons on subjects of religious and political concern. Almost always there would be a cannonade, and in the ports the shipping would hoist its colours, and might also fire salutes. Often, officials provided a treat of alcohol and roast meat for the masses, as when the governor of Antigua treated the white population to 'two Oxen Roasted whole, and ... a great Quantity of Liquor'. There would be balls for the elite in the evening, and bonfires for the artisans and yeomen. The towns would be illuminated, with residents placing candles in their windows to demonstrate their loyalty to their Protestant princes. A finale involving fireworks usually ended the day. The only major formal holiday that deviated from this by mid-century was 5 November, Pope's Day. Rites on this day involved informal artisanal confraternities creating and parading effigies of Satan and the Stuart Pretender in many port towns. In some cases these displays devolved into rowdy street brawling between rival groups.[10]

The celebration of Protestant monarchy in such elaborate fashion dominated the yearly political calendar and created a cycle of veneration repeated year after year. The visual and community-centred character of these celebrations allowed monarchical political culture to reach deep into the social order; women, children, slaves, the semi and illiterate saw the Hanoverian dynasty celebrated in the streets throughout the year. Little boys marched around on 5 November with their own hideous little papal effigies; slaves, servants and sailors pushed the mighty carts on the same day, appeared for ox roastings and toasting on the royal birthdays and watched imperial processions wind themselves through the streets of the port towns several times a year. The fear of popish enslavement, of Catholics and of Catholic powers, central to the empire's identity and political culture, was expressed in the rites; and the rites further amplified and spread these values into society.

---

[9] McConville, *The King's Three Faces*, p. 63; *The South-Carolina Gazette*, 26 Feb.–4 March 1731/32.

[10] McConville, *The King's Three Faces*, pp. 49–80 discusses at length the emergence of these holidays, their origins, character and geographic spread into the smaller population centres of British America. For ox roasting in Antigua, see *Boston Weekly News-Letter*, 13–20 Sept. 1733, and McConville, *The King's Three Faces*, pp. 110–11.

By the 1730s, even small frontier communities were holding these celebrations. When William Stephens became administrator of the crude British settlements in Georgia in the early 1740s, he introduced these imperial holidays to an ethnically polyglot population. Although most of the settlers were not apparently English, in the spring of 1742 Stephens hoisted the British flag and provided alcohol to the assembled yeomen on St George's Day, 23 April; St George was the English patron saint. That autumn, he staged a more elaborate celebration on 30 October to mark George II's birthday, with 'Gun firing', the drinking of royal health and other marks of the day; and six days later he led the celebration of Pope's Day or Guy Fawkes Day, memorialising the foiling of a 1605 Catholic plot against James I and parliament. Even in areas of dispersed settlement like the Carolina interior, frontiersmen drank the king's health on his birthday, to the point they could not attend religious services the next day.[11]

The person peering from the port town window to view an expanding cycle of formal imperial holidays would have also seen a forest of ship masts carrying British consumer goods into the harbours of North America. This ship-borne consumer revolution spread cosmopolitan sensibilities and tastes to the empire's furthest corners, and allowed individuals and families to personally express their identification with the Hanoverian dynasty. Many of these pots, and plates and prints had symbols of the British nation or portrayals of the kings and queens emblazoned on them. Delftware arrived in the colonies emblazoned with the Hanoverian dynasty's mottos, 'Dieu et Mon Droit' and 'Honi Soit Qui Mal Y Pense'; stoneware jugs came bearing 'GR' – George Royal, or the royal arms, or crowns and rising suns. Wedgwood and other mass producers began pouring out ceramics with the royal likeness, and flooded the market when the young English-born George III inherited the throne in 1760.[12]

---

[11] McConville, *The King's Three Faces*, pp. 74–5; E. Merton Coulter, ed., *The Journal of William Stephens, 1741–1743*, 2 vols (Athens, GA, 1959), I, pp. 101, 132, 134, 135; II, p. 222. For a description of the celebration marking the anniversary of George II's coronation, see Coulter, ed., *Journal*, I, p. 92; Richard J. Hooker, ed., *The Carolina Backcountry on the Eve of the Revolution: The Journal and Other Writings of Charles Woodmason, Anglican Itinerant* (Chapel Hill, NC, 1953), p. 39.

[12] Leslie B. Grigsby, *English Pottery: Stoneware and Earthenware, 1650–1800* (London, 1990), pp. 104–5, 156, 423; id., *English Slip-Decorated Earthenware at Williamsburg* (Williamsburg, VA, 1993), p. 48; Michael Archer, *Delftware, the Tin Glazed Earthenware of the British Isles: A Catalogue of the Collection in the Victoria and Albert Museum* (London, 1997), p. 429; Leslie B. Grigsby, *The Longridge Collection of English Slipware and Delftware*, 2 vols (London, 2000), esp. I, p. 62; David Drakard, *Printed English Pottery: History and Humour in the Reign of George III, 1760–1820* (London, 1992), pp. 146, 148–51.

The flood of consumer goods carrying royal likenesses encouraged the royalisation of households. There had been, of course, royal portraits displayed in government buildings since the late 1680s, and they continued to be important in political rites up to the Revolution. For example, Governor William Franklin of New Jersey displayed 'the fine portraits of their Majesties [George III and his queen, Charlotte]' to gathered worthies in West Jersey during celebration of the king's birthday in 1765.[13] By then, mass-produced portraits provided provincials with visual access to their distant rulers. Provincials proudly displayed Hanoverian kings' portraits in their homes. In Benjamin Franklin's Philadelphia residence the king and queen appeared next to a likeness of his brother John, and the Sage of Philadelphia was far from the only one to display the royal likenesses. By the 1740s, even small stores in rural Edgecombe County, North Carolina, along the Albemarle Sound, sold likenesses of the royal family.[14]

This political and cultural machinery all helped create loyalty to the Hanoverian dynasty, but one factor outside human control in the eighteenth century, longevity, cemented the loyalty and enabled a growing cult of monarchy in the colonies. George II took the throne in 1727, and he remained on it for 33 years. By the time he died in 1760, most British Americans had known no other monarch, or had only the dimmest memory of George I or Queen Anne.

It is hard to overstate George II's popularity in British America. Scholars of eighteenth-century Britain or Germany would no doubt be shocked to discover just how affectionate Americans were towards him. He married a popular queen, Caroline; he personally led troops to victory in battle against the French at Dettingen in Germany in June 1743 during the War of the Austrian Succession. Much to the colonists' relief, he survived Bonnie Prince Charlie and the '45 Jacobite rebellion, crushed the rebels and led the empire into King George's War. He lived just long enough to see the empire to its greatest victory in the Seven Years War; and he had the good sense to die in 1760, with that victory assured, and before the war's aftermath embittered relations between the colonies and the London ministry. From the American perspective, George II had excellent timing.

The ministers in their pulpits, the royal officials and the newspapers in the colonies all celebrated this monarch as the empire's model paternal parent. The colonial press, even if they knew about his less than desirable traits, erased his mistresses, his conflicts with his British ministers and his frequent absences from

---

[13] *Pennsylvania Gazette*, 6 June 1765.
[14] McConville, *The King's Three Faces*, p. 133; Alan Watson, 'Society and Economy in Colonial Edgecombe County', *North Carolina Historical Review*, 50 (1973), pp. 231–55, at p. 234.

Britain (visiting Hanover in Germany), all well known and resented in the home islands. For them, he was before all a Protestant prince, a Briton like many of them by choice and religion rather than by birth. George II developed a halo that never wore off. This is why he and his queen continued to smile down on the Virginia House of Burgesses in 1777, even as that same assembly helped lead a rebellion against his grandson.[15]

America's eighteenth-century imperialisation had been enabled and accomplished by a celebration of Protestant monarchy and the Hanoverian dynasty. Its lifecycle, its past and a particularly Protestant history that ran back towards the Reformation provided the foundation stones for the framework through which provincials viewed the world and shaped political and public time. It created an imperial-Protestant worldview the full contours of which are still not widely understood. The Hanoverians were represented to a colonial population who would never see them or their palaces as embodying the empire's best values; the defenders of balance in the British constitution; and the champions of the Protestant interest.

One key aspect of that worldview, or one grown from it in an immediate sense, was an affection political discourse, a political language of love that linked the monarch to his most distant American subject. Protestant princes were supposed to rule via love, the affectionate loyalty of their subjects wherever they might be. Provincials were told constantly of the Hanoverian's love for them. When George II ascended the throne, for instance, American papers reported that he declared he only wished 'to Merit the Love of my people'. Imperial subjects were referred to as 'our loving subjects'. The loving chain of Protestant political affection, as more than one provincial put it, connected the entire empire, from the most distant subjects right to the king.[16]

Love made the empire go round, holding it together, binding it, enabling people at all levels of society and in all places to perceive it as a whole. The affection was real, or seems so. As Thomas Pownall noted in 1764 in his famed

---

[15] Andrew C. Thompson, *George II: King and Elector* (New Haven, 2013) is the most up-to-date study of this under-examined ruler; see also Jeremy Black, *George III: America's Last King* (New Haven, 2006) and id., *George II: Puppet of the Politicians?* (Exeter, 2007). Immigration into British America from northern Europe, and forced immigration from Africa, accelerated sharply in the eighteenth century.

[16] *American Weekly Mercury*, 7–14 Sept. 1727; 'Colonial Militia, 1740, 1748', *Maryland Historical Magazine*, 6 (1911), pp. 44–59, 180–95, at p. 44; see, for instance, Thomas Pownall, *The Administration of the Colonies* (London, 1764), p. 25. For sensibility in the American Revolution, see Sarah Knott, *Sensibility and the American Revolution* (Chapel Hill, NC, 2008) and Nicole Eustace, *Passion is the Gale: Emotion, Power, and the Coming of the American Revolution* (Chapel Hill, NC, 2011), esp. pp. 107–50.

Administration of the Colonies, it seemed at that moment that 'nothing can eradicate from their [provincials'] hearts their natural ... affection to Great Britain'.[17] But even before that fateful year, provincial thinkers were aware that an empire based on the passions needed to be carefully buttressed, in a manner that allowed emotions to flow only in certain restricted channels. Affections and passions, as one provincial writer noted as early as 1729, needed to be 'directed to proper Objects'. Emotions, they continued, needed to be 'Regulated'.[18]

Regulated they were, by the public rites, the consumer goods, the pulpits – all guided emotions to flow towards the Hanoverian dynasty. It would seem, on the surface of things, to have inhibited any ideas of imperial dissolution. In fact, though, it became dangerous in the Seven Years War's aftermath, when debt and the imperatives of control led the London government to attempt to partially integrate the American colonies into the home islands' tax and fiscal structures. When they did, the true danger of the devotion to the Hanoverian kings became apparent.

II

The strangest thing about the imperial crisis, though perhaps the most obvious, is that no one wanted it. Proud Britons, the colonists had participated eagerly in the imperial effort during the Seven Years War, and routinely expressed their passionate loyalty to the empire and the Hanoverian monarchy. The young king, George III, the first Hanoverian king born in England, was popular in the home islands, and, initially, extremely popular in the colonies. He had inherited the throne just in time to bask in the glow of victory in a long, bloody and exhausting global war, and married a young queen who would quickly become as (temporarily) popular as her husband. The London authorities had no overt hostility towards the American colonists, and rightly saw them as loyal Protestant subjects as well as the source of incredible wealth via commerce and, in some cases, land speculation.[19]

The breakdown of this harmony grew from the war itself. The financial demands of global war had created a massive debt, an unstable paper money supply in the colonies as well as new problems of imperial control. While

---

[17] Pownall, *Administration*, p. 25.
[18] *American Weekly Mercury*, 11–18 Sept. 1729.
[19] Andrew Jackson O'Shaughnessy, *The Men Who Lost America: British Leadership, the American Revolution, and the Fate of the Empire* (New Haven, 2013) is an excellent study into the issues of governance that led to the imperial collapse, and the personalities involved.

American historians, with considerable justification, have tended to focus on the former issue, money, the latter issue, institutional-constitutional disorder, was just as important, and maybe more so. The empire had never been uniform; local traditions, differences in charters and local circumstances had created a hodgepodge of structures, their diversity creating subjective understandings of the unwritten British constitution. Ireland had its own parliament; Scotland had had one, too, until the Act of Union early in the eighteenth century. The American colonies on the mainland and in the West Indies had divergent charters and had built institutions on them that differed significantly one from the other.

The empire's administrative and political convulsions in the seventeenth and eighteenth centuries had revolved around this heterodoxy and attempts to standardise institutions and tighten the metropolis's control. The London authority made progress in this vein across the eighteenth century, anglicising institutions by decree and in many cases passively, simply by example. Facing the reality of an empire that now stretched from the Indian Ocean to the Great Lakes, the London authorities struggled to govern their massive new possessions, and their ever more diverse populations. With native Americans, French speakers in Canada and advancing English-speaking settlers to rule, they expanded the garrison in North America at the same time that they pleaded poverty, planned new taxes and appointed a new layer of royal officials.[20]

The result of course was the Stamp Act crisis, as provincials refused to pay the tax and attacked those appointed to administer it. That crisis, and those which would follow in the 10 years between 1764 and 1774, saw angry colonists denounce imperial legislation, the British ministry and parliament again and again, often in the most lurid terms.[21]

---

[20] For efforts to reform the empire before the Revolution, see Heather Schwartz, 'Rewriting the Empire: Plans for Institutional Reform in British America, 1675–1791' (PhD dissertation, Binghamton University, 2011). For the relationship of the British constitution to American constitutionalism, see Charles McIlwain, *The American Revolution: A Constitutional Interpretation* (New York, 1924).

[21] See McConville, *The King's Three Faces*, pp. 249–312. For a cogent study of the 1773–1776 period, see T.H. Breen, *American Insurgents, American Patriots: The Revolution of the People* (New York, 2011); Woody Holton, *Forced Founders: Indians, Debtors, Slaves and the Making of the American Revolution in Virginia* (Chapel Hill, NC, 1999). For the period as a whole, see Edmund and Helen Morgan, *The Stamp Act Crisis* (Chapel Hill, NC, 1995); Pauline Maier, *From Resistance to Revolution: Colonial Radicals and the Development of American Opposition to Britain, 1765–1776* (New York, 1992). For the role of anti-popery in the crisis, see Frank D. Cogliano, *No King, No Popery: Anti-Catholicism in Revolutionary*

However, what is most notable about this deluge of denunciation is the virtual lack of any indictment of George III or the Hanoverian dynasty directly. The opposite proved true. The monarchy received increased support from provincials, precisely because they had absorbed the message of the Protestant political culture developed in the eighteenth century: mainly that the Protestant princes of the Hanoverian dynasty united the far-flung empire, not the parliament, and these kings defended it from internal political popery as well as Catholic powers abroad. As late as 1774, a New England writer declared that the colonists' disputed parliamentary authority had 'no controversy with the king' or disputed 'his regal authority over us'.[22] As a writer for the New York assembly put it in 1764, the Hanoverians, far from being bent on tyranny, had from the beginning of their reign acted as 'the guardians of British liberty'.[23]

For provincials, these princes embodied the empire's best values and held their place by a kind of divine appointment. As early as 1727, Boston preacher Benjamin Coleman had declared 'Our faithful zeal for and adherence to the Protestant Succession in the House of Hanover, is our fidelity to CHRIST and his holy religion.'[24] That belief, and a related perception that the Hanoverians were divinely appointed to save the British nation, gave them a prestige that the Stamp Act crisis did not really diminish.[25]

The eighteenth-century empire's history, and the constitutional tenet that the monarch could do no wrong, enabled provincial faith in the king in the face of this crisis over taxation and the imperial constitution. The continual efforts of the Jacobites to undermine the Hanoverians via conspiracy and foreign-backed covert invasions, tied to the belief that divinely anointed monarchs might be fooled by evil ministers and administrative mandarins – who, it was known from Britain's seventeenth-century history, could do quite a bit of wrong – insulated George III from criticism early in the imperial crisis. Feeling under assault, provincial Americans appealed to George III as 'Guardian of their Rights and Liberties'.[26]

New England (Westport, CT, 1995). See also Peter Shaw, *American Patriots and the Rituals of Revolution* (Cambridge, MA, 1981).

[22] Samuel Sherwood, *A Sermon, Containing, Scriptural Instructions to Civil Rulers, and All Free-Born Subjects ...* (New Haven, CT, 1774), p. 30n.

[23] *South Carolina Gazette*, 26 Nov. 1764.

[24] Benjamin Colman, *Fidelity to Christ and to the Protestant Succession in the Illustrious House of Hannover ...* (Boston, 1727), p. 1.

[25] McConville, *The King's Three Faces*, pp. 192–219 discusses this process. See especially pp. 209–17.

[26] Isaac Skillman, *An Oration on the Beauties of Liberty; or, The Essential Rights of the Americans ...* (Boston, 1773), p. 60.

They wanted the king to intervene, even to use the royal prerogative to veto parliamentary legislation, something that had not occurred since Queen Anne's reign. In 1769, the Virginia House of Burgesses called on their 'King and Father' to somehow stop parliament's 'invasions of dearest privileges'.[27] In short, these Americans did not believe in the unitary sovereignty of the King-in-Parliament that was the understood settlement of the Glorious Revolution in the British Isles. They saw the Hanoverian kings as essentially retaining autonomous constitutional power that extended to the royal negative over parliamentary legislation. In reality, such a negative would have caused a constitutional crisis of epic proportion in London, and there was never any hope of it.

Faith in the king remained strong through 1773. The king's birthday and the other holidays that celebrated the Hanoverian dynasty continued to be popular, and participation in the holidays may have swelled between 1764 and 1773. Certainly, large crowds appeared at celebrations in a number of colonies right up until that latter year.[28]

This empire of love, centred on devotion to the Hanoverian dynasty, began to come apart with the Intolerable Acts and the Quebec Act. In January 1774, loyalty to George III and the House of Hanover remained strong. To be certain, a tiny radical minority stood ready for a rupture. Freeholders in Dinwiddie County, Virginia, though, expressed more typical sentiment when they declared their 'unfeigned Affection and Loyalty for his Majesty' even while revealing their deepening apprehension about 'some ... dangerous innovations' implemented by the British House of Commons.[29]

Events, though, were moving too fast, and with the new legislation designed to punish Boston for the Tea Party, and to settle Quebec's constitutional structure, America's king began to die. Seen from London, these acts were reasonable, tempered responses to two serious problems: the unrest in the English-speaking colonies, and the integration of French-speaking Catholics into an increasingly sprawling, diverse empire traditionally hostile to French-speaking Catholics. Americans saw these acts differently. The Quebec Act, the Maryland-based

---

[27] *South Carolina and American General Gazette*, 17–20 July 1769. As late as 1774, Jefferson suggested just such an intervention by the king, though he realised that the practice had effectively lapsed.

[28] Massachusetts Historical Society, Boston, John Rowe Diary, 4 June 1773; Harold E. Davis, *The Fledgling Province: Social and Cultural Life in Colonial Georgia, 1733–1776* (Chapel Hill, NC, 1976), p. 167; McConville, *The King's Three Faces*, pp. 259–60. For the king's birthday celebration in the aftermath of Stamp Act's repeal in Rhode Island, see William R. Staples, *Annals of the Town of Providence, From its First Settlement, to the Organization of the City Government, in June 1832* (Providence, 1843), pp. 214–15.

[29] *Virginia Gazette*, 21 July 1774, p. 5.

Englishman William Eddis wrote in 1774, had become 'as unpopular here as the Boston Port Bill and adds greatly to the universal discontent'. It seemed to be the absolutist state they had feared, now incarnate in North America. Roman Catholic principles now guided the British ministry, one New Yorker wrote in 1775, precepts that meant popish enslavement for Britons everywhere, beginning in the colonies.[30] A young Alexander Hamilton, writing from New York City, argued that the Quebec Act established 'arbitrary power and its great engine, the Popish religion' in British America. Hamilton believed that the vast American interior would soon fill with Catholics who would surround the existing British American colonies. 'How dangerous', he warned, 'their situation would be, let every man of common-sense judge'.[31]

The king became indicted in this. Americans saw the acts as pointing to the creation of a royal absolutist state; and the mobilisation of imperial forces to enforce the Intolerable Acts implicated George III, as the military was seen as a royal prerogative. The rites that celebrated the Hanoverian dynasty collapsed as news of the Intolerable and Quebec Acts spread and a new symbolic order began to appear by mid-1774. In that year, 'scarcely, if any, notice was taken' of the king's birthday in Philadelphia; no bells rang, few if any imperial pennants flew. A year later, the king's birthday died in New York City; while the garrison cheered and the warship *Asia* fired a royal salute, the town's population held no ceremonies and emitted no cheers. Even at this central imperial outpost, love had become fear and loathing.[32]

Open fighting accelerated this trend. After learning about the Lexington and Concord fighting, Whig leaders in Georgia determined that the king's birthday, 4 June, should not be remembered. On 2 June, Savannah Whigs spiked the artillery in the town in order to prevent the firing of a royal salute on the 4th. The colony's able governor, James Wright, managed to get a few guns working on 5 June and fired a salute. In response, the colony's Liberty Boys erected a Liberty Pole in the town.[33]

---

[30] William Eddis, *Letters from America*, ed. by Aubrey C. Land (Cambridge, MA, 1969), p. 90; *The Norwich Packet and the Connecticut, Massachusetts, New-Hampshire and Rhode Island Weekly Advertiser*, 4 Dec. 1775, p. 3, piece entitled 'New York, November 27'.

[31] Richard B. Vernier, ed., *The Revolutionary Writings of Alexander Hamilton* (Indianapolis, 2008), pp. 141, 151.

[32] William Duane, ed., *Extracts from the Diary of Christopher Marshall, 1774–1781* (New York, 1969), p. 6; I.N. Phelps Stokes, *The Iconography of Manhattan Island, 1498–1909*, 6 vols (New York, 1915–1928), IV, p. 890.

[33] Charles C. Jones, *The History of Georgia*, 2 vols (New York, 1883), II, p. 176.

Ritual collapse quickly gave way to the breaking of a major political taboo, the open denunciation of the king in print. A petition to George III published first in the *Pennsylvania Gazette*, and subsequently republished in several papers, denounced princes who forfeited their 'dignity and respect' either by way of inattention to office or by 'willful male-administration of that authority'. Any prince whose actions endangered the people must stand 'a culprit before the awful tribunal of the public'. George III, he clearly implied, now needed to stand in that shameful docket.[34] The rhetorical devices used to normalise royal authority came under assault by a militant few in the same moment. An October 1774 writer to the *New York Journal* sarcastically attacked the practice of celebrating the British monarch's superiority to other kings. Was it, he asked, 'not rather too severe on the other crowned heads' of Europe to keep claiming 'that the King of England is, by far, the best Prince in Christendom'? A Rhode Island writer used the *Newport Mercury* to ask the public, 'you say to submit to King George and his laws – Suppose King George should bid you not to wear breeches, would you go bare a – d all your life time?'[35]

It all came to a crashing end in late 1775 and 1776 as royal symbols and images were destroyed in a wave of iconoclastic violence. The most famous of these incidents was the destruction of George III's equestrian statue on New York City's Bowling Green in July 1776; but there were dozens, perhaps hundreds, of similar events. Tavern signs with crowns, pictures of the king, glassware with royal symbols, George III effigies; all were destroyed, with the king denounced by mobs embittered by what they saw as a monarchical turn towards tyranny.[36]

III

The iconoclasm marked the first British Empire's end, but it did not mean George III had no loyal subjects left; nor did it mean that Americans' belief in the benefits of monarchy had ended. The fate of the loyalists is well known, but the continuing belief in the values of well-working, balanced monarchy by some of those who supported the cause of independence is less appreciated. Typical of

---

[34] *The Norwich Packet and the Connecticut, Massachusetts, New-Hampshire, and Rhode Island Weekly Advertiser*, 27 Oct. 1774, p. 4.

[35] *The New York Journal; or the General Advertiser*, 27 Oct. 1774, p. 1; *Newport Mercury*, 20 Feb. 1775, p. 2.

[36] McConville, *The King's Three Faces*, pp. 281–311; see also David Waldstreicher, *In the Midst of Perpetual Fetes: The Making of American Nationalism, 1776–1820* (Chapel Hill, NC, 1997), esp. pp. 30–31.

the views on this question of a significant portion of the mid-Atlantic elite were those expressed by Jerseyman Elias Boudinot, soon to be president of Continental Congress. A legislator, he and many others believed, best displayed his genius 'adapting his form of Government to the Genius, Manners, Dispositions & other circumstances of the people' of the society he helped govern. Americans, he continued, were Britons and 'Brittons could never bear the extreams, either of monarchy or of republicans'.

Tyrannical kings had been overthrown in the past, with mixed results. Boudinot believed that the one effort at a commonwealth in the English-speaking world, during the Interregnum, led to Cromwell's despotism and the widespread popular support for restoration of monarchy in 1660. 'This wou'd', he continued, 'most probably be the Case of America, were A Republican form of government adopted in our present ferment'. The best form of government for Britons, which he still thought Americans were, was 'Limited Monarchy', for it was 'most favourable to Liberty, which is best adapted to the Genuis & Temper of Brittons'.[37]

Little wonder, then, that colonial Americans should continue to express love for George I and George II. For people like Boudinot, and there were many in the American camp as the war broke out, the problem was a monarch, not monarchy. George III, his ministers and his parliament had gone all wrong, for certain, but that did not mean monarchy as a system or even all British monarchs had been bad. There had been tyrants, especially in the Stuart family; and there had been heroic kings, like George II. But because they did not see democracy or republics without flaws, so they did not understand monarchy as permanently discredited by bad monarchs. A balanced monarchy kept power in check, and allowed for innovation, even as it reinforced patriarchy and preserved tradition.

It was thus that George II was allowed to continue his reign over Virginia's republican burgesses. Only over time, as the generation that remembered that venerated monarch died out, did the republicanisation and democratisation of American culture become complete, early in the nineteenth century. For the decades between 1776 and that new century, Americans would live in a strange paradox, many of them fondly remembering a monarchical past shaped by their devotion to the Hanoverian dynasty while living in a present in which they perceived themselves as champions of a global revolution. They became in those decades something no longer fully British, but un-free of the memory of that identity.

---

[37] Larry Gerlach, ed., *New Jersey in the American Revolution: A Documentary History* (Trenton, NJ, 1975), pp. 206–8.

Chapter 10
Visions of Kingship in Britain under George III and George IV

G.M. Ditchfield

The theme of 'visions of kingship' in the later eighteenth and early nineteenth centuries provides a reminder of the means by which 'visions' could turn into 'idealisation', and the frequency of the opportunities for the expression of those visions. It allows us to consider the ways in which the British monarchy could associate itself with, and be turned to account by, the aspirations of numerous interest groups in society. One thinks immediately of the philanthropic, the artistic and cultural visions of kingship, each of which received considerable enhancement during the period reviewed in this chapter.[1] Georgian monarchs and their consorts were expected to provide cultural patronage, to sponsor artistic initiatives and at the same time to entertain. There was, in addition, a growing presumption that the monarchy would offer moral leadership, by precept and (perhaps less probably) by example. The moral vision could be credited with some plausibility to George III; his successor, by contrast, achieved a measure of distinction – not always intentionally – in the realm of entertainment.[2] This chapter, however, takes a rather different form and focuses on the three most enduring visions of late Georgian kingship which were central to the years of the Personal Union, namely the Anglo-Hanoverian vision, the military (and naval) vision and, finally, the Protestant vision. These three visions were closely interconnected and each was heavily contested. The balance between them,

---

[1] See, in particular, Matthew Kilburn, 'Royalty and Public in Britain 1714–1789' (DPhil dissertation, University of Oxford, 1997), especially chs I, V and VI; Frank Prochaska, *Royal Bounty: The Making of a Welfare Monarchy?* (New Haven, 1995).

[2] For a rather surprising example of this distinction, see Charles Lloyd, *Particulars of the Life of a Dissenting Minister ... Written by Himself* (London, 1813), pp. 82–5. Lloyd admitted that, as a student for the ministry at the Swansea Presbyterian academy during the 1780s, he was dazzled by the extravagance and flamboyance of the future George IV. Subsequently a Unitarian minister, Lloyd belonged to a denomination associated with radical politics and criticism of the trappings of monarchy.

moreover, changed fundamentally during this period, so that by the late 1820s the Protestant vision, both in terms of 'high' politics and in the public domain, had come to predominate.

I

The importance of Hanover in British diplomacy and foreign policy in the late eighteenth and early nineteenth centuries has received much recent scholarly attention; this chapter looks at the ways in which the Hanoverian connection was regarded in Britain and how it fitted into the 'visions of kingship' implicit in the Personal Union. The French occupation (1803–1805) and the Prussian occupation (1806) of Hanover carried major implications for Georgian monarchy. For all George III's insistence on the separation of his Hanoverian from his British interests and advisors, such a separation was very much more difficult to sustain in the new circumstances. The king and elector still needed British power to restore and protect his electorate. However, while the Ministry of All the Talents (as Brendan Simms showed) used the Hanover issue to win the support of George III for its continuance in office, it was equally anxious to avoid public discussion of its pro-Hanoverian stance against Prussia.[3] And, for all the effectiveness of the Hanoverian faction at the court of George III, there was no latent sentiment of public pro-Hanoverian feeling to which the Talents or any other ministry could appeal. It is true that anti-French horror stories about French behaviour during the brief occupation of Hanover circulated in Britain in 1803, and that George III, according to Lord Auckland, was 'greatly affected' by the sufferings of his Hanoverian subjects in that year.[4] Similarly, there were some parliamentary complaints about the insult to British kingship posed by the Prussian occupation in April 1806; Charles James Fox, in his capacity as foreign secretary, described the occupation as 'an outrage, unprecedented in the history of the worst times of Europe'.[5] But there is not

---

[3] Brendan Simms, '"An Odd Question Enough": Charles James Fox, the Crown and British Policy during the Hanoverian Crisis of 1806', *Historical Journal*, 38 (1995), pp. 567–96.

[4] Cf. *Gentleman's Magazine*, 58 (1803), p. 676; *Annual Register*, 1803, p. 257; *A Peep into Hanover, or, a Faint Description of the Atrocities Committed by the French in that City* (London, 1803); *The Journal and Correspondence of William, Lord Auckland*, 4 vols (London, 1861–1862), IV, p. 177.

[5] T.C. Hansard, *The Parliamentary Debates from the Year 1803 to the Present Time ... Forming a Continuation of the Work Entitled 'The Parliamentary History of England from the Earliest Period to the Year 1803'*, 41 vols (London, 1803–1820), VI, p. 887.

very much evidence from the newspaper press or elsewhere in the spring of 1806 of a sense of public outrage in Britain at the Prussian occupation. Suspicion in Britain of Hanover as an unnecessary and costly commitment, with implications of secret influence and authoritarianism, lingered. It surfaced from time to time in public comments, such as that of the woman of Lambeth who in 1798 attended one of the charity events of the Evangelical Marianne Thornton. 'To be sure', she informed her host, 'the Queen does the same at Frogmore, but then hers is not so much, for she is but a *foreigner*, & has nothing but what is given her. This is all your own.' Unsurprisingly, Marianne Thornton saw in this remark 'the seeds of that disrespect for royalty, which in low minds, leads to violence & insubordination'.[6] When in June 1804 George, Prince of Wales, insisted on the need for the preservation of the British connection with Hanover on the basis that the electorate was 'the key to the King of Prussia's dominions and enables Buonaparte to keep him in complete check', Lord Auckland ventured to disagree. He asserted that any offer of Malta, British sovereignty over Flanders and independence for the Dutch from the French emperor, in return for French control of Hanover, would be more acceptable than retention of the electorate in the British royal house, adding:

> In my opinion it [Hanover] is merely a field of battle, easy to be occupied by a strong army at any time, but from which it may be as easily expelled by a stronger, being an open plain, where nothing further can be gained than ravishing the women and pillaging undefended property.[7]

Nor, more speculatively, does there seem to have been much evidence of more sympathetic public attitudes towards Hanover because of the occupations, with their attendant insecurity and losses, experienced by Hanover between 1801 and 1814. The lessening of the types of public expressions of hostility to Hanover which had been familiar in the earlier eighteenth century, and which asserted that Hanoverian interests played too great a part in the formulation of British foreign policy, did not seem to translate into more positive and sympathetic attitudes towards Hanover.

---

[6] Quoted in Anne Stott, *Wilberforce: Family and Friends* (Oxford, 2012), p. 139.
[7] See the report of this conversation in Francis Bickley, ed., *The Diaries of Sylvester Douglas, Lord Glenbervie*, 2 vols (London, 1828), I, p. 383. This was the occasion on which the Prince of Wales was reported as saying: 'I should insist upon Hanover. I am as mad on that subject as my father.' For the prince's support for the robust response of Fox and the Talents ministry to the Prussian occupation, see Simms, 'An Odd Question Enough', pp. 583–4.

A series of particularly important occasions for the exaltation of the British connection with Hanover arose in 1814–1815. Once finally free from French occupation, Hanover could be proclaimed a kingdom by the Prince Regent on 26 October 1814 and be recognised as such by the Congress of Vienna, as were Saxony, Bavaria and Württemberg. The Prince Regent's youngest surviving brother, the Duke of Cambridge, was appointed as governor-general, while in April 1815 the Prince Regent himself instituted the Royal Guelphic Order to reward the wartime service of his Hanoverian subjects, with Count Ernst von Münster – George III's German minister in London and the key figure in the post-1814 administration of Hanover – as its first chancellor. The Prince Regent, indeed, began to evince a detailed interest in the German genealogy of his family, perhaps as a means of using Hanover to emphasise the historic legitimacy of the dynasty, in response to the 'usurper' Napoleon's abolition of the Holy Roman Empire.[8] At the same time, he was reported to have endowed the University of Göttingen, where the Duke of Cambridge received the degree of doctor of philosophy, with 'a copy of every English work of importance that has appeared during the last ten years'.[9]

In this context, and with the (as yet temporary) victory over Napoleon, the centenary of the Personal Union on 1 August 1814 took on a wider and more significant dimension. A highly publicised event, it was regularly referred to in the newspaper press as the 'Jubilee', the 'Grand Jubilee',[10] the 'National Jubilee',[11] or even, in some press advertisements, as the 'Universal Jubilee',[12] or, as in the print by John Fairburn, the 'Grand National Jubilee'.[13] A public holiday for employees in government offices was declared, and the construction of the pagoda and bridge in St James's Park was entrusted to John Nash, the Prince Regent's personal architect. Queen Charlotte presided over a 'grand entertainment' at Buckingham House, where 'the frame work and table ornaments were entirely new for the occasion, and applicable to the times and joyous event of its being exactly a century since the House of BRUNSWICK

---

[8] See the excellent essay by Clarissa Campbell Orr, 'The Feminization of the Monarchy 1780–1910: Royal Masculinity and Female Empowerment', in Andrzej Olechnowicz, ed., *The Monarchy and the British Nation, 1780 to the Present* (Cambridge, 2007), pp. 76–107, at pp. 81–3.

[9] *Gentleman's Magazine*, 84 (1814), pt. II, p. 551; *Morning Post*, 12 Dec. 1814.

[10] *Kentish Gazette*, 29 July 1814.

[11] *Morning Chronicle*, 2 Aug. 1814; *Gentleman's Magazine*, 84 (1814), pt. II, pp. 179–84.

[12] Advertisements in *Morning Chronicle*, 20 June 1814; *Morning Post*, 1 July 1814.

[13] See also *Grand National Jubilee*, a single-sheet commemorating the peace between Britain and France, printed in Hyde Park, London, 1814.

reigned in England'.¹⁴ With the three royal parks of London illuminated with fireworks and rockets, a spectacular ascent by the celebrated balloonist James Sadler, and a re-enactment of the battle of Trafalgar on the Serpentine (happily with the same outcome as in 1805), the association between the Personal Union and victory in warfare was demonstrated to large and apparently enthusiastic crowds. It received additional emphasis by the coincidence of the jubilee with the 16th anniversary of Nelson's victory at the battle of the Nile. The jubilee was associated, too, with the peace settlement, on the eve of the Congress of Vienna, as the Castle of Discord in the Green Park spectacularly yielded to the Temple of Concord. The artist Joseph Farington, a sympathetic observer, was highly impressed by the whole spectacle. He thought that 'the fireworks were beautiful & the People appeared to be highly gratified'; and that through the performances as a whole, 'the public curiosity appeared to be indulged to the utmost degree, & I saw or heard nothing but what shewed general satisfaction'. But, significantly, he found it necessary to add that the celebration 'by no means justified the sour, caviling remarks profusely made in the opposition newspapers, particularly those which devote their pages to traducing the Prince Regent, viz: Morng. Chronicle – Examiner – Champion &c',¹⁵ for there were indeed such 'sour' comments: sure enough, the Whig *Morning Chronicle* dwelt on the less than successful features of the ceremonies, including the fatalities caused by the collapse into flames of the illuminated pagoda in Hyde Park.¹⁶ William Cobbett's *Weekly Political Register* described the jubilee as a 'piece of mummery' and complained of the cost to the civil list and, thus, to the taxpaying public, while the occasion drew derision from the satirical pen of 'Peter Pindar'.¹⁷ The *Morning Post*, by contrast, loyally insisted that 'It was the Jubilee of Loyalty, Peace, and universal Good Will'.¹⁸ Nine days later, perhaps carried away by the spirit of the jubilee, the ministerial supporter William Dundas declared on his re-election to the House of Commons for the city of Edinburgh, that 'The heart of a Prince of the house of Brunswick was a stranger to fear, and the language of submission our gallant countrymen disdained to learn.'¹⁹

---

¹⁴   *Morning Post*, 3 Aug. 1814.
¹⁵   Angus D. Macintyre and Kathryn Cave, eds, *The Diary of Joseph Farington*, 16 vols (London, 1984), XIII, pp. 4569–70.
¹⁶   *Morning Chronicle*, 2 Aug. 1814.
¹⁷   *Cobbett's Weekly Political Register*, 6 Aug. 1814; *The P ... e's Jubilee; or Royal Revels! A Poem by Peter Pindar* (London, 1814).
¹⁸   *Morning Post*, 2 Aug. 1814.
¹⁹   *Caledonian Mercury*, 11 Aug. 1814. Dundas was a lord of the Admiralty from 1812 to 1814; his re-election was necessitated by his nomination as Keeper of the Signet for Scotland.

Yet, significantly, while the celebration in London was widely reported throughout the British Isles, it seems not to have been replicated substantially on anything comparable to the national scale of the jubilee of George III as he approached the 50th anniversary of his accession in 1809.[20] It is true that there were specific instances of local and regional celebrations which made the jubilee of the Personal Union their *raison d'être*. Elaborate preparations for the event, for example, were undertaken at Cork and at Dublin.[21] The Protestant rationale of the Personal Union was much in evidence at Castledillon, County Armagh, where the performance began with a reading of Dr Daltry's ode:

> A hundred years are past and gone
> Since BRUNSWICK sway'd the British throne;
> O may their honour's scepter last,
> Till time itself be gone and past!

Thereafter, 'bumpers of Champagne were raised to every lip, to the heart-cheering toast of – "*The glorious 1st of August, and the Illustrious House of Hanover*"'.[22] The occasion was graced by the presence of Mary Juliana Stuart, the daughter of William Stuart, Archbishop of Armagh and primate of Ireland, and the granddaughter of George III's 'dearest friend', John Stuart, third Earl of Bute.

Beyond London, however, while there were many local celebrations of the peace, hardly any of them explicitly, or even implicitly, linked the victories to the jubilee. In Canterbury, the address of congratulation to the Prince Regent from the Mayor and Common Council referred to 'the splendid achievements of British arms ... in the sacred cause of national independence'; and the only dynasty which it mentioned was the Bourbon, now restored by the allies to the throne of France.[23] Many other Kentish celebrations of the peace took a similar form, with the traditional bell-ringing, the provision of free food and liquor by local elites and the drinking of patriotic toasts. At Charing, for example, the toasts included 'The Roast Beef' and 'The Duke of Wellington', together with the singing of 'Rule Britannia'; at Ickham 'Oh the Roast Beef of Old England' was sung.[24] Predictably, the bill of fare on these occasions frequently included

---

[20] See Linda Colley, 'The Apotheosis of George III: Loyalty, Royalty and the British Nation 1760–1820', *Past & Present*, 102 (1984), pp. 94–129.
[21] See *Morning Post*, 19 Aug. 1814.
[22] These ceremonials were reported in detail in *Morning Post*, 30 Aug. 1814.
[23] *Kentish Gazette*, 9 Aug. 1814.
[24] *Kentish Gazette*, 5 and 9 Aug. 1814; these two issues of this newspaper contain similar reports of celebrations in Ditton, Rochester, Chislet and Westerham.

roast beef. In several Suffolk villages 'Peace Festivals' were reported with no element of 'Jubilee'.[25] Significantly, the *York Herald and General Advertiser* described the celebrations in St James's Park on 1 August 1814 as 'The London Jubilee'.[26] Patriotic expressions of this kind throughout the English provinces, accompanied by relief at the (albeit temporary) conclusion of hostilities, were, in all probability, not deliberately and pointedly exclusive of Hanover, although expressions of gratitude to Hanover and its inhabitants for their contribution to the victory were almost entirely absent. The overall effect of these celebrations was to confirm older attitudes towards the cost of the continental commitments inherent in the Personal Union.

Otherwise, only on specific and officially stimulated occasions was there much British public interest, even of a spasmodic kind, in Hanover. One such occasion was the departure of George IV to Hanover from Ramsgate harbour on 25 September 1821, where a still-surviving obelisk was erected to commemorate the event. But although the visit was well publicised and reported,[27] it also provided opportunities for sardonic disapproval.[28] In terms of positive and approving public interest in the German connections of the Hanoverian dynasty, it is clear that the metropolitan spectacle of 1 August 1814 was the exception which proved the rule. Indeed, shortly thereafter several provincial newspapers reported, with evident equanimity, the increasing likelihood of the separation of Britain from Hanover in view of the likelihood of marriage between Ernest Augustus, Duke of Cumberland, and Duchess Friederike of Solms-Braunfels. They pointed out, correctly, that, should the birth of a son result from this marriage, that son would succeed in Hanover if the Prince Regent and the dukes of York and of Kent failed to produce a legitimate male heir – as they did. If Princess Charlotte, as seemed likely, succeeded her father (or grandfather if the Prince Regent predeceased him) to the British thrones, she could not, 'by the laws of Germany', succeed in Hanover.[29] Such coolness amounted to a further reminder that the Personal Union was precisely that, with none of the incorporating features of the unions of England with Scotland and with Ireland. It was also consistent with the way in which the dissolution

---

[25] *Bury and Norwich Post*, 3 Aug. 1814. For similar reports, see *Derby Mercury*, 4 Aug. 1814; *Jackson's Oxford Journal*, 6 Aug. 1814; and *Leeds Mercury*, 6 Aug. 1814.

[26] *York Herald and General Advertiser*, 6 Aug. 1814.

[27] For example, in the *London Gazette*, 29 Sept. 1821; *Morning Post*, 5 and 19 Oct. 1821; *Trewman's Exeter Flying Post*, 4 Oct. 1821.

[28] For example, in *Cobbett's Weekly Political Register*, 6 Oct. 1821.

[29] For example, *Bury and Norwich Post*, 31 Aug. 1814; *Derby Mercury*, 1 Sept. 1814; *Kentish Gazette*, 2 Sept. 1814.

of the Union in 1837 occurred 'almost without comment on either side' and 'without any great fuss'.[30] That the personal dimension itself had lost much of its significance in the public memory is suggested by the dispassionate nature of Queen Victoria's reported comment on the Prussian annexation of Hanover in 1866: that a protest to Prussia would be inexpedient and that 'a reunion of Hanover with this country is by no means an event to be desired'.[31]

II

It was no coincidence that the Anglo-Hanoverian centenary celebration in 1814 was used to commemorate military and naval success. With the warfare of 1793–1801 and 1803–1815 it was impossible for the monarchy not to be associated with the armed forces. As Hannah Smith has shown, the concept of the soldier-king had been essential to the construction of the monarchical image of George I and George II.[32] And although George III and George IV (for all their youthful aspirations) never personally participated in warfare, they engaged in symbolic alliance with the army and navy, and, in a more practical sense, took a direct part in the appointment of senior military and naval personnel. George III's interest in the navy, for example, from the 1770s onwards, notably with his visits to Portsmouth, became well known. This identification went much further than portraiture in military uniform, or in George IV apparently thinking he and not Wellington won the battle of Salamanca, and claiming that he had taken part in the battle of Waterloo.[33] Such an elevated profile was a public expectation, just as support for the monarchy during the war was preached as a public and patriotic duty. Warfare in the 1790s necessarily involved an even higher public profile for the monarchy since the enemy had proclaimed itself a republic and executed its former king. On 19 April 1793 the Evangelical Anglican Charles

---

[30] Christopher D. Thompson, 'The Hanoverian Dimension in Early Nineteenth-Century British Politics', in Brendan Simms and Torsten Riotte, eds, *The Hanoverian Dimension in British History, 1714–1837* (Cambridge, 2007), pp. 86–110, at p. 108; Mijndert Bertram, 'The End of the Dynastic Union, 1815–1837', ibid., pp. 111–27, at p. 126.

[31] Quoted in Jeremy Black, *The Hanoverians: The History of a Dynasty* (London, 2004), p. 212. For Queen Victoria's lack of sympathy with the exiled Hanoverian royal family after 1866, see P.H.H. Draeger, 'Great Britain and Hanover, 1830–66' (PhD dissertation, University of Cambridge, 1998), p. 428.

[32] Hannah Smith, *Georgian Monarchy: Politics and Culture, 1714–1760* (Cambridge, 2006), pp. 104–16, 182–5.

[33] Lytton Strachey and Roger Fulford, eds, *The Greville Memoirs, 1814–1860*, 7 vols (London, 1838), I, p. 327.

Edward de Coetlogon used his fast day sermon to make an impassioned plea for the populace to rally to the 'Defence of our amiable Sovereign – for the Comfort of his Queen and Family – for the Security of the Constitution – for the Honour of the Nation – and for the Destruction of its Enemies'. Prominent among those enemies were republicanism and atheism, and de Coetlogon was appealing to the same visions of kingship as those invoked by the loyalist Church and King clubs which sprang up during the winter of 1792–1793.[34]

Public commemorations of victory – such as that of 19 December 1797 at St Paul's Cathedral to celebrate the battles of St Vincent and Camperdown – were necessary means for the monarchy to associate itself with the successes of the armed forces. George III took a personal interest in the form of service ('a good old *Te Deum & Jubilate*') for occasions of public celebration, and in 1805 he gave strong support for Nelson's funeral to be held in St Paul's Cathedral.[35] The Prince Regent, by honouring Wellington and making him – at least for a time – a personal friend, was in effect conferring vicarious distinction upon himself. After Waterloo he was wont to claim of his commanders that 'I set them all to work'.[36] When as George IV he began his famous Scottish visit in 1822, his sea journey from Greenwich to Leith aboard the *Royal George* identified him ostentatiously with the navy, and led the advocate and author James Simpson, in a letter to Sir Walter Scott, to enthuse that the regal landing was 'suitable to our naval character, associated with thoughts of victory', and that when the king appeared on the half-moon battery of Edinburgh Castle, there, with 'the royal standard waving over his head, the artillery flashing under his feet … stood the commanding figure of the British Monarch, the father of his people'.[37] The link with the armed forces could still allow the presentation of kingly authority as performance, and, indeed, as entertainment.

---

[34] Charles Edward de Coetlogon, *The Patriot King, and Patriot People: A Discourse, Occasioned by the General Fast* (London, 1793), pp. 33–4.

[35] *A Form of Prayer and Thanksgiving to Almighty God … on Tuesday the Nineteenth Day of December 1797, Being the Day Appointed by His Majesty's Royal Proclamation for a General Thanksgiving to Almighty God, for the Many Signal and Important Victories … [to] His Majesty's Fleets* (London, 1797); G.M. Ditchfield, *George III: An Essay in Monarchy* (Basingstoke, 2002), p. 86; The National Archives, Kew, PRO 30/8/104/2, fos 461–2, George III to William Pitt, 11 Nov. 1805; Jeremy Black, *George III: America's Last King* (New Haven, 2006), p. 396.

[36] Quoted in Christopher Hibbert, *George IV: Regent and King 1811–1830* (Newton Abbot, 1975), p. 79.

[37] James Simpson, *Letters to Sir Walter Scott, Bart., on the Moral and Political Character and Effects of the Visit to Scotland in August 1822, of His Majesty King George IV* (Edinburgh, 1822), pp. 44, 84–5.

Yet even with the successes of British arms by 1814–1815, a public demonstration of proximity between monarchy and the armed forces, especially the army, as Christopher Thompson has observed, carried potentially dangerous implications for visions of kingship.[38] The wars of 1793 to 1815, much more than the War of American Independence, aroused internal opposition, which one historian has highlighted as a series of 'peace movements'.[39] Some of the disapprobation of war, admittedly, emanated from predictable sources. Here, for example, is the response of William Storrs Fry to seeing George III in London in June 1799:

> I arrived in Whitechapel about half past 10 – & just as I got opposite Charles Palmer's I was informed the King was coming by ... I had a good View of him; the Guards attended him with sundry Great Men & I hear his Sons the Duke of York & Clarence were with him – I must own I felt no real pleasure at the sight altogether, but should have enjoyed the sight of the King in private – for I have for Years past disliked to see Men drest up in martial Clothes because I annex thereto the horrid Ideas of War.[40]

Fry was a Quaker, and his opinion hardly surprising. But the General Baptist and Unitarian minister Joshua Toulmin provides an illustration of changing opinions since mid-century. In 1765 he preached and published a eulogistic sermon on the death of the Duke of Cumberland, full of adulation for his martial qualities and of pride over his defeat of the Jacobites at Culloden:

> Among the noble actions which signalized the Duke of Cumberland: You have not forgot ... with what Skill, Fortitude and Success he rode triumphant over the Foes of his Royal Father, and of these devoted Isles! ... A lawless and unnatural Race took up Arms against their amiable and venerable Sovereign ... At the alarming Prospect every Face grows pale; every knee trembles! Till the princely Youth, animated with filial Affection, fired with the Ardor of Fortitude, with the love of Britain and of Liberty ... [and] the Voice of Triumph and Conquest is heard thro' our Lands ... His conquering Arm saved you from Popery and Chains.[41]

---

[38] Thompson, 'Hanoverian Dimension', p. 90.
[39] J.E. Cookson, *The Friends of Peace: Anti-war Liberalism in England, 1793–1815* (Cambridge, 1982).
[40] British Library, London, Egerton Ms 3672A, fo 50, William Storrs Fry to his daughter Elizabeth Fry, 21 June 1799.
[41] Joshua Toulmin, *Reflections on the Death of a Prince and a Great Man, in a Sermon, Preached at Taunton, Nov. 10, 1765, on Occasion of the Death of His Royal Highness William Duke of Cumberland* (London, 1765), pp. 10–12.

But 11 years later, Toulmin preached another sermon, significantly entitled *The American War Lamented*, in which he declared that: 'The principles of Christianity should beget in every bosom a veneration for the human race, which should stay the hand lifted up to slaughter and destroy any part of it.'[42] During the Napoleonic War Toulmin disapproved of British participation in the conflict, took a sternly critical view of George III's jubilee in 1809 and bemoaned his entire reign. According to his memoirist, Toulmin:

> could not regard that reign as, upon the whole, prosperous and happy. It was pre-eminently a warlike reign; and, recollecting the rivers of human blood that had been spilt during the half century preceding 1809, he could not, with his abhorrence of war, in Christian sincerity make it the subject of religious thanksgiving.[43]

The linkage between monarchy and war was explicit in several petitions for peace, particularly from Lancashire and Yorkshire in 1807–1808, which were directed not to the king but to parliament, seeking to persuade it to exercise restraint upon the crown and its ministers, in whose hands lay the responsibility for a 'War of Aggrandizement'.[44] This type of attitude was taken further by the dissenter Thomas Colfox of Bridport, Dorset, who thundered in 1820: 'One may almost say that this Country has been infatuated, *quite besotted*, for the last 30 years. Indeed it began with the American War. Oh, the wicked, cruel, iniquitous reign of George III!!!'[45]

The traditional fear of standing armies in peacetime as instruments of repression continued. While the service of many Hanoverians in the King's German Legion, mostly in Portugal and Spain, probably helped to ease anti-Hanoverian prejudice in Britain during the Napoleonic War,[46] William Cobbett condemned the presence of the Legion in Britain as a wholly unnecessary expense and a potential threat to liberty; he was prosecuted and imprisoned in

---

[42] Joshua Toulmin, *The American War Lamented: A Sermon Preached at Taunton, February the 18th and 25th, 1776* (London, 1776), p. 4.

[43] R.B. Aspland, *Memoir of the Life, Works and Correspondence of the Rev. Robert Aspland of Hackney* (London, 1850), pp. 239–40.

[44] Cookson, *Friends of Peace*, 208. As the author points out, the dissenting (particularly Unitarian) presence in the support for these petitions is of particular significance.

[45] Thomas Collins Colfox of Bridport, 27 Oct. 1820, quoted in Basil Short, *A Respectable Society: Bridport 1593–1835* (Bradford-on-Avon, 1976), p. 53.

[46] As suggested by Black, *The Hanoverians*, p. 207.

1810 after criticising the flogging of English militiamen by German soldiers.[47] It was common form for radical elements regularly to associate war with monarchical ambition and extravagance. The Duke of York's case in 1809 had revived the issue of corruption in the award of military promotions, while the cost of the armed forces had reached unprecedented heights by 1815. In that year the *Morning Chronicle* complained that because the German Legion was recruiting in Flanders, '[t]he British Nation is paying bounties for a foreign levy, in the time of a profound peace'.[48] In the immediate post-Waterloo years of economic and social distress, the soldiery was more prominent than before in the response to public disorder. At the same time, the well-publicised campaigns of Sir Francis Burdett during and immediately after the Napoleonic War and of Joseph Hume in the 1820s and 1830s to abolish flogging in the army did not improve the army's image.[49] The libertarian tradition of a civilian militia as against a standing army in peacetime was of long duration, exemplified, for example, in John Cartwright's *England's Aegis* (1806), which linked a citizens' military force to civil freedom. The 'warrior prince' vision of kingship necessarily declined in value to the monarchy in the early nineteenth century, especially as the role of champion of the Protestant interest in Europe was hardly available to the Hanoverian monarchy after 1815.[50]

III

The functions of kingship included the supreme governorship of the Church of England. The coronation oath prescribed the maintenance of 'the Protestant Reformed Religion established by Law', while the oath taken by the Prince Regent in 1811 required that he 'inviolably maintain and preserve the settlement

---

[47] Leonora Nattrass, ed., *William Cobbett: Selected Writings*, 6 vols (London, 1998), II, pp. 249–74; Nicholas B. Harding, 'Hanover and British Republicanism', in Simms and Riotte, eds, *The Hanoverian Dimension*, pp. 301–23, at pp. 320–22.

[48] *Morning Chronicle*, 20 Jan. 1815. The reference to 'profound peace' was slightly premature.

[49] See J.R. Dinwiddy, 'The Early Nineteenth-century Campaign against Flogging in the Army', *English Historical Review*, 97 (1982), pp. 308–31, and Victoria Arnold, 'The Reputations of Sir Francis Burdett' (PhD dissertation, University of Kent, 2010), pp. 81–3.

[50] A relatively rare exception was the expression of concern expressed by the General Body of Protestant Dissenting Ministers for the Protestants in the south of France during the first years of the Bourbon Restoration; see Dr Williams's Library, London, MS 38.107, pp. 125–6 (21 Nov. 1816).

of the true Protestant religion'.⁵¹ That George III took both of these obligations with the utmost seriousness is well known, and his personal piety and insistence on doctrinal orthodoxy were public knowledge and regularly praised by the Anglican clergy.⁵² Although hardly emulating his father in terms of his spiritual life or moral conduct, George IV accepted the formal responsibilities towards the Church. There is not much evidence that he envisaged his role as its head as fundamentally different from that of George III, especially after his endorsement of the continuation in office after 1811 of the Tory ministries of Spencer Perceval and Lord Liverpool. The official impression was one of continuity between monarchs; for example, the customary royal proclamation at the beginning of a new reign enjoining morality was issued in 1820 as in 1760. Moreover, the *raison d'être* of the Personal Union had been the Protestant religion and succession, and it is impossible to examine visions of kingship in this period without some consideration of the confessional dimension.

However, we can identify more than one Protestant vision of kingship. It is not easy, for example, to reconcile the enlightenment Christianity in its Anglo-Hanoverian context as patronised by Queen Charlotte and convincingly elucidated by Clarissa Campbell Orr with an intolerant and exclusively Protestant vision of kingship.⁵³ In some quarters the Anglo-Hanoverian union was interpreted as signifying a libertarian and pluralist vision of religion. Protestantism, according to this perception, was inconsistent with intolerance. Moreover, there was evidence that such intolerance of Catholicism was unnecessary in practice as well as objectionable in principle. From the time of the French Revolution there had been fulsome declarations of loyalty to George III from English Catholics: a notable example was Vicar-Apostolic John Milner's praise for the 'wise and just counsels' of George III in the peroration of his funeral sermon for Louis XVI in 1793.⁵⁴ And the loyalty of pro-Catholics such as Henry Bathurst, Bishop of Norwich from 1805 to 1837, could hardly be doubted. The Unitarian Robert Aspland praised what he called 'the tolerant

---

⁵¹ 51 Geo. III, c. 1 ('An Act to provide for the Administration of the Royal Authority during the Continuance of His Majesty's Illness'); and see John Reeves, *Considerations on the Coronation Oath to Maintain the Protestant Reformed Religion, and the Settlement of the Church of England* (London, 1801).

⁵² See Ditchfield, *George III*, ch. 4.

⁵³ Clarissa Campbell Orr, 'The Late Hanoverian Court and the Christian Enlightenment', in Michael Schaich, ed., *Monarchy and Religion: The Transformation of Royal Culture in Eighteenth-Century Europe* (Oxford, 2007), pp. 317–42, esp. pp. 331–5.

⁵⁴ John Milner, *The Funeral Oration of His Late Most Christian Majesty Louis XVI* (London, 1793), p. 62.

disposition of the successive Monarchs of the Hanover family',[55] while the *Monthly Repository* in 1814 commended the jubilee of the Anglo-Hanoverian union with the comment: 'The gradually improved state of religious freedom during the last century, is a fact of which no man of observation can be ignorant, a blessing for which no sincere and reflecting nonconformist can be unthankful.'[56] This was a type of Protestant vision which, noting that the Catholic minority in eighteenth-century Hanover was less disadvantaged than that in eighteenth-century Britain, regarded religious intolerance as outdated, and inconsistent with a more enlightened age.[57] In 1828 Henry Gally Knight urged George IV to emulate Henri IV of France by granting Catholic Emancipation, as his French counterpart had granted the Edict of Nantes to the Huguenots 230 years earlier.[58] Anti-Catholicism, undoubtedly, was still a powerful social and cultural force in Britain. Some anti-Catholics even favoured emancipation on the grounds that Catholicism thrived on a sense of persecution and that the removal of this sense of grievances would diminish its support. But anti-Catholicism, as I have suggested elsewhere, did not amount to anything like a solid Protestant consensus.[59]

For the crisis over Catholic Emancipation in the late 1820s led to a reassertion of the original principle of the Personal Union. The social reformer and MP for Newark, Michael Sadler, declared in the House of Commons on 17 March 1829 that: 'The privileges of Protestantism, as hitherto maintained, constitute the Royal Title-Deeds of his [George IV's] august family.'[60] In even more apocalyptic terms, on 4 November 1828 Dennis Kelly of Castle Kelly told the first annual meeting of the Brunswick Constitutional Club of Ireland that Catholic Emancipation would remove the claim of the Brunswick family to the British throne; what he called the 'Savoy family' would then take precedence

---

[55] Aspland, *Memoir*, p. 256.
[56] *Monthly Repository*, 9 (1814), p. 610.
[57] Colin Haydon, *Anti-Catholicism in Eighteenth-Century England: A Political and Social Study* (Manchester, 1993), ch. 5.
[58] Henry Gally Knight, *Foreign and Domestic View of the Catholic Question* (4th edn, London, 1828), p. 78.
[59] G.M. Ditchfield, 'Church, Parliament and National Identity, c.1770–c.1830', in Julian Hoppit, ed., *Parliaments, Nations and Identities in Britain and Ireland, 1660–1850* (Manchester, 2003), pp. 64–82, at pp. 65–70.
[60] *The Speech of M.T. Sadler, M.P. for Newark, in the House of Commons; on the Second Reading of the Roman Catholic Relief Bill* (London, 1829), p. 25. See also the speech of Sir Edward Knatchbull in the House of Commons, 17 March 1829, T.C. Hansard, *The Parliamentary Debates ... New Series*, 25 vols (London, 1820–1830), XX, pp. 1125–7.

over the house of Brunswick.[61] In the House of Lords Baron Colchester, a former speaker of the House of Commons, took the appeal to the monarchy a stage further, declaring:

> Of the August Sovereign now happily on the throne of these Realms, we are precluded by the principles of our Constitution from stating his Personal Opinions upon matters depending in Parliament, which those now under our consideration are so soon to become. But we all know the solemn nature and form of the Coronation oath which He has taken. We know also the fixed and recorded opinions of his revered Predecessor, upon the full Extent of that Obligation.[62]

Privately he added that the passage of the Act 'puts an end to the Protestant monarchy of Great Britain'.[63] His clear implication was that George IV should withhold royal assent from the Catholic Emancipation bill, a course of action comparable to that suggested to George III over the Talents ministry's proposed measure for Catholic relief in 1807.

The Brunswick clubs of the late 1820s formed to resist Catholic Emancipation by invoking Hanover and the Brunswick line to support a particular Protestant vision of kingship, and which helped to bring the term 'Ultra' into broader use, did receive some royal support, notably from George IV's brother, the Duke of Cumberland – although two other royal dukes, those of Clarence and of Cambridge, supported emancipation. But rather than a conscious attempt by the monarchy to place itself at the head of a Protestant nation, movements of this nature amounted to an effort to create, or reinvent, an older type of vision of Protestant kingship and to impose, with a substantial element of popular support, this vision upon the monarchy of George IV. In that sense the monarchy of George IV was hijacked by anti-Catholic elements – a development made easier by the king's increasing conservatism as well as his declining political activity from the mid-1820s. But it was hijacked not only by Tory Ultras such as Lord Eldon but also by many Anglican Evangelicals, such as Joseph Mendham, curate of Sutton Coldfield, who, in *The Protestant King* (1820), compared George III to the Old Testament King David, added that 'he was a truly *Protestant* king', and hoped that George IV would maintain his coronation oath. He thought

---

[61] *A Full and Authentic Report of the Proceedings of the First Annual Meeting of the Brunswick Constitutional Club of Ireland* (Dublin, 1828), p. 12.

[62] *Speeches upon the Roman Catholic Claims: Delivered in Parliament, by Charles, Lord Colchester* (London, 1828), p. 5.

[63] *The Diary and Correspondence of Charles Abbot, Lord Colchester ... : Ed. by His Son Charles, Lord Colchester*, 3 vols (London, 1861), III, p. 373.

that Edward VI and George III were the best kings since the Norman Conquest. It was, he believed, through the 'true fortitude' of George III that 'the subjects and zealots of a foreign, a corrupt, an arrogant, and sanguinary church, have not become part of the legislature of a protestant country'.[64]

One finds a similar anti-Catholic mentality among much of the recently evangelicised Protestant Dissent, increasing in numbers and in many cases strongly anti-Catholic: evident, for example, in the Protestant Society, founded in 1811, and expounded vehemently by leading preachers such as the Particular Baptist Joseph Ivimey, who feared that the death of Princess Charlotte in 1817 would weaken the Protestant succession.[65] The confidence of many dissenters in the Protestantism of the Church of England was shaken by the decline of Latitudinarianism and what they saw as the growing strength of high churchmanship; and it was not surprising that in these circumstances they turned from the established Church to the monarchy as preservers of the Protestant religion. It is true that much of the Anglican hierarchy – including the Archbishop of Canterbury, the high churchman Charles Manners Sutton, and his successor William Howley – were hostile to Catholic Emancipation in the late 1820s, and that most of the bishops who attended the crucial division in the House of Lords in 1829 voted against emancipation. But perhaps we are seeing here, nonetheless, the beginnings of a nonconformist sense – soon to be given a powerful stimulus by the Oxford movement – that the established Church of England was not only fundamentally at odds with the essential voluntary principle of Protestant Dissent, but also that it could no longer be fully trusted as the guardian of the Protestant religion. Hence the desperate appeal to the Hanoverian monarchy in 1829 as a last hope.

IV

By the 1820s, then, many positive visions of kingship in Britain still drew upon highly traditional sources and arguments. So, too, did many hostile depictions of kingship. There is no shortage of examples. On 29 February 1768 the

---

[64] Joseph Mendham, *The Protestant King, with a View of the Coronation Oath, and of Certain Papal Oaths: A Sermon Preached in the Parish Church of Sutton Coldfield, on Sunday, February 27, 1820* (Birmingham, 1820), pp. 9, 11.

[65] Joseph Ivimey, *Reasons why the Protestant Dissenters in Particular Lament the Death of Her Royal Highness the Princess Charlotte Augusta* (London, 1817), p. 26. See also Joseph Kerby, *The Voice of God to Great Britain: A Funeral Sermon Occasioned by the Much Lamented Death of Her Royal Highness the Princess Charlotte* (London, 1817), p. 17.

posturing republicanism of Sylas Neville led him to record of his visit to Drury Lane theatre:

> Got into the pit with great difficulty, stood in the most disagreeable situation and bore the abhorred sight of George and Charlotte to have the pleasure of seeing Garrick and Mrs Pritchard play Hamlet and the Queen. Many in the Pit were so intoxicated with monarchical principles as to remain uncovered between the Acts.[66]

While the regicide of 1793 discredited republicanism in some previously sympathetic circles, George IV, especially in his earlier incarnations as Prince of Wales and Prince Regent, incurred a more strident and populist republican hostility than that of the commonwealth Whigs of the eighteenth century.[67] And although the radical adoption of Queen Caroline's cause in 1820–1821 was evanescent, it damaged the image of the monarchy far more than Tory attacks on the equally disastrous marriage of George I. At the same time, Whig and radical suspicions of 'Hanoverian encroachments on British sovereignty' persisted.[68] Similarly, the Primitive Methodist William H. Stephenson, preaching in Newcastle upon Tyne on 19 July 1821, the day of George IV's coronation, cited the Old Testament example of Rehoboam's threat to chastise his subjects with scorpions, with thinly veiled allusions to the Hanoverian monarchy. Strongly critical of passive obedience and non-resistance, Stephenson declared that when the king becomes a tyrant, 'rebellion is lawful, and resistance becomes a public duty', adding 'I have always been at a loss to know why people should be so horror struck, when the word revolution is named'.[69]

The influence of the crown was continually under attack, especially after 1783–1784; as an issue it was kept in politics by the paranoia and resentment of the opposition Whigs. Hence visions of kingship remained highly contested. George III and George IV were not 'above party': from George III's personal intervention to secure the appointment of Pitt in 1783, through George IV's effective repudiation of the Whigs in 1811–1812, after which, indeed, some

---

[66] Basil Cozens-Hardy, ed., *The Diary of Sylas Neville* (Oxford, 1950), p. 30.
[67] See Iain McCalman, *Radical Underworld: Prophets, Revolutionaries, and Pornographers in London, 1795–1840* (Oxford, 1993), esp. ch. 8.
[68] Harding, 'Hanover and British Republicanism', p. 323.
[69] William H. Stephenson, *A Sermon, Preached in the Independent Methodist Chapel, Newcastle, on the Nineteenth of July, 1821, the Day of the Coronation of His Majesty George IV* (Newcastle upon Tyne, 1821), pp. 13–14, 17, 19. His biblical text was 2 Chronicles, x. 12–14.

opposition Whig politicians began to look to Princess Charlotte for a possible revival of the reversionary interest.[70] Both kings were personally identified with the ministerial regime which – however grumblingly at times – they sponsored, supported and, of course, needed. Kingship above party might have been a vision – or idealisation – of monarchy, but it was as far from reality and practice under the last two Anglo-Hanoverian Georges as it had been under the first two. However, the connection with Hanover was one reason why neither George III nor George IV was completely the prisoner of ministers, and why George III in particular was more than simply a John Bull symbol of anti-revolutionary stability from the 1790s. As well as the continuing importance of the crown in domestic politics, the connection with Hanover gave the crown a potential measure of independence from its ministries, even if there were relatively few opportunities for its exercise in practice, despite George III's independent action over the *Fürstenbund* in 1785. So does the Anglo-Hanoverian union, in its later stages under George III and George IV, reinforce or undermine the fashionable concept of a 'long eighteenth century'? On the whole a good case could be made for the argument that – especially in its international and confessional dimensions – it tends to reinforce that concept; not, indeed, by a Whiggish insistence on pushing the nineteenth century back into the eighteenth, but by recognising that many values and attitudes – or visions – of kingship associated with the eighteenth century retained much of their influence well into the nineteenth.

---

[70] See E.A. Smith, *George IV* (New Haven, 1999), pp. 157–8.

PART IV
Contested Loyalties

Chapter 11
The Hanoverian Succession and the Politicisation of the British Army

Hannah Smith*

In January 1729, Colonel Francis Negus MP recounted to John, Viscount Percival, how close Britain had been to a military coup 15 years earlier in the feverish final months of Queen Anne's reign. According to Negus, Henry St. John – Viscount Bolingbroke, Secretary of State – plotted to bring over the Pretender by military force with the approval of the queen and her Tory confidante, Abigail, Lady Masham. To achieve this, Bolingbroke proposed 'the modelling the army'. But Bolingbroke's great rival, Anne's Lord Treasurer, Robert Harley, first Earl of Oxford:

> knew the impossibility of doing that suddenly and opposed it … However, the Duke of Ormond, who was Lord Bollingbroke's man and general, in pursuance of this scheme began to debauch the officers. He thought himself sure of the Tories and undertook to debauch the Whigs among them, but he found a strong resolution in these last not to serve the Queen *her own way*, which was the expression used to them, and the touchstone of their inclinations. And many who yielded to keep their posts and military governments, privately gave assurance to those who managed the interest of the House of Hanover that they would never forsake it. Many of them even signed the association to rise and seize upon Oxford and Bollingbroke on a certain day, and by a bold but necessary step preserve the Hanover succession. General Withers was one and told it Negus.[1]

---

* This chapter is based on a paper given at the 'Dynastic Politics, Monarchical Representation and the Union between Hanover and Britain' conference, London, October 2012. I wish to thank the conference's participants for their comments and questions on it. Material from the Cholmondeley (Houghton) papers is cited by kind permission of the Syndics of Cambridge University Library.

[1] Historical Manuscripts Commission, ed., *Manuscripts of the Earl of Egmont: Diary of Viscount Percival, Afterwards First Earl of Egmont*, 3 vols (London, 1920–1923), III, p. 334.

In the event, the Hanoverian succession was preserved without the need for such a 'bold but necessary step'. As Anne lay dying, from 30 July to 1 August 1714, the Privy Council seized the political initiative to ensure the Elector of Hanover's accession to the throne, which was overseen by a Regency Council prior to Georg Ludwig's arrival in England on 18 September. While military precautionary measures were put in place, most notably the standard procedures of securing garrisons and ports, it was the acquiescence of politicians from a broad range of political perspectives, including Bolingbroke, Ormonde and Oxford, in late July and early August 1714 which ensured the smooth transition from the Stuart to the Guelph dynasties.

Yet in the spring and summer of 1714, this outcome appeared uncertain to contemporaries. A civil war, accompanied by a foreign invasion, was widely feared. Fears were fuelled by memories of how military intervention secured a particular political and dynastic outcome in 1660 and 1688–1689; by alarm over the constitutional dangers that a 'standing army' posed; and by the existence of large numbers of serving and disbanded officers and soldiers. Fears were also inflamed by the politicisation of the British army, a phenomenon that historians of Anne's reign have considered from the perspectives of ministers, MPs and the officer corps.[2] In the 'age of party', the army's politicisation was similar to that experienced by British society more generally. But the army's politics were exacerbated by tensions and anxieties that were special to military life. Few livelihoods demanded so much possible or actual pain – death, disablement, injury, capture and periods of prolonged separation from family and friends – yet might return so little by way of recompense. After 1706, the army generally did not grow in size, reducing opportunities for promotion.[3] The fate of officers and soldiers looked precarious as a peace seemed possible. Such stresses were heightened by the army's limited access to reliable and regular news while on

---

[2] Particularly important have been the History of Parliament Trust volumes covering the period 1690 to 1715 published as D.W. Hayton, Eveline Cruickshanks and Stuart Handley, eds, *The House of Commons, 1690–1715*, 5 vols (Cambridge, 2002) and http://www.historyofparliamentonline.org/research/members/members-1690-1715. All subsequent references are to the online version: *HoP, 1690–1715*. See also I.F. Burton, '"The Committee of Council at the War-Office": An Experiment in Cabinet Government under Anne', *The Historical Journal*, 4 (1961), pp. 78–84; Geoffrey Holmes, *British Politics in the Age of Anne* (revised edn.; London, 1987); Henry L. Snyder, 'The Duke of Marlborough's Request of His Captain-Generalcy for Life: A Re-Examination', *Journal of the Society for Army Historical Research*, 45 (1967), pp. 67–83; Edward Gregg, 'Marlborough in Exile, 1712–1714', *The Historical Journal*, 15 (1972), pp. 593–618.

[3] Ivor F. Burton, *The Captain-General: The Career of John Churchill, Duke of Marlborough from 1702 to 1711* (London, 1968), pp. 166–8.

campaign, especially in Spain. The army had its own intense microclimate, influencing the politics of its members.

This chapter explores the politicisation of the British army from the latter half of Anne's reign to the opening years of George I's, as successive ministries, with the crown's backing, attempted to 'model' the army to support their own authority and political aims. These initiatives were not novel. Since the founding of a permanent professional army in 1660–1661, every regime had paid careful attention to the army's political loyalties. Nor was political division within the army a new phenomenon. James II's army had become factionalised as a result of the king's pro-Catholic policies by 1688, and the collapse of James's regime was partly owing to the defection of some of his officer corps to William of Orange.[4] But the last four years of Anne's reign in particular represent a singular period in the political history of the British army that reflect the tensions unique to the reign of the last Stuart. Never again would the army be so riven by party politics; nor would military appointments be quite so determined by party allegiance. The significance of this moment was immediately recognised, and became of crucial importance to justifying 'standing armies' after the Hanoverian succession, and bolstering the early Georgian army's communal self-perception as a corps of patriots committed to protecting Protestantism and political liberty.

I

Anne's parliaments contained a considerable number of MPs who were serving, or had served, in either the army or navy. This number reached 18 per cent of MPs in the parliament of 1707 – 1 per cent more than the noticeably militarised 1685 parliament of James II's reign.[5] Contemporaries were quick to criticise this development, which suggested that the war was creating a new socio-economic and political group. They were alarmed by army officers contesting parliamentary seats in counties and boroughs where they had previously had no or little influence or interest. As perturbing was the army officer MP's perceived status as a placeman, dependent upon a ministry for advancement in his career.[6] Such concerns had a solid basis, particularly for Tories. Of the 144 army officers who were MPs for English and Welsh constituencies between 1690 and 1715, 77 can

---

[4] John Childs, *The Army, James II, and the Glorious Revolution* (New York, 1980), pp. 138–64.
[5] http://www.historyofparliamentonline.org/volume/1660-1690/survey/i-composition-house; *HoP, 1690–1715*, 'Members'.
[6] Holmes, *British Politics in the Age of Anne*, pp. 126–9, 132, 149, 182, 223.

be identified as Whigs and 43 as Tories.[7] Furthermore, as Geoffrey Holmes has remarked, 'by 1710 not merely political but parliamentary voting considerations were clearly dictating Whig recommendations for army promotion'. Of the 21 commissions for the posts of major-general or lieutenant-general between 1 May 1707 and 1 January 1709, 12 went to Whigs – including MPs William Cadogan, Thomas Farrington, Emanuel Howe, Thomas Meredith, Harry Mordaunt, Francis Palmes, Viscount Shannon, James Stanhope and Sir Richard Temple. The Tories were a much smaller cohort, with John Richmond Webb the only MP.[8]

As captain-general, and a long-serving soldier himself, John Churchill, first Duke of Marlborough, fully appreciated the need for promotions to reflect military merit and experience – 'of not doing injustice in putting anybody over the heads of officers that may have deserved very well' – to ensure the army's military effectiveness, the morale of the senior officer corps and his own authority within the army.[9] However, Marlborough's attempts to protect the interests of long-standing and suffering officers might conflict with his own political needs. Marlborough was opposed to the lord lieutenant of Ireland, Lord Wharton's, request to raise a new Irish regiment in 1709. 'Considering the great number of officers the Queen has to provide for, I can't think anybody should have a redgiment that has not nor never can serve', he wrote to Godolphin in July 1709, who pointed out the scheme's political advantages in smoothing their relations with Wharton. The regiment was duly raised, Wharton filling it with his own political following.[10] Marlborough also had to grapple with the needs and repercussions of the Act of Union of 1707. A number of influential Scottish noblemen were ambitious senior army officers whose relatives and clients held commissions. The most notable and troublesome was John Campbell, second Duke of Argyll, who commanded his own coterie of army officer MPs and whose

---

[7] *HoP, 1690–1715*, 'Members'.

[8] Holmes, *British Politics in the Age of Anne*, p. 27; Geoffrey S. Holmes, *Augustan England: Professions, State and Society, 1680–1730* (London, 1982), pp. 268–9; P.W.J. Riley, *The English Ministers and Scotland, 1707–1727* (London, 1964), pp. 108, 143–4.

[9] Henry L. Snyder, ed., *The Marlborough-Godolphin Correspondence*, 3 vols (Oxford, 1975), III, p. 1278.

[10] Snyder, ed., *Marlborough-Godolphin Correspondence*, III, pp. 1299, 1299, n. 5, 1306, 1346; *HoP, 1690–1715*, 'Wittewronge, Sir John'. For the lord lieutenant's military patronage in Ireland see D.W. Hayton, 'Dependence, Clientage and Affinity: The Political Following of the Second Duke of Ormonde', in Toby Barnard and Jane Fenlon, eds, *The Dukes of Ormonde, 1610–1745* (Woodbridge, 2000), pp. 211–41, at pp. 232–3.

powers of patronage and capricious personality proved a pain for successive ministries both before and after 1714.¹¹

The increasingly partisan environment in which army officer MPs operated is strikingly demonstrated by the case of the three Windsor brothers. In 1705, Captain Dixie Windsor stood in the hard-fought election for a University of Cambridge seat against Godolphin's son, Francis. Notwithstanding the ministry's efforts, the Godolphins lost to Windsor, a Tory churchman. The political tensions between the ministry and the Windsors came to a head in 1707, when Dixie's elder brother, Thomas, Viscount Windsor, also an army officer, failed to support the ministry. This was a dangerous course for an officer to take, dependent as he was upon the crown and its ministers for military patronage – as Windsor could not but have been aware. Indeed, at the time of the 1705 Cambridge election, it was alleged that Dixie Windsor had been threatened with the loss of his commission for standing against Francis Godolphin. In April 1707 the ministry moved swiftly. Lord Windsor lost his regiment, and Dixie Windsor his captaincy. The dismissal of two officers – the sons of an earl, and one a peer with a long history of military service – solely because of their politics caused wide consternation in the army. 'My Lord Windsor is much espoused by the gentillmen of the army of all partes, there not being many examples of that kind amoung us', wrote Lieutenant-General Henry Lumley to fellow Tory Sir Thomas Hanmer in June 1707.¹² That the ministry was intent on providing a political lesson to army officer MPs is also suggested by its handling of Thomas's and Dixie's brother, Andrews Windsor. Unlike his elder brothers, Andrews Windsor had yet to join the Commons. His military career survived, with Marlborough promoting him in October 1709.¹³

Yet, as the years between 1709 and 1712 demonstrate, Marlborough's own political and professional survival was dependent on royal favour since military appointments had to be approved by the crown. Prior to the spring of 1709 Anne was generally prepared to accept Marlborough's recommendations for appointments and promotions. The queen's willingness to do so may not only have

---

¹¹ Christopher Storrs, 'The Union of 1707 and the War of the Spanish Succession', *Scottish Historical Review*, 87 (2008), pp. 31–44, at pp. 38–40; Riley, *English Ministers and Scotland*, pp. 20–21, 95; John Stuart Shaw, *The Management of Scottish Society, 1707–1764: Power, Nobles, Lawyers, Edinburgh Agents and English Influences* (Edinburgh, 1983), pp. 8–9.

¹² *HoP, 1690–1715*, 'Windsor, Thomas, 1st Vist. Windsor'; 'Windsor, Hon. Dixie'; Henry Bunbury, ed., *The Correspondence of Sir Thomas Hanmer, Bart.* (London, 1838), p. 106; W.A. Speck, *Tory and Whig: The Struggle in the Constituencies, 1701–1715* (London, 1970), p. 107.

¹³ *HoP, 1690–1715*, 'Windsor, Hon. Andrews'; Snyder, ed., *Marlborough-Godolphin Correspondence*, III, p. 1394.

reflected her confidence in her captain-general but also in her husband, Prince George of Denmark, who screened Marlborough's lists. On her succession, Anne had immediately appointed George of Denmark as 'Generalissimo of all Her Majesty's Land Forces', as well as Lord High Admiral.[14] While George did not distinguish himself in either role – he was particularly viewed as being under the influence of Marlborough's brother, George Churchill, in Admiralty matters – the involvement of the prince in army promotions may have given Anne some reassurance that the crown's interests were being protected. George of Denmark's function in this capacity is clearly indicated after his death in late October 1708, which, as Robert Walpole, Secretary at War, informed Marlborough, had 'putt a Stop to the Course of business in this Office. I presume all applications now must be made directly to Her Ma^{ty}.'[15] Like Anne, George of Denmark was also willing to defer decisions until he had received Marlborough's advice, only occasionally taking an initiative. In early June 1708, when Marlborough's own candidate for preferment failed to take up his post in the West Indies, George ordered the commission for another, 'by whose intercession', Walpole reported to Marlborough, 'I doe not know'.[16] Royal involvement might not have been unwelcome to Marlborough. The queen's handling of those applications for appointments and promotions made to her in person could prove useful to her captain-general. When Marlborough received a letter in April 1704 from Thomas Livingstone, Viscount Teviot, concerned at the disposal of his regiment to Lord John Hay, he waved Teviot towards Anne: 'The Queen herself will have informed your Lordship what were the motives that induced her Majesty to it ... her Majesty may have assured you at the same time of her regard to your services.'[17]

However, the spring of 1709 saw the beginning of a change in the queen's approach to patronage. With George of Denmark no longer at her side, ostensibly to oversee Marlborough's lists, Anne possibly felt the need to adopt a more wary attitude. More significantly, it was in the spring of 1709 that the duke made the first of his unsuccessful requests to the queen to be appointed captain-general for life.[18] While Marlborough's desire for permanency stemmed from

---

[14] R.E. Scouller, *The Armies of Queen Anne* (Oxford, 1966), pp. 5, 55.

[15] Cambridge University Library, Cambridge (hereafter CUL), Walpole (Houghton) MSS Ch (H) Pol. Papers 6, Robert Walpole to John Churchill, Duke of Marlborough, 2 Nov. 1708.

[16] Ibid., Walpole to Marlborough, 1 June 1708. See also George Murray, ed., *The Letters and Dispatches of John Churchill, First Duke of Marlborough, from 1702 to 1712*, 5 vols (London, 1845), I, p. 248.

[17] Murray, ed., *Letters and Dispatches*, I, pp. 248–9.

[18] Edward Gregg, *Queen Anne* (2nd edn; New Haven, 2001), p. 300.

his increasing uneasiness about the security of his position, he only succeeded in heightening Anne's suspicions about his political ambition.[19]

Anne publicised her mistrust in January 1710 when she made two important promotions against Marlborough's wishes, triggered by the death of the second Earl of Essex, constable of the Tower of London and colonel of a regiment of dragoons.[20] Marlborough was lobbied by Richard Savage, fourth Earl Rivers, for the office of constable. Rivers had been a Whig for most of his political life but had become increasingly disillusioned with the ministry after its failure to back him in a quarrel with the first Earl of Galway, commander in the Peninsula, or to promote him further. Rivers also had a small parliamentary following of his own within the army in Henry Bradshaigh and, more briefly, Henry Bradshaigh's brother, Sir Roger Bradshaigh, both MPs for Wigan.[21] Marlborough had no wish to promote Rivers; but, rather than turn him away, Marlborough permitted him to speak to the queen about the vacancy, assuming that Anne would discuss it with the duke. Anne did not, and appointed Rivers directly.[22]

Even worse from Marlborough's perspective was the queen's next action. Anne gave Essex's regiment to Abigail Masham's brother, John Hill, again without consulting Marlborough. An irate Marlborough, who believed that Harley had instigated both nominations, left London in a fury, threatening to resign if Anne did not dismiss Abigail Masham, the Duchess of Marlborough's great rival for the queen's favour. An unhappy Anne eventually backtracked on Hill's appointment, but not before queen and duke had been driven to rally their supporters in a competing and traumatic show of political strength. Marlborough tried – and failed – to instigate enough backing for a parliamentary address demanding Abigail Masham's dismissal, and his own appointment as captain-general for life.[23]

Marlborough's victory was pyrrhic, not least because his actions prompted damaging rumours about his political intentions. Peter Wentworth, later equerry to Queen Anne and then to George I, told his brother, Lord Raby, on 24 January 1710 that the 'General officers has been sounded by both sides to

---

[19] Snyder, 'Duke of Marlborough's Request', pp. 67–83.
[20] For accounts of this episode upon which the following paragraphs are based see Snyder, 'Duke of Marlborough's Request', pp. 75–81; Gregg, *Anne*, pp. 300–305; Frances Harris, *A Passion for Government: The Life of Sarah Duchess of Marlborough* (Oxford, 1991), pp. 164–6.
[21] *HoP, 1690–1715*, 'Savage, Richard, Visct. Colchester', 'Bradshaigh, Henry', 'Bradshaigh, Sir Roger'; Holmes, *British Politics in the Age of Anne*, p. 325.
[22] Snyder, 'Duke of Marlborough's Request', p. 75.
[23] Ibid., pp. 75–81.

discover what they wou'd do if things shou'd come to extremitys'.²⁴ Three days later, Wentworth wrote that:

> what was reported as to the Duke's friends sounding all the General Officers as to their inclinations of standing by him and that 'twas found he cou'd depend upon none but Codagan [Cadogan] and Merideth [Meredith] is said to be all false and an invention of the Tories to alarm the Q_n with designes of the Duke which he never had.²⁵

Moreover, the duke's ability to block the rise of the Harley–Masham interest was temporary. Shortly after Anne's final, bitter meeting with the Duchess of Marlborough in early April 1710, Marlborough decided to omit Hill, and Masham's husband, Samuel Masham, from the current round of promotions for brigadier-general and colonel respectively. The queen countered by commanding Marlborough, through Walpole, to promote them.²⁶ Godolphin pointed out to the duke on 19 May that Marlborough had given a handle to his enemies in denying Anne's request, and urged him not to refuse it but 'rather to make a complement of it'.²⁷ Marlborough finally bowed to Anne's wishes in early June, as the queen was in the process of firing Marlborough's son-in-law, Charles Spencer, third Earl of Sunderland, from office as Secretary of State.²⁸

Godolphin's dismissal in August 1710, his replacement by Harley and the massive victory of the Tories in the parliamentary elections in the autumn of that year exacerbated the growing factionalism within the army. The new ministry promoted officers with known Tory or anti-Marlborough leanings. As the newswriter Abel Boyer remarked, 'it was thought necessary, in order to strengthen the Hands of the *New Ministry*, and the *Church Party*, to do Justice to some *Military* Gentlemen, who seem'd to have been neglected under the last Ministry'.²⁹ Where no such rancour existed, attempts were made to create it. In early August 1710 the Whig Anne Clavering cried up the 'glorious young rogue, Lord Ashburnham', who was 'as good as closetted' by the Harleyite Earl Poulett:

---

²⁴ James J. Cartwright, ed., *The Wentworth Papers, 1705–1739* (London, 1883), p. 103.
²⁵ Ibid., p. 104.
²⁶ Gregg, *Anne*, pp. 311–12; Snyder, ed., *Marlborough-Godolphin Correspondence*, III, pp. 1410, 1461, n. 6; William Coxe, *Memoirs of the Life and Administration of Sir Robert Walpole, Earl of Orford*, 3 vols (London, 1798), II, pp. 13–17, 21–4; J.H. Plumb, *Sir Robert Walpole: The Making of a Statesman* (London, 1956), pp. 153–5.
²⁷ Snyder, ed., *Marlborough-Godolphin Correspondence*, III, p. 1500.
²⁸ Gregg, *Anne*, pp. 312–14.
²⁹ [Abel] Boyer, *Quadriennium Annæ Postremum; Or the Political State of Great Britain*, 8 vols (London, 1718), I, p. 8; Holmes, *British Politics in the Age of Anne*, p. 28.

to endeavour to perswade him he ought to resent Lord Portl[an]d's being preferd to Lord Albem[arle's] Troop of Guards before him ... and that he hoped his Lordship woud not enter into the schemes of some men, but woud always be a zealous server of his country and joyn with the Queen and her Party.

Ashburnham refused to be drawn, although Clavering's enthusiasm was misplaced. Two months later Ashburnham married Mary, Ormonde's daughter, and gravitated to the Tories.[30]

The most prominent beneficiary of regime change was the Tory David Colyear, first Earl of Portmore. Portmore was appointed to command in Portugal in place of Galway, 'whose advanc'd Age and Infirmities, render'd him unfit for Action; not to mention his Intimacy with the late Treasurer', Godolphin.[31] But malcontents saw their chance too. In June 1710, Charles Boyle, fourth Earl of Orrery, complained to Harley that he had been blacklisted in the current round of army promotions, and ingeniously explained that he only pressed for advancement 'for our common cause ... that the Queen may show she will not suffer his Highness to wrong the service or prejudice any person that does not misbehave himself to her or the public'.[32]

Orrery's friend, Argyll, was another ambitious senior officer who believed that Marlborough had failed him. It was widely alleged at the time of the political crisis in January 1710 that Argyll had offered Anne that 'whenever she commanded, to seize the Duke at the head of his troops, and bring him away either dead or alive'.[33] In late April 1710, Marlborough reported to Godolphin that Argyll was giving the impression of 'having an entier power' with the queen, and that Marlborough was only permitted to continue in office since he was indispensable to the war effort. Marlborough retaliated by making it clear that Argyll lay under his displeasure. A month later, Marlborough was pleased to report that nobody conversed with Argyll 'but such as are angry' with Marlborough.[34] This very public rupture brought its own rewards for Argyll from the new ministry. The duke was invested with the Order of the Garter in

---

[30] H.T. Dickinson, ed., *The Correspondence of Sir James Clavering* (Gateshead, 1967), pp. 88–9; *HoP, 1690–1715*, 'Ashburnham, Hon. John'.
[31] Boyer, *Quadriennium*, I, p. 8; Holmes, *British Politics in the Age of Anne*, p. 28.
[32] Historical Manuscripts Commission, ed., *The Manuscripts of His Grace the Duke of Portland, Preserved at Welbeck Abbey*, 10 vols (London, 1891–1931), IV, p. 544.
[33] Cited in Snyder, 'Duke of Marlborough's Request', p. 80.
[34] Snyder, ed., *Marlborough-Godolphin Correspondence*, III, pp. 1474, 1499.

late December 1710 and appointed to the dubious honour of commander-in-chief of the British army in Spain in early 1711.[35]

But possibly the most striking case of a frustrated careerist of these years was Lieutenant-General John Richmond Webb. Webb had quarrelled with Marlborough back in September 1708 after Marlborough had mistakenly credited his protégé and quartermaster-general, William Cadogan, with what was Webb's moment of *gloire* at the Battle of Wynendael. Webb's case was picked up by his fellow Tories as a way of attacking Marlborough.[36] In September 1711 Webb requested that Oxford continue an earlier awarded pension, bearing in mind his services and sufferings, and since he had been poorly rewarded 'by the late Ministry'.[37]

The political divisions within the army received maximum publicity in December 1710, when Anne ordered three of Marlborough's favourites – Thomas Meredith, George Macartney and Philip Honywood – to dispose of their regiments for drinking toasts to the damnation of the new ministry. As Wentworth informed Raby:

> 'tis said 'twas not a health drunk in a drunken fitt, but a constant health among them – Confussion to the present ministry, and Damnation to all that had a hand in the change, without exception, and damn all that wou'd not stand by the Duke of M_ with their lives and fortunes ... 'tis said these healths were drank at Cadogan's house, and that when they came to them [Charles] Ross and Billy Care [Col. William Kerr] flew out of the company in a passion.[38]

Wentworth remarked, 'the Officers begin to curse again the president the late Ministry gave in turning out Lord Windsor, whose talking never came up to the Extravagance of these gentlemen'.[39]

The evocation of the Windsor case was apt. Meredith had briefly been a Whig MP until he lost his seat in the 1710 election, the Tory Commons ignoring his petition of appeal.[40] By contrast, although Kerr's politics were Whiggish, his support for Tory acquaintances and causes ensured he gained a

---

[35] Riley, *English Ministers and Scotland*, pp. 146–8, 160, 236; John Stuart Shaw, *The Political History of Eighteenth-Century Scotland* (Basingstoke, 1999), pp. 46–52.
[36] Cartwright, ed., *Wentworth Papers*, p. 69; *HoP, 1690–1715*, 'Webb, John Richmond'.
[37] Historical Manuscripts Commission, ed., *The Manuscripts of His Grace the Duke of Portland*, V, p. 87.
[38] Cartwright, ed., *Wentworth Papers*, 163–4.
[39] Ibid., p. 162.
[40] *HoP, 1690–1715*, 'Meredyth, Thomas'.

reputation as a Tory. Charles Ross, meanwhile, was committing himself to the Tories.[41] Arthur Maynwaring, the Whig writer and political confidante of the Duchess of Marlborough, pointed to Ross as 'one of [the] Informers against the poor Gentlemen that were broke' and sarcastically ascribed Ross's promotion in the army in May 1711 as richly deserved for that reason.[42] The case was immediately played out in the periodical press, in Jonathan Swift's *The Examiner* and Maynwaring's *The Medley*.[43]

The trio's dismissal demonstrated the determination of both Anne and her ministry to control Marlborough's influence within the army. As Anne told her physician, Sir David Hamilton, she was happy for Marlborough to remain in post '*if he would go into her* Measures, and not divide and make partys'.[44] Anne's ministers appear to have shared such sentiments. As Swift reported:

> The ministry is for gentler measures, and the other Tories for more violent. Lord Rivers, talking to me the other day, cursed the paper called *The Examiner*, for speaking civilly of the duke of Marlborough; this I happened to talk of to the secretary [St. John], who blamed the warmth of that lord and some others.[45]

Harley was attempting to resist Tory demands to turn out Whigs from their posts; St. John wished to restrain rather than remove the duke.[46] Harley's creation of 'the Committee of Council which sits at the War-office', in operation from late February 1711 until its demise at the end of July, was a consequence of this policy of containment.[47] The committee considered a range of military administrative matters, including the regulation of promotions and sale of commissions, and so presented a direct if short-lived challenge to Marlborough's influence, before St. John's intriguing appears to have terminated its existence.[48]

---

[41] Ibid., 'Kerr, Hon. William', 'Rosse (Ross), Hon. Charles'.

[42] Cited in Frank H. Ellis, ed., *Swift vs. Mainwaring: The Examiner and The Medley* (Oxford, 1985), p. 107, n. 110.

[43] Cartwright, ed., *Wentworth Papers*, p. 165; Ellis, ed., *Swift vs. Mainwaring*, pp. 107–18, 136–8, 163–9.

[44] Gregg, *Anne*, p. 327; Philip Roberts, ed., *The Diary of Sir David Hamilton 1709–1714* (Oxford, 1975), p. 21.

[45] Jonathan Swift, *Journal to Stella*, ed. by Harold Williams, 2 vols (Oxford, 1948), I, p. 195.

[46] Sheila Biddle, *Bolingbroke and Harley* (London, 1975), p. 191; H.T. Dickinson, *Bolingbroke* (London, 1970), pp. 76–7.

[47] Burton, 'Committee of Council', pp. 78–84, although see Holmes, *British Politics in the Age of Anne*, p. 462, n. 78.

[48] Burton, 'Committee of Council', pp. 82–4; Dickinson, *Bolingbroke*, p. 76.

II

The politicisation of the army entered a new phase at the start of 1712 with Marlborough's dismissal and his replacement by the Tory hero, James Butler, second Duke of Ormonde. Nevertheless, the ministry had to proceed cautiously in any attempt to remodel the army. Between 1712 and 1713, experienced personnel were still required to staff the British army in the field, such as Cadogan. 'No man knows the Spanish Low Countries better than he does, nor is more expert in the affair of quarter-master general', the first Earl of Strafford (formerly Lord Raby), remarked to Oxford of Cadogan around the time that Cadogan finally lost his appointments in the winter of 1712–1713 after he had requested ministerial permission to travel abroad with the now self-exiled Marlborough.[49] Thus, it was only in the autumn of 1713, with the Peace of Utrecht signed and stable, that the government could think seriously about altering the political composition of the army.

The extent to which Bolingbroke, Oxford and Anne were plotting a Jacobite succession was debated at the time and thereafter. While both Bolingbroke and Oxford were intermittently in negotiation with the Pretender to persuade him to convert to Protestantism, Anne seems to have had little enthusiasm for a potential 'James III', whatever was alleged after her death by Hanoverian and Jacobite adherents alike.[50] Anne's support for remodelling the army was, of course, vital to implementing any changes; she may have seen it as necessary to make her army her own.

In early November 1713, Argyll alleged to the Hanoverian envoy to London, Georg von Schütz, that Oxford was interrogating officers and broke them 'when their answers did not please him'.[51] The opening months of 1714 saw sweeping changes, with 'persons put in that are for the interest of her Majesty and Ministry', as a newsletter of March 1714 remarked.[52] It was alleged that 16 'Whigg Collonells' were ordered to sell out. Rumours abounded that Lord Windsor, a Hanoverian Tory, would be dismissed again, as would General Henry Lumley, then commander-in-chief in Flanders, whose support for the Tories and friendship with Bolingbroke also encompassed a commitment to

---

[49] Cited in *HoP, 1690–1715*, 'Cadogan, William'.
[50] Edward Gregg, 'Was Queen Anne a Jacobite?', *History*, 57 (1972), pp. 358–75.
[51] James Macpherson, *Original Papers; Containing the Secret History of Great Britain from the Restoration to the Accession of the House of Hannover*, 2 vols (London, 1775), II, p. 511.
[52] Historical Manuscripts Commission, ed., *The Manuscripts of His Grace the Duke of Portland*, V, p. 401; Holmes, *British Politics in the Age of Anne*, pp. 28, 462.

the Hanoverian succession.⁵³ Prominent Whig officers – including Lieutenant-Colonel William Egerton, MP for Brackley– were dismissed.⁵⁴ Such reports understandably 'caus'd no small Uneasiness among the Military Men'.⁵⁵ The most politically prominent scalp was Argyll's. The duke's relations with the ministry had deteriorated since its high point in early 1711 when he had been appointed commander-in-chief in Spain. His army had suffered numerous setbacks, which Argyll blamed on the ministry for failing to provide adequate supply. The Whiggish Argyll returned to London in opposition by 1713, and lost his posts in the spring of 1714.⁵⁶

The tense atmosphere of this period is captured in accounts written after the Hanoverian succession. *An Apology for the Army*, 'Written by an Officer' and published in 1715, related how officers were:

> *closeted*, and extreamly pressed with large Promises of Preferment, &c. to *Enter into the Queen's Measures*. When they replyed, *That they were Her Majesty's Dutiful Subjects, and wou'd readily Obey Her, in every Thing consistant with the Dictates of their Honour and Conscience*: This was not admitted as a satisfactory Answer. They were to engage *Implicity*, which they shewing an Aversion to, (as suspecting the Drift of the Proposers) then *Innuendo's* were let fall, that *Posts* in the *Army* were only *during Pleasure*, not *Places for Life*.⁵⁷

Captain Robert Parker recounted in his memoirs how a fellow officer had been closeted by an uncle, a lieutenant-general, 'in great vogue with the Party', and promised a company in the guards provided that he would 'serve the Queen faithfully'. When Parker's acquaintance countered that he had 'always served my Queen and Country faithfully, and well', his uncle responded:

> Sir ... your Country is not what I propose: But will you serve your Queen *without any reserve*? I replied, that I had always supposed, that in serving my Queen,

---

⁵³ Margaret Maria Verney, ed., *Verney Letters of the Eighteenth Century from the MSS. at Claydon House*, 2 vols (London, 1930), I, p. 274; *HoP, 1690–1715*, 'Windsor, Thomas'; 'Lumley, Henry'.

⁵⁴ Robert Parker, *Memoirs of the Most Remarkable Military Transactions from the Year 1683, to 1718* (London, 1747), pp. 251–2; *HoP, 1690–1715*, 'Egerton, Hon. William'; Boyer, *Quadriennium*, VII, pp. 263–4, 409–10; Macpherson, *Original Papers*, II, p. 588.

⁵⁵ Boyer, *Quadriennium*, VII, p. 264.

⁵⁶ Riley, *English Ministers and Scotland*, pp. 236, 239–40, 244, 246; Shaw, *Political History*, pp. 24–5, 52–3.

⁵⁷ *An Apology for the Army: In a Short Essay on Fortitude, Etc. Written by an Officer* (Dublin, 1715), p. 38.

my Country was at the same time included, and that I could never serve one without including the other. Then, said the General, you are to expect no further preferment; but be thankful if you keep what you have.

'These were the arguments they used to cajole, or frighten the Gentlemen of the Army', Parker reported. 'Nay, they had Spies in all the Coffee-houses that were frequented by Officers, to inform against such as condemned their proceedings.'[58]

It was not only the officer corps that came under political pressure. According to the *Apology for the Army*'s author, the ministry, disappointed in their attempts to 'corrupt' the officer corps, tried to divide it by 'encouraging the common Soldiers against their Officers, in order to weaken and disarm, if possible, these last'.[59] Parker similarly commented on the dissatisfaction of the rank and file, concerned by Ormonde's failure to engage with France, the 'badness of their bread' and fears that they were to be disbanded without their arrears of pay, which led to mutiny.[60]

Against this backdrop of politically motivated dismissals and promotions, it seemed that a Hanoverian (or Jacobite) succession was reliant upon military backing – from foreign troops or those in foreign service, or from troops at home. One upshot was Oxford's proposed bill in the Lords in mid March 1714 making it high treason to invite foreign troops into Britain without parliament's support, which had implications for both Hanoverian and Jacobite supporters. (Bolingbroke, meanwhile, promoted a bill creating it high treason for anyone to enlist soldiers for the Pretender.)[61] As Edward Gregg has shown, Marlborough had mooted an allied invasion to protect the Hanoverian succession and stop the peace settlement in December 1712. The exiled duke's plan would see Hanoverian troops in Dutch and Imperial pay sent to England. Cadogan would manage the expedition, assisted in England by James Stanhope and Sunderland. Although Marlborough's scheme was dismissed by the Dutch, the emperor and the Elector of Hanover, he continued to hope for an invasion in the summer of 1713, before carrying on negotiations with the Jacobites in the autumn.[62] While the Elector of Hanover wished to appear neutral in English politics, he was willing, in March 1713, to consider military action on Anne's death and

---

[58] Parker, *Memoirs*, pp. 248–9.
[59] *Apology for the Army*, p. 6.
[60] Parker, *Memoirs*, pp. 221–2.
[61] Biddle, *Bolingbroke and Harley*, pp. 268–9; Brian W. Hill, *Robert Harley: Speaker, Secretary of State and Premier Minister* (New Haven, 1988), pp. 210–11; Dickinson, *Bolingbroke*, p. 125; Gregg, *Anne*, p. 383.
[62] Gregg, 'Marlborough in Exile', pp. 599–600, 602–6.

discussed plans with Marlborough and Cadogan. They recommended that they should be authorised to secure and assess the political reliability of the British troops abroad. Cadogan was to go to London to command the Tower of London, administer oaths of allegiance to the English troops and break politically suspect officers. Cadogan also advised on the political character of the commanders of the British garrisons on the continent.[63] Marlborough and Cadogan once again liaised with the Dutch in early 1714, when Anne was seriously ill, about an invasion in the event of her death.[64]

Pro-Hanoverian former or serving army officers in England also seem to have drawn up plans for a military *coup d'état*. According to the Jacobite George Lockhart of Carnwath, 'great sums of money were advanc'd by the heads of the party towards providing arms and ammunition, which were accordingly got ready to be distributed amongst their friends'.[65] In September 1738, John Hampden MP told the first Earl of Egmont (formerly Viscount Percival) that his brother, Richard Hampden, an associate of Stanhope, had recalled how:

> my Lord Stanhope, a soldier and a hot and desperate man ... advised that in the House of Commons the Whigs should draw their swords and murder such of the Ministry and their friends as should be in the House upon the day that the person pitched on by the Ministry to move the repeal of the Hanover succession ... should ... make that motion.[66]

Much later in the century, it was claimed that:

> General Stanhope was to have commanded the army, and lord Cadogan to have seized the tower. All the officers on half-pay ... had signed the association. The place of *rendez-vous* was appointed behind Montagu House. The officers held their arms in readiness in their bedchambers, and were prepared to obey the summons at a minute's warning.[67]

---

[63] Ibid., pp. 601–2; Macpherson, *Original Papers*, II, pp. 475–8.
[64] Gregg, 'Marlborough in Exile', pp. 609–10.
[65] *The Lockhart Papers: Containing Memoirs and Commentaries Upon the Affairs of Scotland from 1702 to 1715*, 2 vols (London, 1817), I, p. 462.
[66] Historical Manuscripts Commission, ed., *Manuscripts of the Earl of Egmont*, II, p. 509.
[67] M[atthew] Maty, ed., *Miscellaneous Works of the Late Philip Dormer Stanhope, Earl of Chesterfield*, 2 vols (London, 1777), I, pp. 15–16; Basil Williams, *Stanhope: A Study in Eighteenth-Century War and Diplomacy* (Oxford, 1932), pp. 143–4.

In the event, the Hanoverian succession occurred without the need for military assistance at home or from abroad. The regents secured garrisons and ports, sending half-pay officers and Chelsea out-pensioners to Portsmouth, where General Thomas Erle, a veteran supporter of the Revolution, was reinstalled in place of the Jacobite Lord North and Grey.[68] The new king reinstated a number of senior officers who had been removed by the last ministry, most notably Marlborough. However, George I resisted efforts to remodel the army at the outset, in keeping with his initial policy of attempting to maintain some semblance of a politically balanced ministry. While key posts were filled or retained by known Hanoverian supporters, Tories, such as Webb, were kept on. Wentworth reported in mid October 1714 that:

> when some people prest hard to have Web outed of all, the King ask'd if he had not done his Duty well in his several posts, wch cou'd not be denied. Then the King said he wou'd have no regard to people's private piques, and ordered Web to be continued and to wait upon the D. of M[arlborough].[69]

Lord Windsor, likewise, stayed in post, as did several of Ormonde's army supporters, notably Thomas Pearce. Henry Withers was another who successfully made the move between the regimes, despite his association with Bolingbroke. Withers remained as governor of Sheerness until his death in 1729, as a result of his longstanding favour with Marlborough and his alleged plotting to secure the Hanoverian succession.[70]

It was the deterioration of the political situation from the spring and summer of 1715, with the prosecution and flight of Bolingbroke and Ormonde, which made imperative the dismissal of politically suspect Tories from positions of military command and their replacement with proven loyalists.[71] Webb's Toryism ensured his removal from the governorship of the Isle of Wight in June 1715 and he later lost his regiment, becoming a pronounced Jacobite in the process.[72] Lieutenant-General Robert Echlin, a Tory MP closely tied to Ormonde, was deprived of his regiment in early 1715. Echlin then joined the Pretender abroad, fought in the '15 and died in exile. James Barry (fourth Earl of Barrymore), Sir

---

[68] Boyer, *Quadriennium*, VIII, p. 634.
[69] Cartwright, ed., *Wentworth Papers*, p. 430.
[70] *HoP, 1690–1715*, 'Pearce, Thomas', 'Windsor, Thomas', 'Withers, Henry'; Hayton, 'Dependence, Clientage and Affinity', pp. 239–41.
[71] Holmes, *Augustan England*, p. 274.
[72] *HoP, 1690–1715*, 'Webb, John Richmond'; *Weekly Journal with Fresh Advices Foreign and Domestick*, 18 June 1715.

Henry Goring, Major-General John Hill, General Charles Ross and Brigadier Richard Sutton were also dismissed in the summer and autumn of 1715, as the '15 rebellion broke out.[73]

The ministry not only confined its attention to senior officers. 'We hear there are Orders from Above for a great Reform of the Officers in the first and second Regiment of Foot-Guards', reported the *Weekly Journal* on 18 June 1715.[74] The same month, George I approved the removal of an officer from the half-pay list: 'Information having been given against him of publishing & Dispersing Scandalous & Seditious Libells'.[75] In August 1715, the Secretary at War, William Pulteney, instructed that four captains in Lord Shannon's Regiment were to be suspended while their political loyalties were investigated, ordering that if the allegations were true, officers currently on half pay should replace them.[76] Fears over the loyalties of the rank and file also troubled the regime, stemming from ministerial concerns about support for the Hanoverian succession amongst the populace more generally in the wake of High Church and Jacobite rioting in late 1714 and in 1715.[77] In November 1715, when Pulteney sent a regiment to police Jacobite Oxford, he not only instructed its commanding officer to ensure that the troops did not offend Oxford's scholars and townspeople; he also urged him to make sure that neither the officers nor soldiers were 'Corrupted' by Oxonians.[78] Pulteney's concerns could scarcely have been assuaged by the report which reached him in February 1716 that soldiers from a company of Colonel Kirk's regiment, quartered at Bridgnorth, Shropshire, had roamed the town in the absence of all but one of their officers, crying 'damn the Whigs, down with the Roundheads'.[79] The king, his ministers and army officers set about tackling sedition within the ranks through oaths of allegiance and harsh punishment. One old soldier in receipt of a military pension was disciplined in January 1716 for drinking the Pretender's health by the permanent withdrawal of his allowance.[80]

But the regime's fears during the '15 were unrealised. The majority of the officer corps and private soldiers remained loyal to the Hanoverian regime.

---

[73] *HoP, 1690–1715*, 'Barry, James', 'Echlin, Robert', 'Goring, Henry', 'Hill, John', 'Rosse (Ross), Hon. Charles', 'Sutton, Richard'; *HoP, 1715–1754*, 'Sutton, Richard'.
[74] *Weekly Journal with Fresh Advices Foreign and Domestick*, 18 June 1715.
[75] The National Archives, Kew (hereafter TNA), WO4/17/127.
[76] Ibid., WO4/17/174.
[77] Nicholas Rogers, 'Popular Protest in Early Hanoverian London', *Past and Present*, 79 (1978), pp. 70–100.
[78] TNA, WO4/17/261.
[79] Ibid., WO4/18/46.
[80] Ibid., WO71/34/42–3, WO4/18/2, 9.

Few serving officers have been identified as joining the '15.[81] Relatively few cases of sedition appear in surviving court martial records. Indeed, it was the Whig Schism rather than the '15 which proved a more politically testing time for the officer corps. Argyll was dismissed in July 1716 for perceived political troublemaking, his lack of vigour in putting down the '15 and his feud with Cadogan, his successor as commander-in-chief in Scotland. A year later, the Stanhope–Sunderland ministry was only able to fight off the opposition's attack on Cadogan for embezzlement in June 1717 by 10 votes. These developments led to the removal of a number of Argyll's friends and followers who had been staunch in their support of the regime during the '15, such as Lieutenant-Colonel John Middleton, Lieutenant-Colonel Robert Munro and, most prominently, Orrery, who was subsequently in touch with the Jacobite court by mid 1717, as well as other officers who had voted against the government. Lord Windsor, who having lost his regiment to party politics a decade earlier, was turned out once again for his political opposition.[82] This was closely followed by the rupture between the king and the Prince of Wales in December 1717, which led to army officers with posts in the prince's household banned from holding both employments.[83]

III

In the years after George I's accession, the perceived role that pro-Hanoverian officers played in defending the Hanoverian succession quickly became integral to the army's self-image, trumpeted in print and via anecdotes such as the one told to Percival in 1729. As the author of *An Apology for the Army* declared:

> so just a Sense had these Gentlemen [the Officers] of their own Honour, so great a Regard to the Welfare of their Country, and so clear an Apprehension of these Men's wicked Designs, that they scorned all Offers on one Side, and Threats on the Other, bravely resolving, to hazard their Posts, (their only Maintenance) rather than lay violent Hands on a Constitution they had so often ventured their Lives to defend.[84]

---

[81] Daniel Szechi, *1715: The Great Jacobite Rebellion* (New Haven, 2006), pp. 122, 128.
[82] Riley, *English Ministers and Scotland*, pp. 263–4; Shaw, *Political History*, pp. 57–8; Szechi, *1715*, p. 162; *HoP, 1690–1715*, 'Middleton, John II', 'Munro, Robert', 'Boyle, Hon. Charles II', 'Windsor, Thomas'.
[83] TNA, SP 35/1/67–8.
[84] *Apology for the Army*, p. 5.

Similarly partisan interpretations of the army's recent political history were important to the army's defenders in the post-war years, since this narrative emphasised the officer corps' patriotic commitment to the Protestant succession, and the constitutional structure that upheld it. Such claims were also professionally useful to individual officers, not only in the opening years of George I's reign, prior to the proscription of the military Tories, but in the final years of George II's. As late as 1756, Sir John Rushout, when angling for a peerage, alleged that he had resigned his captaincy four decades earlier in January 1712 to avoid being dismissed by Ormonde for supporting the Hanoverian succession.[85]

The politicisation of the British army reached a high point in the last four years of Anne's reign. Never again were so many army officers so open in their opposition to the crown's ministers and policies; nor was there so much potential for a military *coup d'état*. The conditions that created this situation were specific to Anne's reign: an uncertain and disputed succession to the crown weighted with significant ideological baggage; a large wartime army engaged in a conflict which was viewed as part of the struggle to defend the revolutionary settlement; and, in the figure of Marlborough, an influential and politically serpentine captain-general, increasingly at odds with his sovereign. The period between the outbreak of the '15 and the end of the Whig Schism also saw a series of dismissals from the army on political grounds. Moreover, Jacobite plotters remained unduly optimistic that enough of the officer corps and private soldiers could be persuaded to support a rising in favour of the Pretender, notably during the Layer Plot of 1722–1723.[86] But the political circumstances of the late 1710s were different to those earlier in the decade. After 1716, it was reversionary interest rather than dynastic politics, and tensions between Stanhope, Cadogan and Argyll over who would eventually succeed Marlborough as captain-general, that preoccupied particular members of a much smaller peacetime officer corps.[87] From around 1720 onwards, politics – and the political involvement of the army – changed again. Argyll was rehabilitated in 1719 and, after another blip in his political fortunes, once again in 1721. Some of his followers, and those of the Prince of Wales, were reinstated. Army officers usually supported the ministry, a development reflecting the tenor of politics in an age of oligarchy and

---

[85] *HoP, 1690–1715*, 'Rushout, Sir John'.

[86] See *A Report from the Committee Appointed by Order of the House of Commons to Examine Christopher Layer and Others* (London, 1722); *The Whole Proceeding Upon the Arraignment, Tryal, Conviction and Attainder of Christopher Layer, Esq; for High Treason, in Compassing and Imagining the Death of the King* (London, 1722 [1723]).

[87] Shaw, *Political History*, pp. 58–60; Williams, *Stanhope*, pp. 409, 439.

the curtailed opportunities for advancement which peacetime brought.[88] While those opposed to 'standing armies' continued to articulate their fears about the possibility of military 'tyranny' in the regular parliamentary debates over the size of the military establishment, the moment for an army-led *coup d'état* in British politics had passed.

---

[88] Riley, *English Ministers and Scotland*, pp. 268–72; http://www.historyofparliament online.org/volume/1715-1754/survey/appendix-vii-members.

Chapter 12
Jacobitism and the Hanoverian Monarchy

Gabriel Glickman

On 6 August 1714, the Tory parliament at Westminster proclaimed loyalty to George, Elector of Hanover, as king of Great Britain and Ireland, pledged enmity to all opponents of his 'undoubted right to the imperial crown' and secured the Protestant succession peacefully by a unanimous vote. Yet only a year after this triumphant moment, the dynastic horizons appeared notably less propitious. By the autumn of 1715, Scotland was ablaze with rebellion: an insurgency that soon snaked south to engulf Lancashire and Northumberland. *Habeas corpus* had been suspended amid fears of foreign invasions, and the commanding personalities of the old Tory ministry had been impeached, banished or thrown into the Tower. Before the end of the year, a rival prince was sailing across from the continent, resolved to plant his claim upon British shores. The eventual, comprehensive failure of the 1715 Jacobite rebellion appeared markedly less certain in the chaotic months that followed its inception, and its effect was to force a shift in the mood of Hanoverian rule, away from the serene consensus of August 1714. For the remainder of the new king's life, and long into the reign of his son, the British state stood on a war footing, unsettled by the twin perils of internal subversion and external assault. Thirty years later, when a second pretender occupied Edinburgh, the Whig Earl of Marchmont believed his monarch to be only one defeat away from being toppled.[1] Stirring Marchmont's alarm, moreover, was the anxiety that Jacobitism had burgeoned because of defects in the principles and practices shaping Hanoverian rule. The greatest threat to the dynasty, he had argued, lay in an 'absence of zeal' among its advocates, when the court had fallen sway to the 'interested persuasions of Favorites and Ministers'; when parliament now resembled the 'corrupt and adulating Senate' of imperial Rome; and when 'the Royal Family every Day more and more estranges the good Will and Fidelity of their Subjects'.[2]

---

[1] George Henry Rose, ed., *A Selection from the Papers of the Earls of Marchmont, Illustrative of Events from 1685 to 1750*, 3 vols (London, 1831), I, p. 102.

[2] Earl of Marchmont, *A Serious Exhortation to the Electors of Great Britain* (London, 1740), pp. 10–11, 29.

Long into the century, the exiled house of Stuart menaced the Hanoverian monarchs with a shadow court, a subterranean intelligence network and an alternative regal and political vision. Secondary re-evaluations have struck likewise against the received narratives of eighteenth-century Britain. Once dismissed as a movement of grimly archaic nostalgia, Jacobitism has, since the 1970s, been exposed to a process of scholarly recovery. Its ideological hinterland has been recaptured as richer and more consistent, its polemical literature placed within the canopy of Augustan satire and its support base characterised more extensively than was hitherto imagined.[3] Jacobites probed at the limits of Hanoverian authority; they fostered alternative ideas of how a monarch should govern and whom he should govern for; and they imported mistrust into the political process. How the strength or otherwise of the Stuart cause is to be adjudged carries, moreover, potent implications for larger interpretations of the cultural and political mentality that underpinned the three kingdoms within the 'long eighteenth century'.[4] The picture put forward in revisionist writings – of a kingdom caught in a protracted succession crisis, and a polity so wedded to the principle of 'legitimacy' that its bonds could be fractured by dynastic conflict – cleaves far apart from the older representations of an Augustan age of secular, modernising stability.

However, the significance of Jacobitism has proved a subject of contention, plagued by ambiguous extant material. To study the Stuart cause outside its militant heartlands in the Highland and north-eastern regions of Scotland and the European diaspora is to enter a hall of mirrors, a world of obliquely shifting sympathies in which contemporaries proved rarely more certain than secondary scholars as to who among them might carry the Pretender's shilling. 'The appellations of Tory and Jacobite ... are always ridiculously given to any man who does not bow to the brazen image the king has set up', complained one apostate to the cause, Henry St. John, Viscount Bolingbroke. Yet Bolingbroke acknowledged too that the roll-call of subversives was not easy to pin down, when 'every Jacobite in England sinks his master's divine right in the popular topics of debts, taxes, and corruption', cloaking the cause in the language of 'constitutional' opposition.[5] Accordingly, the historiography of Jacobitism has

---

[3] Paul Kléber Monod, *Jacobitism and the English People, 1688–1788* (Cambridge, 1989); Daniel Szechi, *The Jacobites: Britain and Europe 1688–1788* (Edinburgh, 1986).

[4] J.C.D. Clark, 'On Moving the Middle Ground: The Significance of Jacobitism in English Historical Studies', in Eveline Cruickshanks and Jeremy Black, eds, *The Jacobite Challenge* (Edinburgh, 1988), pp. 177–85.

[5] [Henry St. John, Viscount Bolingbroke], *Remarks on the History of England* (London, 1743), pp. 22, 35.

threatened to become almost as treacherous as the cause itself. The Jacobite movement has enjoyed many afterlives. Within half a century of their defeat, the Stuarts in exile had been memorialised for the purposes of legitimist 'throne and altar' politics in revolutionary Europe.[6] Latterly, the cause has been recruited for the eternal quest to discover an elusive 'world we have lost', and identified as a form of 'social banditry' levelled against the 'polite and commercial' values of the age.[7] This judgement would perhaps have surprised the host of bankers, planters and merchants who funded, toasted or fought for the exiled princes. The Stuart cause undeniably fostered ideas of civic patriotism in Ireland and Scotland, yet in eliding this stance with the content of separatist, nationalistic ideologies emerging in later centuries, historians risk overshadowing a more complex reality in which even fervent Irish Jacobite commentators proclaimed themselves subjects of the 'British monarchy' and part of the 'British Empire'.[8] If the attempts to characterise Jacobitism socially and ideologically have proved problematic, the question of how to calibrate its support base is even thornier. A long succession of scholarly blasts and counterblasts has seen rival fragments of evidence stacked up for or against the contention that after 1714, a faction in English politics, principally within the Tory party, was motivated by seditious dynastic considerations.[9] Yet the decisive evidence remains elusive. Recent debates have, especially, failed to settle upon a shared consensus over exactly what constituted a Jacobite; of where, in the slippery space between claret-fuelled 'loyal toast' and the taking-up of rebel arms, could be found the cast-iron will to rock the Hanoverian throne.

Scholarly doubt over the scale of the Jacobite threat should not blind us to the importance of dynastic rivalry in the evolution of Hanoverian rule. This chapter aims to establish a means of thinking about the battle of Stuart and Hanover that eschews the knotted problem of classifying exactly who was or was not a Jacobite. I will look at the demonstrable ways in which the princes over the water impinged upon the relationship between the new dynasty and its domain, and exerted an influence visible in foreign and domestic policy. The

---

[6] James J. Sack, *From Jacobite to Conservative: Reaction and Orthodoxy in Britain c.1760–1832* (Cambridge, 1993), pp. 60–61.

[7] For a measured assessment of this association, see Monod, *Jacobitism*, pp. 115–9.

[8] Royal Archives, Windsor (henceforth RA), Stuart Papers, Miscellany, VII, pp. 129–35, Thomas Sheridan, 'Political Reflexions', 1710; Bodleian Library, Oxford (henceforth Bodl.), Carte Ms 229, fo 275, Nicholas Plunkett, 'A Light to the Blind', 1711. The Royal Archives are cited with kind permission of Her Majesty the Queen.

[9] See, for example, Andrew Hanham, '"So Few Facts": Jacobites, Tories and the Pretender', *Parliamentary History*, 19 (2000), pp. 233–58; Eveline Cruickshanks, 'Jacobites, Tories and "James III"', *Parliamentary History*, 21 (2002), pp. 247–54.

Jacobite gambit may have rested upon the untried potential of a line of exiled Catholics, but it was taken seriously by monarchs and ministers, not least because it could not be contained within domestic confines. Stability in any kingdom in eighteenth-century Europe was an all too flighty holy grail, when predatory impulses in state relations drew other powers into exploiting the internal ruptures of their neighbours. At home, recent literature has shown that the old depiction of bewildered princes wading through a sea of xenophobia represents at best an incomplete understanding of the shifting moods present in English popular politics.[10] Yet Jacobitism highlighted limitations on the dynastic appeal nonetheless, and drew attention to weaknesses in the governmental armoury, many of which harked back to conflicts that had riven the multiple-kingdom British monarchy across the previous century. The Stuart cause could become a locus of opposition for religious, cultural and political identities threatened by the expansion of a centralising, fiscal-military state. Concurrently, the fear of Jacobitism inhibited relations between Hanoverian monarchs and their subjects in Scotland and Ireland, and left the integrity of politics at Westminster undermined by fears of veiled allegiances and hidden motivations. The chapter will conclude by showing how concern over the peril spurred Hanoverian champions and propagandists into appropriating elements in the rhetoric of Jacobite kingship, to shape the representation of the incumbent princes. I will suggest that if Jacobite boasts often corresponded with ministerial anxieties to magnify the actual peril from the displaced princes, the effect was still to stamp a lasting mark upon the political identity of the Hanoverian crown.

I

Between 1715 and 1745, public commentaries dramatised the dangers for a kingdom wooed by two 'suitors', as the Jacobite poet Jane Barker saw it: 'whilst each Pretender thinks himself alone/ ... Nay, well it is, if such will grant/ That there is one elsewhere Triumphant'.[11] For the dynasty's supporters, the battle against Jacobitism provided the *raison d'être* of Hanoverian rule: failure would, as one author put it, result in 'the Ruin of half the Nation ... the Protestant

---

[10] Hannah Smith, *Georgian Monarchy: Politics and Culture, 1714–1760* (Cambridge, 2006).

[11] Jane Barker, 'A Patchwork Screen for the Ladies, or Love and Virtue Recommended' (1723), in C. Shiner Wilson, ed., *The Galesia Trilogy and Selected Manuscript Poems of Jane Barker* (Oxford, 1997), pp. 80, 151.

interest and the Liberties of Christendom'.¹² The Hanoverian succession had decisively affirmed the political reality established in the British Isles after the 1689 Revolution: the religious identity of a monarch was now more important than the laws of hereditary succession. In transmitting their call to arms, Whig ideologues linked the clash over the throne to a still-febrile strain of historic anti-popery. After the 1715 rising, the declaration from the Anglican bishops invoked the memory of Mary I, and the most notorious massacres of the European religious wars, to allege that the restoration of James III, '[t]ogether with the long train of Papists in the Succession, can bode nothing but fatal and Irrecoverable Ruin'.¹³ The case for George I was fixed within international as much as domestic horizons, engaging the sensibilities of Whigs such as Sir John Percival who looked to the preservation of Protestant monarchies across Europe for evidence that 'God has promised never to abandon his Church, and that Church (when we oppose the Protestant to the Popish) is certainly the Former'.¹⁴

Yet in spite of their confidence in its moral rectitude, Hanoverian rule appeared still to rest, too often for Whig sensibilities, on a knife-edge. For the Earl of Stair, every instance of popular disaffection bred 'dangerous consequences to the Protestant succession in the house of Hanover'.¹⁵ Bernard Mandeville agreed that the throne was surrounded by 'enemies to our tranquillity'; and confessed himself anxious that those 'who at the [1688] Revolution were either Children, or are born after it' were evincing cavalier disregard for its essential verities of 'Moderation', 'peace and union'.¹⁶ A sense of fragility stirred the generation who had cut their political teeth during the War of the Spanish Succession, who had seen governments forced to affirm the principle of the Protestant succession on five separate legislative occasions after 1689 and perceived themselves living in the shadow of Catholic danger on the continent. The consciousness 'that Jacobitism is rising ... and that spirit has ever subsisted under the ashes' was the star that steered the policies of Robert Walpole, as architect of a vast and far-

---

¹² Bernard Mandeville, *Free Thoughts on Religion, Church and National Happiness* (London, 1720), p. 328.

¹³ *Declaration of the Archbishop of Canterbury, and the Bishops in and near London, Testifieing their Abhorrence of the Present Rebellion* (London, 1715); Colin Haydon, '"I love my King and my Country, but a Roman Catholic I hate": Anti-Catholicism, Xenophobia and National Identity in Eighteenth-Century England', in Tony Claydon and Ian McBride, eds, *Protestantism and National Identity: Britain and Ireland c. 1650–c.1850* (Cambridge, 1998), pp. 33–52.

¹⁴ British Library, London (henceforth BL), Add Ms 47031, fo 81, Sir John Percival to Edward Southwell, 1 Dec. 1725.

¹⁵ Rose, ed., *Marchmont Papers*, II, p. 76.

¹⁶ Mandeville, *Free Thoughts*, pp. xiv, 317–18.

flung intelligence network constructed against threats within and without.[17] While Whig polemics sought to rouse the nation into Protestant fervour, Walpole's struggle against the Stuarts would be fought out as intensely in the secret worlds of agents and informers, the taverns, forests and fishing ports as on the battlefield; laws against smugglers and poachers arose in part as attempts to disrupt the supply lines through which Jacobite ciphers entered the British Isles.[18] The maintenance of a 70,000 strong standing army in times of peace proved that Hanoverian governance scarcely rested on a note of complacency.

The challenge from the Stuarts was more persistently ideological than military. The political arguments of Jacobitism had been conceived in the penitential prayers and jeremiads of the Anglican Non-jurors who rejected the 1688 Revolution; by 1715, however, the movement had undergone an internal reinvention. Lit up by its portraits, medals and pageantry, the cause of the exiled Stuarts melded patriotic slogans with a culture of joyfully subversive revelry. From the chants heard within High Church riots in Norwich, Bristol and Manchester, to the sprigs of oak pinned up by the Duchess of Norfolk over her family's Worksop estates on the Pretender's birthday, to the tartan worn by Tories at race meetings across the Midlands, the Stuart cause transmitted a festive calendar at once patrician and plebeian, monarchic and anarchic.[19] Public parading of these quirkily ritualised tokens of misrule was not itself a sound indicator of treasonable activity. The garments, songs and floral trinkets did, however, reflect the efforts of Jacobite artists and authors to achieve the improbable feat of recasting the heirs to James II as '[t]hose Sweet and Royal Roses ... the Darlings of Old England', the heralds of popular opposition towards Whig governments.[20] In the exiled

---

[17] H.T. Dickinson, *Walpole and the Whig Supremacy* (London, 1973), p. 158; Historical Manuscript Commission, ed., *Manuscripts of the Earl of Egmont: Diary of Viscount Percival, Afterwards First Earl of Egmont*, 3 vols (London, 1920–1923), I, pp. 361, 424 (henceforth HMC, *Egmont Diary*).

[18] Eveline Cruickshanks and Howard Erskine-Hill, 'The Waltham Black Act and Jacobitism', *Journal of British Studies*, 24 (1985), pp. 358–65; John Broad, 'Whigs and Deer-Stealers in Other Guises: A Return to the Origins of the Black Act', *Past and Present*, 119 (1988), pp. 56–72.

[19] Arundel Castle, Howard of Norfolk MSS, miscellaneous correspondence, no. 114, Phillis Balguy [i.e., Maria, Duchess of Norfolk] to 'Mr Heaton Junior at Sheffield', 24 March 1717; History of Parliament Trust, London, transcripts, diary of Sir Dudley Ryder (henceforth Ryder Diary), 16 May 1747; Nicholas Roger, *Whigs and Cities: Popular Politics in the Age of Walpole and Pitt* (Oxford 1989), p. 81. Citation from the Arundel MSS comes with the kind permission of His Grace the Duke of Norfolk; the Ryder Diary is quoted with thanks to the History of Parliament Trust.

[20] [George Flint], *The Shift Shifted*, 7 July 1716.

court, pragmatic voices produced new Jacobite manifestos that disowned the 'imprudences of the late K. James's reign', promised free parliaments, religious toleration and respect for Anglican privilege.[21] In England, Jacobite newsbooks latched emotively onto signs of oppression and corruption, as hallmarks of a time when 'Right and Wrong changed Names, Party Revenge was protected under the veil of Publick Justice; Loyalty one year was Treason in the next'. For George Flint, the author of *The Shift Shifted*, the condition of England – 'our gaols are cramm'd'; Jacobite suspects subject to 'the axe, the halter, the pillary'; and London turned into a 'Garrison'd Town' – confirmed the baleful evidence of history that all 'usurpations' succeeded only when they had 'drain'd the Oceans of the best blood in the Nation'.[22]

Jacobite correspondents represented Hanoverian England less as a monarchy than an oligarchy. Weak foreign potentates provided only the mask for a clique of notables who had attained such 'mighty power' that 'they can make a king out of a broomstick' and win acquiescence on 'the same principle of corruption that we often see man ... suffer indignities from a base creature called a mistris, that they would think themselves dishonoured if they suffered from a lawfull wife'.[23] For the oligarchs, they were unable to suppress a certain admiration. 'Write in your hand to Mr Walpole', the Pretender was urged by his former chaplain, Lewis Innes: 'offer him all he can reasonably desire ... make him see his own honour in the just cause'.[24] But the diagnosis of 'ministerial despotism' also encouraged the Stuarts' supporters to pitch dynastic claims within the grammar of Augustan civic thought; to attack the unbalancing of the constitution by factions; and to argue that the restoration of the rightful prince marched hand in hand with the recovery of the people's freedoms. Jacobite polemics shadowed patriot opposition discourse, caught the cadence of *Cato's Letters* and Bolingbroke's *Craftsmen*, and decried the national loss of virtue that, as they saw it, entrenched the injustices of Hanoverian rule.[25] The Septennial Act had placed Britain in thrall to another 'long parliament'; swelling taxes and standing armies recalled past Cromwellian tyranny. Foreign polices had been

---

[21] Archives of the Archbishop of Westminster, Kensington, Epistolae Variorum V/48, E. Dicconson to Mayes, 17 March 1714; Lord Middleton, 'On the Hanoverian succession', 1709, in Historical Manuscript Commission, ed., *Calendar of the Stuart Papers ... at Windsor Castle*, 7 vols (London 1902–1923), VII, p. 597.

[22] [Flint], *The Shift Shifted*, 12 May 1716, 23 June 1716.

[23] RA, Stuart Papers, 108/49, Thomas Southcott to John Graeme, 7 July 1727; ibid., 107/151, Lewis Innes to James Edward Stuart, 30 June 1727.

[24] Ibid., 121/72, Lewis Innes to James Edward Stuart, 27 Dec. 1728.

[25] William King, *Literary and Political Anecdotes of His Own Time* (London, 1818), pp. 39, 57; Christine Gerrard, *The Patriot Opposition to Walpole: Politics, Poetry and National Myth 1725–42* (Oxford, 1994).

distorted towards the service of a German electorate, leaving Britain's Atlantic fleet 'neglected and dishonoured' while a government that evinced the ferocity of 'lions' against 'liberty and property' at home acted like 'feeble spaniels' overseas.[26] Jacobite rhetoric played upon paradoxes: the republican author Thomas Gordon was perturbed to see his 'numerous Pamphlets published against the Administration ... all forced into their service', while the London journalist Nathaniel Mist seized with relish upon Lockean arguments to exhort 'resistance' from 'the freeholders of England' towards the 'haughty tyrants' seated in their midst.[27] In the exiled court, Stuart princes showcased their affiliations with Archbishop Fenelon, the critic of Louis XIV, to sketch out an idea of a Jacobite monarch as a virtuous, law-giving, anti-Machiavellian counterblast to contemporary tyranny and absolutism.[28] Indeed, the Pretender would increasingly be defended less on hereditary grounds than as a patriot prince, exalted by one versifying Benedictine monk as a hero who 'neglects his own to heal his people's wounds' and 'weeps to see his groaning subjects lie/ In fetters that they might themselves untie'.[29] In the despondent decades between the rebellions of 1715 and 1745, the audacity of its printed voice was critical to keeping the Jacobite cause alive.

II

'The plausible appearance under which the modern Jacobite hath of late chosen to represent his cause', as the Oxford Whig Edward Bentham observed, caused exasperation in governing circles. If the Jacobite case rested, for Bentham, on the outlandish proposition that the return of James Edward Stuart would make 'the Seasons ... bloom in one perpetual Spring', its potential to indulge a spectrum of opinion – from 'the Resentment of the Disappointed ... to the generous warmth of the patriot' – provoked a statutory attack upon seditious writings that, nominally at least, exceeded the rigour of laws framed after the

---

[26] *Revolution Politicks being a Compleat Collection of All the Reports, Lyes and Stories, Which Were the Fore-runners of the Great Revolution in 1688* (London, 1733), p. 31; David Morgan, *The Country Bard, or the Modern Courtiers* (London, 1738), pp. 11, 23, 30.

[27] Rose, ed., *Marchmont Papers*, II, p. 345; Thomas Gordon, *A Short View of the Conspiracy* (London, 1723), p. 9; Paul Chapman, 'Jacobite Political Argument in England, 1714–1766' (PhD thesis, University of Cambridge, 1983).

[28] Andrew Michael Ramsay, *Life of François de Salignac de la Motte Fénelon Archbishop and Duke of Cambray* (London, 1723); Gabriel Glickman, 'Andrew Michael Ramsay, the Jacobite Court and the English Catholic Enlightenment', *Eighteenth-Century Thought*, 3 (2007), pp. 294–329.

[29] Douai Abbey, Woolhampton, 'Memoirs of the Society of St Edmunds', p. 303.

French Revolution.³⁰ In reality, the confidence of the Jacobite voice drew only the thinnest of veils over frailties planted within the heart of the movement. The religion of the Pretender provided an obstacle to extracting serious terms from Tory leaders in the closing years of Anne's reign, and a source of rancour affirmed in the 1715–1716 rebellion, when James Edward estranged his military council with refusal to assist in an Episcopalian *Te Deum*.³¹ National and religious antagonisms struck at Jacobite unity in and outside Britain, when Stuart manifestos had scattered their promises indiscriminately across partisan causes and particular grievances, to engage at once Catholic calls for toleration and High Church fears for the loss of clerical power, Tory anxieties over the danger of imperial decline and Scottish reactions against the Act of Union. Such positions brought into the cause a variety of conflicting and divergent impulses, and turned the exiled court into a site of bitter factional competition.³²

In the British Isles, Jacobites worked to purge themselves of associations only with the revanchist and the opportunistic. While a later historiography has connected the expression of Stuart loyalty with a reaction against eighteenth-century modernity, Jacobite works tended more often to shadow rather than reject the intellectual culture of Hanoverian Britain – one portrait captured the Pretender in a library filled with volumes of Locke.³³ But insofar as this initiative made headway, it created a new conundrum – the worldlier cast of characters coveted by the exiled court was unlikely to risk its stake in the kingdom for the dubious honour of martyrdom. The historian Edward Gibbon recalled his childhood in a household filled with Non-juring prayers and devotions, where spiritual convictions ran up nonetheless against professional choices that anchored the family in the world of post-Revolution politics, as financiers and contractors for the British army.³⁴ If sympathy for the Stuart remained rife among Scottish and Irish merchants in Montserrat, Jamaica and St Kitts, its expression was judiciously stifled as trading connections brought both communities within the orbit of the City of London.³⁵ The career of the Irish Catholic author

---

30   Edward Bentham, *A Letter to a Fellow of a College* (London, 1749), pp. 8, 34–5; Nicholas Rogers, *Crowd, Culture and Politics in Georgian Britain* (Oxford, 1998), pp. 21–57.

31   James Edward Stuart, 'Reasons for not assisting in the *Te Deum* at Perth', January 1716, in Historical Manuscript Commission, ed., *Stuart Papers*, IV, pp. 12–13.

32   Pauline McLynn, *Factionalism Among the Exiles in France: The Case of Bishop Atterbury and Chevalier Ramsay* (Huntingdon, 1989).

33   Monod, *Jacobitism*, p. 84.

34   J. Murray, ed., *The Autobiographies of Edward Gibbon* (London, 1896), p. 10.

35   John Oldmixon, *Memoirs of Ireland from the Restoration to the Present Times* (London, 1716), p. 250; James Livesey, *Civil Society and Empire: Ireland and Scotland in the Eighteenth-Century Atlantic World* (New Haven, 2009), pp. 111–12.

Nathaniel Hooke, who served as amanuensis for the Duchess of Marlborough, exemplified the balancing act sustained within a great part of the Jacobite world, as it brushed against Hanoverian openings and opportunities.[36] Taxes must be paid and 'order and peace' preserved even under a usurper, argued the Chevalier Andrew Michael Ramsay, a thinker in favour at the exiled court, even while 'Obedience must never go soe far, as to approve the Injustice of the Usurpation'.[37] In exile, Bishop Francis Atterbury could never countenance the descent of a 'popish army' into England.[38] Most of the leading Jacobites were not by instinct desperadoes: accordingly, and problematically for the exiled court, they were unlikely to welcome the prospect of a country plunged into a new civil war. Even as the 1715 rebellion gathered pace, Alexander MacDonnell of Glengarry moved to assure the Whig commander at Fort William that a dynastic dispute was 'not the quarrel of private gentlemen': in contrast to the civil conflicts of the previous century, the Jacobite risings were short on burnings, lootings and sackings.[39]

Set against these inhibitions, the Jacobite cause has to be located within a larger canvas to understand why it managed so successfully to spark anxiety within court and government. The Jacobite threat was perhaps explicable less through the intrinsic merits of the cause than its exploitation of deeper vulnerabilities, divisions and animosities that underlay the governance of Britain, and which prevented the new monarchs from resting securely upon their thrones. Assessed in an insular context, the Stuart cause appeared a sporadic and containable threat. Its salience increased when Jacobitism spilled out into a European landscape in which succession contests functioned as the engine of geopolitical conflict, and when displaced dynasties could be turned into instruments for the ambitions of rival powers. The Hanoverian succession was secured in parliament in 1701 on the eve of a Europe-wide conflagration over the Spanish crown. Twice, between 1709 and 1738, Polish monarchs were restored through Russian agency against rivals backed by other powers. In 1741, French factions helped orchestrate the coup that swept Elizabeth Petrovna to the Russian throne; simultaneously, continental armies mustered to contest the right to the Holy Roman Empire. The 'strange jumble of interests in Europe at present', as observed by Sir John Percival – a matrix of shifting alliances, with

[36] Joseph Spence, *Anecdotes, Observations and Characters of Books and Men, Collected from the Conversation of Mr. Pope and Other Eminent Persons of his Time*, ed. by Samuel Weller Singer (London, 1964), pp. 199, 211; Rose, ed., *Marchmont Papers*, II, p. 206, Alexander Pope to Viscount Polwarth, 9 Jan. 1740.
[37] Andrew Michael Ramsay, *An Essay upon Civil Government* (London, 1722), p. 58.
[38] RA, Stuart Papers, 81/168, James Murray of Stormont to John Hay, 30 April 1725.
[39] Daniel Szechi, *1715: The Great Jacobite Rebellion* (New Haven, 2006), p. 111.

no single dominating power – lifted continental affairs to a point of primacy in ministerial calculations, and made domestic politics in a divided kingdom liable to manipulation by foreign agency.[40] The fears expressed by Whig ministers that the opposition in parliament danced to a Jacobite tune became more logical when placed in parallel with the internal politics of Sweden, where party conflict was destabilised by the support given to rival factions by French, Russian or English agency.[41] When the monarchs of western and central Europe had entered into a joust for commercial and territorial supremacy that stretched over three continents, any kingdom exposing its fissures to the world could expect its enemies to capitalise.

At the point of the Hanoverian succession, Jacobite émigrés were already strung out across Europe. With their numbers reconstituted by dispersals from Scotland after the 1715 rebellion, the tally would grow to an estimated 40,000, lodged inside institutions from the Gallican Church to the Russian military establishment, to the Swedish East India Company, bearing letters of endorsement from James Edward Stuart and broadcasting awareness of the wrong they believed had wrested them from their native shores.[42] 'Great severities have been used to the Catholics by the Usurpers', the Jacobite court informed its agents; exiles could serve the cause by working to 'remonstrate the cruel oppressions they lie under to the Catholic potentates in Europe'.[43] The Jacobite diaspora enhanced the martial resources available to potential Hanoverian enemies. Scottish soldiers reactivated old networks in northern Europe, and followed Marshal George Keith on a career trajectory from service of the Russian Empress Anna to the court of Frederick II of Prussia.[44] The 'wild geese' who made up the principal Irish contribution to the Jacobite cause clustered ominously in French bases on the Channel coast. As late as 1750, the Duke of Newcastle was disquieted to find Dunkirk 'filled with rebels', with three

---

[40] BL, Add Ms 47031, fos 78–82, Sir John Percival to Robert Southwell, 1 Dec. 1725; Brendan Simms, '"Ministers of Europe": British Strategic Culture, 1714–1760', in Hamish Scott and Brendan Simms, eds, *Cultures of Power in Europe during the Long Eighteenth Century* (Cambridge, 2007), pp. 110–32.

[41] Michael Roberts, *Swedish and English Parliamentarism in the Eighteenth Century* (Belfast, 1973).

[42] RA, Stuart Papers, 44/13, orders to William Dicconson, 22 June 1719; Edward Corp, *A Court in Exile: The Stuarts in France 1689–1718* (Cambridge, 2003), pp. 201–14.

[43] 'Instructions sent by Captain John Ogilvie', Aug. 1716, in Historical Manuscript Commission, ed., *Stuart Papers*, IV, p. 63.

[44] Rebecca Wills, *The Jacobites and Russia: 1715–1750* (East Linton, 2002), pp. 74–8; Steve Murdoch, *Network North: Scottish Kin, Commercial and Covert Associations in Northern Europe, 1603–1746* (Leiden, 2005).

regiments quartered 'just on the other side of the water, in order to recruit in time of peace, and to be ready to invade us, in time of war'.[45] Jacobitism stood not simply as a threat in itself, but as the spearhead for the regional and imperial rivals of the new dynasty: enemies who were mainly, but – as the 1718 plot concocted by the Swedish ambassador served to illustrate – not exclusively Catholic.[46] If the failure to convert these connections into a concrete military alliance eventually started to wear away at the Stuart cause, the slightest possibility nonetheless kept the movement registered at the forefront of British diplomacy.

The effect of the Jacobite challenge was therefore to internationalise Hanoverian rule: to render it not merely a strategic choice but a dynastic imperative to 'form such a confederacy ... as will make it dangerous for any power in Europe to disturb the tranquillity thereof', in the words of Lord Hardwicke.[47] After 1715, dynastic needs pushed ministers into overturning 40 years of Whig thinking about the wider world, courting the war-weary kingdom of France with the appointment of a former Jacobite exile, Earl Waldegrave, as ambassador to Versailles, alongside the encouragement of ecumenical dialogue between Anglican and Gallican ecclesiastics and promises to prevent the persecution of British and Irish Catholics.[48] European allies were valued too as potential outlets for Irish Catholic soldiers who were otherwise liable to enter into the Jacobite fold: active recruitment for the house of Austria had been initiated in the reign of Queen Anne, and continued intermittently through the following half-century, with the blessing of Whig ministers.[49] On these foundations, the government welded together the Quadruple Alliance – for Jacobites, 'that four-footed monster' – drafting Austria and the United Provinces into an accord

---

[45] BL, Add Ms 32720, fo 278, Duke of Newcastle to Henry Pelham, 7/18 May 1750; J.G. Simms, 'The Irish on the Continent, 1691–1800', in Theodore William Moody and W.E. Vaughan, eds, *A New History of Ireland*, vol. 4: *Eighteenth-Century Ireland* (Oxford, 1986), pp. 629–56.

[46] Szechi, *Jacobites*, pp. 104–7.

[47] Brendan Simms, *Three Victories and a Defeat: The Rise and Fall of the First British Empire, 1714–1783* (London, 2007), pp. 133, 76, 187.

[48] BL, Add Ms 47031, fos 77–8, Sir John Percival to Daniel Newman, 1 Dec. 1725; RA, Stuart Papers, 64/171, Thomas Southcott to James Edward Stuart, 24 Jan. 1723; Norman Sykes, *William Wake, Archbishop of Canterbury: 1657–1737*, 2 vols (Cambridge, 1957), I, pp. 261–75.

[49] Narcissus Luttrell, *A Brief Historical Relation of State Affairs from September 1678 to April 1714*, 6 vols (Oxford, 1857); BL, Add Ms 32720, fo 278, Duke of Newcastle to Henry Pelham, 7/18 May 1750.

outlined as the bedrock of domestic as well as European stability.[50] Anglo-French relations held, against assorted mutual provocations, up to 1744, and their strategic premise was vindicated after the fall of Walpole, when the parting of the ways over the Austrian succession provoked Louis XV into a major naval build-up, and prised open the space for a new Jacobite rebellion.[51]

The importance of European affairs informed not merely ministerial priorities but dictated the wider visual and rhetorical presentation of the reigning dynasty, when a genre of popular verses and images valorised Hanoverian monarchs as martial, confessional heroes, glossing over the alliances with Catholic powers and linking the security of the Protestant succession at home to the health of the Protestant interest abroad.[52] Yet the danger was to tie the identity of Hanoverian monarchs to the same policies that placed the greatest strains on their domestic reputation – the treaties, subsidies and interventions that threatened, for Viscount Bolingbroke to channel 'ye small remainder of our wealth where we have thrown so much already, into ye German guelph'.[53] The challenge from the house of Stuart compelled Hanoverian monarchs to remain European in their outlook: in turn, it obliged them to adopt the very policies that reinforced their 'foreignness' and kept the readiest material for Jacobite critiques intact.

III

If the threat from the exiled Stuarts defined the stance of monarchs and ministers abroad, so it also mapped out the limits of the Hanoverian state at home. Jacobite sympathies in the British Isles were concentrated among an ideological core of supporters, comprised of the Anglican Non-jurors and sections of the Catholic communities of England, Scotland and Ireland, in whose devotional literature, the call to arms for the Pretender was presented through a cosmic narrative of trial and redemption. For Charles Radcliffe, heir to the attainted earldom of Derwentwater, James II had conferred upon his supporters 'a Crown of Thorns given him by Allmighty God in place of those Crowns He took from

---

[50] Historical Manuscript Commission, ed., *Stuart Papers*, VII, pp. 659–60, George Jerningham to Earl of Mar, 20 Dec. 1718.

[51] Jeremy Black, 'Foreign Policy in the Age of Walpole', in id., ed., *Britain in the Age of Walpole* (London, 1994), pp. 145–72.

[52] Hannah Smith, 'The Idea of a Protestant Monarchy in Britain 1714–1760', *Past and Present*, 185 (2005), pp. 91–118.

[53] BL, Add Ms 37994, fos 13–14, Bolingbroke to Marchmont, 26 March 1741; Simms, *Three Victories*, pp. 239–75.

Him to punish us unworthy of so good a Prince'.[54] In 1715, the recusants who dominated Jacobite forces in northern England raised banners streaked with the image of a pelican feeding her young with her own blood, as a symbol of Christian sacrifice; in parts of Gaelic Ireland, poems and prayers fixed upon the Stuarts as agents of millennial deliverance.[55] Outside the pietistic inner sanctum, a second Stuart restoration was envisioned as a chance to reconfigure relations between the three kingdoms: the historian Nicholas Plunkett called upon the Pretender to overthrow the Navigation Acts and liberate the Dublin Parliament in Catholic hands, so enabling Ireland to 'overtop' the English 'in a general and free trade', when 'it is a great Debilitation to the Brittish Empyre to have the third Part of her might kept purposely feeble'.[56] For the new dynasty, the threat from recusant quarters was perceived potent enough to preserve the legal bars and privations of the anti-papist penal laws, and to keep the bulk of the British army permanently stationed across the Irish Sea.[57] In the event, however, the place of Catholic Ireland in Jacobite strategy was largely confined to its promise as a crucible for exiled soldiers, while the collapse of the rebel armies at Preston in 1715 exposed the limitations on northern English recusancy as an insurgent force. Far more combustible, in the eyes of Hanoverian governments, were the attitudes of other communities, less inherently wedded to the exiled dynasty since 1689 than spurred on by different grievances, which had estranged them from the turn of post-revolutionary politics. The strongest scope for disaffection came from the schism at the heart of Scottish Protestantism – the principal factor in explaining why the northern kingdom so exceeded Ireland in its centrality to Jacobite strategic thinking.

The Act of Union had been sealed in 1707 with a pledge of continuing Presbyterian domination over the Kirk: deemed the vital precondition to salvage support within the community hitherto most given to separatist sentiment.[58] The

---

[54] RA, Stuart Papers, 70/29, Charles Radcliffe to James Edward Stuart, 23 Nov. 1723.

[55] Samuel Hibbert Ware, *Lancashire Memorials of the Rebellion, 1715* (Edinburgh, 1845), pp. 97–8; F.J. McLynn, 'Ireland and the Jacobite Rising of 1745', *Irish Sword*, 13 (1977–1979), pp. 339–52.

[56] P.H. Kelly, ed., 'The Improvement of Ireland', *Analecta Hibernica*, 35 (1992), pp. 45–84, at p. 54.

[57] Eamonn O'Ciardha, *'A Fatal Attachment': Ireland and the Jacobite Cause 1688–1788* (Cambridge, 2001); Gabriel Glickman, *The English Catholic Community 1688–1745: Politics, Culture and Ideology* (Woodbridge, 2009), pp. 55–9.

[58] Jim Smyth, *The Making of the United Kingdom 1660–1800: State, Religion and Identity in Britain and Ireland* (London, 2001), pp. 115–16; R. Mitchison, 'Patriotism and National Identity in Eighteenth-Century Scotland', in T.W. Moody, ed., *Historical Studies*, vol. 11 (Belfast, 1978), pp. 73–95.

Union had, paradoxically, survived its troubled infancy by widening Scotland's inner divisions, its architects banking on the premise that Presbyterians would accept religious safety and a Protestant succession over the uncertainties of continual independence in a conflicted kingdom. 'The desire I have to see our Church secured makes me in love with the Union as the most probable means to preserve it', affirmed William Carstares as Principal of Edinburgh University; elsewhere, as David Hayton has commented, the 'higher visibility of the Catholic and Jacobite threat' rendered Scottish Whiggery 'correspondingly more violent' towards its adversaries.[59] In the 1715 rebellion, a Calvinist case for loyalty, embedded in civic ceremonies, sermons and printed broadsides, transplanted old Covenanting motifs onto a new conception of Protestant 'Britain', saluting George I as leader of an embattled Israel besieged by Assyrian tormentors.[60] Scotland's Episcopalians lingered at the margins of this new order, denounced as agents of the popish Babylon, and engorged with memories of Scotland's seventeenth-century civil conflicts. The fragile Toleration Act in 1712 was the only concession won since the Revolution, and it did not put to sleep the traumas of a community who perceived themselves disabled in the kingdom of George I.[61] The prayers uttered in their north-eastern strongholds yearned instead that God 'give not up this Church and Nation to destruction ... restore true Religion and Piety'. When ministers evoked the same Hebraic imagery that informed the sermons of the Kirk, their Israel was not a rising Britain but a suffering Scotland, deprived of its parliament, stripped of its true church and, as was increasingly perceived, wrenched apart from its rightful prince.[62] The domination of post-Revolution Scottish politics by a feuding, duelling caste of magnates had wrought disorder even in times of peace: by 1715, the injection of new confessional and patriotic grievances had turned the nation into a tinderbox, sliding, as one Jacobite agent warned, towards 'a war of religion'.[63] The landing

---

[59] Bruce P. Lenman, 'A Client Society: Scotland between the '15 and the '45', in Black, ed., *Britain in the Age of Walpole*, pp. 69–93; David Hayton, 'Constitutional Experiments and Political Expediency 1689–1725', in Steven G. Ellis and Sarah Barber, eds, *Conquest and Union: Fashioning a British State 1485–1725* (Harlow, 1995), pp. 276–305, at p. 291; Carstares quoted in Karin Bowie, *Scottish Public Opinion and the Anglo-Scottish Union, 1699–1707* (Woodbridge, 2007), p. 112.

[60] Linda Colley, *Britons: Forging the Nation 1707–1837* (London, 1992), pp. 31–2.

[61] Szechi, *1715*, pp. 24–65.

[62] Patrick Cockburn, *A Penitential Office for the Use of Those who Mourn for the Sins and Calamities of this Church and Nation* (London, 1721), pp. 4–5; Bruce Lenman, 'The Scottish Episcopal Clergy and the Ideology of Jacobitism', in Eveline Cruickshanks, ed., *Ideology and Conspiracy: Aspects of Jacobitism, 1689–1759* (Edinburgh, 1982), pp. 36–48.

[63] Ryder Diary, 8 Oct. 1746; Szechi, *1715*, p. 68.

of the Pretender added only the final component to a clash of cultures, creeds and consciences that stretched beyond the issue of which family held the crown.

The shock delivered by a rebellion so soon after the king's accession brought major inhibitions into Hanoverian rule over Scotland. Episcopalians, retreating from public worship into a recondite nexus of chapels and meeting houses, were accommodated only minimally within the structures of the polity.[64] Those few clergymen who did challenge dynastic sympathies received little ministerial encouragement, and struggled to articulate reasons for switching allegiance. The Aberdeen parson Patrick Cockburn flitted uneasily between contractualist, Hobbesian and providentialist grounds to acknowledge George I, and aroused congregational animosity for his efforts.[65] For many members of the confession, political transitions were accomplished more easily across the Atlantic – Gabriel Johnston, James Glen and William Keith emerged from Jacobite backgrounds to take offices in Carolina and Pennsylvania.[66] With legal, administrative and ecclesiastical preferment deemed to be most safely placed in the hands of trusted local undertakers, much of Scotland remained treated as an outlying province, kept as separate as was feasible from the metropole.[67] The Highlands were in effect handed over to Archibald Campbell, Lord Islay, who, as Dudley Ryder held it: 'governed Scotland for twenty years, and in order to be able to do that has courted the Jacobites, brought many of them into places'. In practice, this approach meant devolving governmental functions on regional magnates of, at best, dubious loyalty – individuals such as Norman MacLeod of Dunvegan and Simon Fraser, Lord Lovat, who maintained a steady correspondence with the exiled court.[68] This policy, Ryder believed, bore significant responsibility for the insurrection of 1745, when Islay had casually ushered into his service individuals who had 'either underhand fomented the rebellion or connived at it or not being heartily

---

[64] Daniel Szechi, 'Constructing a Jacobite: The Social and Intellectual Origins of George Lockhart of Carnwath', *Historical Journal*, 40 (1997), pp. 977–96.

[65] Patrick Cockburn, *On the Duty and Benefit of Praying for Our Governors* (Edinburgh, 1728); *The Duty of Praying for Our Superiors Consider'd, in Remarks on Mr. Patrick Cockburn's Printed Sermon* (n.p, 1728); [John Lindsay], *An Expostulatory Letter to the Rev. Mr. Patrick Cockburn* (London, 1740).

[66] Ned Landsman, 'The Legacy of British Union for the North American Colonies: Provincial Elites and the Problem of Imperial Union', in John Robertson, ed., *A Union for Empire: Political Thought and the Union of 1707* (Cambridge, 1995), pp. 297–317.

[67] Lenman, 'Client Society', pp. 69–90.

[68] Ryder Diary, 1 Jan. 1747; I.F. Grant, *The MacLeods: The History of a Clan* (London, 1959), pp. 402–4; Allan I. MacInnes, *Clanship, Commerce and the House of Stuart, 1603–1788* (London, 1996).

against it'.⁶⁹ The dramatic swing from the Argathelian stratagem of coaxing loyalty through traditional Highland patronage to the systematic challenge to the institutions of clanship rolled out after 1745 revealed governmental uncertainty over how to contend with Scottish disturbances, and a concomitant failure to nurture the Union as any more than a narrowly strategic arrangement. The ability of Charles Edward Stuart to move a rebel army from Glenfinnan to Edinburgh with barely a shot fired in anger connoted, as Lord Marchmont lamented, an 'absence of zeal' for George II on a national scale.⁷⁰ In English politics, the Jacobite aspersions flung at the lords Mansfield and Bute, together with the denial of militia rights to Scottish burghs in 1756, showed such diffidence fully reciprocated. For half a century, fears of rebellion constrained the growth of a more inclusive British identity within the parameters of the Hanoverian state.⁷¹

IV

Compared to the militant Jacobitism running through the northern kingdom, sympathy for the Stuart cause in English politics was a fugitive phenomenon. For Robert Patten, the Non-juring eyewitness to the rebellion in Lancashire, 'the Roman Catholicks died like men, never varying from their principles', while Tory high churchmen, being 'Never right heavy for the cause, til they are mellow, as they call it, over a bottle or two ... do not care for venturing their carcasses further than the tavern'.⁷² In 1745, the Oxford MP Thomas Rowney, who, according to the Earl of Egmont had 'drunk ye Pretender's health 500 times', was 'frightened out of his wits' when 'the Pretender's Son came into England ... and ordered his chaplain to pray for King George'.⁷³ But if Tory Jacobitism remained, for the most part, a dog that resolutely refused to bark, its reality was adamantly insisted upon by contemporary critics. George II believed the phenomenon to be endemic; so did most Whigs in government office, as well as Patriot opposition leaders such as Egmont.⁷⁴ So too did Frederick, Prince of Wales, when

⁶⁹ Ryder Diary, 1 Jan. 1747; MacInnes, *Clanship*, pp. 160–70.
⁷⁰ Bruce Lenman, *Jacobite Risings in Britain 1689–1746* (London, 1980), pp. 105–6.
⁷¹ John Robertson, *The Scottish Enlightenment and the Militia Issue* (Edinburgh, 1985); Kathleen Wilson, *The Sense of the People: Politics, Culture and Imperialism in England, 1715–1785* (Cambridge, 1998), pp. 175, 210–11.
⁷² Robert Patten, *The History of the Late Rebellion* (London, 1717), p. 72.
⁷³ BL, Add Ms 47012, D 12, Earl of Egmont, 'notes on the Tories'.
⁷⁴ BL, Add Ms 47012, D 12, fos 8–17; BL, Add Ms 61467, fos 11–12, George II to Prince Frederick, 10 Sep. 1737.

he brought the sister of the young Pretender's mistress into his household, and voiced support for the London conspirator Alexander Murray – both conceived as measures to win over Tory sympathies at Westminster.[75] That they did so reflected the continuously destabilising character of a 'rage of party' kindled in the reign of Queen Anne, in which conflict over questions of foreign and domestic policy was heightened by brutal displays of brinkmanship following the rise and fall of rival factions. Amid the rosy consensus of August 1714, the Earl of Mar had assured his brother that if George I's old Whig correspondents 'may get the better with him at first ... he has better understanding than to make himself king of one partie'.[76] But a raft of Tory promotions did not happen, and any chance of its occurrence was scattered to the winds within a year, when Mar himself could be found at the head of a rebel army, followed by the MP Thomas Forster in Northumberland, and loyal suspicions brought about the impeachment of the old ministerial cadre: Bolingbroke, Harley and Ormonde. After the Septennial Act had dented their electoral challenge, the ejection of local and national Tory officeholders turned from an emergency measure into an identifying feature of Hanoverian politics.[77] The Cambridge MP John Hynde Cotton was insistent that Stuart sympathies had been tepid within the party of Harley and Bolingbroke: the new reality of proscription ensured that when parliament reconvened, he found 'all his friends turned Jacobite'.[78] The Earl of Bath reflected that when it was 'common to represent every man as a Jacobite who opposed the measures of the court', the effect was to 'propagate a belief' among Tories 'that the Jacobites are now become the only friends to liberty'.[79] In providing the best provocation for actual Jacobite sympathies, the exclusion of the Tories had indeed created a political circle thoroughly vicious to all except its main ministerial beneficiaries.

---

[75] John Carswell and L.A. Dralle, eds, *The Political Journal of George Bubb Dodington* (Oxford, 1965), p. 34; Ryder Diary, 16 May 1747; W.S. Lewis, ed., *The Yale Edition of Horace Walpole's Correspondence*, 48 vols (New Haven, 1937–1983), XX, p. 131.

[76] Historical Manuscript Commission, ed., *Report on the Manuscripts of the Earl of Mar and Kellie, Preserved at Alloa House, N.B.*, 2 vols (London, 1904–1930), I, pp. 505–6, Earl of Mar to James Erskine, 7 Aug. 1714.

[77] For the Tories under proscription, see G.V. Bennett, *The Tory Crisis in Church and State 1688–1730: The Career of Francis Atterbury* (London, 1975); Linda Colley, *In Defiance of Oligarchy: The Tory Party 1716–1760* (Cambridge, 1982).

[78] *Bishop Burnet's History of His Own Time: With ... Notes by the Earls of Dartmouth and Hardwicke, and Speaker Onslow*, 6 vols (Oxford, 1823), I, p. 17.

[79] William Cobbett, ed., *The Parliamentary History of England*, 20 vols (London, 1806–1820), XIV, pp. 454–5.

After 1715, the fear of a Jacobite 'fifth column' was soon determining the practice of English high politics, to an extent that outstripped proven reality. Claims of rampant sedition within High Church Oxford provoked the ministers into unfulfilled plans for the reform of a university where, according to one local Whig, 'the Principles here taught, and the Practises here encourag'd, are of the utmost consequence to the religious and civil Happiness of this Nation.'[80] In 1722, the exposure of Tory support for the Atterbury Plot served to deflect parliamentary attention from the crisis unleashed over the South Sea Company. The effect of all of these tumults was to stir severe antagonism between the reigning monarchs and the principal faction within the parliamentary opposition: illustrated when George II blocked repeated opportunities to widen the ministerial base by bringing Tories into government. Behind the blast of allegations, however, the evidence of treacherous conduct was plagued by enigmas. Tory politics was certainly steeped in loyalty to the house of Stuart: an inheritance potent enough to leave many party authors uncomfortable in their judgements upon the recent past. 'The Revolution was necessary but it broke our constitution', mused Samuel Johnson; 'Usurpers will be Usurpers, though sitting in St. Stephen's Chapel, and calling themselves Representatives of the good People of England', concluded Thomas Salmon.[81] Contemporary politics created quotidian tensions: Tories railed against the Hanoverian influence in English foreign policy and largely rejected the pan-Protestant vision that engaged the court of George I, with its affinity for Lutheran or Calvinist brethren abroad and dissenters at home.[82] After the fall of Walpole had failed to break proscription, Tory leaders made themselves accessible to Jacobite agents; and when these consultations were exposed at the Jacobite trials of 1747, Dudley Ryder's diary disclosed that John Hynde Cotton was closer than perhaps he realised to facing arrest.[83] 'A race of foreigners' was how Cotton viewed the ruling dynasty, in a letter to *The Craftsman*: a line 'whose title', he swiftly added, 'we do not

---

[80] *A Letter to Doctor King, Occasion'd by His Late Apology* (London, 1755), p. 24; John Gascoigne, 'Church and State Allied: The Failure of Parliamentary Reform of the Universities 1688–1800', in A.L. Beier, David Cannadine and J. Rosenheim, eds, *The First Modern Society: Essays in English History in Honour of Lawrence Stone* (Cambridge, 1989), pp. 401–29.

[81] James Boswell, *The Life of Samuel Johnson LL.D*, 10 vols (London, 1835), IV, pp. 170–71; Thomas Salmon, *A Review of the History of England*, 2 vols (London, 1724), II, pp. 32–3.

[82] Cobbett, ed., *Parliamentary History*, IX, p. 190, XIII, p. 221; Sack, *From Jacobite to Conservative*, pp. 46–63.

[83] Ryder Diary, 23 Feb. 1747; Philip Yorke, ed., *The Life and Correspondence of Lord Chancellor Hardwicke*, 3 vols (Cambridge, 1913), I, p. 583.

dispute, but whose want of affection' merited comparisons to 'the tyranny of Tiberius'.[84] Yet for those who sought to vindicate the party, a sufficient number of contradictions clouded the claims of treason. Cotton's Jacobite liaisons arose simultaneously with efforts to lever himself into government, resulting in an unhappy spell inside the 'Broadbottom' ministry of 1744–1745. The closing years of his career were dedicated to the campaigns of Frederick, Prince of Wales, pressing fellow Tories into the opposition circle centred on Leicester House.[85] If twentieth-century traitors could be executed for less, the Jacobite material produced against Cotton and his allies at the High Court showed men anxious to leave only the lightest of footprints over the Stuarts' conspiracies: 'against setting their hands and seals to anything but [they] gave assurances in case of assistance from abroad'.[86]

Rival accounts of the party's evolution have judged the preservation of Tory unity after 1714 to have stemmed principally from encouragement by the prospect of office under either George or James.[87] It is perhaps better to see Tories searching rather for the restoration of *any* monarch in the image of their beloved, deceased Stuart Anglicans than actively privileging the Catholic Pretender over the Hanoverian King.[88] 'We have had our day, it ended with Queen Ann', feared the Earl of Orrery; the emotive memorialisation of Charles I that persisted in Tory households certainly suggested a yearning for a form of politics unrepresented in the court at Whitehall or its exiled counterpart.[89] But if these sentiments did not commonly translate into rebellion, the estrangement risked opening up problems for the new monarchs in English politics, when, as one Whig regretted, '[t]he spirit of the gentry of the nation is Toryism' and, in the verdict of Bishop Atterbury, the gentry remained the 'political blood' of the kingdom.[90] 'Nothing but ill usage and despair has made men Jacobites', the

---

[84] BL, Cotton Ms C17, Sir John Hynde Cotton to 'Caleb Danvers', n.d.
[85] Gabriel Glickman, 'The Career of Sir John Hynde Cotton (1686–1752)', *Historical Journal*, 46 (2003), pp. 817–41.
[86] BL, Add Ms 35363, fo 200, Philip Yorke to Joseph Yorke, 17 March 1747.
[87] See especially Linda Colley's *In Defiance of Oligarchy* argues that the party remained in essence Hanoverian. The case for Tory Jacobitism is put by Eveline Cruickshanks, *Political Untouchables: The Tories and the '45* (London, 1979) and Ian R. Christie, 'The Tory Party, Jacobitism and the 'Forty-Five: A Note', *Historical Journal*, 30 (1987), pp. 921–31.
[88] Cambridgeshire County Record Office, Cambridge, Cotton of Madingley Ms 588/DR/F1, fo 40, historical notes.
[89] Countess of Cork and Orrery, ed., *The Orrery Papers*, 2 vols (London, 1903), II, pp. 116–17.
[90] John Kenyon, *Revolution Principles: The Politics of Party, 1689–1720* (London, 1977), p. 203; Francis Atterbury, 'English Advice to the Freeholders of England' (1714), in

MP Wrightson Mundy informed Egmont.[91] Most commonly, 'despair' revealed itself simply in an absence of loyalist zeal. 'I am so totally alienated from my native country', wrote Orrery, after the collapse of the '45 rebellion: 'A man's country may prove ungrateful, may degenerate from itself, may become an asylum of slaves.'[92] In 1745, as the Highland army probed south, the leading Tory notables in Oxfordshire refused to sign the Association of Loyalty drawn up to George II; if the cause was distaste for a document composed by local Whigs, such disengagement still offered a salient contrast to the success of the 1696 Association offered to William III.[93] Moreover, when allegiance was widely construed by contemporaries as a virtue requiring more than just passive submission, such neglect would be construed in a suspicious light.[94] When a party founded on principles of non-resistance seemed so uncomfortable with the question of precisely which monarch not to resist, the result above all was to threaten dysfunction in politics, and undermine royal confidence in parliament, as a place where hidden agendas seemed to roam, 'distressing the King in his administration and making it difficult or impossible for him to carry on the government', as Dudley Ryder alleged.[95] For over 40 years after the accession of George I, the basic presumption underpinning government in Britain was, in the words of Horace Walpole, of a Protestant succession 'built upon Whig principles, and alone supported by Whig zeal'.[96]

V

Politically agile in a way that belied its obscurantist reputation, Jacobitism was eclipsed by military and diplomatic weaknesses more than ideological exhaustion, and by the partial closing-off of the old sources of exclusion that had inclined individuals to the Stuarts out of despair of an alternative. Soon

---

Walter Scott, ed., *A Collection of Scarce and Valuable Tracts*, 13 vols (London, 1809–1815), XIII, p. 541.

[91] BL, Add Ms 47012, D 9, Earl of Egmont, 'notes on the Tories'.

[92] Cork and Orrery, ed., *Orrery Papers*, I, pp. 301–2.

[93] R.J. Robson, *The Oxfordshire Election of 1754* (London, 1949), pp. 6–11; Steve Pincus, *1688: The First Modern Revolution* (New Haven, 2009), pp. 464–9.

[94] For contemporary views on the meaning of allegiance, see BL, Stowe Ms 121, 'Papers relating to a scheme for inducing the English Catholicks in general to become, by degrees, truly and heartily well-affected to His Majesty's Government', 1719.

[95] Ryder Diary, 26 Nov. 1748.

[96] Bodl., Dashwood MSS, B7/1/10a, Horace Walpole, 'A memorial of several noblemen and gentlemen of the first rank and fortune', [1750s].

after the accession of George III, the gradual widening of the ministerial net to draft in Tories at Westminster encouraged one excitable commentator to hail the greatest moment of national reconciliation since the uniting of 'the Red and White Roses' by Henry VII.[97] In the 20 years following the Battle of Culloden, the rising wealth and closer integration of Scotland into British politics and the Atlantic economy began to drain the seditious swamps further north.[98] Memories had faded sufficiently by the close of century for the Jacobite cause to drift into memory less as a cause of subversion than quixotic sentiment: rendered, paradoxically, a part of Scotland's rugged attraction when the offspring of Culloden veterans stormed through North America in the name of the British Empire, and appearing docile indeed compared to the challenges issued from revolutionaries after 1789. Echoes of the Jacobite appeal endured longest, paradoxically, in the dominion most neglected by the exiled court, when the glimpse of white cockades amid the Whiteboy tumults in Munster and Leinster showed a polycentric cause mutating into a final form, as one voice within the visual and rhetorical culture of Irish Catholic protest and agitation.[99]

A more ironic testimony to the aesthetic power of the Stuart cause emerged when traces of Jacobite rhetoric, symbols and motifs began to appear within English courts and palaces, to craft the image, and communicate the virtue, of a purified Hanoverian kingship. When courtiers within the circle of Frederick Lewis and, later, the young Prince George, sought ways to widen the appeal for the dynasty, they borrowed the Stuarts' clothes – almost literally in 1747, when the heir to the throne donned tartan among a Tory crowd at the Middlesex elections, commissioning a bust of Charles I and bringing patronage to erstwhile Jacobite pamphleteers.[100] Frederick's Leicester House circle snatched the idea of 'patriot kingship' from Jacobite literature, importing for Hanoverian consumption the maxim central to Jacobite arguments, that 'the voice of a single man of probity and understanding, ought frequently to be preferred to the sentiments of ten judges, who are weak and cowardly, or

---

[97] *Terrae Filius. Number IV. Friday 8th July 1763*; Aubrey N. Newman, ed., 'Leicester House Politics, 1750–60: From the Papers of John, Second Earl of Egmont', *Camden Miscellany*, 4th ser., 23 (1969), pp. 85–228.

[98] T.M. Devine, *The Scottish Nation, 1700–2000* (London, 2000), ch. 6.

[99] Vincent Morley, *Irish Opinion and the American Revolution, 1760–1783* (Cambridge, 2002), pp. 1–8; David Dickson, 'Jacobitism in Eighteenth-Century Ireland: A Munster Perspective', *Éire-Ireland*, 39 (2004), pp. 38–99.

[100] Richard Rolt, *A Monody, on the Death of His Royal Highness Frederic-Louis Prince of Wales* (London, 1751); Stephen Jones, *Frederick, Prince of Wales and His Circle* (Sudbury, 1981), pp. 15–18; Betty Rizzo, 'In Pursuit of a Bedfordshire Author', *Bedfordshire Magazine*, 16, no. 128 (1979), pp. 333–6.

obstinate and corrupt'.¹⁰¹ For the Earl of Egmont, who based Frederick's entire campaign upon the capture of waning Jacobite sentiments, the strategy was essential to set up a proper combatant against the Pretender, so that despite 'general dissatisfaction and contempt for his Majesty, the people did preserve a due regard for some of the Royal family of Hanover'.¹⁰² Erstwhile Jacobites could pass through to Hanoverian allegiance by adorning the prince in an image pitched deliberately against his father's court: 'a King of England', in words of the Scottish Episcopalian satirist William Guthrie, who would animate 'all those who sway the British sceptre, and have a due influence on the measures of his government'.¹⁰³ The trend was noticeable enough to provoke some contention in the body politic. Four years after Frederick's death, Horace Walpole warned fellow Whigs that unconstitutional influences had struck roots in the household of the future George III, where 'preceptors of Jacobitism' had taken charge of royal education, 'inculcating the worst maxims of Government, and defending the most avow'd Tyrannies'.¹⁰⁴ Such words anticipated the political storms of a later generation. But if it rattled its opponents no less, the 'Jacobitism' to which Walpole referred was not a dynastic threat but a domesticated ideology, a style of high-flown kingship that showed above all the rising confidence of Hanoverian rule after its nervous birth pangs.

Surveying the state of the nation in 1720, Bernard Mandeville had lamented the attachment of too many British subjects to 'an Eutopia' proffered by 'villains' who 'tell us on the least Disaster, that the Land can expect no Blessing til the right Heir is restor'd again'.¹⁰⁵ For Mandeville, the experience of Hanoverian rule was bound inseparably to competition with a shadowy rival, whose ranks stretched from ideologues to an outer circle of malcontents and opportunists. It is the contention of this essay that Jacobitism provided a challenge to the governance of Britain no less formative to Hanoverian policy for the fact that its triumph was improbable. That a family of Catholic claimants was able to unnerve the occupants of a Protestant throne showed the depth of old fault-lines, political,

---

¹⁰¹ *Proper Heads of Self-Examination for a King* (London, 1747), pp. 8–9; Simon Varey, 'Hanover, Stuart and the *Patriot King*', *British Journal of Eighteenth-Century Studies*, 6 (1983), pp. 163–72.
¹⁰² BL, Add Ms 47067, fo 10, Egmont journal, 13 Nov. 1736.
¹⁰³ William Guthrie, 'A Character of His Royal Highness Frederick, Prince of Wales', *Weekly Miscellany; or, Instructive Entertainer*, 21 Feb. 1750, p. 496; Alexander Allardyce, *Scotland and Scotsmen in the Eighteenth Century*, 2 vols (Edinburgh, 1888), II, pp. 547–9.
¹⁰⁴ Bodl., Dashwood MSS, B7/1/10a, Walpole, 'A memorial of several noblemen'; H. Penruddock Wyndham, ed., *The Diary of the Late George Bubb Dodington* (London, 1784), p. 200.
¹⁰⁵ Mandeville, *Free Thoughts*, pp. 354–5.

religious and national, that had riven the British Isles in the previous century, and illustrated how far the fortunes of monarchs were dictated in the greater theatre of European diplomacy. In British politics, support for the Stuarts materialised more commonly as a symptom than a cause of dynastic problems. But the fear of Jacobitism, whether expressed sincerely from the throne or more tendentiously from the mouth of Sir Robert Walpole, shaped public affairs so intensely that it threatened to become a self-fulfilling prophecy. The real danger of the Stuart cause was to make the Hanoverians resort to partisanship in their methods of governance, to rely upon proven loyalists – Whigs in England, Presbyterians in Scotland – and risk converting the resentments of the excluded into permanent disaffection. It required not just military defeat, but the lifting of the ideological siege and the widening of the Hanoverian political world, finally to banish the shadow king and cast the exiled court beyond the margins of eighteenth-century Britain.

Chapter 13

The Alternative to the House of Hanover: The Stuarts in Exile, 1714–1745

Edward Corp

Any discussion of the Stuarts in exile after the Glorious Revolution involves a willingness to consider that British history might have developed in a different direction during the first half of the eighteenth century. This is not easy because, viewed from the perspective of the twenty-first century, there seems a certain inevitability about the sequence of events after the deposition of the Catholic James II. The Bill of Rights excluded all Catholics from the royal succession; the Act of Settlement excluded all non-Anglicans; and consequently the Elector George of Hanover succeeded as King George I of Great Britain in 1714. We all know, and perhaps take for granted, that George II peacefully succeeded his father in 1727, to be succeeded in turn by his own grandson, George III, in 1760. The Hanoverian dynasty, despite its German origins, was by then established and accepted, so that its descendants have continued to occupy the British throne until the present day.

However, when George I succeeded Queen Anne in 1714 it was by no means certain that he and his family would retain their new British possessions. James III, the only son of James II, was living on the continent, determined to regain the thrones lost by his father. The fact that he never succeeded tempts us to assume that there was never any real prospect of a Stuart restoration. But so long as the exiled James III and his family lived abroad and maintained their claims there was a viable and recognised alternative to the House of Hanover. Between 1714 and the 1740s the Hanoverians remained deeply unpopular with a significant proportion of the British people, which secretly retained its loyalty to the deposed Stuart royal family.

James III had succeeded his father as the exiled Jacobite king in 1701, when the Stuarts were living in France at Saint-Germain-en-Laye.[1] At that time he was

---

[1] For the Stuart court in France, see Edward Corp, *A Court in Exile: The Stuarts in France, 1689–1718* (Cambridge, 2004).

only 13 years old, living with his mother (Queen Mary of Modena) and his sister (Princess Louise-Marie) as a guest of Louis XIV. By 1714 he had been obliged by the terms of the Treaty of Utrecht to move his court to the duchy of Lorraine. His mother was still alive (and had four more years to live), but his sister had died unmarried in 1712. The future prospects of the Stuarts as an alternative to the House of Hanover therefore rested exclusively on the continued good health of James III himself, and his ability to find a wife and have children.

If James had died at any time between 1712 and 1720 there would have been no viable alternative to the Hanoverians.[2] In the late summer of 1719, however, he married Princess Maria Clementina Sobieska, granddaughter of King John Sobieski of Poland. The first of their two children, named Charles and created Prince of Wales, was born in December 1720. The second, named Henry and created Duke of York, followed in March 1725. By then the Stuarts had left Lorraine and were living in Rome as guests of successive Popes.[3] James himself did not die until 1766, and his two sons lived respectively until 1788 and 1807, so there remained a real dynastic alternative to the House of Hanover. But neither of James's two sons had legitimate children, and it was during the reign of George III that the Hanoverians were completely established as the only possible royal dynasty for the throne of Great Britain.

The problem confronting historians is to decide how much support the Stuarts retained in England and Scotland during the eighteenth century, and to judge to what extent and for how long they remained, from a practical political point of view, a real threat to the House of Hanover. We might speculate that most people in Ireland, and possibly most people in Scotland, remained pro-Jacobite until at least the 1740s, but historians cannot agree about the dynastic sympathies of the people of England. Similarly, there is disagreement concerning the chances of a Stuart restoration, whether in 1714, 1715–1716, 1719, 1722 or 1745–1746, some regarding one or another attempt as a real possibility, while others dismiss the whole idea as a romantic illusion. These questions have divided British and American historians for many years, and no clear consensus is likely to emerge, beyond the general conclusion that Jacobitism was

---

[2] The Jacobite heiress presumptive during these years was Anne-Marie de Bourbon Orléans, wife of Vittorio Amadeo, Duke of Savoy and (after 1713) king of Sicily. The latter was committed to maintaining the dynastic settlement reached in the treaties of Utrecht and Rastadt which not only recognised him as king of Sicily but also recognised George I as king of Great Britain and Ireland.

[3] For the Stuart court when James III married Princess Maria Clementina, see Edward Corp, *The Jacobites at Urbino: An Exiled Court in Transition* (Basingstoke, 2009).

a more significant movement than previous nineteenth- and twentieth-century historians supposed.[4]

When Charles II was restored in 1660 he was greeted by a popular enthusiasm which astonished some contemporaries, and which revealed secret supporters in unexpected places. It is useful to remember this, because it is so difficult to assess what the attitude of the English people really was in the first half of the eighteenth century. It was no doubt changeable and even contradictory, but there are perhaps two generalisations which can be made about most of the people: first that they were strongly anti-Catholic, knew that the exiled Stuarts were Catholic, yet regarded them as the legitimate kings; second that they were not enthusiastic about the Hanoverians, yet were not prepared to rise in rebellion against them to assist the Stuarts. We might possibly go further and speculate that most people would have shown great enthusiasm for the return of the Stuarts if they had been restored as Charles II was in 1660, and felt little loyalty to the dethroned Hanoverians. This last point can be no more than conjecture. It is more productive to examine the Stuarts themselves as an alternative royal family rather than attempt to delve into the evolving attitudes of the English people.

To understand the position of James III himself we have to bear in mind that the Stuarts faced several serious handicaps. In the first place they were dynastically isolated. The marriages of Charles II and James II had brought no dynastic benefits for the Stuarts, and the absence of Stuart princesses – except of course for Mary II and Anne, who had both deserted their father – had originally left the exiled family totally dependent on the support of Louis XIV, his son and grandsons. The premature deaths of the Dauphin and his sons, the duc de Bourgogne and the duc de Berri, following the departure of the duc d'Anjou to become King Philip V of Spain, thus deprived James III of the French support upon which he had until then totally relied. Then the fact that the duc d'Orléans, the Regent of France after the death of Louis XIV, had strong personal reasons for making an alliance with George I meant that the French government became positively unhelpful during the restoration attempts of 1715–1716, 1719 and 1722.[5]

The second disadvantage facing James III, as an alternative to George I, then George II, was that he was forced to live in exile. Here we might usefully compare his position with that of the Archduke Charles, both before and after

---

[4] For a discussion of the Jacobite debate, see Daniel Szechi, *The Jacobites: Britain and Europe, 1688–1788* (Manchester, 1994), pp. 1–6.

[5] For the duc d'Orléans' attitude to James III before 1715, see Corp, *A Court in Exile*, p. 172. His hostility was then increased by his dependence on George I and the other guarantors of the Utrecht settlement to exclude Philip V from the French succession.

his election as the Emperor Charles VI. Charles claimed to be the rightful king of Spain, just as James claimed to be the rightful king of England. Yet Charles was able to fall back on the Habsburg territories in central Europe, and pursue his ambitions from the safety of Vienna.[6] James never had that security, and was obliged to live as a guest of successive popes in the Papal States. We might also compare his position with that of his Hanoverian rivals. Let us imagine that George I or George II had been deposed as the result of a Stuart restoration. They would have returned to the hereditary possessions of their electorate within the Holy Roman Empire and, like Charles VI, would then have pursued their ambitions to regain their thrones from there, in no way dependent on the goodwill of any host government.

The third disadvantage which confronted the Stuarts was geographical, because partition was out of the question. By the Treaty of Rastadt it was possible to partition the Spanish Empire, giving Spain and its colonies to Philip V, and the Netherlands and parts of Italy to Charles VI. One might by analogy have given England and its colonies to George I, with Scotland and/or Ireland reserved for James III. Yet such a partition was simply out of the question for strategic reasons, even without the recently enacted Treaty of Union between England and Scotland. For James III, and of course for George I, it was all or nothing. It was inconceivable that any government in London would or could ever have accepted a compromise settlement based on the partition of the three kingdoms of the British Isles. And this simple fact influenced all the Stuart restoration attempts between 1689 and 1746. England was the target, and possession of Ireland or Scotland was never regarded as more than a means to that end. It is true that there were Jacobite risings in Scotland against George I in both 1715 and 1719, but in reality they were planned as no more than diversions. The main risings were to have taken place in England, where the so-called Atterbury Plot of 1722 was also located. This can be seen most obviously in 1745 when Prince Charles, the elder son of James III, succeeded in taking control of most of Scotland. Instead of remaining there, consolidating his position as ruler of Scotland and thus of course leaving George II for the time being as king of England, the prince immediately marched his army south into England in November and December – a time of year when the campaigning season should have ended – and with disastrous results. For Prince Charles, Scotland without England was not worth having, or at least not viable. And of course the Stuarts,

---

[6] See William O'Reilly, 'A Life in Exile: Charles VI (1685–1740) between Spain and Austria', in Philip Mansel and Torsten Riotte, eds, *Monarchy and Exile: The Politics of Legitimacy from Marie de Médicis to Wilhelm II* (Basingstoke, 2011), pp. 66–90.

whatever their historical origins, had already become primarily an English dynasty by the end of the previous century.

Yet we should not exaggerate this, as neither George I nor George II ever visited Scotland, and James III sought consciously to show that he was king of Scotland as well as of England. One obvious way in which he did this, apart from employing some Scots at his court, was to enhance the importance of the Order of the Thistle, the premier chivalric order of Scotland. Just as the Habsburgs and the Spanish Bourbons maintained rival Orders of the Golden Fleece, so the Stuarts and the Hanoverians maintained rival Orders of the Garter and of the Thistle. The innovation made by James III in 1717 was to wear both the Garter and the Thistle at the same time, something which neither he nor his father had previously permitted, and which was not practised in early Hanoverian Great Britain. James commissioned a great many portraits of himself and his two sons, to be reproduced in multiple copies, engraved and sent secretly to England or Scotland, and in all of them the St Andrew medal of the Thistle can be seen with the blue sash and St George medal of the Garter.[7]

As already stated, James III was living in exile. That statement, however, needs to be qualified, because James actually lived in a double exile. He and his court had been based in France at Saint-Germain-en-Laye, to the west of Paris, until 1712 when, by the Treaty of Utrecht, he was exiled from France and had to live in the duchy of Lorraine. Then, after the failure of the Jacobite rising of 1715–1716, the Regent of France, under pressure from George I, obliged him to move south to Avignon, and finally, after the Triple Alliance of January 1717, to cross the Alps and live in the Papal States, briefly at Urbino and then permanently in Rome. James, therefore, had to pursue a double aim. Of course he wanted to be restored to his kingdom of England, but he also wanted to persuade the French government to let him return to live at Saint-Germain or some other royal château in France within striking distance of England. Just as Ireland and Scotland were regarded as stepping stones back to England, so France was regarded as a desirable and even necessary stepping stone back to all parts of the British Isles.

This became very apparent to James III after the Spanish fleet that had been assembled to invade England was destroyed by storms in the Atlantic in 1719, and after the revelation of the Atterbury Plot in 1722. With the support of Cardinal de Polignac, the French ambassador at Rome, he hoped that France's

---

[7] For the portraits, see Edward Corp, *The King over the Water: Portraits of the Stuarts in Exile after 1689* (Edinburgh, 2001); Corp, *A Court in Exile*, ch. 7; and Edward Corp, *The Stuarts in Italy, 1719–1766: A Royal Court in Permanent Exile* (Cambridge, 2011), chs 5 and 14.

foreign policy might be reversed after the death of the Regent to become pro-Jacobite, thus allowing the Stuart court to return to Saint-Germain. In 1725 serious hopes were entertained in Rome that this was about to happen, following the marriage of Louis XV to Princess Maria Leszczynska, daughter of the exiled king of Poland and a cousin of James's wife Clementina Sobieska. These hopes were then dashed by the Treaty of Hanover of September 1725, whereby Great Britain and France, with Prussia, renewed their anti-Jacobite alliance.[8]

James III, therefore, had no option but to await the death of George I, hoping that the opposition between the Whig ministers headed by Walpole and the Hanoverian Prince of Wales might open the way for a Stuart restoration. When George I died at Osnabrück in June 1727 the moment seemed to have arrived. James immediately left the Papal States and made his way north as quickly as possible, not as he would have wished to France, but instead to Lorraine. When he arrived there he received the news that George II had succeeded his father without any apparent opposition, and that Walpole had been confirmed as the new king's prime minister. History then repeated itself. The French government, now directed by Cardinal Fleury, obliged the Duke of Lorraine to make James leave his duchy and move south to Avignon. Six months later Fleury forced James to leave Avignon and return to the Papal States.[9] It was thus the death of George I at Osnabrück which finally convinced James III that he himself would never be restored to his kingdoms of England, Ireland and Scotland. And from that point onwards he resigned himself to a life of permanent exile.

We should not conclude, however, that all hopes for a Stuart restoration were therefore abandoned. On the contrary, they were passed on to the next generation and therefore postponed for about 15 years. James III's elder son, Prince Charles, would reach manhood in the 1740s, so Stuart hopes rested on the possibility of a breakdown in Anglo-French relations, resulting in an Anglo-French war, at that time. If no such war broke out, then all hopes for a Stuart restoration would no doubt have to be completely abandoned – for ever. As it happened, the fall of Walpole and the death of Fleury *did* lead to the involvement of Great Britain and France on opposite sides in the War of the Austrian Succession. France therefore became willing to support the Stuarts militarily, for the first time since 1713.

During the intervening years, the 1720s and particularly the 1730s, it was essential for James III that enough people in the Papal States should believe that a Stuart restoration was still likely to take place, sooner or later. Opposition to the

---

[8] Corp, *The Stuarts in Italy*, pp. 72–4.
[9] Ibid., pp. 32–3.

House of Hanover depended on credibility, and on a balancing act. The Stuart court in Rome had to be maintained on a relatively lavish scale, though with a degree of moderation.[10] Regular entertainments, including balls and concerts of high-quality music, had to act as a magnet both for the Roman princely families and for the visiting Grand Tourists. The organisation of the court had to resemble what it had been at Whitehall and Saint-Germain, though with various modifications or simplifications to reflect the reality of living in exile on a limited budget. James himself had to be seen to be a devout Catholic, even a bigoted one in the eyes of some people, so that he could employ Protestant servants in important positions, and even have an Anglican chapel within the Palazzo del Re, without calling into question his own religious orthodoxy. And he had to show himself as the legitimate king of all the people of Great Britain and Ireland, not just the Jacobites. In this he was helped by the attitudes and behaviour of most of the Grand Tourists who visited Rome, because the Stuart court served as a surrogate British embassy. It provided passports, Anglican services, including public burials in the Protestant cemetery which successive popes permitted James to use, and English-speaking doctors. The fact was that the British and Irish Grand Tourists preferred to socialise in Rome with people of their own nationality who could speak English, rather than with the Italians and other foreigners who could not. Political and dynastic preferences gave way to practical convenience, and lost their significance for young men who were a long way from home and who wanted to meet and mix with people with whom they could talk easily.

In this context it was also very important for the credibility in Rome of James III as a real alternative to the House of Hanover that he was treated with full royal honours by the French and Spanish ambassadors. Whatever might have been the official policies of the governments at Versailles and Madrid, the ambassadors behaved as though they had been accredited to the Stuart as well as the papal court. Men like Cardinal de Polignac, the duc de Saint-Aignan, Cardinal de Tencin and the two Cardinals Aquaviva d'Aragona (uncle and nephew) became James's personal friends, and even acted as his ministers. So long as the representatives of both France and Spain treated James in this way, it was only reasonable to believe that a Stuart restoration might well be achieved sooner or later. Even the attitude of the Imperial ambassador became more positive after the Habsburg–Lorraine marriage of 1736. And we might observe that although the Stuart family had previously been dynastically isolated, James III's marriage to Maria Clementina Sobieska had brought an important

---

[10] See Corp, *The Stuarts in Italy* for this and the following paragraphs.

connection, not only with the Habsburgs but also with the Bourbons of Spain, Parma and Naples, and with the Wittelsbachs of Bavaria and Cologne, among others. James III himself had few relations, but his two sons, Prince Charles and Prince Henry, had many. The children of a Sobieski and Neuburg princess, they were both popular and highly esteemed by their cousins in Vienna, Madrid and Munich, as well as in Italy.

Yet in other respects James III's marriage to that princess, who became Queen Clementina, was a great disappointment. One aspect of James's image as an alternative to the House of Hanover was that he provided a contrast to the turbulent family life of George I, his estranged wife and his son, and then to the strained relations between George II and his son Frederick. During the early 1720s all seemed well, and the Stuarts in Rome did indeed compare very favourably with their rivals in London. However, this came to an abrupt end in 1725, when Queen Clementina left the Palazzo del Re in Rome and took refuge in a convent over the river in Trastevere. When George I died at Osnabrück in June 1727, and James made his final attempt to recover his thrones, he had not seen his wife for nearly two years, and it was to be another six months before he was able to effect a superficial reconciliation and once again live with her under the same roof.

As already stated, the long period of waiting for a new Anglo-French war finally came to an end just in time, in the early 1740s. It was now or never if the Stuarts were ever to dethrone King George II, and in 1745 Prince Charles arrived in Great Britain to start a new Jacobite rising. Its initial success, when Charles managed to control most of Scotland and prepare his ill-fated invasion of England, provides us with a glimpse of what might have happened if he, like his great-uncle Charles II, had managed to recover the English throne. The reports of his initial success which reached Rome convinced many people that the long-anticipated Stuart restoration was now about to take place. The English minister at Florence reported in October 1745 that the Grand Tourists had always 'paid great court' to James III's two sons, encouraged by their governors, most of whom were Jacobites.[11] As he put it a few weeks later, when Prince Charles was in Edinburgh: 'hitherto our English have either behaved weakly or scandalously. Those who have abstained from going to [the Stuart court] have paid profound court to his sons.'[12] At the end of December the British Grand Tourists in Rome took part in a great celebration to mark Prince Charles's 25th birthday, and in

---

[11] W.S. Lewis, W.H. Smith and G.L. Lam, eds, *Horace Walpole's Correspondence with Sir Horace Mann*, 3 vols (New Haven, 1954), III, p. 112, Horace Mann to Horace Walpole, 5 Oct. 1745.

[12] Ibid., p. 135, Mann to Walpole, 26 Oct. 1745.

January 1746, when the news of the prince's invasion of England reached Italy, the minister reported that 'our travellers have so good an opinion of their success that they are gone to Rome to pay homage among the first'.[13] As late as March 1746, before it was realised that the Jacobite invasion of England had failed, the minister reported that the Grand Tourists 'made *junkets* and got drunk with rejoicing with the ... servants' of James III for the success of his son.[14] These celebrations were premature, and the news soon arrived of Prince Charles's disastrous retreat back to Scotland, followed by his defeat at Culloden in April 1746. But they are useful for us, because they provide fascinating evidence of the latent opposition to the House of Hanover, demonstrated in a place where it was safe to show it, and a glimpse of what might have been the reaction of English people if there really had been a Stuart restoration in 1746.

James III, of course, knew that all hopes for a restoration had to be abandoned. There is evidence from both English and French sources that many people in Rome and elsewhere still believed 'that something may or will be done',[15] but James was not one of them. He now knew that neither he nor his son would ever be restored, so he concentrated on providing his family with financial security in permanent exile, instead of vainly attempting to overthrow the Hanoverians. In 1747 he and Pope Benedict XIV agreed that Prince Henry, James's younger son, should become a cardinal. The plan had first been made with Pope Clement XII back in 1732, and had been held in readiness ever since, in case no restoration had been achieved by about 1746, when Prince Henry would be 21 years old.[16] By then the Stuarts had been in exile for 58 years, and the Hanoverians had been on the throne in London for over 30. A new generation had grown up which had begun to develop new loyalties, which accepted the judgement of Divine Providence in favour of the Hanoverians and which had become less committed to the Stuart cause.

A significant point was reached when Frederick, the Hanoverian Prince of Wales, died in 1751. Back in the 1720s and early 1730s this would have been an occasion for rejoicing. But after Culloden there was no point. A Prussian living in Italy reported that 'the Jacobites have shown an extreme pleasure at the news of the Prince of Wales. But James has personally and publicly reprimanded

---

[13] Ibid., p. 191, Mann to Walpole, 4 Jan. 1746.
[14] Ibid., p. 218, Mann to Walpole, 15 March 1746.
[15] Ibid., p. 399, Mann to Walpole, 16 May 1747; Royal Archives, Windsor, Stuart Papers 287/4, James III to Tencin, 29 Aug. 1747.
[16] Corp, *The Stuarts in Italy*, pp. 219–20, 225, 229, 230–31.

any of his servants who have shown their pleasure in his presence.'[17] By 1746 King James III, living his double exile, accepted that the union of Great Britain and Hanover was destined to continue and that the Hanoverians were now regarded by more and more British people as the new legitimate kings of Great Britain and Ireland.[18] And we all know that the dynastic union survived both the eighteenth and early nineteenth centuries. We should remember, however, that history might have taken a different direction; that between 1714 and 1745 the union might well have been prematurely terminated; and that there was indeed an alternative British royal dynasty.

---

[17] The National Archives, Kew, State Papers 98/58, fo 38, Philip von Stosch to Wriothesley Russell, 3rd Duke of Bedford, 7 May 1751.

[18] It was accepted by James III and his son Henry, but not by his son Charles; see Corp, *The Stuarts in Italy*, pp. 232–4, 348.

Chapter 14
Radical Popular Attitudes to the Monarchy in Britain during the French Revolution

Amanda Goodrich

In September 1794 two members of the radical London Corresponding Society (LCS) were arrested for plotting to assassinate George III with a poisoned arrow from an air-gun disguised as a walking stick. Much was made of this so-called 'Pop-Gun Plot' in the loyalist press, but confusion ensued as to the truth of the allegations and the intentions of the alleged perpetrators, two artisans – Peter Lemaitre and George Higgins. Had they 'imagined the king's death' and thus committed treason, or did no such conspiracy exist?[1] The evidence was unclear and confused and the truth of the event obscured by the murky manoeuvrings of the government, in the famous Treason Trials of 1794.[2] This episode and the context of loyalist and government fear and paranoia within which it may be set illustrate the difficulties for both contemporaries and historians in establishing popular attitudes to the monarchy during the turmoil of the French Revolution. It is also not easy to gain a sense of the people, from what appears to be 'a multitude of individuals with a multitude of experiences' and political views.[3] That 1790s radicalism was a diverse movement with a fragmented ideology has been argued by John Dinwiddy, Mark Philp and others. Neither radicals

---

[1] See John Barrell, *Imagining the King's Death: Figurative Treason, Fantasies of Regicide, 1793–1796* (Oxford, 2000), ch. 14.

[2] At these trials a number of radical leaders were acquitted of treason. See for example Barrell, *Imagining the King's Death*; F.K. Prochaska, 'English State Trials in the 1790s: A Case Study', *Journal of British Studies*, 13 (1973), pp. 63–82; Alan Wharam, *The Treason Trials, 1794* (Leicester, 1992); Clive Emsley, 'Repression, "Terror" and the Rule of Law in England during the Decade of the French Revolution', *English Historical Review*, 100 (1985), pp. 801–25.

[3] E.P. Thompson, *The Making of the English Working Class* (London, 1991), p. 11. See Kathleen Wilson, *The Sense of the People: Politics, Culture and Imperialism in England, 1715–1785* (Cambridge, 1998), pp. 17–22.

nor loyalists adhered to clear and consistent ideologies.[4] Radicalism reflected a variety of views about what was wrong with the British state and what should be done about it.[5] Moreover, anti-monarchist sentiment may or may not have reflected a desire for regicide and the establishment of a republic. Indeed, radicals who called for reform of government may still have remained loyal to the monarch, or at least indifferent.

Nevertheless, during the 1790s and into the nineteenth century monarchy was to varying degrees a focus of radical attention both in popular writing and actions and also within the pamphlets of radical political thinkers.[6] Historians have primarily argued that radicals portrayed two positions: republicanism and constitutionalism. This chapter first explores the republicanism which invited revolution, anti-monarchist rhetoric and, possibly, regicide – a strand of republican thinking particularly common in popular radicalism. The second focus is a universalism evolving from the French Revolution and promoting universal rights and freedoms for all mankind, and a 'world of revolutions'. Finally, radical constitutionalism is explored, that formulated proposals for practical reform within which monarchy was less prominent than in the republican agitation. Also apparent here were certain forms of 'constitutionalist action' that were familiar to the people and attracted popular support.[7]

It is the contention of this chapter that while some radicals explored and promoted the possibilities of republicanism and universalism, the majority of reform proposals for Britain focused increasingly on the existing constitution. This constitutionalism ensured that reform remained within the framework of the existing mixed constitution of which the monarchy was an essential component. Corruption in government, the domination of government by an elite 'aristocracy' as Thomas Paine labelled it, that was seen as retaining rights

---

[4] John Dinwiddy, 'Conceptions of Revolution in the English Radicalism of the 1790s', in Eckhart Hellmuth, ed., *The Transformation of Political Culture: England and Germany in the Late Eighteenth Century* (Oxford, 1990), pp. 535–60; Mark Philp, 'The Fragmented Ideology of Reform', in id., ed., *The French Revolution and British Popular Politics* (Cambridge, 1991), pp. 50–77; id., 'Disconcerting Ideas: Explaining Popular Radicalism and Popular Loyalism in the 1790s', in Glenn Burgess and Matthew Festenstein, eds, *English Radicalism, 1550–1850* (Cambridge, 2007), pp. 157–85; James A. Epstein, *Radical Expression: Political Language, Ritual and Symbol in England, 1790–1850* (Oxford, 1994), p. 6.

[5] Radicalism as used here incorporates all those promoting revolution or reform of government. And loyalism refers to those who supported the political status quo and Britain against France, often declaring themselves for 'church and king' or 'king and constitution'.

[6] Marilyn Morris, *The British Monarchy and the French Revolution* (New Haven, 1998), ch. 3.

[7] Epstein, *Radical Expression*, p. 11.

and riches for the few, meant that 'aristocracy' remained at the forefront of radical criticism rather than monarchy.[8] Thus, within radical constitutionalism and related popular action continuities may be identified in radical attitudes to monarchy.

I

Turning first to relevant contextual debates, historians have emphasized that despite the limitations placed on the monarchy at the Glorious Revolution of 1688–1689 and the Act of Succession (1701) the Hanoverian monarchs still retained considerable power.[9] Of course it was not always expedient to use such power; nor did it ensure popular respect or support.[10] The continuing popular acceptance of monarchy through the turbulent years of the later eighteenth century was by no means guaranteed. Indeed, there has been much debate about attitudes to monarchy and how far its' survival through the eighteenth century and into the nineteenth was due to the skills and hard work of the monarch, an 'invented tradition', a mythologizing of monarchy or to the 'institutional conservatism' of the English people.[11] Hannah Smith noted a sustained loyalism and a hitherto 'unrealized degree of popularity' for George I and II.[12] Linda Colley and Marilyn Morris both identified something of an apotheosis of George III during the later years of the eighteenth century; describing a dramatic rise in the popularity of the king.[13]

---

[8] See Amanda Goodrich, *Debating England's Aristocracy in the 1790s: Pamphlets, Polemics and Political Ideas* (Woodbridge, 2005).

[9] See Julian Hoppit, *A Land of Liberty? England, 1689–1727* (Oxford, 2002), pp. 37–8, 161–2; Linda Colley, *Britons: Forging the Nation, 1707–1837* (London, 1994), p. 196.

[10] See for example, Colley, *Britons*, p. 208; Anthony Taylor, *'Down with the Crown': British Anti-Monarchism and Debates about Royalty since 1790* (London, 1999).

[11] See for example, Morris, *British Monarchy*; Tom Nairn, *The Enchanted Glass: Britain and Its Monarchy* (London, 1988); David Cannadine and Simon Price, eds, *Rituals of Royalty: Power and Ceremonial in Traditional Societies* (Cambridge, 1987); Steve Poole, *The Politics of Regicide in England, 1760–1850* (Manchester, 2000). Also Cynthia Herrup, 'Beyond Personality and Pomp: Recent Works on Early Modern Monarchies', *Journal of British Studies*, 28 (1989), pp. 175–80.

[12] Hannah Smith, *Georgian Monarchy: Politics and Culture, 1714–1760* (Cambridge, 2009), pp. 9–16.

[13] Colley, *Britons*, ch. 5; ead., 'The Apotheosis of George III: Loyalty, Royalty and the British Nation 1760–1820', *Past and Present*, 102 (1984), pp. 94–129; Morris, *British*

For Colley this apotheosis was about promoting a favourable nationalistic royal image rather than a resurgence of royal power in political terms. Indeed, she argued that after the American War the political influence of the king declined considerably and the elite rather than the king were held responsible for the loss of the American colonies.[14] Peter Jupp has also noted a significant shift in power away from monarchy and towards government from the 1780s due to the growth in the administration and increasing independence of ministers.[15] And, John Cannon argued that George III survived the upheaval of the French Revolution and gained the support of the majority by reinventing himself as the 'bastion of conservative patriotism', a 'patriot king' above party and 'father to his people'.[16] Morris noted that the British monarchy was a 'focal point in political argument' in the 1790s, and came under intense 'vulgar scrutiny' by radicals such as Paine. Yet, this did not have a detrimental effect in the long run but served to 'humanize' the monarchy and to pave the way for the newly important role it came to play as head of the social hierarchy.[17] Certainly, later in his reign George III was lampooned for his parsimony, domesticity and interest in farming rather than his involvement in politics.[18] Such interpretations provide useful insights into reasons for the survival of the institution of monarchy through the turbulent Georgian period, and beyond.

II

It was a radical focus on republicanism that brought monarchy into the foreground of debate. The declaration of France as a republic in 1792 and the execution of Louis XVI in January 1793 clearly influenced radical thinkers in Britain. In 1790s popular radical ideology a republic was a form of government without a monarch, and republicanism was 'straightforwardly anti-monarchical'.[19] Epstein noted 'an angry raw republicanism' in the streets and taverns of Britain

---

Monarchy. But, as Colley in particular related, some considerable effort to promote the king, by the establishment and the authorities, was needed to achieve this.

[14] Colley, *Britons*, pp. 212, 148.

[15] Peter Jupp, 'The Landed Elite and Political Authority in Britain, c. 1760–1850', *Journal of British Studies*, 29 (1990), pp. 53–79, at pp. 57–60.

[16] John Cannon, 'The Survival of the British Monarchy', *Transactions of the Royal Historical Society*, 36, (1986), pp. 143–64, at pp. 149–50.

[17] Morris, *British Monarchy*, pp. 11–12.

[18] Colley, *Britons*, pp. 209–10.

[19] Mark Philp, 'English Republicanism in the 1790s', *Journal of Political Philosophy*, 6 (1988), pp. 235–62, at p. 240.

during 1793–1795;[20] and Iain McCalman identified a small group of 'ultra-radicals', forming a 'revolutionary-republican underground' movement from the mid 1790s to early Chartism that condemned monarchy 'loudly and lewdly'.[21] A profusion of printed material from pamphlets to broadsides, handbills, squibs, songs and prints that aimed to attract popular attention provides plenty of examples. Many promoted regicide, such as Richard 'Citizen' Lee's pamphlets *The Happy Reign of George the Last* and *King Killing* (both 1795), and his poem *A Cure for National Grievances. Citizen Guillotine, A New Shaving Machine*. In *King Killing* Lee declared that 'tyrants ... are all alike; their fraternity consists in a partnership of prey and rapine ... united, to torment and destroy mankind'. He called on the people to 'destroy this huge Colussus' of monarchy.[22] A Norwich pamphleteer declared in 1795: 'Off with the King's head! And a REPUBLIC in Great Britain!'[23] Daniel Eaton's *Hog's Wash, Pig's Meat* and *Politics for the People: or, a Salmagundi for Swine* (1794) provided many examples of anti-monarchist sentiment, such as 'The Land of the Apes – A Fable' which included much criticism of the king of the apes and his corrupt and dissipated court.[24] One famous squib that was read out at Thomas Hardy's trial for treason in 1794 advertised: 'At the Federation Theatre in Equality Square ... a new and entertaining farce La Guillotine! Or George's Head in the Basket! ... The whole to conclude with a grand decapitation of placemen, pensioners and German leeches.'[25]

Much theatricality can be detected in such writings and in the radical toasts reportedly made, damning the king in taverns and alehouses. The well-known orator John Thelwall allegedly 'blew the head off his pot of porter and declared, "Thus I would serve all Kings"'.[26] One John Nuttal toasted: 'Here's Damnation to the King and the Constitution.'[27] Edward Swift declared: 'Damn the King and Queen, they ought to be put to death the same as the King and Queen of France ... Damn and bugger the King ... Damnation and blast the king, I would

---

[20] Epstein, *Radical Expression*, p. 8.
[21] Iain McCalman, *Radical Underworld: Prophets, Revolutionaries, and Pornographers in London, 1795–1840* (Oxford, 2002), p. 2.
[22] [Citizen Lee], *King Killing* [London, 1795], p. 1. See Poole, *Politics of Regicide*, p. 102.
[23] Ibid., p. 96.
[24] Daniel Isaac Eaton, *Politics for the People: or, a Salmagundi for Swine*, 2 vols (London, 1792), I, p. 80–83.
[25] Quoted in Glynn A. Williams, *Artisans and Sans-culottes: Popular Movements in France and Britain during the French Revolution* (London, 1981), p. 72.
[26] Morris, *British Monarchy*, p. 93.
[27] Epstein, *Radical Expression*, pp. 8–9. See also Barrell, *Imagining the King's Death*, p. 102.

as soon shoot the king as a mad dog.'[28] As John Barrell has pointed out, however, it is uncertain how many of such verbal outbursts were accurately reported or fabricated by witnesses or spies in the frenzy of loyalist alarmism about radicalism and treason.[29] The British Club of radicals in Paris at a dinner in November 1792 to celebrate the Revolution made thirteen toasts, including those for the French Republic founded on the rights of man and for a union of France, Britain and many other nations sharing the same revolutionary sentiments.[30] Albert Goodwin described the toasts drunk at the dinner as 'chivalrous, egalitarian and treasonable'.[31] Such republican enthusiasm can also be identified later in 1797–1798 among those hoping for a French invasion and a revolution in Britain. The revolutionary radicals of the United Englishmen and United Scotsmen began underground meetings in 1797 and were in contact with the United Irishmen who were plotting the 1798 insurrection.[32] One contemporary print states that it is '[i]ntended to convey the Army of England from the Gallic Shore, for the purpose of exchanging French Liberty! For English happiness!' and claims to be '[a]ccurately copied from a plan presented to the Executive Directory' in France.[33] Radical action such as the Pop-Gun Plot, attacks on the king's coach in 1795 and 1817 and Colonel Despard's conspiracy to blow up the king in 1802 drew alarmist loyalist reaction. Evidence at the Treason Trials of radical societies, particularly in Sheffield and Manchester, arming to march on London to incite an uprising, also suggested a consistent and widespread republicanism.[34] It was alleged that pikes, as used in France, were being manufactured in Sheffield and sold for 10d a piece, although this was never proven.[35]

---

[28] Clive Emsley, 'An Aspect of Pitt's "Terror": Prosecutions for Sedition during the 1790s', *Social History*, 6 (1981), pp. 155–84, at p. 157.

[29] Barrell, *Imagining the King's Death*, pp. 102–3.

[30] David Erdman, *Commerce des Lumières: John Oswald and the British in Paris, 1790–1793* (Columbia, MO, 1986), pp. 230–31. See also John G. Alger, 'The British Colony in Paris, 1792–93', *English Historical Review*, 13 (1898), pp. 672–94.

[31] Albert Goodwin, *The Friends of Liberty: The English Democratic Movement in the Age of the French Revolution* (London, 1979), p. 249.

[32] Morris, *British Monarchy*, pp. 95–9.

[33] [Citizen Monge], *The Grand Republican Balloon* (1798), at http://www.britishmuseum.org.

[34] For evidence from the treason trials see e.g. the trials of Thomas Hardy and Henry Redhead Yorke in Thomas Bayly Howell and Thomas Jones Howell, eds, *A Complete Collection of State Trials and Proceedings for High Treason*, 34 vols (London, 1816–1828), XXIV and XXV.

[35] 'The Second Report of the Secret Committee', in *An Account of the Treason and Sedition, Committed by the London Corresponding Society, the Society for Constitutional Information, the Other Societies of London, Sheffield, Norwich, Manchester, Bristol, Coventry,*

Nevertheless, no concerted and sustained radical physical resistance to the monarch was actually carried out, despite the rumours, threats and rhetoric.[36]

Such popular republicanism did not for the most part reflect on the complexities of political analysis based on concepts of classical republicanism that had a long tradition in eighteenth-century political thought.[37] A few radical pamphleteers did engage with such issues, Thomas Spence providing one example. In his periodical, *One Pennyworth of Pig's Meat* (1793), Spence discussed the history of republicanism from the classical world, French and American concepts of republicanism and advocated for Britain, along with agrarian reform, a 'beautiful and powerful New Republic' with a national assembly.[38] Yet, J.G.A. Pocock and others have questioned the extent to which significant numbers of radicals in the debate on the French Revolution in Britain can be identified as truly republican.[39]

Certainly radicals expressed admiration for the American and French systems, but concrete plans for a republic in Britain were notably absent from radical writings.[40] Even Paine did not provide such a blueprint in *Rights of Man* (1791–1792), despite his later claim that 'I have always considered the present Constitution of the French Republic the *best organized system* ... yet produced.'[41] A broad and often vague set of ideas were proposed to follow the advocated abolition of the monarchy and government, including some form of direct democracy, agrarian collective or new anarchic society.[42]

Nottingham, Derby, Birmingham, Leeds, Newcastle, Hereford, York, Edinburgh, Dublin &c. &c. (London, 1794), The National Archives, Kew, T.S. 11/892/3035, p. 53.

[36] Poole, *Politics of Regicide*, p. 15.

[37] See Philp, 'English Republicanism', p. 240.

[38] Thomas Spence, *One Pennyworth of Pig's Meat; Or, Lessons for the Swinish Multitude*, 3 vols (London, 1793), I.

[39] J.G.A. Pocock, 'Varieties of Whiggism', in id., *Virtue, Commerce, and History: Essays on Political Thought and History, Chiefly in the Eighteenth Century* (Cambridge, 1985), pp. 215–310, quoted in Philp, 'English Republicanism', p. 238. But see also Gregory Claeys, *Thomas Paine: Social and Political Thought* (London, 1990); id. 'The French Revolution Debate and British Political Thought', *History of Political Thought*, 11 (1990), pp. 59–80.

[40] See for example, George Dyer, *The Complaints of the Poor People of England* (London, 1793); John Thelwall, 'Peaceful Discussion, and Not Tumultuary Violence, the Means of Redressing National Grievance' (1795), in Gregory Claeys, ed., *Political Writings of the 1790s: The French Revolution Debate in Britain*, 8 vols (London, 1995), IV, p. 401.

[41] Thomas Paine, 'Letter to the Legislature and Executive Directory of the French Republic', attached to his 'Agrarian Justice', 1796, in M. Foot and I. Kramnick, eds, *The Thomas Paine Reader* (London, 1987), p. 472, quoted in Goodrich, *Debating England's Aristocracy*, p. 125.

[42] See for example, John Oswald, *The Government of the People: or, a Sketch of a Constitution for the Universal Common-Wealth* (Paris, 1793); Thomas Spence, 'The Real

III

Moreover, in the writings of radical thinkers such republicanism is less common than a strong universalism that celebrated revolution and republicanism generally but not directly for Britain.[43] This more subtle ideology also often implied rather than expressed republican ideas within a dramatic rhetoric. In the early stages of the French Revolution, in particular, a number of English radicals followed Paine and adopted much of the new universalist vocabulary of France, promoting universal rights of man, freedom from despotism and tyrannical oppression, and focusing on all people in Europe or the world as a whole.[44] One pamphleteer, 'Citizen Randol', celebrated the French for waving 'the celestial banners of the rights of man, over the tottering bastiles of Europe; to break the shackles of despotism from the ankles of millions, and destroy those yokes of oppression, vainly reserved by the impious ministers of misguided monarchs.'[45] The LCS's joint *Address to the French National Convention* of September 1792 reflected such universalism[46] and the *Address* of the Derby Society for Constitutional Information expressed aims of 'universal liberty' and declared: 'By the fall of Despotism, you have reared the drooping head of suffering nations; and given to Tyrants an awful example.' The 'gallant ... French citizens ... contended not for France alone but the whole human race.'[47] And Thomas Cooper condemned all hereditary rule , including 'hereditary Monarchy', claiming that 'TYRANNY IS THE SURE OFFSPRING OF HEREDITARY OFFICE.'[48] Central here was the concept of tyranny and despotism, associated particularly with absolute

---

Rights of Man' (1790), and id., 'The Rights of Infants' (1796), in H.T. Dickinson, ed., *The Political Works of Thomas Spence* (Newcastle upon Tyne, 1982). William Godwin, *Enquiry Concerning Political Justice, and Its Influence on Modern Morals and Happiness* (1793; 3rd edn, 1798), ed. by Isaac Kramnick (Harmondsworth, 1985). See Goodrich, *Debating England's Aristocracy*, pp. 123–9, 137–8.

[43] See Amanda Goodrich, 'Radical "Citizens of the World" 1790–1795: The Early Career of Henry Redhead Yorke', *Journal of British Studies* 53 (2014), pp. 1–25.

[44] See Epstein, *Radical Expression*, p. 9.

[45] [Citizen Randol, of Ostend], *A Political Catechism of Man* (London, 1795), p. 8.

[46] London Corresponding Society, 'Joint Address' (1792), in Goodwin, *Friends of Liberty*, p. 503. This was a joint address of the London Corresponding Society, Manchester Constitutional Society, Manchester Reformation Society, Norwich Revolution Society and others.

[47] Henry Yorke, 'Address to the National Convention of France', in 'Reason Urged against Precedent: In a Letter to the People of Derby' (London, 1793), in Claeys, ed., *Political Writings*, IV, pp. 80–81.

[48] Thomas Cooper, *A Reply to Mr. Burke's Invective against Mr. Cooper and Mr. Watt* (London, 1792), p. 17.

rulers, and much of this rhetoric was focused on France or the wider world and represented a cosmopolitan idealism. Indeed, in the mid 1790s, John Thelwall called on radicals to be 'citizens of the world!' for '[t]he happiness of the human species is the only object virtue has in contemplation'.[49]

Some pamphleteers clumped together a collection of 'hereditary rulers' for their condemnation. Eaton's *Politics for the People*, for example, accused 'Kings, Princes, Courtiers and Pharisaical Priests' of corruption.[50] And an anonymous pamphleteer condemned 'HEREDITARY KINGS AND GOVERNORS'.[51] But, as I have argued elsewhere, within the texts of the French Revolution debate in England anti-aristocratic rhetoric became dominant.[52] Paine started this trend in *Rights of Man* by declaring that in England the House of Lords was 'beyond the control of the nation'; it was an 'aristocracy' more powerful than that in France before the Revolution. This aristocracy was at the root of corruption and all that was wrong with the English government.[53] He also identified aristocracy as a class or caste unacceptable for its hereditary nature, excessive wealth and social privileges.[54] Until this moment the term 'aristocracy' had in Britain retained a largely neutral meaning within political philosophy, reflecting ancient Greek, of 'government by the few'.[55] Paine had taken the term and imbued it with broader negative meaning and brought it into common usage. 'Aristocracy' then became a term of abuse and a highly charged rhetorical device in radical literature and popular language. According to radicals, 'aristocracy' plundered the wealth of the nation and was keeping ordinary people from their rights, their share in the democracy. The term also conflated a hereditary class with government as a whole. As radicalism increasingly focused on economic inequalities, particularly after the outbreak of war with France in 1792, it was an all-embracing 'aristocracy' that prevented

---

[49] John Thelwall, 'Tribune', 18 Apr. 1795, pp. 132–3, quoted in Epstein, *Radical Expression*, p. 8.

[50] Eaton, *Politics for the People*, I, p. 3.

[51] Anon., *An Address to the Jacobine and Other Patriotic Societies of the French* (London, 1792), p. 45.

[52] Goodrich, *Debating England's Aristocracy*, ch. 2. See also Michael S.C. Smith, 'The French Revolution, British Cultural Politics, and Recent Scholarship across Disciplines', *Huntingdon Library Quarterly*, 63 (2000), pp. 407–28, at p. 424.

[53] Thomas Paine, *The Rights of Man* (1791–1792), ed. by Eric Foner (London, 1985), p. 59. On this point, see Dror Wahrman, *Imagining the Middle Class: The Political Representation of Class in Britain, c. 1780–1840* (Cambridge, 1995), pp. 35–6.

[54] Goodrich, *Debating England's Aristocracy*, pp. 61–2.

[55] Amanda Goodrich, 'Understanding a Language of Aristocracy, 1700–1850', *Historical Journal*, 56 (2013), pp. 369–98.

greater political, economic and social equality in Britain.[56] Of course, accusations of corruption against the crown and government were common during much of the eighteenth century, but in the 1790s, and thereafter until at least the demise of Chartism, a class of 'aristocracy', rather more than monarchy became the focus of broad radical condemnation.

IV

A further strand in radical discourse identified constitutional reform as the solution to Britain's political ills. Here radicals claimed the historically universally revered central feature of the English government system, much defended by loyalists, and made it their own. They advocated reform of the constitution generally in terms of an end to corruption in parliament, annual parliaments, universal male suffrage and a fairer representation. Such proposals for reform within the established constitutional structure and law were often the only concrete plans to be found in radical writings.[57] Moderate radicals, such as Major Cartwright, had consistently proposed constitutional reform, in his case since 1776; and in 1795 he claimed that 'to restore the constitution at home' was the only way to 'contend with republican *France*'.[58] Many called for the restoration of a true balanced English constitution, as one pamphlet stated: 'not a breach, but a renovation of our constitution'.[59] Most notably such reform proposals rarely focused on monarchy but on 'aristocracy'. Morris has noted that Pitt and his ministers came under greater attack than George III, as political caricatures from the time illustrate.[60] The target was not so much the mixed government with a monarchy and two houses of parliament, but corruption in government and the hegemony of an oppressive 'aristocracy' who exploited the people and suppressed the democratic components of government.[61]

Thus radical writings incorporated a seemingly uncomfortable combination of republican or universalist statements, vitriolic anti-aristocratic rhetoric and

---

[56] See John Thelwall, 'Rights of Nature against the Usurpations of Establishments' (1796), in Gregory Claeys, ed., *Politics of English Jacobinism: Writings of John Thelwall* (University Park, PA, 1995), p. 476; Goodrich, *Debating England's Aristocracy*, ch. 4.

[57] See Goodrich, *Debating England's Aristocracy*, ch. 4; Epstein, *Radial Expression*, ch. 1.

[58] John Cartwright, 'The Commonwealth in Danger' (1795), p. 44, quoted in Goodrich, *Debating England's Aristocracy*, pp. 125–6.

[59] Joseph Gerrald, 'A Convention the Only Means of Saving us from Ruin' (1793; 3rd edn, London, 1794), in Claeys, ed., *Political Writings*, IV, p. 193.

[60] Morris, *British Monarchy*, pp. 161–3.

[61] Smith, 'The French Revolution', p. 416.

pragmatic constitutional reform for Britain. Correspondingly, one radical or radical society can be found promoting universalism at one moment and reform of the English constitution at another, or together in one pamphlet. The Society for Constitutional Information and the LCS, who had also embraced universalism if not republicanism, increasingly promoted for Britain peaceful reform not revolution. John Thelwall, whilst lauding 'the brave republic of France', advocated for England 'annual parliaments and universal suffrage; by which, and which alone, plenty and happiness can ever be extended to the majority of the people of this country'.[62] Similarly, an anonymous pamphleteer celebrated the republics in France, Holland, Switzerland and America but promoted reform of the existing government in England.[63] The British Convention at Edinburgh, having provocatively modelled itself on the French convention, claimed in its *Address* that it wished only for '[t]he restoration of annual parliaments and universal suffrage. We go no further.'[64]

V

As mentioned above, this inconsistency in ideology has generally been explained as a symptom of the times: the 1790s identified as a 'decade of ideological diversity, experimentation and flux' as Epstein put it;[65] a time when views were frequently altered and political allegiances changed; when outside factors such as government action and loyalist competing propaganda pushed radicalism in one direction or another and reinterpreted and misinterpreted its aims and ideology. Philp has pointed to 'diversity and division' among radicals and the complex relationship between 'radicals' aspirations, their commitments and their rhetoric'.[66] Certainly, the juxtaposing in one pamphlet of universalist rhetoric with constitutionalist proposals for reform in Britain often renders it difficult to understand the ideological position of the writer. Epstein and Karr have explained such a dual position as enacting a 'Jacobin performance' which involved adopting the 'styles and ultra-radical codes of speech' of French

---

[62] Thelwall, 'Peaceful Discussion', p. 401.
[63] Anon., 'The Political Crisis: Or, a Dissertation on the Rights of Man' (1791), in Claeys, ed., *Political Writings*, IV, pp. 148, 134.
[64] British Convention, 'The Address of the British Convention, Assembled at Edinburgh' (1793), in Claeys, ed., *Political Writings*, VI, p. 89.
[65] Epstein, *Radical Expression*, p. 6.
[66] Philp, 'Fragmented Ideology, p. 53.

revolutionaries, together with English constitutionalism.[67] Such performance reflected a desire to explore how far radicals could 'play outside the lines of safe formality'.[68] Whilst promoting a genuine constitutionalism, many also wished to engage with the 'political desires of a moment that appeared to hold extraordinary democratic promise'.[69]

Another common explanation for such inconsistencies is the repression of radicals during Pitt's 'reign of Terror' of 1794–1795 and the government's introduction of the crime of 'figurative treason', of 'imagining the king's death', which meant that radicals were at greater risk of being convicted, in particular, for anti-monarchical rhetoric.[70] Moreover, the rhetoric of popular loyalism indiscriminately condemned all reformers as Jacobin levellers and republicans with regicidal tendencies. Even classical republican discourse was no longer a topic for open discussion now that it was linked directly to regicide, tyranny and anarchy; it was the casualty of the repression of radicalism.[71] As one pamphlet put it, 'Republican, a word ... which to an enlightened head and an honest heart, was wont to convey every generous and manly sentiment, is now made to signify all that is abominable and wicked.'[72] This, it is argued, resulted in a need for greater caution, and ingenuity, among radicals and their societies. It became expedient to obscure one's true meaning if it ran the risk of incurring a criminal charge. Many, including radical societies, responded by promoting only constitutional reform in their later writings, and others had fallen silent by 1796.

While there is no disagreement here with these contentions, there is also an argument for consistency. Whether or not radicals took part in a 'Jacobin performance' or adopted universalist rhetoric, the majority, for whatever reason, promoted in their writings constitutional reform for Britain. And such reform proposals were largely consistent in content. Moreover, in arguing not just for reform but also restoration of the constitution many radicals sought evidence of the true English constitution in a familiar narrative of English history. They invoked Magna Carta and/or the reign of King Alfred as a time when true English liberty and rights since lost could be found, and thus restored. Many adopted

---

[67] Epstein and Karr are suggesting a 'mood' or 'temper' here rather than the existence of 'real' or 'fully fledged Jacobins'. See James Epstein and David Karr, 'Playing at Revolution: British "Jacobin" Performance"', *Journal of Modern History*, 79 (2007), pp. 495–530. See also Goodrich, 'Citizens of the World', for a discussion of 'Jacobin performance'.
[68] Epstein and Karr, 'Playing at Revolution', pp. 500–501, 530.
[69] Ibid., p. 530.
[70] Barrell, *Imagining the King's Death*, pp. 29–36.
[71] Philp, 'English Republicanism', pp. 258–9.
[72] Anon., *A Political Freethinker's Thoughts on the Present Circumstances* (London, 1795), p. 18, quoted in Barrell, *Imagining the King's Death*, p. 2.

ideas expressed in influential pamphlets such as the anonymous *Historical Essay on the English Constitution* (1771), Cartwright's *Take Your Choice* and Paine's *Common Sense* (both published in 1776). The *Historical Essay* claimed that the 'Saxon form of government ... was founded on the common rights of man', with all the 'elective power constitutionally placed in the people of England'; but this was destroyed by the Norman Conquest when tyranny was imposed.[73] In *Rights of Man*, Paine claimed that at the Norman Conquest tyrannical French rule had been imposed on England and the 'hatred' that 'invasion and tyranny begat' became 'deep rooted in the nation ... not a village in England has forgotten it', although he also claimed here that England had no constitution.[74] Joseph Gerrald admired the 'Golden days of Alfred, a patriot King' and sought the roots of a convention in the Saxon 'folk-mote' where *'the majority of wills'* dominated government.[75]

Furthermore, radicals' promotion of the revolution settlement of 1689, and its centenary in 1789, provided further evidence of such constitutional continuities. The Glorious Revolution was celebrated as a source of the power of the people to effect political change within the constitution.[76] The writings of political philosophers, particularly John Locke, were also invoked by radicals as evidence of the sovereignty of the people and the right of resistance. The Reverend Richard Price had triggered the French Revolution debate between radicals and loyalists in Britain with a sermon given on the centenary of the Glorious Revolution and celebrating the outbreak of revolution in France. Price claimed that in Britain sovereignty lay in the people who had the right to choose and remove governments and monarchs if they proved unfit for purpose. To Price, both government and the monarch were servants of the people but he was not advocating revolution.[77] Radicals continued to promote such ideas, and Paine stood almost alone in directly claiming that Britain had no constitution.[78] This sense of legitimate public control over the constitution, including the right to overthrow components of it in certain circumstances, conversely

---

[73] Christopher Hill, 'The Norman Yoke', in id., *Puritanism and Revolution: Studies in Interpretation of the English Revolution of the Seventeenth Century* (London, 1958), pp. 50–102, at pp. 95–9.

[74] Paine, *Rights of Man*, p. 168.

[75] Joseph Gerrald, *A Convention the Only Means of Saving Us from Ruin* (London, 1794), pp. 91, 111.

[76] See Kathleen Wilson, 'Inventing Revolution: 1688 and Eighteenth-Century Popular Politics', *Journal of British Studies*, 28 (1989), pp. 349–86, at pp. 355–8.

[77] Richard Price, *A Discourse on the Love of Our Country* (London, 1789), pp. 22, 23.

[78] See for example, Paine, *Rights of Man*, pp. 140–47. See also Godwin, *Enquiry Concerning Political Justice*, p. 475.

enabled radicals to contemplate working within the existing constitutional framework and within the law. One example of such ideology can be identified in the widespread radical response to the restrictive Two Acts of 1795. Radicals identified these acts as the government's attempt to establish something resembling an absolute monarchy with Pitt on the throne. Meetings were held in protest, and the LCS declared that the acts were a violation of Magna Carta and the Bill of Rights. It was suggested that radicals should invoke the 'right of resistance' as a 'natural right' and a 'constitutional duty'.[79] To some extent, then, as Michael Smith has argued, 'radicalism was tempered by the conceptual limitations of its constitutional and political discourse ... It could not escape the political and cultural worlds it was designed to transform.'[80]

Moreover, in addition to this constitutionalist ideology, a consistent 'constitutionalist action' was adopted by radicals that reveals an adherence to conventional practices in relation to monarchy. Such action, including mass petitioning and remonstrances to the king, were established methods of popular action that had been practised for centuries.[81] It was generally believed that the right to petition government and the king was guaranteed by the Bill of Rights (1689) and petitioning was widely adopted during the eighteenth century. Steve Poole has further identified a recognized contractual relationship between the monarch and the people: that it was the king's role to address the grievances of the people when they appealed to him. As a result, popular criticisms in the late eighteenth and early nineteenth centuries were made primarily on the basis of the king's failure to fulfil his contractual duties rather than an attack on the monarchy per se. Correspondingly, Poole argued, the people generally viewed the monarchy as a separate entity to parliament, and thus above faction and party control and also the corruption so closely associated with government.[82] Despite Paine's complaint that petitioning smacked of slavery, during the 1790s popular radical societies often invoked the right to petition.[83] And, importantly, radicals first petitioned parliament, rather than the king, as the target for reform.

---

[79] The Treasonable Practices Act and the Seditious Meetings Act (1795) expanded the scope of treason and restricted public meetings. See Goodwin, *Friends of Liberty*, pp. 387–97.

[80] Smith, 'The French Revolution', p. 417.

[81] Epstein, *Radical Expression*, p. 11. See also James Vernon, *Politics and the People: A Study in English Political Culture, c.1815–1867* (Cambridge, 2009), 'Introduction'.

[82] Steve Poole, *The Politics of Regicide in England, 1760–1850* (Manchester, 2000), pp. 7–11.

[83] Paine argued that the Bill of Rights allowed government to divide amongst itself all powers and profits. The nation was merely left with the right of petitioning, which was an insult. Paine, *Rights of Man*, p. 193.

In 1793 radical societies led by the LCS petitioned parliament; and a number, including the Sheffield Constitutional Society, decided to petition the king only once the petition to parliament had failed. In the 1795 radical response to the Two Acts, mass petitions were presented to parliament, and upon their failure a remonstrance to the king was proposed. John Baxter suggested that the LCS once again resort to 'Addresses, Petitions, or Remonstrances' as the means to provoke reform.[84] Thus continuities can be traced within radical constitutionalism and the actions it promoted.

VI

In brief, similar attitudes to monarchy and radical continuities can also be identified in the early nineteenth century. Whilst revolutionary republicanism could be found within radicalism, constitutionalism remained dominant until at least the demise of Chartism in about 1848. The Chartist Declaration of Rights (1839) was clear in its adherence to the constitution:

> The sovereignty of this United Kingdom is monarchical; not despotic, but limited ... the prerogatives of the imperial crown of this United Kingdom are a constitutional trust vested in the person of the monarch for the benefit and service of the people, and may be controlled, modified, and limited by the will of parliament.[85]

As Paul Pickering has pointed out, Chartist radicalism was no more coherent and clear in its aims and ideologies than earlier radicalism, but for the majority of Chartists the monarch was 'not the problem'.[86] Frank Prochaska argued that from 1832 'virtually all radicals now assumed that their principal enemy was the oligarchy not the Crown'.[87] Certainly, 'Old Corruption' remained a contentious issue and 'aristocracy' was still a major target of attack in calls for reform. An

---

[84] John Baxter, 'Resistance to Oppression: The Constitutional Rights of Britons Asserted' (1795), in Claeys, ed., *Political Writings*, VI, p. 439.

[85] Paul Pickering, '"The Hearts of Millions": Chartism and Popular Loyalism in the 1840s', *History*, 88 (2003), pp. 227–48, at p. 243.

[86] Ibid., p. 227. Dorothy Thompson also observed that Chartists were not much concerned with monarchy. Dorothy Thompson, *The Chartists* (Hounslow, 1984), p. 6. See also Malcolm Chase, *Chartism: A New History* (Manchester, 2007), pp. 106–7.

[87] Frank Prochaska, *The Republic of Britain, 1760–2000* (London, 2000), pp. 30–31. See also Robert Poole, 'French Revolution or Peasant's Revolt? Petitioners and Rebels in England from the Blanketeers to the Chartists', *Labour History Review*, 74 (2009),

enduring anti-aristocratic rhetoric was adopted and adapted into new areas of radical debate.[88] But, as radicals became more closely associated with the demands of the emerging working class, their antagonists also reflected broader groups. Chartist writings invoked 'aristocracy' broadly to include not just the governing elite, but also a capitalist middle class that oppressed the working class and denied them economic as well as political rights. New terms were also adopted – such as 'millocracy', 'shopocracy', or 'millocrat', 'cotton lord', 'steam aristocracy'. In 1839 *The Charter* condemned 'the malevolence of aristocratic and shopocratic tyranny'.[89]

Familiar forms of constitutionalist action were also consistently adopted in the early nineteenth century.[90] With greater control now exerted by the authorities over access to public spaces and the development of a 'bourgeois public sphere', those promoting revolutionary action found themselves marginalized. Radicals needed access to the 'public sphere' to influence a broader public opinion, and constitutionalism was increasingly the only action and discourse available within such shared spaces.[91] In 1817 constitutionalist action can be seen in meetings at Manchester, Spa Fields in east London and with the Hampden Club attempting a mass national petition to the House of Commons for reform. As in the 1790s, when the petition failed to even gain recognition by the government, petitioning the king was promoted. The subsequent attempted march of the Blanketeers famously carried petitions from Manchester to London to present to the Prince Regent. One speaker at a meeting of marchers declared: 'We will let them see it is not riot and disturbance we want ... and we will apply to our noble Prince as a child would to its father ... so lawful and constitutional a proceeding'.[92] Again in 1839 Chartists first petitioned parliament and then, anticipating failure,

---

pp. 6–26, at p. 21. See also Pickering, 'The Hearts of Millions'; Taylor, *Down with the Crown*; Goodrich, 'Understanding a Language of Aristocracy'.

[88] Goodrich, 'Understanding a Language of Aristocracy'.

[89] Gareth Stedman Jones, *Languages of Class: Studies in English Working Class History, 1832–1982* (Cambridge, 1993), p. 153.

[90] Poole, 'French Revolution or Peasants' Revolt?', pp. 8, 22. See also Paul Pickering, '"And Your Petitioners etc.": Chartist Petitioning in Popular Politics, 1838–48', *English Historical Review*, 116 (2001), pp. 368–88.

[91] See Vernon, *Politics and the People*, pp. 6–11; Jon Mee, *Romanticism, Enthusiasm and Regulation: Poetics and the Policing of Culture in the Romantic Period* (Oxford, 2003), p. 10. For a succinct synthesis of the debates on the 'public sphere' see J.A. Downie, 'Public and Private: They Myth of the Bourgeois Public Sphere', in Cynthia Wall, ed., *A Concise Companion to the Restoration and Eighteenth Century* (Oxford, 2005), pp. 58–79.

[92] Poole, 'French Revolution or Peasants' Revolt?', p. 15; Poole, *The Politics of Regicide*, pp. 147–9.

promoted approaching Prince Albert to become 'the People's Champion' like King Alfred. The queen was also asked to put herself above government and support the people's petition for adult suffrage;[93] 1840 saw mass petitioning to the queen by Chartists calling for the reprieve of the radical John Frost.[94] These examples suggest that appeals were commonly made to the monarch as a figure outside and above government.

VII

The argument here is that anti-monarchism and regicidal threats are to be found in popular radical culture and republican tracts. The fact that many radicals promoted republican or universalist ideas suggests that they were excited by the possibilities of a world made afresh in line with democratic and egalitarian principles.[95] That their ideas often remained somewhat nebulous and were not taken further to develop a framework for a republic or an entirely new democratic constitution in Britain is not surprising. Not only were government suppression and the broad legal interpretation of treason serious deterrents, but it is also clear that English radicalism had not reached a moment of crisis at which concrete plans for an entirely new government were imperative. Revolution had left the American colonies and France without legitimate governments, and this accelerated their need to create a new constitution. Furthermore, the continuing turmoil of the Revolution and the French Wars meant that France did not provide a suitable model of a fully functioning republic; and the Americans were still undecided as to what to call their fledgling government and how to fully unite the federal states. An acceptable universal form of democratic government had not yet emerged, and would not do so during the 1790s.[96] Thus, the radical proposals for revolutionary change were diverse, experimental and shifted in response to the tumultuous times. Ultimately, such proposals did not amount to a united call for regicide or a republic in Britain. Rather, they were overtaken by a wider radical movement for reform of the existing constitution focused on the governing elite of 'aristocracy'.

---

[93] Poole, French Revolution or Peasant's Revolt?', p. 20. See also Thompson, *The Chartists*, p. 58.
[94] Chase, *Chartism*, pp. 139–40.
[95] See Mee, *Romanticism*, p. 294.
[96] See John Dunn, *Setting the People Free: The Story of Democracy* (London, 2005), esp. ch. 2.

The evidence also suggests, that continuities may be identified in radical attitudes to monarchy in the adherence to English constitutionalism. During the French Revolution and beyond the majority of British radicals continued to agitate for a greater democracy by adopting a consistent ideology of constitutional reform set within a recognized framework of English history, law and political philosophy. They also adopted familiar practices and forms of constitutionalist action to assert the popular voice that fell within established popular political protocols and paradigms. Such action engaged with the monarch in conventional ways that tended to represent the king as a separate entity to parliament, and on occasion, a longstanding 'friend to the people'. Moreover, such constitutionalism hindered the development of anti-monarchical action beyond rhetoric and 'performance', significant thought these aspects may have appeared at the time. Reform or restoration of the English mixed constitution necessarily entailed retention of the monarch but also a recognition of the limitations of monarchical power. For radicals, then, it was the 'aristocracy', encompassing the two houses of parliament and government of the day, that was condemned as the bulwark preventing the people from asserting their rights to a role in politics, a place in the 'public political sphere' and to greater social and economic equality. The monarchy ,was pushed to the wings of the political stage. It is not the intention here to revert to a vision of a consistent and continuous radicalism in the English past.[97] Rather, it is to suggest that within a fragmented and diverse radicalism, continuities may also be identified in relation to attitudes to monarchy.

---

[97] See e.g. Thompson, *Making*.

Index

acts and bills
    Act of Association (1584), 25, 26
    Act of Settlement (1701), 7, 25, 41,
        95–6, 251
    Act of Union (1707), 41, 181, 210–11,
        235, 240–41, 254
    Bill of Rights (1689), 95, 251, 274
    Intolerable Acts (1774), 183–4
    Occasional Conformity Act (1711),
        74–5, 86–7
    Quebec Act (1774), 10, 122–4, 183–4
    Schism Act (1714), 75, 87
    Seditious Meetings Act (1795), 274, 275
    Septennial Act (1716), 233, 244
    Stamp Act (1765), 181, 182, *183*
    Toleration Act (1712), 75, 79, 88, 241
    Treasonable Practices Act (1795), 274, 275
Adolphus Frederick, 1st Duke of
    Cambridge, 22, 190, 201
Albert of Saxe-Coburg and Gotha, 277
Alfred the Great, 143, 272–3, 277
Anglican Church, *see* Church of England
Anna, Empress of Russia, 237
Anne, Queen, 25, 38, 77, 95, 129, 178, 183, 253
    and army, 207, 209, 211–14, 215, 216,
        217, 218
    body, 148, 149, 150, 151, *163*, 169
    and Church of England, 38, 114, 116,
        117, 121
    court, 155
    death, 73, 208
    and Hanoverian succession, 75–6, 79,
        207–208, 220–21, 225
    image, 148, 149, 150, 151, *163*, 169,
        171
    and royal touch, 12, 38, 138
anti-Catholicism, 8, 131–3, 138, 200–202, 253

Aquaviva d'Aragona, Pasquale, 257
Aquaviva d'Aragona, Troiano, 257
Archer, John, 77–9
Aretin, Karl Otmar von, 60
Argyll, John Cambell, 2nd Duke of, 210–11,
    215–16, 218, 219, 224, 225
aristocracy, 21, 47–8, 65–8, 262–3,
    269–70, 275–6, 277–8
Arndt, Johannes, 64
Arne, Thomas, 143
Ashburnham, John, 1st Earl of, 214–15
Aspland, Robert, 197, 199–200
Atterbury, Francis, 236, 246
Auckland, William Eden, 1st Baron, 188, 189
Augustus II, King of Poland and Elector of
    Saxony, 94, 105
Austria, 39, 54, 59, 64, 65, 70, 97, 102, 104,
    105–106, 238, 254, 257–8
Avignon, 19, 255, 256

Banks, Joseph, 18
Baptists, 76, 81, 82, 196, 202
Barker, Jane, 230
Bärninger, Otto Friedrich, 50–52, 66, 68
Barrell, John, 266
Barrymore, James Barry, 4th Earl of, 222–3
Bath, William Pulteney, Earl of, 223, 244
Bathurst, Henry, 199
battle of
    Camperdown, 195
    Cape Saint Vincent, 195
    Conzer Brücke, 44, 50, 51, 56, 60, 69
    Culloden, 196, 248, 259
    Dettingen, 15, 16, 70, 164, 178
    Nile, the, 17, 18, 191
    Oudenarde, 18
    Salamanca, 194

Teutoburg Forest, the, 50
Trafalgar, 17, 18, 191
Waterloo, 194, 195
Wynendael, 216
Bavaria, Electorate of, 45, 63, 190, 258
Baxter, John, 275
Belcher, Jonathan, 112
Bell, James B., 114, 122
Benedict XIV, Pope, 259
Bentham, Edward, 234–5
Berlin, 63, 96, 99, 101, 102, 237
Blair, Tony, 149
Le Blanc, Jean-Bernard, 130
Bolingbroke, Henry St. John, 1st Viscount, 129, 207–208, 217, 218–19, 220, 222, 228, 233, 239, 244
Bonnie Prince Charlie, *see* Charles Edward Stuart
Book of Common Prayer, 30, 96, 117, 118, 119, 124, 125
Boston, 107, 111–12, 113, 116, 118, 119, 121, 123–4, 182, 183–4
Boudinot, Elias, 186
Bradbury, Thomas, 73, *79*, 80
Bradley, James E., 88
Bradshaigh, Henry, 213
Bradshaigh, Roger, 213
Bremen, Duchy of, 57, 61
Brewer, John, 134
Bridenbaugh, Carl, 109–10
Bristol, 83, 117, 156, 232
Brunswick-Lüneburg, Electorate of, *see* Hanover, Electorate of
Brunswick-Wolfenbüttel, Duchy of, 45–6, 63, 64
Bull, Peter, 163, 164
Burdet, Francis, 198
Burnet, Gilbert, 129–30
Bute, John Stuart, 3rd Earl of, 192, 243

Cadogan, William, 210, 214, 216, 218, 220, 221, 224, 225
Calamy, Edmund, 83, 84, 86
Cambridge, 82
 university, 211
Cambridge, Mass., 121
Campbell Orr, Clarissa, 5, 199
Cannon, John, 2, 264
caricature, art of, 149–50, 165, 270
Carl Philipp of Brunswick-Lüneburg, 56
Caroline of Brandenburg-Ansbach, Queen, 7, 13, 80, 83, 137, 138, 139, 142, 154, 166, 171, 175–6, 178, 179
Caroline of Brunswick-Wolfenbüttel, Queen, 21, 149–50, 203
Carstares, William, 241
Carte, Thomas, 74
Cartwright, John, 198, 270, 273
Catherine of Braganza, Queen, 7, 138
Catholic Emancipation, 40, 123, 200–202
Catholicism, 29–30, 33–6, 93–4, 122–3, 135–6, 183–4
Caudle, James, 111, 112
celebrations, public, 74, 79–81, 112–13, 136, 175–7, 184, 190–93, 195, 258–9
Celle, 50, 52, 57, 60, 61, 62, 63, 64
Charles I, King, 7, 11, 30, 33, 41, 79–80, 87, 129, 246, 248
Charles II, King, 7, 11, 12, 26, 28, 30, 31, 32–3, *35*, 79, 87, 140, 141, 169, 253, 258
Charles VI, Holy Roman Emperor, 7, 39, *94*, 104, 137, 253–4
Charles Edward Stuart, Jacobite Prince of Wales, 19, 136, 167, 178, 243, 252, 254, 256, 258–9, *260*
Charles Louis, Elector Palatine, 66–7
Charlotte of Mecklenburg-Strelitz, Queen, 5, 14, 178, 190, 199, 203
Charlotte Augusta, Princess of Wales, 193, 202, 204
Chartism, 275–7
Chauncy, Charles, 111–2
Chenevix-Trench, Charles, 161
Chesterfield, Philip Dormer Stanhope, 4th Earl of, *154*, 159, 221
Christian Louis of Brunswick–Lüneburg, 45
Church of England, 29–32, 35–6, 38, 39–41, 86–7, 88, 198–9, 202, 231

colonial, 107–110, 114–22, 124–5
Churchill, George, 212
Clark, Samuel, 77, 78, 79
Clavering, Anne, 214–15
Clement XII, Pope, 259
Clinton, Bill, 149
Cobbett, William, 191, 193, 197–8, 244
Cockburn, Patrick, 241, 242
Coetlogon, Charles Edward de, 194–5
Coleman, Benjamin, 182
Colfox, Thomas, 197
Colley, Linda, 13, 132–3, 149, 263–4
Collins, Jeffrey, 28
Congregationalists, 9, 82, 107–108, 109, 110, 112, 121
Constitutionalism, 262–3, 270–78
Conti, Louis-François de Bourbon, prince de, 43
Cooper, Thomas, 268
coronation oath, 123, 198–9, 201–202
Corpus Evangelicorum, 7, 93, 97–8, 99–102, 104–6
Cotton, John Hynde, 244, 245–6
coup d'etat, military, 218–24, 225
court culture, 10–13, 19–20, 32–3, 257
Cowper, William, 87
Cox, Richard, 133
Cranmer, Thomas, 136
Créqui, François de Blanchefort de, 44
Cromwell, Oliver, 37, 186, 233
Cruickshank, George, 149, 150
Cumberland, William, Duke of, 154, 193, 196, 201

Defoe, Daniel, 168
Denmark, 56–8, 61, 62
Dinwiddy, John, 261
dissent, religious, 8–9, 28–9, 30, 35, 36, 40, 73–88, 107–108, 110–12, 120, 123, 135, 136, 174, 197, *198*, 202, 245
Dublin, 83, 192, 240
Dundas, William, 191
Dutch Republic, 26–7, 103, 104, 189, 220, 221, 238–9
Dyck, Anthony van, 171

Eaton, Daniel, 265, 269
Echlin, Robert, 222
Eddis, William, 184
Edinburgh, 191, 195, 227, 243, 258, 271
Edward VI, King, 202
Edward, Duke of Kent and Strathearn, 18, 193
Edward of Woodstock, the Black Prince, 143
Egmont, John Percival, 1st Earl of, 207, 221, 224, 231, 236–7, 243, 247, 249
Elizabeth I, Queen, 11, 25, 37, 38, 129
Elizabeth, Empress of Russia, 236
Elizabeth Charlotte, Princess Palatine, 43, 66
Elizabeth Christine, Holy Roman Empress, *94*
Epstein, James, 264–5, 271–2
Erastianism, 27–8, 37, 40
Erle, Thomas, 222
Ernest Augustus, Duke of Cumberland, 193, 201
Ernest Augustus, Elector of Hanover, 43–4, 45–6, 49, 50, 51, 52, 54–6, 58, 60–61, 62–3, 65, 66, 70, 94–5
Eveleigh, Josiah, 80

Faes, Johannes, 50–51, 53–4
Farington, Joseph, 191
Farrington, Thomas, 210
Fenelon, Francois, 60, 234
Ferdinand Maria, Elector of Bavaria, 47
Fleury, André Hercule, Cardinal de, 256
Flint, George, 232–3
Fontainebleau, 43, 47
Forster, Thomas, 244
Fox, Charles James, 188, *189*
France, 36, 102, 192; *see also* French Revolution
  alliance with England, 238–9, 253, 255
  aristocracy, 65, 66–7
  Catholicism, 29–30, 34, 39
  food, 130
  Huguenots, 39, 131, *198*, 200
  Jansenism, 141
  relations with German princes, 43–4, 46–8, 54, 58, 61–4, 69, 70, 100
  royal rituals, 33

and Stuart exile court, 135, 136, 251, 255–6, 257
wars with England, 2, 37, 38, 133, 143, 171, *190*, 220, 269
Francophobia, 46–8, 50, 62–3, 68, 69, 130–32, 133, 143, 168
Franklin, Benjamin, 173, 178
Franklin, William, 178
Frederick II, King of Prussia, 16, 96, 102, 139, 237
Frederick, Duke of York and Albany, 193, 196, 198
Frederick Augustus of Brunswick-Lüneburg, 56
Frederick Lewis, Prince of Wales, 13, 20, 96, 115, 142–3, 144, 243–4, 246, 248–9, 258, 259
Frederick William I, King of Prussia, 39, 102, 103
Frederick William, the Great Elector, 54, 57
French Revolution, 133, 134–5, 194, 199, 203, 204, 229, 234–5, 248, 262, 264, 265–9, 270–73, 277, 278
Friedrich II, Landgrave of Hesse-Kassel, 104–105
Fry, William Storrs, 196
Fryer, John, 84–5
Funck, Friedrich, 50–51, 52–3, 66
Fürstenberg, Franz Egon von , 47, 48
Fürstenberg, Wilhelm Egon von, 47, 48

Galen, Christoph Bernhard von, 47, 48, 64
Gay, John, 137–8
George I, King, 5, 26, 45, 139, 142, *252*, 254–5, 256
 body, 150–51
 celebrations of, 73–4, 76, 80–81, 107–108, 136
 and Church of England, 114–22, 125
 court, 5, 11–13, 139–40, 142, 155
 defender of Protestantism, 38–9, 76–9, 101–103, 105–106, 107–108, 109–14, 122, 138, 241, 245
 family life, 258
 and France, 253
 and Frederick William I, 102
 image, 2, 7, 20, 38–9, 51–2, 60, 69, 76–9, 109–14, 122, 136, 138, 125, 152, 155–63, 168–9, 194
 and military, 14–17, 51–2, 194, 209, 222–5
 and political parties, 244, 245, 246
 popularity, 5, 13, 74, 145, 171–2, 177, 186, 251, 263
 and public sphere, 141–2
 religiosity, 8–9, 96, 140
 religious policies, 7–10, 82–8, 95, 108, 140–41, 241
 and Scotland, 241, 242, 254–5
George II, King, 5, 142, 254–5, 256
 body, 150–51, 163–4
 celebrations of, 177
 and Church of England, 114–22, 125
 court, 5, 11–13, 139–40, 142, 155
 defender of Protestantism, 104–106, 109–14, 122, 125, 137
 family life, 258
 image, 2, 7, 20, 60, 69–70, 109–14. 122, 125, 137, 153, 163–9, 194
 marriage policies, 104
 and military, 14–17, 70, 137, 194, 224, 225
 and political parties, 243, 245, 247
 popularity, 5, 13, 88, 145, 171–2, 77–9, 186, 243, 251, 263
 and Prussia, 102
 and public sphere, 141–2
 religiosity, 8–9, 96, 140
 religious policies, 7–10, 83–4, 140–41
 and Scotland, 242–3, 254–5
George III, King, 41, 144–5, 187, 251, 252
 Anglican faith, 7, 8–9, 88, 144, 199
 assassination attempt on, 261
 body, 149
 and Catholicism, 122–3, 199–202
 and Church of England, 41, 88, 108–109, 116, 120–25
 criticism of, 108–109, 171, 183–6, 197, 264, 270
 defender of Protestantism, 182, 198, 201
 and Electorate of Hanover, 188
 image, 2–3, 149

kingship above party, 20–21, 203–204, 248, 249
and military, 14–15, 17–18, 194–7, 198
popularity, 13, 110, 145, 177–8, 180, 182–3, 192, 263, 264
religious policies, 9–10, 88
and University of Göttingen, 18
George IV, King, 192, 193
body, 149–50, 169
and Catholic Emancipation, 200–202
and Chartism, 276
and Church of England, 198–9
criticism of, 191, 203
and Hanover, 21–2, 189, 190, 193
image, 3, 149–50, 151, 169, 187
kingship above party, 203–204
and military, 15, 194–5, 198
and Queen Caroline affair, 21, 203
and Royal Guelphic Order, 190
and University of Göttingen, 190
George of Denmark, consort of Queen Anne, 212
George William, Duke of Brunswick-Lüneburg, 44, 45, 49, 50–51, 52–3, 54, 56, 57, 58, 60, 61, 62, 70
Georgia, 103, 114, 115, 177, 184
Gerrald, Joseph, 270, 273
Gibbon, Edward, 235
Gibson, Edmund, 116
Gillray, James, 149
Glen, James, 242
Glorious Revolution, 1, 25, 34, 40, 62, 81, 95, 129, 131, 133–5, 140–41, 143, 173, 183, 222, 231, 232, 241, 245, 251, 263, 273
Godolphin, Francis Godolphin, 2nd Earl of, 211
Godolphin, Sidney Godolphin, 1st Earl of, 210, 211, 214, 215
Goldie, Mark, 27–8
Goring, Henry, 223
Göttingen, University of, 18, 190
Granger, Stewart, 163
Gregg, Edward, 220
Griffiths, Richard, 168

Gustav II Adolph, King of Sweden, 91–2
Gwynn, John, 140

Haldane, James, 101
Halifax, George Savile, 1st Marquess of, 133
Hamburg, 56, 57, 58, *100*
Hamilton, Alexander, 184
Hamilton, David, 217
Hampden, John, 221
Hampden, Richard, 221
Handel, George Frideric, 11, *155*
Hanmer, Thomas, 211
Hanover, Electorate of, 2, 14, 15, 21–2, 45–6, 56, 144, 204, 220
English attitudes towards, 4, 5, 21, 169, 178–9, 188–94, 197, 203
imperial policy, 57–62, 64, 69, 94–5, 98–9, 101–106
religion, 8–9, 108, 200
Harding, Nathanael, 76, 77, 78
Hardwicke, Philip Yorke, 1st Earl of, *105*, 238
Hardy, Thomas, 265, *266*
Harley, Robert, *see* Oxford, 1st Earl of
Harris, Tim, 134
Hatton, Ragnhild, *84*, 161
Hayton, David, 241
Hazard, Ebenezer, 171–2
Henrietta Maria, Queen, 7, 133, 138
Henry VII, King, 248
Henry VIII, King, 10, 25, 31, 36, 129, 169
Henry Benedict, Jacobite Duke of York, 136, 252, 258, 259, *260*
Henry the Lion, Duke of Saxony and Bavaria, 58
Henry, Patrick, 116
Higgins, George, 261
Hill, John, 213–4, 223
Hoadley, Benjamin, 86
Hobbes, Thomas, 28
Hogarth, William, 130–32, *169*
Honywood, Philip, 216
Hoppit, Julian, 39
Howe, Emanuel, 210
Hutchinson, Thomas, 120–21

Ihalainen, Pasi, 38–9
Imperial Diet, *see Reichstag*
Innes, Lewis, 233
Ireland, 8, 20, 83, 92, 123, 132, 135, 181, 192–3, 200, 210, 229, 230, 235, 237, 238, 239–40, 248, 252, 254, 255, 257, 266
Islay, Archibald Campbell, Lord, 242–3
Ivimey, Joseph, 202

Jacobitism, 12, 18–21, 81, 85, 135–6, 141, 151, 227–60
   ballads, 4, 154–6, 158–60, 163, 166
   European dimension, 230, 236–9
   exile court, 19–20, 235, 237, 251–60
   and Ireland, 20, 135, 229, 230, 240, 254
   and political parties, 218–22, 223–4, 225, 243–8
   rhetoric, 232–6, 248–9
   and Scotland, 20, 136, 229, 230, 240–43, 254–5
James I and VI, King, 25–6, 177
James II and VII, King, 12, 15, 20, 26, 33–7, 41, 95, 116, 129, 131, 133, 134, 135, 136, 143, 209, 232–3, 239–40, 251
James Francis Edward Stuart, styled James III, 95, 135–6, 137, 156, 218, 231, 234–5, 237, 251–2, 253–60
Jervas, Charles, 163
Jesse, John Heneage, 160, 166–7
John Frederick, Duke of Hanover, 45, 47, 49, *56*, 57, 61, *94*
Johnson, Robert, 175
Johnson, Samuel, 136
Johnson, Samuel, 138, 159, 245
Johnston, Gabriel, 242
Jupp, Peter, 264

Kantorowicz, Ernst, 147–8
Karl Philipp, Elector Palatine, 100–101, 103
Karr, David, 271–2
Keith, George, 237
Keith, William, 242
Kelly, Dennis, 200–201

Kelsey, Sean, 30
Kent, William, 12
Kielmannsegge, Sophia Charlotte von, 154, 156, 158
King James Bible, 119
king's evil, 12, *16*, 19, 31, 34–5, 38, 138–9
king's two bodies, 147–8
Kneller, Godfrey, *156*, 157
Knight, Henry Gally, 200
Kreienberg, Christian Friedrich, 75

Lafontaine, Georg Wilhelm, *151*, 152
Lauenburg, Duchy of, 56, 58–9, 62, 69
Lee, Richard, 265
Leibniz, Gottfried Wilhelm, *49*, 62–3
Lemaitre, Peter, 261
Leopold I, Holy Roman Emperor, 53, *59*, 65–6
Leslie, Doris, 163
Leszczynska, Maria, 256
Lewis, Jenkin, 85
Lillo, George, 168
Liverpool, Robert Banks Jenkinson, 2nd Earl of, 199
Locke, John, 234, 235, 273, 140–41
Lockhart, George, 221
London, 73, 80, 81, 82, 83, 84, 104, 117, 119, 130, 131, 139–40, 141, 143, 191, 192, 193, 196, 213, 221, 233, 235, 261, 266, 276
London Corresponding Society, 261, 266, 268, 271, 274, 275
Lorraine, Duchy of, 19, 252, 255, 256
Louis XIV, King of France, 7, 16, 34, 37, 39, 43–4, 46–7, 48, 49, 50, 54, 61–2, 63, 64, 65, 68, 69, 94, 130, 131–2, 133, 139, 140, 168, 234, 252, 253
Louis XV, King of France, 239, 256
Louis XVI, King of France, 138–9, 199, 264
Louvois, François Michel le Tellier, marquis de, 48
Lovat, Simon Fraser, 11th Lord, 242
loyalism, 13–14, 21–2, 73–88, 107–22, 171–80, 182–4, 185–6, 194–5,

200–201, 224–5, 247, 250, 261–2, 263–4, 266, 270, 272
Lumley, Henry, 211, 218–19
Lutheranism, 8–9, 93, 96, 100, 107, 111, 115, 245

Macartnay, George, 216
Macaulay, Thomas Babington, 135, 136
McCalman, Iain, 265
McCarthy, Justin, 160
MacDonnell, Alexander, 236
MacLeod, Norman, 242
Manchester, 81, 232, 266, *268*, 276
Mandeville, Bernard, 231, 249
Marchmont, Hugh Hume Campbell, 3rd Earl of, 227, 243
Marlborough, John Churchill, 1st Duke of, 16, 210, 211–18, 220–22, 225
Marlow, Joyce, 161
Marshall, Dorothy, 161
Mary I, Queen, 231
Mary II, Queen, 25, 95, 116, 123, 129, 253
Mary, Landgravine of Hesse-Cassel, 104–105
Mary of Modena, Queen, 138, 252
Mary Stewart, Queen of Scots, 25
Masham, Abigail, Lady, 207, 213–14
Masham, Samuel, 214
Mather, Cotton, 9, 107, 108
Max Heinrich, Elector of Cologne, 47, 48
Mayhew, Jonathan, 114, 121, *122*
Mehemet von Königstreu, Georg Ludwig Maximilian, 139, 154
Mendham, Joseph, 201–202
Meredith, Thomas, 210, 214, 216
Merkel, Angela, 149
Michael, Wolfgang, 160–61
Miller, Martin, 167
Milner, John, 199

monarchy, 1–2
    composite, 4–6, 26–7
    limited, 27, 123–4, 185–6, 262–3, 270, 278
    military, 14–18, 37–8, 39, 194–8

philanthropic, 14, 187
sacral, 26, 27, 30–32, 33–7, 38–41, 76–9, 107–108, 123, 150, 182
Montagu, Mary Wortley, 159
Mordaunt, Harry, 210
Morris, Marilyn, 149, 263, 264, 270
Munro, Robert, 224
Münster, Ernst von, 190
Mustapha, Ernst August, 139, 154

Nash, John, 190
nationalism, English, 129–32, 143–4
Nelson, Horatio, 17, 191, 195
Neville, Sylas, 203
Newcastle, Thomas Pelham-Holles, 1st Duke of, 121, 237–8
Newcastle upon Tyne, 117, 203
Nicholson, William, 87
Niven, David, 167
Nottingham, Daniel Finch, 2nd Earl of, 75
Nuttal, John, 265

Obama, Barack, 149
d'Olbreuse, Éléonore Desmier, 62
Order
    of the Garter, 19–20, 119, *155*, 215–16, 255
    of the Golden Fleece, 255
    Royal Guelphic, 190
    of the Thistle, 19–20, 255
d'Orléans, Anne-Marie, *252*
Ormonde, James Butler, 2nd Duke of, 208, 215, 218, 220, 222, 225, 244
Orrery, Charles Boyle, 4th Earl of, 215, 224, 246, 247
Osnabrück, Bishopric of, 43, 45, 50, 51, 52, 256, 258
Owen, Jeremiah, 80
Owen, Jonathan, 77, 78
Oxford, 81, 223, 234, 243, 245, 247
    university, 82, 223
Oxford, Robert Harley, 1st Earl of, 150, 207, 208, 213, 214, 215, 216, 217, 218, 220, 244

Paine, Thomas, 124, 262, 264, 267, 268, 269, 273, 274
palaces, royal, 10–13, 83, 138–40, 142
Palmes, Francis, 210
Panayi, Panikos, 168
papacy, 31, 36, 252, 254–7
Paris, 140, 255, 266
Parker, Robert, 219–20
Parry, Mark, 82
'patriot opposition', 20, 141, 144, 195, 233, 234, 243, 248–9, 264, 273
patriotism, imperial, 45, 50–70
patronage, military, 209–17, 222–4, 225–6
Patten, Robert, 243
peace treaties of
    Nijmegen (1679), 49, 61
    Rastadt (1714), *252*, 254
    Ryswick (1697), 97–8
    Utrecht (1713), 102, 218, 252, *253*, 255
    Westphalia (1648), 45, 52, 91–4, 98, 99–100, 102, 105
Pearce, Thomas, 222
Perceval, Spencer, 199
Peter the Wild Boy, 154
petitioning, 82–7, 121, 122, 124, 185, 197, 274–5, 276–7
Philadelphia, 116, *125*, 178, 184
Philip V, King of Spain, 253, 254
Philippe II, duc d'Orléans, 253, 256
Philp, Mark, 261, 271
Pickering, Paul, 275
Pincus, Steve, 33–4, *36*, 129, 133, 134
Pine, Robert Edge, 153, 164
Pitt, William, 203, 270, 272, 274
Plumb, J.H., 134, 142, *150*, 151, *154*
Plunkett, Nicholas, 229, 240
Pocock, J.G.A., 267
Polignac, Melchior, Cardinal de, 255, 257
political plots, 19, 21, 25, 238
    Atterbury Plot, 19, 245, 254, 255
    Gunpowder Plot, 79, 177
    Layer Plot, 225
    Pop–Gun Plot, 261, 266
    Popish Plot, 26
Poole, Steve, 274

Pope, Alexander, *159*, 166
Portmore, David Colyear, 1st Earl of, 215
Portugal, 7, 197, 215
Poulett, John Poulett, 1st Earl, 214–15
Pownall, Thomas, 179–80
Presbyterians, 8, 28, 30, 31–2, 74, 80, 81, 82, 83, *85*, 86, 87–8, 111, 135, *187*, 240–41, 250
Preston, 82, 240
Prévost, Antoine François, 141–2
Price, Benjamin, 110
Price, Richard, 273
Priestley, Joseph, 88
Prince, Thomas, 136
Protestantism, 135–6
    and Hanoverian dynasty, 6–10, 41, 89–90, 94–106, 107–22, 125, 137–8, 174–5, 178–9, 198–202, 231, 239
Prussia, 57, 61, 97, 102–103, 105–106, 188–9, 194, 256
public sphere, 13, 141–2, 172–3, 276
Pulteney, William, *see* Earl of Bath
Puritanism, 28–9, 35

Quakers, 81, 112, 196

Radcliffe, Charles, 239–40
radicalism, 21, 41, 197–8, 261–78
Ralph, James, 139
Ramsay, Andrew Michael, 236
Regensburg, *see Reichstag*
Reichstag, 46, 64, 92–4, 97, 98–9, 100, 101, 104, 105
republicanism, 21, 26, 37–8, 88, 124, 141, 171–2, 184–6, 194–5, 202–203, 234, 262, 264–8, 270–71, 272, 275, 277
Riotte, Torsten, 5
Roberts, Clayton, 161
Roberts, David, 161
Rome, 19, 135, 252, 254–9
Rosewell, Samuel, 83
Ross, Charles, 216–17, 223
Rowney, Thomas, 243
Ryder, Dudley, 232, 242, 244, 245, 247

Sacheverell, Henry, 82
Sadler, James, 191
Sadler, Michael, 200
Saint-Aignan, Paul-Hippolyte de Beauvilliers, duc de, 257
Saint-Germain-en-Laye, 19, 251, 255
Saint-Saphorin, François Louis de Pesme de, 102
Saxony, Electorate of, 45, 94, 97, 98, *100*, 101, 190
Schnath, Georg, *2*, 49, 59, 60
Schulenburg, Friedrich Wilhelm von der, *86*
Schulenburg, Melusine von der, 154, 156, 158
Schütz, Georg von, 218
Scotland, 8, 10, 19–20, 25, 28, 31–2, 33, 41, 84, 111, 132, 136, 171, 181, *191*, 193, 195, 210–11, 224, 227, 228, 229, 230, 235, 237, 239, 240–43, 248, 250, 252, 254–5, 258–9, 266
Scott, Walter, 195
scrofula, *see* king's evil
Secker, Thomas, 121
Seeman, Enoch, 163
Seymour, Francis, 142
Shackleton, John, 164
Shannon, Richard Boyle, 2nd Viscount, 210
Sherman, Roger, 173
Simms. Brendan, 5, 8, *122*, 188
Simpson, Helen de Guerry, 163
Simpson, James, 195
Smith, Hannah, 5, 7, 74, 113, 138, 140, 194, 263
Smith, John, 86
Smith, Michael, 274
Sobieska, Maria Clementina, 252, 256, 257–8
Sobieski, John, 252
Society for Constitutional Information, 271
Society for the Promotion of Christian Knowledge, 103
Society for the Propagation of the Gospel, 114, 115, 116–17, 121, *122*
Solms-Braunfels, Friederike von, 193
Sophia, Electress of Hanover, 6, 43–4, 47, 56, 69, 95–6

Sophia Dorothea of Celle, 163
Sophie Charlotte, Queen of Prussia, 44
Sowerby, Scott, 36
Spain, 143, 171, 197, 209, 216, 219, 254, 257, 258
Spence, Thomas, 267
Stair, John Dalrymple, 2nd Earl of, 231
standing army, fears of, 15, 17, 197–8, 208–209, 226, 233
Stanhope, James Stanhope, 1st Earl, 86, 210, 220, 221, 224, 225
Stinton, Benjamin, 76–7, 79, 83
Stuart, Charles Edward, *see* Charles Edward Stuart
Stuart, James Francis Edward, *see* James Francis Edward Stuart
Stuart, Maria Juliana, 192
Stuart, William, 192
succession, 3, 25–6
    Protestant, 75–9, 207–208, 218–24, 227, 228, 231, 251
Sunderland, Charles Spencer, 3rd Earl of, 214
Sutton, Charles Manners, 202
Sutton, Richard, 223
Sweden, 27, 57, 61, 86, 99–100, 237
Swift, Edward, 265–6
Swift, Jonathan, 217

Temple, Richard, 210
Tencin, Pierre-Guérin de, 257
Teviot, Thomas Livingstone, Viscount, 212
Thelwall, John, 265, 269, 271
Theobald, David, *123*, 124
Thompson, Christopher, 196
Thorn, blood-bath of (1724), 132
Thornton, Marianne, 189
Thornville, James, 17
Tingley, Samuel, 125
Toland, John, 151
Tories, 20, 27, 31, 33, 38, 74–5, 87–8, 142, 159, 199, 201, 203, 207, 209–11, 214–18, 222, 225, 227, 228, 229, 232, 235, 243–8
Toulmin, Joshua, 196–7

treason, 220, 232, 246, 261, 265–6, 272, *274*, 277

Unitarians, *187*, 196, *197*, 199

Vanbrugh, John, 140
Verden, Duchy of, 57
Versailles, court of, 65, 69, 133, 138, 140
Victoria, Queen, 22, 150, 169, 194
Vienna, 13, 63, 65, 92
Vittorio Amadeo, Duke of Savoy, *252*

Wake, William, 87
Waldegrave, James Waldegrave, 1st Earl, 238
Wallmoden, Amalie Sophie von, 166
Walpole, Horace, 150–51, 154–5, 247, 249
Walpole, Robert, 121, 141, 144, 150, 154, 212, 214, 231–2, 233, 239, 245, 250, 256
wars, 16, 38, 49, 63, 69, 113, 118, 133–4, 135, 143, 172, 196, 197, 198, 209
   American Independence, 3, 17, 112, 125, 144, 171, 173, 196, 197, 264
   Austrian Succession, 15, 69–70, 178, 256, 258
   Devolution, 46
   Dutch, 43, 44, 46, 47, 49, 57, 61, 64
   English Civil, 26, 27, 31–2
   Nine Years, 47, 61–2, 97–8
   Revolutionary and Napoleonic, 14, 15, 17, 190, 191, 194, 196, 197, 198, 269, 277
   Second World, 161, 169
   Seven Years, 17, 70, 122, 172, 178, 180
   Spanish Succession, 15, 64, *98*, 137, 215, 231
   Thirty Years, 45. 54, 91–2, 93
   Turkish, 54, 56, 61, 69, 137
Washington, George, 124–5

Webb, John Richmond, 210, 216, 222
Wellington, Arthur Wellesley, 1st Duke of, 194, 195
Wentworth, Peter, 213–14, 216, 222
Whigs, 25, 27–8, 32, 40, 75, 84, 86–7, 145, 155, 159, 184, 191, 203–204, 207, 210, 213, 214, 216–17, 218, 219, 221, 223, 224, 225, 227, 231–2, 234, 236, 237, 238, 241, 243–4, 245, 246, 247, 249, 250, 256
Whitelocke, Bulstrode, 35
Whitworth, Charles, 99, 101
Wilhelm I, Landgrave of Hesse-Kassel, 104
Wilkes, John, 129
William III, King, 16, 25, 26–7, *36*, 37–8, 41, 79, 83, 95, 113–14, 116, 117, 123, 129, 134, 136, 138, 143, 169, 175, 209, 247
William IV, King, 3, 22, 150, 196, 201
William Augustus, Duke of Cumberland, 154, 196
Williams, Basil, 161, 163
Williams, Daniel, 83, 84
Williams, R. Folkestone, 162, *167*
Winchester, 11–12, 140
Windsor, Andrews, 211
Windsor, Dixie, 211
Windsor, Thomas, Viscount, 211, 216, 218, 222, 224
Withers, Henry, 207, 222
Woolverton, John, 114
Worlidge, Thomas, 164
Wren, Christopher, 17
Wright, James, 184
Wrisberg, Rudolf Johann Freiherr von, 101, 102

Zenger Crisis, 172–3